COMPETING WITH IDIOTS

COMPETING WITH IDIOTS

Herman and Joe Mankiewicz

A Dual Portrait

Nick Davis

ALFRED A. KNOPF ˜ | NEW YORK 2021

THIS IS A BORZOI BOOK
PUBLISHED BY ALFRED A. KNOPF

www.aaknopf.com

Knopf, Borzoi Books, and the colophon are registered trademarks of
Penguin Random House LLC.

Library of Congress Cataloging-in-Publication Data
Names: Davis, Nick, [date] author.
Title: Competing with idiots : Herman and Joe Mankiewicz,
a dual portrait / Nick Davis.
Description: First edition. | New York : Alfred A. Knopf, 2021. |
Includes bibliographical references and index. |
Identifiers: LCCN 2020052645 (print) | LCCN 2020052646 (ebook) |
ISBN 9781400041831 (hardcover) | ISBN 9780593319703 (ebook)
Subjects: LCSH: Mankiewicz, Joseph L. | Mankiewicz, Herman J.
(Herman Jacob), 1897–1953. | Motion picture producers and directors—
United States—Biography. | Screenwriters—United States—Biography. |
Motion pictures—United States—History—20th century.
Classification: LCC PN1998.2 .D378 2021 (print) | LCC PN1998.2
(ebook) | DDC 791.4302/33092273 [B]—dc23
LC record available at https://lccn.loc.gov/2020052645
LC ebook record available at https://lccn.loc.gov/2020052646

Jacket images: (top) Herman Mankiewicz during production of *Laughter,*
1930. Billy Rose Theatre Division, The New York Public Library for the
Performing Arts; (bottom) Joseph L. Mankiewicz during production of
Cleopatra, 1962, by Philippe Le Tellier / Paris Match / Getty Images
Jacket design by Jenny Carrow

Manufactured in the United States of America
First Edition

For Jane

Contents

PROLOGUE

IT'S ONLY WHEN YOU STOP KNOWING EVERYTHING THAT YOU CAN START to know anything at all.

It was 1988. I was twenty-three years old and walking through Central Park with my dad. We were coming from the French Consulate, it was a lovely spring day, and Great Uncle Joe had suddenly turned into a Mystery.

All my life, Joe Mankiewicz had played a distant second fiddle. In no way could his work or life measure up to that of his big brother Herman, my maternal grandfather, the beloved legendary Hollywood figure who, while drinking himself into a memorable early grave, scattering brilliant one-liners like chicken feed for everyone to peck at, had also written some of the best screenplays in Hollywood's golden age, cowriting with Orson Welles what was quite clearly the greatest movie of all time, *Citizen Kane.* My grandfather's legend was secure, at least in my mind.

The sense I'd inherited about his younger brother Joe, on the other hand, was that first of all, Joe wasn't nearly as good a writer as Herman. To begin with, my understanding was that Joe's 1963 epic, *Cleopatra,* starring Elizabeth Taylor and Richard Burton, was as big a bomb as the Hollywood system ever churned out, and that basically everything else Joe had ever done, with the grudging exception of *All About Eve,* was almost embarrassingly overwritten, whereas nothing in Herman's oeuvre, including of course *The Pride of the Yankees* (highlighted by the immortal line "Lou! Lou! Lou! Gehrig! Gehrig! Gehrig!") was anything other than eminently quotable. But more than that, there was the notion that Joe simply wasn't a very good guy; it was part of the air I breathed that Joe Mankiewicz was a man who had misplaced his decency at birth and never even bothered to look for it.

But now this afternoon at the French consulate was changing everything. In the first place, that the entire nation of France had honored Joe

Joe and Claudette Colbert at the French Consulate
at the ceremony where Joe was honored with the
Chevalier de la Légion d'Honneur, 1988

with something called the Chevalier de la Légion d'Honneur, struck me as totally amazing. How could a man who'd made two or three good movies (I was dimly aware that Joe should get credit for a couple other movies I'd never much bothered with, like *A Letter to Three Wives* and *Suddenly, Last Summer*) and one historically rotten epic, actually be awarded a national honor by an entire country? I knew of France's bewildering devotion to Jerry Lewis, so I recognized the nation had a questionable barometer when it came to matters of cinematic taste—ah, youth—but were the French standards such that they would venerate the man who'd made *The Barefoot Contessa,* (which I'd once passed while flipping channels, cringed at the florid and ham-handed dialogue, and moved scornfully past)? As I considered the simple ribbon and medal that the French ambassador had pinned to Joe's lapel that afternoon, the highest honor the nation bestowed and one rarely given to foreigners, I started to sense that maybe it wasn't entirely fair to have reflexively condemned the man to the outer ring of movie directors, relishing the category in which Andrew Sarris had lumped Joe's work: "Less than Meets the Eye."

But in the second place, and more important, was Joe himself. This kind, unassuming, seemingly modest older man who had greeted me so warmly that afternoon, who twinkled with delight as he'd introduced me to Claudette Colbert, the man who had spoken so wittily and self-deprecatingly when the French ambassador asked him to say a few words, shaking his head and smiling down at the ornate yellow carpet when others praised his work . . . he looked gentle and decent, and quite a lot like my beloved Uncle Frank. Frank was Herman's younger son, my mother's brother and one of my favorite relatives—funny and smart and humane, and in my imagination probably the closest thing to what Herman himself must have been like. But that afternoon it was Joe, pudgy and wrinkled like a chewed-up dog toy, who seemed to emanate nothing but gentleness and humanity. He had grasped my hand warmly when we parted, and patted my hand with his sandpapery fingers, a gesture of such intimacy that it made me miss, completely and utterly, my mother, who had died when I was nine. He was my flesh and blood, this Great Uncle Joe, and he was lovely and warm and real.

So why had we never seen this man growing up? Why, when he lived less than an hour from our home in Greenwich Village, was this only the third or fourth time in my life I could remember seeing him, and the first since Mom's funeral more than a decade before? None of it made any sense.

Dad took a deep, theatrical sigh when I asked him these questions, the kind a certain kind of man loves to take when he's about to lay some serious shit on his son. Then he told me a story about my mom.

Dad had always been careful not to overwhelm me with stories about her. He knew I missed her, knew I'd loved her, but I think he also felt that since she'd died when I was so young, my own memories of her were fragile treasures, things that might break or, worse, alter and be replaced, if too many other people's memories were larded on top of my own. So Dad and I had settled into a comfortable respect for my memory of my mother, and stories about her were told sparingly. But this one, he said, could no longer be avoided, especially since I was asking about Joe. It was something, Dad told me, that he was sure Mom would have wanted me to know if she had lived. . . .

In the fall of 1958, Johanna Mankiewicz had just graduated from Wellesley, and she had come to live in New York City. She could have decided to go back to California, where she was from, but I'm not sure it even occurred to her. She had inherited from Herman a general distaste for most things California had to offer, and besides, New York was where Joe lived.

Since Herman had died when she was fifteen, Uncle Joe had become the closest thing Mom had to a father. He'd sent her to Europe the summer after Herman's death, and she and Joe had both relished the evenings when she was at Wellesley and would bring her friends down to the city for the weekend to meet him. They would sit at his feet and he would tell witty stories about his experiences with Hollywood starlets, making them feel at once superior to the Hollywood world and also included in its undeniable glamour.

He was nothing if not entertaining, Mom said, and in those three or four coeds who would sit at his feet, you could see he'd found a perfect audience—educated, earnest young women who knew about the things Joe cared about—Literature, Art, Theater—but weren't so snobby, unlike other members of the New York intelligentsia, that they would reject Joe outright just because he was a successful Hollywood movie director. In fact, to them he was able to downplay his success out west and present himself as someone who'd shunned the whole damn business—Joe had moved east for good in 1951—even as he continued to direct successful movies. It's easy to imagine Joe getting serious points and puppy dog stares from the young ladies at his feet as he modestly put off any suggestions that he was actually a quite principled fellow, tapping his pipe occasionally before sticking it back in his jaw, clenched and grinning. Young women had always been fond of Joe, not merely as a sexual creature, but as an educated, literate, psychologically astute older man who listened to them and made a much greater effort to understand them than their boyfriends, husbands, or fathers did.

And in the months after Mom had graduated from college, Joe remained the paragon. At the time, Joe and his wife Rosa were splitting their time between two homes—one a grand eleven-room apartment on Park Avenue, and the other an elegant nineteenth-century stone structure they rented in Mount Kisco. During the frequent absences of Rosa, who had long been characterized as mentally unstable and that autumn seemed to have fallen into one of her periodic ruts, Joe would often ask my mother to step in and play the role of hostess at his cocktail parties and dinners. For Mom, all of twenty-one years old and newly out in the world, it was heady stuff, having to decide whether the Moss Harts should sit next to or across from the Bennett Cerfs, and where exactly to place the Averell Harrimans. She loved it, but at the same time she recognized the basic unreality of it; during the day she was working for forty-five dollars a week at *Time* magazine and starting to learn a few things about the real world. But rubbing shoulders with the sort of people she did at Joe's was always thrilling, and a party at Joe's was never dull. After all, *All About Eve*'s Margo Channing's famous pre-party warning—"Fasten your seat belts, it's going to be a bumpy night!"—hadn't come from nowhere. It had come from the life of Joe Mankiewicz.

And when the party was over? Like her father, Joe wasn't any less witty when the liquor stopped flowing and the guests grabbed their coats and left. In fact, Mom said that Joe one-on-one was as crisp as ever. His wit was in many ways as sharp as Herman's—more moralizing, to be sure, less free-wheeling and spontaneously brilliant—but it had a consistency and a grounded quality that Herman's lacked. There was, in both Joe's work and his life, a solidity above all else that my mother had never experienced from her own father. The truth is, Joe was an unqualified success, unlike her dad—but more than that he was *of* the world, *in* the world, a contributor to the way things actually were, not a fantasist of the way things might have been. Unlike Herman, he dwelt in the real world, even though he may have loathed so many of its narrow-minded conventions.

So it was with no small alarm that on the autumn Saturday in question Mom received so many calls from her usually stoic uncle. Joe was staying at the Park Avenue apartment, and he couldn't seem to rouse Rosa on the telephone up in Mount Kisco, where he'd left her the evening before. Rosa had been troubled for a long time, and Joe's house had witnessed many uncomfortable scenes between Joe and the former Rosa Stradner, some involving knives, some involving scissors, all involving a good deal of screaming. Rosa had been in and out of sanatoriums from 1941 on, and while today we might have classified her as bipolar, and found the sensitive combination of antidepressants, antipsychotics, and mood stabilizers to keep her steady at least, back then the sensitivity was a more general "tut, tut, poor Rosa" that surely left the poor woman feeling just as isolated.

When they finally spoke, Joe told Mom that he was worried. He'd been unable to reach Rosa and he asked, almost casually, if she'd be able to accompany him up there to see if everything was okay. Mom dropped her plans for the afternoon—later she said she couldn't remember for sure but thought they might have involved Bonwit Teller—and met Joe at his apartment. They called Mount Kisco again and reached a caretaker who told Joe that Rosa was asleep and that everything was fine, but Joe told my mom that that didn't sound right, so the two of them decided to travel up to Mount Kisco together.

The drive takes no more than fifty minutes, and on a brisk autumn afternoon, the leaves along the Saw Mill River Parkway were turning a nice golden yellow, with the sun dappling shadows on the cars that sped along on their weekend jaunts. But the mood in the car could hardly have been pleasant. Of course, the two Mankiewiczes in the car did not discuss what they were doing or their feelings or trepidations about what they might find in Mount Kisco. My family has long enjoyed an easy irony about itself: for people who made their living through words and communication, almost nothing of any real importance got discussed in a serious way. So while the mood may have been tense, it was undoubtedly masked by quips, witticisms, even stories from both of them—things that would bring to the Mankiewicz mouth a customary grin, a curling up of those flattish lips into a smile that can never be wholly divorced from pain. For the Mankiewiczes, it's a wonderful, real feeling—the feeling that the listener and the speaker share the certainty that the world is an absurd place, filled with morons, and that the best we can do is point it out to each other and share laughs at the world's unknowing expense. In fact, to a Mankiewicz, what went on in that car on the drive to Mount Kisco—heading together toward an uncertain fate, pushing away feelings of anxiety and dread with lively talk and playful digressions—was pretty much the definition of intimacy.

The house at Mount Kisco was a large stone structure with hardwood floors, a massive fireplace, and exposed oak beams. The yard was expansive, part wooded, part lawn, and surrounded by a winding stone wall straight out of Robert Frost. On pulling the car into the driveway and walking toward the front door, Joe told my mother to check upstairs while he looked downstairs. The bedroom, of course, was upstairs.

Years later Mom still described it as the great horror of her life, walking into that bedroom and seeing what she saw: the corpse of her aunt, askew on the mattress, the room in disarray, a stench already wafting. The feeling of having been used in the incident, though, took a few years to hit Mom fully—Dad reminded me that when he and Mom got married the next year, it was Joe who walked Mom down the aisle—but when it did, she found it hard to forgive Joe for those simple words: *Josie, go upstairs*. It wasn't just that she felt the whole thing had been a setup—she suspected that Joe had known Rosa was dead the entire day—but that Joe had chosen *her* to be the instrument by which a suicide would be discovered.

Why had Joe felt the need to orchestrate the scene that way? If he really suspected his wife was dead, why couldn't he have asked someone to go check on her? Or, better yet, check on her himself? Isn't that what husbands do for wives they worry about? What kind of man does that to his niece?

Dad wasn't able to tell me too much more that afternoon, but I knew that the answers to these questions could probably be found in the relationship between Joe and Herman. They were two of the most accomplished brothers Hollywood had ever seen—even now, more than sixty years after their greatest successes, most people still know about Joe's *All About Eve* and Herman's *Citizen Kane* (the battle over screenplay credit would rage far beyond Herman's lifetime, and neither Pauline Kael's famous essay "Raising Kane" nor David Fincher's movie *Mank* will ever put an end to the debate over what Herman contributed and what Orson Welles did)—but at bottom, they were brothers, born nearly twelve years apart, bound together in a relationship of such complexity—full of passion and pride, hatred and love, jealousy and rage—that even five years after Herman's death, it's possible Joe simply couldn't resist the urge to direct a scene where the focus of all the horror and pain he could muster would be his late brother's daughter.

But what drives a man to such extremes? What did Herman do to Joe to engender such unconscious hostility? Was Herman such a powerful figure for Joe that years after his death, he was still calculating his every move through a prism of how it might play to the Herman in the back row of his imagination?

Or was Joe merely in need of human connection? Was his sending Mom upstairs merely a quick suggestion, almost a meaningless reflex?

Years before Mom's horrifying discovery in Mount Kisco, her father had laid down the rules for film construction for his friend Ben Hecht. They included the basic moral strictures of good guys winning, bad guys losing, and both the hero and heroine remaining virgins, which stood in direct contrast with the villain, who, at least until the final reel, "can have as much fun as he wants—cheating and stealing, getting rich and whipping the servants."

But in his litany of storytelling chestnuts, Herman neglected one of the most familiar: an opening scene that leaves us with nothing but question marks, followed by a flashback dissolve . . .

PART ONE

———————⚭———————

WILL YOU ACCEPT THREE HUNDRED PER WEEK TO
WORK FOR PARAMOUNT PICTURES? ALL EXPENSES
PAID. THE THREE HUNDRED IS PEANUTS. MILLIONS
ARE TO BE GRABBED OUT HERE AND YOUR ONLY
COMPETITION IS IDIOTS. DON'T LET THIS GET
AROUND.

—TELEGRAM, HERMAN J. MANKIEWICZ
TO BEN HECHT, 1926

CHAPTER ONE

— ✿ —

ROSEBUD

Maybe Rosebud was something he couldn't get or something
he lost. Anyway, it wouldn't have explained anything. I don't
think any word can explain a man's life. No, I guess Rosebud
is just a piece in a jigsaw puzzle, a missing piece.

—*CITIZEN KANE*

AS A YOUNG BOY, HERMAN MANKIEWICZ FOUND HIMSELF IN TROUBLE
nearly every day, and for one infraction or another, he often found himself virtually imprisoned in his room to think about what he had done.
It was practically an afternoon ritual. But as he later told a psychoanalyst
in Hollywood, what remained most vivid about those enforced solitary
confinements was not the thought he gave to his alleged misdeeds or any
shame over having committed these dastardly acts, or even the deep and
profound rage at his father (or, less frequently, mother) for the enforced
exile, though the anger was severe indeed and would remain with him
forever, but the exquisite feelings he felt in being alone, the sights he saw
and the smells and sounds that surrounded him outside his window in
New York City. Most of all what he remembered was a powerful, almost
primal urge to share those feelings with the whole world. He thought
that if he were somehow able to convert his actual, entire experience—
the orange tint of the afternoon sun on the bricks on the building
opposite his window, the sound of a breeze, the snapping sound of
the lines of laundry in the tenement courtyard—into something the
whole world could also feel, life would be worth living. Anything else
would be a misery. To share this life, he thought, to get the world to see
through his eyes—that was all he wanted in the world, but to his young
mind it was also quite obviously an impossibility. How could one *will*

Herman in NYC, c. 1903

the entire world to see what he saw? The situation made him deeply depressed.

So while Herman Mankiewicz later said that there was no better time to be born in New York City than 1897, he was equally convinced in the first few years of his life that he would rather have been anywhere else in the world. As well as a deep and urgent need to get the world to share his vision, the feeling of being in not quite the right spot was one that he would grow painfully familiar with throughout his life. But what Herman didn't know, at least not in so many words, was that the trait was an inherited one, passed from generation to generation like blue eyes in a Norwegian family or red hair in a Scottish one, the not-quite-belonging trait, Mankiewiczian to the core. It was what Herman woke to every morning of his young life in New York City.

New York at the turn of the twentieth century was not so different from New York today, or at any point between then and now: the center of the world for those living there, a colorful, swirling, mad, loud, impossible, smelly place riven by wild class divisions and unacceptable cruelty jutting up against magnificent examples of the most graceful humanity imaginable; and for those elsewhere, a spot to be avoided, or at best tolerated if one had to pass through. The almost permanently discomfited expression on the face of Herman's dad, Professor Franz Mankiewicz, always suggested to Herman that he too wished to be elsewhere. He wished to be elsewhere than in New York in the first few years of Herman's life, wished to be other than a schoolteacher, wished to be married to a woman other than Herman's mother, wished to be born in a different century, a different country, into different skin.

Franz's discomfort had as much to do with the world as it did with himself. Like many dogmatic personalities, he was often bewildered by the realm outside his head. Raised in Frankfurt by a domineering father himself, Franz had inhaled a Teutonic sense of self-discipline and order, and the world's inability to follow along never ceased to amaze and infuriate him. As a schoolteacher, he was beloved by the students, who cared as passionately as he did about his subjects. Those who didn't he heaped with contempt, as well as a profound and deep inability to understand their lassitude or lack of interest. This discomfort—what Herman and Joe used to love to make fun of when they were out in Hollywood in the 1930s and Franz would come for one of his infrequent visits—was plainly etched on Franz's face, and while hundreds of students passed through Franz Mankiewicz's classrooms over the years, he had only one first son. One first son on whom he could pin all his hopes and dreams—one son to disappoint and enrage him.

Franz Mankiewicz

Young Herman learned early on that he had become a magnet for his father's displeasure. It wasn't just that Herman was a continual disappointment to his father—he was, of course; Herman all his life would tell of bringing home a 97 on an exam only to be barked at: "Where are the other three points?" (It was the "where" that got Herman going. "Where? They fell out of my pants, I dropped them in the gutter, I stuffed them up my nose . . .") If Herman responded by saying that nobody else in class got more than a 90, Pop would say, "The boy who got 90, maybe it was harder for him to do that than for you to get 97. It's not good unless it's your best." To Franz, Herman later said, bragging about being smart was no different than bragging about "having blue eyes. It's just a characteristic. It's what you do with it that matters." On those rare occasions when Herman did meet the high standards his father had set for him, Franz never praised him. It's hard to imagine it even crossed his mind to do so.

Looking at pictures of the man when I was growing up, or, more menacingly, the portrait of the stern face that stared down from its pride of place hanging above my grandmother's mantel in Brentwood, it was almost impossible to imagine that Franz Mankiewicz was ever young. In picture after picture, the frown, the worry, the concern of age weigh heavily on every single feature. He was married at the age of twenty-four, but could he ever have walked with a bounce in his step, or sung in the bathtub, or had a moment of genuine passion with his wife, or anyone else for that matter, that didn't involve yelling? As a young immigrant in New York, the highly educated Franz had become a reporter for one of the three hundred German language papers in the city. He was effective, smart, and hardworking, with a fierceness for life that inspired in those around him a genuine feeling of respect. For his firstborn, though, that

The portrait of Franz, seen here on Joe's mantel in Bedford,
New York, in the 1980s

feeling was closer to fear. "Pop was a tremendously industrious, brilliant,
vital man," Herman said later. "A father like that could make you very
ambitious or very despairing. You could end up by saying, 'Stick it, I'll
never live up to that and I'm not going to try.' That's what eventually
happened to me."

To Herman, Franz was the hot and unrelenting sun around which he
rotated and which threw all of Herman's most unpleasant features into
relief, for Franz and everyone else to see; thus exposed, Herman would be
met with the fiercest disapproval, judgment, and discipline. Above all, discipline. Like most German immigrant fathers, Franz didn't spare the cane,
and his regular beatings of Herman became part of family lore. It got so
when Herman saw his father with a look in his eyes, he would merely go
to Franz and bend over, even when he had no idea what particular sin
he'd committed. While Herman later spun it into an amusing anecdote,
and more than that, wove it into the fabric of his existence, behind the
funny story was an undeniable truth: Herman Mankiewicz had come to
loathe his father. Indeed, though he knew it wasn't true, he later felt that
he had almost no memory of feeling anything but hatred for the man.
So dominant was the feeling, and so thorough was his assumption that
children hated their parents, it became the source of one of the Hermanic
witticisms that was passed down in the family as if it were Talmudic logic.

The example given was always spinach, that most detested of vegetables. "I hate spinach," the young child would say, only to be told by Herman, "No, you don't hate spinach. You *despise* spinach. You *hate* your parents."

That story was told frequently when I was growing up, just about whenever my older brother Timmy or I said we hated something, like spinach or sweet and sour pork. My problem, early on, was I didn't get the joke. It took me years to understand that it was based on the strange truth that Herman assumed, profoundly and deeply, that you *did* hate your parents, that everyone did, and as a result that trait got baked into the family DNA, as much as the humor. In fact, only if you admitted you hated your parents would you fall into line, in line with all the Mankiewiczes of course, but most of all in line with Herman. And nothing was better than to be like Herman.

For from the beginning of my own life, I knew one thing: Herman J. Mankiewicz, Mom's dead father, the "Gopa" we never knew (to the "Goma" we did, the "poor Sara" of so many long-suffering years in Hollywood), was the funniest man who ever lived. Uncle Frank told funny stories, Uncle Don was funny responding to others, but their father—Herman—he was nonpareil.

Two quick examples, the kind you find in books about Hollywood's earliest batch of screenwriters from back East and their notorious self-loathing. First: a studio head fires Herman, tells him that not only will Herman never work at the studio again but the man assures him he'll make sure Herman never works at any studio in town. Herman looks at the man and says, "Promises, promises."

Second: watching Orson Welles walk by on the studio lot: "There but for the grace of God, goes God."

Of course Herman was far from the first to transform pain into comedy, but what seems to have given Herman his greatest satisfaction growing up was his stealth comedy, a sense that he could mock someone—usually his father—without the target's even realizing it. To the end of his life, Franz would be the butt of both of his sons' humor, and what they loved most was how little he seemed to understand why what he did was funny to them.

In the early 1930s, Herman and Joe were in Hollywood working on a script together—some biographers might say declaratively that it was *Million Dollar Legs,* the W. C. Fields movie on which Joe received a writing credit, and for which Herman was one of the producers, but there's no knowing what movie it was—and they came across the French word for town, *ville,* which Herman took delight in pronouncing "veal," an obviously Americanized pronunciation. Joe would quietly correct his big brother, leaving off the *l*'s and making it sound overly Gallic: "Vee-yah." The brothers go back and forth on it for a while, Joe insisting that by French rules of pronunciation it should be "veeya," Herman insisting right back it's an exception to the rule. Then they realize that the man who would know the answer happens to be in New York City, a brilliant professor and linguist just a long-distance phone call away. So they call Franz, he picks up the phone and says hello, they say "It's Herman and Joe, Pop. We're having an argument over the correct pronunciation of the French word v-i-l-l-e, is it 'veeya' or 'veal'?" Franz says "veal" and hangs up the phone.

Herman and Joe both loved telling that story. The man hadn't heard from his sons in weeks, maybe even months. But niceties, warmth, kindness—all of that seemed beyond Franz Mankiewicz. He had answered their question. The purpose of the call had been accomplished. It cost a lot of money to talk long-distance. And so he'd hung up.

But there is a crucial difference between the *ville* story and how Herman experienced Franz in his childhood: the difference was Joe. Joe gave Herman an ally in the lifelong battle for respect from his father, and also another soldier in the silent war against him, a war whose explosions had been fights and one-sided gusts of laughter from Herman until Joe's arrival on the scene. But for Herman, the age difference of nearly twelve years meant that Joe would not be a full ally until adulthood—in childhood, it was Herman against Franz, and it was a bruising battle.

And what of Herman's mother? How can it be that the family lore is so focused on Franz, and that Mama gets such scant attention? As an adult, Herman virtually dismissed his mother, telling one friend that his mother had been a typical German hausfrau, "a round little woman who was uneducated in four languages. She spoke mangled German, mangled Russian, mangled Yiddish and mangled English." Goma later told Herman's biographer Richard Meryman, "For his mother, he had a kind of, not contempt, it's too strong a word, but certainly no great regard." Herman thought of her, or so he said, as little more than someone to darn the socks, cook the meals, and make sure that everything was in its place. He grew, in fact, to be as indifferent to her as his father was—one famous family anecdote tells of the absentminded professor proudly telling his wife that she should be proud of him, for that day, on the street, he had seen two women coming toward him. "I concentrated very hard,"

Franz said, "and I remembered the name and said, 'How do you do, Mrs. Neuschatz?'" And who was the other one, she asked him. He didn't know. "That was me," said his wife.

But a son who wavers between contemptuousness and indifference to his mother had most likely once felt quite differently toward her . . .

The morning had been a pleasant one, and Herman told his wife about it years later with great feeling. Mama had taken him to the butcher's first, where Herman always loved walking on the sawdust-covered floors, imagining he was in some kind of jungle, with the sausages hanging down from the trees and the enormous slabs of animal laid out on the butcher's blocks, white-apron-clad warriors slicing and hacking, cutting away at the beasts, who Herman knew had been quite recently terrorizing the villagers, circling their huts and eating their young. After the butcher's had come a rarer treat still, a visit to Mama's friend, the lady with the flower dress who Mama had tea with. The woman had given Herman a red sourball as a treat, which he'd plugged away in his right cheek until it had caused a small sore there and he'd shifted it to the other cheek. The day had been easy, fun, not even noticeable as a day, and only later, in thinking back, did Herman realize that he must have been dribbling juice from his sourball on his shirt all afternoon. But then, when they came home, there was Papa, inexplicable—why? Why in the middle of the day?—and he'd become incensed at the sight of the stain on Herman's shirt, and directed all his fury toward Herman. When the whip came out, the images were frantic and cruel—Franz unstrapping the belt from over the door handle where he always kept it, and wiping his hands on the belt, as if he were a surgeon and it were a rag and he was drying his hands before an operation—and the whole time, Herman was never particularly worried. He'd been beaten before, of course, and grown so accustomed to the spankings and beatings that he no longer really dreaded them, or even their outcome, which was a bottom that would be sore if not outright numb and paralyzed for a few hours—but this one was different. Because Mama was there. She was there, and she was raising her voice—surely she was raising her voice, she must be—to defend Herman, to tell Franz that it was her fault, not to punish the boy, he's five, and he'd been given the sweet by my friend, Franz, don't take it out on him. If I hadn't taken him with me, this wouldn't have happened. I will wash the shirt, the shirt will be as good as new, you need not worry.

But the words never came. There was no defense. Mama left the room without a word, and when Herman went in to the bedroom later that afternoon to take his nap, the rage flowed like tears, bitter and furious. He would fight his father because he had to, because no one else would. But Mama, he decided, he would no longer think about. She was to be obeyed, fine, but never again respected, never again a source of love. He wouldn't let it happen. The full-throated love and trust was gone forever.

ONE OF THE GREAT DEBATES IN FILM HISTORY, TO SAY NOTHING OF the insane battles waged over the same issue in my family, is who wrote what in *Citizen Kane*. Much of that, of course, had to do with the enormity of Orson Welles's ego, and his insistence, which to be fair was also a shrewd business move, on being known as a one-man band, an auteur before we even knew the meaning of the word. As a result, to Goma's eternal regret, Herman's original contract sold his right to any claim of authorship of *Kane*. While the debate has raged for nearly eighty years with no obvious resolution (despite what Goma felt), two elements of the script's provenance have never been in dispute. The first is its startling structure, with the reporter's quest for getting to the truth about Charles Foster Kane leading to a series of overlapping sequences and chronological restarts that still feels strikingly modern. The second is Rosebud, one of the most famous words in movie history, the word that Kane utters on his deathbed that sets the biographer's search in motion.

Both inventions were Herman's. Even Welles himself admitted: "Rosebud was pure Mank."

Of course, Welles also derided Rosebud as "dollar book Freud." The idea that on his deathbed a great tycoon would dredge up a long-dormant memory of a childhood toy, now all but forgotten, as a symbol for his lost innocence does sometimes seem a simplistic gimmick to stand at the center of filmdom's greatest masterpiece.* But it's also powerful, in part because, as Pauline Kael and others have pointed out, *Citizen Kane* isn't Shakespearean tragedy, but really, at its heart, a great *movie* movie—the greatest movie of all time, maybe, but it earned its A-plus as a B movie, as much an emblem of pop culture as transcendent work of art. And therefore, it isn't in spite of the Rosebud gimmick that the movie works

---

* It's also a gimmick with a maddening inconsistency, for after Kane says the word, he drops the snow globe, which shatters on the floor, and it is only then that the nurse hurries into the room. If he was alone in the room, who heard the man say "Rosebud"?

so well, as Welles may have hoped in his moments of greatest artistic ambition, but rather because of it—because the entire movie's narrative is driven by the meaningless conceit. "Maybe Rosebud was something he couldn't get or something he lost," the reporter Thompson speculates at the end. "Anyway, it wouldn't have explained anything. I don't think any word can explain a man's life. No, I guess Rosebud is just a piece in a jigsaw puzzle, a missing piece."

But if it's a missing piece, it's a piece that was put there by—and taken away from—Herman Mankiewicz.

Herman was, in fact, drawing on his own life. He'd had his very own Rosebud, and unlike Kane's, it wasn't a sled that symbolized the loss of his mother, but a bicycle that stood for the possibility, ever elusive, of paternal acceptance and love—and for escape.

The Mankiewicz family had moved to Wilkes-Barre, Pennsylvania, in 1904. Franz had uprooted the clan from New York and headed west when he'd been hired to edit the Wilkes-Barre German newspaper *Demokratischer Wachter*. But while you could take Franz out of the city, you couldn't take the city out of Franz. He remained as oppressive to Herman even in that verdant valley as he'd been in New York, and in Pennsylvania, there was often no way to get away.

Too, there was school. Herman excelled at the private Harry Hillman Academy, but the pressure from his father to be perfect was enormous. Those missing three points were as crucially disastrous as ever, and worse now, because Franz was breathing down his young son's neck. Literally. Soon after they'd moved to Wilkes-Barre, Franz had become friendly with the headmaster at Hillman, and before long he was earning extra money tutoring some Hillman students in French and German. Shortly after that, the nightmare scenario for all children: the modern language teacher fell seriously ill and Franz became a full-time teacher at Hillman. Herman's demanding father now became his most demanding teacher. In class, according to one of Herman's classmates, Franz would "bulldog Herman as though he wished Herman wasn't around. He wanted Herman to equal or excel everyone else, and he hated it when Herman showed up badly in front of us." For Herman, it was torture. "Those years," Joe later said on Herman's behalf, "must have been terrifying and destructive beyond description."

For Franz, it came down to equipping his young son with the tools he would need to survive: discipline and a good education. No doubt as a German immigrant, Franz would have found laughable the notion that

Herman with his "Rosebud" bicycle in Wilkes-Barre,
c. 1907

he was a cruel father, simply because he demanded his eldest son put forth his best effort during his formative years. But while the brutality of Franz's disciplinary measures could be debated, the significance of one incident cannot be: what happened to Herman's bicycle.

When Herman was ten, his father promised him a bicycle for Christmas. Like many immigrant Jewish families of the time, the Mankiewiczes struggled with their Judaism, a battle that would echo for decades across the family. Joe would later describe his father as a "rip-snorting atheist," but according to Herman and Joe's sister Erna, Pop did accede to the wishes of the Wilkes-Barre Jewish community by having Herman sent to the Reform synagogue for Sunday school. But when the rabbi took issue with Franz's insisting on his family celebrating such long-standing German traditions as Christmas trees and Easter eggs, Franz withdrew his son. Thus, Christmas was celebrated in the Mankiewicz home, and in 1907, when ten-year-old Herman rushed down to the Christmas tree that morning, he came expecting to celebrate the holiday with a promised new bike that he had spied in the window of a local store. For a moment, Herman couldn't find the bike and thought his father was playing a rare joke on him. But alas, no bike was there, probably because Franz was too poor to afford it at the time, though it could also have been merely his famous absentmindedness. The memory of that pit in his stomach, the feeling of emptiness as he looked around the room and realized there was no bicycle, stayed with him forever, even though a few short weeks after Christmas, Franz did provide his firstborn the long-awaited bike. But where the one in the window had a racing stripe Herman would never forget, this one was ordinary and drab. As always with a Mankiewicz, the negativity of the original lack-of-bike would outweigh the positivity of the bike's ultimate, if belated arrival—especially because the bike would not be Herman's for long.

One afternoon, for having committed some forgotten offense, Herman was confined to his house by his mother, and to insure he wouldn't leave, she hid the stockings he needed for his knickers. (Goma later cited this incident as evidence of Johanna's simpleminded incompetence as a mother. "He wasn't going to the pool room," Goma said. "He was going to the library. She should have encouraged that!") Herman retaliated by sneaking into his mother's room, putting on a pair of her stockings, and pedaling off to the library a few blocks away. When he emerged from the library a few hours later, the bicycle was gone, the victim of a rare hiccup of Wilkes-Barre crime. Herman was mortified and embarrassed and trudged home through the snow. When he got there, Franz, for once, didn't beat him.

Instead, as punishment, he never replaced the bicycle.

———————— ✾ ————————

CHAPTER TWO

GERTRUDE SLESCYNSKI

I am nobody's fool. Least of all yours.

—*ALL ABOUT EVE*

TO THE END OF HIS LIFE, JOE MANKIEWICZ INSISTED THAT HIS FIRST memories were of hiding.

He remembered, most acutely, the sound and the feeling. Hiding inside his bedroom closet while he heard shouts titanic and epic. The raging storm outside made him feel like a cabin boy, a stowaway on a ship crossing the Atlantic, cowering in a barrel, while outside he felt the presence of the storm and the high seas, a horrible wind, with him just listening, crouching in fear, resting safe in the closet amid the musty smell of moth-eaten old suits Pop had worn long before Joe had been born. He was safe, but God, that storm! For it wasn't just Pop who was bellowing with anger, but Herman too. Herman was both braving Pop and also giving as good as he got—the yells were so frequent and joined together that at a certain point Joe lost the ability to distinguish between Herman's voice—loud, clear but with that telltale drag at the end of every word, Herman used his voice like a trumpet player—and Pop's, deeper but brusquer, barking almost, a dog with sandpaper stuck in his windpipe. Herman braved the storm so much that he became the storm, and he would wear Pop down, getting louder and louder as the storm raged: "Where in Christ is it written that a boy has to follow every god-damn diktat that . . ." In the closet, Joe, leaning against Pop's suits, knew that if he waited long enough, as he would have to, Herman would have defeated the storm—or ridden it out until at last it would pass and Joe would be safe. He could emerge and resume life until the next storm came.

Joe hid, and was safe—because of Herman.

If Franz was the pole around which Herman rotated, for Joe it was Herman himself who stood as the center of his universe. "Other people have got a father complex," Joe said later. "I've got a Herman complex." To Joe, Herman was the one who got everywhere first—to Columbia University, to Berlin, to Hollywood, to marriage, to kids, to success in the movie business, to the Oscar, and finally of course to the final finish line, the grave. More than eleven and a half years younger, Joe was always competing with a big brother who was larger than he could ever be: larger, louder, funnier, smarter, more outrageous. In every meaningful way Herman simply took up more space. With Herman the acknowledged star of the family, Joe not only idolized him but naturally modeled his behavior on Herman's—with a few crucial differences. For one thing, Joe was keenly aware of the agony Herman's angry and later drunken behavior caused his father, and Joe wanted no part of that. Joe wanted to succeed, always. He could never understand Herman's self-destructive behavior. Drinking, or gambling, or fighting with those who had the power to help you; these things made no sense to Joe. Why would you impede your own progress as Herman seemed to do almost deliberately? Joe's goal was simple: to find out what the game was, and win. Often, the game was to compete with Herman. But given his brother's tremendous head start in life, not to mention nearly a dozen years of people thinking Herman was the cat's pajamas, could the younger brother ever catch up?

To Herman, the answer was easy, a two-letter word that rhymed with Joe. Herman began by viewing his brother as an adorable little plaything, cute and round like a beach ball, and early on he took pride in his young brother's scholastic achievements and then later his rapid early ascent in Hollywood. But having helped Joe get a foot on the Hollywood ladder, he watched, somewhat stunned, as Joe proved himself a master of a game that Herman couldn't stand even to consider, let alone actually play. To the end of his life, Joe insisted that Herman had loved him dearly, and he refused to acknowledge to anyone other than maybe himself how much scorn Herman actually directed at him. Though it was well documented and sometimes seemed that nearly half of Hollywood had heard Herman utter the phrase, Joe pooh-poohed the notion that Herman ever referred

Joe (second row, seated, second from far right)
graduating from eighth grade at the age of eleven

to him as "my idiot brother"—as in "M-G-M made my idiot brother a producer" or "my idiot brother is directing a picture for Fox." But while Joe may have invented a fiction for himself—that he was merely an adoring younger brother and Herman the proud older brother—Herman refused to see Joe as an equal, or anything remotely resembling a threat. He'd given Joe his entrée to Hollywood, taught him where to sit in the Paramount commissary (in the back under the windows, the better to observe the whole room), whom to befriend (the right-hand man to the head of production), whom to avoid (the secretaries to the head of production), what the rules were (never raise your voice in a meeting with the head of production, don't screw the secretaries of anyone in the production building but confine yourself to the outer bungalows), which ones could be flouted with impunity (the secretary rule, broken by nearly everyone), and which would require a defter touch (the politics of the studio were complicated, and Herman loved talking politics). It's as if Herman never really took Joe seriously. Then again, whom did he take seriously, other than himself? Certainly not members of his own family . . .

When psychoanalysis swept Hollywood in the 1930s and '40s, Herman and Joe were both caught in its path. Joe saw a man with the deliciously

analytic name of Dr. Hacker,[*] and Herman saw a man named Dr. Simmel.[†] For two years, Herman went almost religiously, three or four times
a week, lying on Simmel's couch, free-associating, telling the man all that
he felt he could bear to tell another living soul. But finally, Herman had
had enough. After months of complaining to my grandmother about the
lack of progress he was making, he decided to quit. He went in to Simmel
and broke it off. The story my family likes to tell is that he gave Simmel
a bit of a farewell speech. He explained to the man that the analysis had
not worked. Two years earlier, he began, he gambled, he drank, he was
deeply in debt, he felt distant from his wife, and he was miserable about
his career. Now, two years later, he gambled, he drank, he was deeply in
debt, the distance from his wife hadn't lessened, and he was miserable
about his career—plus he'd lost a lot of money to his shrink ("He couldn't
stop my gambling," Herman told friends, "but at least now I know *why* I
gamble."). Simmel, or so it is said, understood and agreed to end the sessions. The two men shook hands and Herman walked to the door. There
he paused and turned back to the doctor. "By the way," he said, "I have
a sister, and I hate her."

Oh yes, the sister: Erna, so forgotten, not just by Herman, but Joe as
well. The Mankiewiczes were a family dominated by men. Born seven
years after Herman and with the distinct disadvantage of being female
in a Prussian household, Erna was clearly and quite obviously shunted
aside in favor of her brothers.[‡] In her youth she had loved them both
fiercely. First Herman, so brilliant, so imposing, so large and dominant
and dazzling—then Joe, more studied, but equally brilliant. And it was
Erna who saw, probably before anyone else, that Joe was determined
above all else to outdo Herman. As for Herman, he admitted ruefully to
Life magazine for a profile of Joe in 1951, "Joe was fiercely ambitious as
a kid," but he'd never really understood what Joe would do with all that

---

[*] For a time, Joe was also analyzed by Dr. Otto Fenichel, who had studied with Freud
in Vienna.

[†] Dr. Ernst Simmel, also a Freudian, was famous for his pioneering work on gambling, though it hardly had an effect on Herman's.

[‡] Erna's lack of status in the family continues, sadly, to the present day. At a recent
family gathering, two of my (male) cousins and I got to talking, and all three of
us admitted that we had never really known Erna at all, and two of us discovered
that growing up neither of us was certain whether her name was Erna or Erma.

ambition. By the time Herman realized Joe might actually be a threat, it was too late.

In the late 1940s, after Herman's peak, he ran into another screenwriter at a men's room in M-G-M. The other writer was a man named Frank Davis, who would in time become my other grandfather[*] . . .

The two men know each other, if only slightly, and don't exchange more than a few pleasantries as Herman completes his business then goes to the sink and washes his hands under the chrome-plated tap. He grabs one of the folded linen towels at the side of the sink, dries his hands, then looks back at Frank Davis, finishing at the urinal. "My brother Joe," Herman says out of nowhere, "is a real shit." He tosses the towel down in the hamper. "And someday you're going to find out why." With that, Herman strides out of the bathroom, and pretty much out of Frank Davis's life, though Frank had reason to recall the moment a decade or so later in Beverly Hills, sitting by the agent Sam Jaffe's swimming pool, watching his twenty-two-year-old son Peter stand stiffly next to a rabbi, and all heads turning to see young Johanna, Herman's now fatherless twenty-one-year-old daughter, walk down the aisle with her uncle Joe Mankiewicz. Was Joe a shit? Why? Frank Davis squinted into the setting sun and watched the young woman who would be his daughter-in-law walk in on the arm of this successful and solid director. A shit? Frank never really knew what Herman had meant. But he never forgot it either.

About midway through *All About Eve,* Bette Davis's Margo Channing throws a welcome-home party for her lover and soon-to-be fiancé, Bill Sampson, who has been off in Hollywood directing a movie. Toward the end of that famously bumpy night, a small group of partygoers sits on the stairway discussing the merits of the theater world and the psyches of its denizens. Addison DeWitt, perhaps the greatest of all of Joe's male characters and the one whom he identified as his mouthpiece, an endlessly cynical critic unable to see the good in anything, comments on how those who populate the theater, from the playwright on down to the costume girl,

---

[*] For me and my brother Timmy, the following scene often recalled a moment in what we considered Herman's second greatest movie, *The Pride of the Yankees,* where Babe Ruth hugged Gary Cooper (playing Lou Gehrig). Here were these two titans, almost from different epochs, different lives, together at last: Herman Mankiewicz, Mom's legendary late drunk of a father, and Grandfather, Dad's dad, handsome beyond belief, solid as an oak. We loved to imagine them at the urinals, these two men—out of whom came the seeds that had carried us to the moment of first hearing this story in or around 1973.

are quite abnormal. The director Bill Sampson disagrees. He contends that any abnormalities theater folk might have are merely a reflection of the abnormalities evident in any aspect of society. In other words, theater people are just like the rest of us, only more so. But Sampson adds, "To be a good actor or actress or anything else in the theater means wanting to be that more than anything else in the world. It means a concentration of desire, ambition and sacrifice such as no other profession demands." At which point Joe's camera cuts to Eve Harrington. She sits just below Bill on the stairs, nodding in almost hypnotic agreement to all he says; she would, and did, do anything to rise to the top of the theater world. Ambition incarnate, she too as much as Addison DeWitt came from the soul of her creator. It was Eve who would give Joe his greatest success, and the film for which he would be most remembered, even if few people knew the depth of its autobiographical sources.

Unlike Herman, Joe enjoyed a mostly happy and successful career, and though like his brother he sometimes yearned for a different life than the one he ended up with, few careers in the movies were as successful or meteoric as Joe's. After coming to Hollywood at his brother's urging in 1929, he had become, at the astonishing age of twenty, by far the youngest member of Paramount studio's writing staff, named one of the ten best dialogue writers of the year after writing a Jack Oakie movie titled *Fast Company*. Two years and dozens of screenplays later, he received his first Academy Award nomination for a now-forgotten picture called *Skippy** (based on a comic strip about a mischievous if sometimes melancholy ten-year-old boy), and three years after that, he was writing for M-G-M, Hollywood's most prestigious studio. A year later he'd risen to producer, and for the next ten years, he oversaw more than twenty films, including Fritz Lang's *Fury*, George Cukor's *The Philadelphia Story*, and George Stevens's *Woman of the Year*. By 1945, he was writing and directing, which a few years later led to a feat that has yet to be duplicated: double Oscars, screenwriter and director, for movies in two consecutive years: *A Letter to Three Wives* in 1949, *All About Eve* in 1950. He continued to write and direct for the next two decades, and while he may never again have regained those heights, he was always on the short list of Hollywood's top directors, directing such movies as *Guys and Dolls; Julius Caesar; Sud-*

---

* One contemporary article argued Joe would have won had producer David Selznick not shown up at the eleventh hour with a handful of votes for his film *Cimarron*. Apparently, Mr. Price had not yet met Mr. Waterhouse.

"There was a time when he was not a monster":
Joe (right) and Rosemary (left) in Rome during the
filming of *Cleopatra,* flanking his sister Erna and
Cleopatra production manager Johnny Johnston

denly, Last Summer; The Barefoot Contessa; and *Sleuth,* for which, at the
age of sixty-two, he captured yet another Academy Award nomination for
his direction of the film's only two actors, Laurence Olivier and Michael
Caine, both of whom received Best Actor nominations. (Joe liked to joke
that he was the first director in history whose entire cast received Academy
Award nominations.)

To his peers, Joe Mankiewicz was virtually beyond reproach, not only
for the merit and quality of his work, but also for his sophisticated and
unimpeachable behavior on the set. Linda Darnell said, "Joe never shouts
on the set, he never even raises his voice." Celeste Holm, one of his *Eve*
stars, said, "He starts out by assuming that you're a professional and
that you have at least reasonably good sense." Richard Burton called Joe
"well-nigh perfect. He let me have my head and curbed me very gently
and subtly when I threatened to tear a passion to tatters." Michael Caine
said Uncle Joe was "bloody marvelous," Sidney Poitier gave endless credit
to him for starting his career and directing him so well, and Bette Davis
said simply, "Mankiewicz is a genius." But it wasn't just the actors. Erna
insisted he always had the best relationships with the people on his sets.
"His crews always adored him. He lived with them and laughed with
them and was always on good terms with them." And Joe's son Tom, who
himself would go on to a successful career in Hollywood as a screenwriter
and script doctor, claimed that there was always kidding and jokes on his
father's sets and more people laughing than on any other set he ever saw.

In sum, Joe achieved supreme success in Hollywood's fickle world, and he did so by applying the "concentration of desire, ambition and sacrifice" that Bill Sampson said the profession, unlike any other, demanded. But it's hard not to wonder at what cost.

The bare facts of Joe's private life would give comfort to any enemies. He divorced his first wife Elizabeth after just three years of marriage, and his marriage to his second wife Rosa was a continuous nightmare that ended with her suicide. He and his father never had much of a relationship, and though he was close to his mother in his childhood, at some point in early adulthood he exorcised her completely from his life. He was estranged from his sister Erna for the latter third of her life, largely because she felt he had become a monster of selfishness and wasn't worth trying to maintain a relationship with, and when she lay dying in the hospital room that she would never leave, even though it was her last wish to be reunited with her only remaining brother, he refused to come. His older brother Herman, never the real champion of Joe's that a younger brother might have wanted, in addition to famously calling him an idiot, was, when he wasn't deriding him, often as not borrowing money from him that he seldom bothered to return. As for his own children, Joe was never close to his two (acknowledged) sons, ending in an uneasy truce with his younger, Tom, while his elder son Chris openly despised him. Then there was the little matter of the other son whose existence he wouldn't admit to publicly, and rumors of a second family in Europe that slithered through our family for years. And though he did end his life seemingly happily married to his third wife, Rosemary, and they'd had a marvelous daughter, there's no denying that as he lived out his days in Bedford, New York, Joe had pretty much alienated everyone who was close to him, and not by accident. "I'm a very, very internal guy," Joe told his biographer Ken Geist in 1973. "I don't think I've ever told the truth or confided in anyone the way external people do." Tom agreed, telling me, "Dad was so controlled that you never knew what he really thought. He lived that whole life without ever sharing what he really felt with anybody."

But it hadn't always been that way. The boy who hid in the closet hearing Herman and Franz rage at each other had possessed a delicacy that would later find its way into the gentlest sections of his screenplays. And despite their later struggles, Erna insisted to the end that he had been "the sweetest child," a fact that utterly shocked some of those who had known Joe only as an adult.

Among those was his own son, Chris. In the 1970s, when Chris was in his thirties, he joined his aunt Erna in Brentwood for lunch at the home of his aunt Sara, Herman's widow. After lunch, Erna asked Chris to take her to the nearby farmer's market, and he obliged. In the parking lot of the market, standing near the car, Erna suddenly told Chris, "It's terrible about your dad, what a terrible monster he became." Chris was shocked. He wasn't aware that there was a time when Joe *hadn't been* a monster. But in fact there was. "He was such a sweet child," Erna told her nephew. "We all loved him so much." Chris realized then that he'd always assumed the monster he'd known was the only Joe Mankiewicz there had ever been. But the tears rolling down Erna's cheeks as she described the angel she'd grown up with told a different story indeed. It was a story with its own echoes in Joe's greatest script. For *All About Eve*'s Eve Harrington, remember, didn't really exist: born Gertrude Slescynski, she invented Eve Harrington to escape a past she wanted nothing to do with. In the end, the story of how Joe evolved is a similar tale of reinvention, more subtle to be sure, the story of a little brother with nowhere else to turn.

JOE HAD LOST TRACK OF THE TIME, WHICH HAPPENED A LOT, ESPE-cially in the summer after the family had moved uptown, closer to Columbia, where Herman went to school and Pop now taught, now that the family had moved back to New York City. Joe had fallen in with a gang of boys who called themselves the Mudcats, and the Mudcats played a lot of stickball out on Seventh Avenue, or on the other side of 110th Street, in Central Park, and prided themselves on playing so late that their mothers would start yelling down at them from surrounding buildings. In fact, Joe never really lost track of time; he only pretended to. He knew when it would start getting late, and he'd sometimes be running around the bases and even stick his tongue out of his mouth in a way that would display, to anyone who might be watching, intense concentration. Joe knew that any third party observing him would absolutely *know* that there was no way the boy could possibly guess what time it was. How was he to sense when it was time for supper? What if he *hadn't* seen that man with the pocket watch about twenty minutes ago? It would have been easy for him not to have seen that, and anyway, what if the mother of that kid with the harelip *hadn't* come looking for him at seven? She didn't usually do that, and it was easy enough for Joe to pretend she hadn't come tonight.

But now that the cat was out of the bag—there had been too many other grown-ups shouting down, and it was practically dark now, the streetlamps were on, and the game had broken up—there was no use in trying to act like Joe didn't know he was late—it was time to head home. He did it slowly. He knew Pop would be waiting, with the strap. Joe figured if he walked slowly enough, maybe he'd figure something out before he got there. Usually, he did.

For one thing, there was Herman. If Herman was home, Joe stood a fighting chance. So Joe would ring the buzzer downstairs, and when someone answered, Joe would call out, "Is Herman there?" If the answer was no, Joe would likely sit on the stoop and wait until Herman did arrive. A few minutes later, there'd come Herman, swinging up the street, his pants too short, looking uncomfortable and even somehow disheveled in his gabardine suit, and he'd smile that crooked smile at Joe and know that it was time to move into protector mode. They'd head up together and Herman would happily argue Joe's case, telling his parents they shouldn't punish Joe. He'd offer any number of reasons for them to excuse Joe's tardiness—the kid is too young, he can't tell time, he'd been waylaid by a peddler who spoke no English and demanded to have the afternoon newspaper read aloud to him front to back. And almost always, the tactic worked. Joe learned, literally, how to bat his eyes, and usually Pop had no time for such nonsense anyway, and Mama liked the play of it all. When Herman had done his duty, he'd give a little two-finger salute to Joe and head toward the kitchen to get a bite to eat: liverwurst if there was any left. Joe would look after him, full of pride and hope.

Herman, Joe said later, was the only one permitted to see the full range of feeling inside him. "When I was a boy, I used to bare my heart in the most childish way—actually open—no defenses—to Herman. He was the father figure I wanted."

Then again, there were the fights, the shouts and yelling, the horror of hearing Franz fulminate at Herman for some infraction, real or perceived. Coming home late, getting a 94 on a test, an incident with a bottle of beer that shamed the professor in front of his colleagues. The litany of embarrassments and horror stories would fill Joe with as much shame as he had pride in the moments of Herman's great accomplishments. Then there was that memorable afternoon when Joe and a pack of younger boys had chased Herman and his friends after the older boys had seemed to make off with some loose change from the ice cream parlor. Theft? Not exactly, but then why was the store owner's cousin so furious as he ran after Herman and the other boys?

Many feelings coursed through Joe as he and the others bounded after

Herman and the older boys: shame, pride, guilt—but there was something else nagging at him as he ran: Was he running with his brother, or was he running with the pack? It wasn't at all clear to Joe whose side he was on.

I am not my brother, nor am I his keeper. I am my own person, and I will not be judged by his actions. It is this, as much as anything, that defines the moment of selfhood that all younger brothers arrive at—this moment of realizing we are separate. This moment when Abel understands he is not Cain, nor even Kane.

Franz Mankiewicz had no time for bad puns, no time for entertainment, and even less for what is now called the entertainment business. It was sheer frivolity—work was something else. Work was hard, demanding, and, above all, serious. To Joe and Herman, growing up in such a home, where Pop's every pore oozed learning and books, education and teaching, it would be a true challenge to escape the path of academic achievement that Franz seemed to have laid out for them. For a time, Herman seemed to be hewing to the path. Missing three points or not, his scholastic career was utterly brilliant. The boy excelled at every school he ever attended, and nearly every subject. He sped through Hillman in record time, graduating when he was only fourteen—making pocket money on the side, ho-hum, by translating friends' Latin homework for a dime. Even more impressive, he'd passed the entrance examinations to Columbia University when he was only thirteen. (Columbia's bylaws prevented him from attending till he was fifteen.)* Still, with Franz Mankiewicz as a father, it was never nearly enough. And how must Herman have felt when Franz seemed to horn in on his own glory by following his acceptance to Columbia by going there himself as a teacher and beginning his tenure on the first day of Herman's freshman year? Of course, Herman likely told himself that Pop was doing what was right; as hard as it was to get into an Ivy League school as a student, think about how many fewer spots there were for teachers.

---

* Herman spent the yearlong interim between Hillman and Columbia in the least Mankiewiczian of ways: he took a job as surveyor's assistant in the Pennsylvania coal mines, a courageous and possibly foolhardy decision; Wilkes-Barre lost an average of 170 men per year in those mines. Still, it was there, among the rawboned Pennsylvanian miners, that Herman toughened up physically. The men called him "Mike" and introduced him to dirty jokes, his favorite being the one about the young girl walking down the street approached by a man who tells her, "You have a hair on your lollipop." "I should have," the girl replies, "I'm fifteen years old."

What's more, Pop was beloved by his students. With the Mankie-wicz home constantly filled with young people seeking his advice on any number of issues, resentment of Franz, or dislike for him, must have felt doubly ungrateful to Herman. Franz was devoted to his students, who loved him back with a ferocity bordering on idolatry. Franz made sure his students chose the best schools to get into, and in a long career that included teaching stints at Columbia, CCNY, and Stuyvesant, one of the city's finest public high schools, he always prepared them to take the proper exams and helped them get scholarships. His roster of students over the years (ranging from the critic Alfred Kazin to the producer-actor Sheldon Leonard) was filled with devotees who remained forever grateful for Professor Mankiewicz's tutelage. My uncle Frank, Herman's second son, told me when I set out on this project: "All through my adult life, I don't think there's a month goes by that somebody doesn't say to me, 'Are you related to a Professor Frank Mankiewicz who taught at CCNY?'" Like any good Mankiewicz, Uncle Frank's delight had some educational bias baked in, and much to do with the fact that he was recognized for a relative who made his name in academics as opposed to the entertain-ment industry.

In fact, Franz's complete disregard for the entertainment industry was the source of both of his sons' conflicted attitude about success in Hol-lywood, as well as of one of the more repeated family anecdotes, about Franz's most famous student, James Cagney. Visiting his sons in Hol-lywood in the thirties, during the height of Cagney's fame, Franz was taken by Joe to the famed Brown Derby for lunch. No doubt Joe thought hobnobbing with the leading lights of Hollywood might impress the impossible-to-impress professor. While they were there, Cagney spotted and approached his former high school teacher. Franz had never been great with names and faces, and so while he vaguely recalled Cagney he couldn't place him. Finally, the former student from Franz Mankiewicz's classes at Stuyvesant High School said, "I'm James Cagney," which at long last jogged Franz's memory. "Of course," Franz said. "How nice to see you again." Franz stared at Cagney a moment, then said, "Tell me, Cagney, what are you doing these days?"

With such a father, it is no surprise that Joe became something of a mama's boy. "By necessity, Joe spent most of his time with our mother," Herman said. "She raised Joe—Pop had no time for him." For Joe, this wasn't necessarily such a bad thing. He had dodged a pretty dangerous bullet, and in its place was his mother, Johanna—who, whatever else she may have been, seems to have been warm and accepting, and Joe's first audience.

From the beginning, Joe Mankiewicz knew how to render his mother absolutely helpless with laughter. As a boy, he had a cherished bathrobe, and the older and more tattered it became, the more he loved it. He used it as the central prop in a comic routine that brought his mother and sister to hysterics. Erna and Johanna would be sitting on the sofa in the living room, talking or listening to the radio or phonograph records, and Joe would emerge with the robe flung over his shoulder like a matador's cape. Hurling himself dramatically down at the feet of his plump mother, who was already shaking with laughter, the little boy would look at her soulfully and then say to her with an unplaceable accent, "I love you. Flee with me to my hacienda. I will learn you to make mad love." Over the years, Joe did this routine many times, but each time it was as if it were happening for the first time, with Johanna doubled over in laughter.[*]

A cute scene, and what a stark contrast with Herman, not just for how much Joe was craving attention and love, and how much he actually got these things from Johanna, but because of the work ethic embedded in it. Joe worked hard on his bathrobe routine, perfecting it and learning through trial and error what particular words to stress as he played the scene. Which word would get Erna in stitches, which one Mama? Never great with accents, Joe soon stumbled across the old vaudevillian's trick when tasked with performing something at which he has no skill: the harder you try, the funnier it is. Thus, the more seriously Joe pushed a Spanish accent, the more ridiculous the effect—and so he drove even harder into mock-Spanish. He also did wonders with the robe—taxing his imagination to come up with different ways of wearing it, of flashing it about or twirling it around him before laying it to rest gently on his shoulder. He tried kneeling, burying his head in his mother's lap, long, soulful looks out the window, then quick turns back to Johanna and Erna. Whatever worked.

To Herman, if it didn't happen naturally, it wasn't worth it. Repeating

---

[*] Despite her love for these comic scenes, Johanna seemed not to revere the robe as Joe did. Once, when he was a teenager away for a weekend, she got rid of the old thing, giving it to one of the charity groups she became involved in later in life. When Joe returned and discovered what had happened, he made his mother return to the charity organization and buy the robe back. How different from Herman's furious acceptance of the fate of the bicycle.

a joke, refining an anecdote, polishing a story until he got it just right, working up a "routine"—these were of less than little interest to him, and worse, in real life struck him as almost morally bankrupt. He'd do it occasionally, and God knows as a professional writer he had to, but he didn't value it, and certainly didn't appreciate a worked-on performance the way his brother did. To him, the spontaneous remark, the bon mot that people would still be talking about days later—this was the pinnacle. In later years, after a particularly brilliant riposte, he got in the habit of turning to someone—anyone—and saying, "You should write that down." The point was, Herman wasn't about to. To write it down was to kill it, to deny it of its essence, the spontaneity and sheer coruscating brilliance of the original remark cheapened by the act of even appearing to work on it. He was funny, he simply *was*. He would not appear to work on it.

To Joe, working on it, refining it until you got the damn thing right, was both a skill and a talent. Hard work *was* a virtue. And in fact, Joe saw little else from Pop other than work. The man was working furiously at a variety of academic posts as well as a few other odd jobs on the side, like translating travel brochures and laxative ads—there's no question that Joe prized his father's tremendous work ethic, even as it pulled Pop away from the family and caused them to keep moving neighborhoods, even after the move back to New York—Franz kept getting new teaching jobs and wanted to move closer to them, and the attendant salary increases allowed for better and roomier digs, to accommodate his ever-increasing need for bookshelves. "I can't remember all the different places we lived in New York City," Joe said. "I know we lived in Bensonhurst, Sheepshead Bay, three or four locations on the Lower East Side, Harlem, and Madison Avenue. We were moving all the time." There were always new neighborhoods, "new gangs of kids, new adjustments. I made no friends." With an obsessive, violent, angry father, a mother who alternated between timid acceptance of the man and rueful avoidance of him, and a household that kept relocating, Joe felt very little stability as a child and made few lasting attachments. Years later, he would look back and say, almost as a regretful boast, "I have no contact today with anyone who knew me as a child."

In fact, like Herman, Joe was quite popular among his peers. "He had friends," Erna said, "but he made friends quickly and then moved on to the next set quickly." In fact, Joe was developing the social skills, the charm and ease of manner, the Mankiewicz wit, that would mask any inner turmoil. Establishing friendships but never close ones and not keeping them long, Joe was learning how to armor himself against the world.

In a house dominated by an exacting, demanding academic with no regard for the frivolities of movie making and the theater, it's easy to see why a young boy might feel lonely, especially if he is in thrall to an older brother who was devoted above all else to entertainment. Entertainment, and being entertaining, which was becoming easier every day.

OF THE GREAT ROMANCE OF HERMAN MANKIEWICZ'S LIFE, ABSO-lutely nothing is known of the moment his lips first parted for alcohol. We know that by the time he'd entered Columbia at the age of fifteen, he was already well familiar with liquor, most likely from the coal miners of Pennsylvania, and we know that his college years only solidified the relationship, so much so that by the time he graduated, he was placing on his senior page not a warbly quote from the Bard, or an earnest Emersonian proclamation about self-reliance, as his contemporaries did in the same way later generations would cite tide-beating boats. No, what nineteen-year-old Herman chose to quote was a couplet from Columbia's own humor magazine, *The Jester*, written by Herman's classmate (and future comrade in Hollywood), Morris Ryskind. The two-line ditty consisted not of words of wisdom, life advice, or sage remarks about Nature, but of a tribute, ironic and arch, to Herman himself:

> *I'll say this much for H. J. Mank,*
> *When anybody blew, he drank.* *

It's not just that Herman was freely admitting his weakness for drinking. It's that he was already crafting an image of himself as worthy of spectacle, creating a persona that he knew might reap as much attention as his actual work. Indeed, it was during his college career that he realized for the first time the enormous effect he could have on people—to make them admire him, love him, wish to be in his presence—all of which was magnified by alcohol.

Of course, at the time, alcoholism was no disease—it was an affliction,

---

* Ryskind used *The Jester* to tweak Herman one other time, writing a column decrying how dull Columbia had become and announcing a contest calling for suggestions for something new at the university. To the best suggestions he received, Ryskind suggested awards—for third place, he'd give the winner a portrait of Herman J. Mankiewicz. For fourth place, he said, he'd give the winner two.

or a character defect, something the lower classes had to worry about and the weaker members of the human race had to be careful about, lest they slip into it. It carried with it both greater societal acceptance—especially among those who, like Herman, could be tremendously funny when drunk—and also more shame, for it wasn't a disease over which one had no power, but rather a weakness in the character of the alcoholic. It may also have been a way to reject his family, and Jewishness. As Dr. Hacker put it, "It was unheard of in the family . . . Jews fool around. They cheat, they steal, they do God knows what, but they don't drink."

At Columbia, Herman's love for booze took hold. One of his main drinking buddies when he was there was a short, somewhat elfin kid from Harlem named Lorenz (Larry) Hart. Before Hart would team with Richard Rodgers to rewrite Broadway history, he was an introverted depressive at Columbia who found a comrade in Herman. On more than one occasion, Larry's father would phone Franz Mankiewicz in the middle of the night, and the two would head out into the city in search of their drunken sons.* In fact, Herman loved drinking at Columbia, and he found to his delight that the campus bars were convivial places to drink and talk, and then drink some more and talk some more. Fifteen years after graduation, Herman happily answered the Columbia Alumni Association's questionnaire about his time at the college. Asked if he belonged to any clubs, he replied that he did not but that he had been blackballed by three and expelled for nonpayment of dues by two others. In that same questionnaire, he also claimed that his recreations were "numerous—without exception illegal" and that his hobbies were "regular attempts to get away with my recreations."†

Hand in hand with drinking went gambling, for like drinking, at Columbia gambling went from being a pleasant diversion to a dominant

---

* Years later, when Hart's drinking made him too dissolute and unreliable for Rodgers to keep working with him, he turned to another lyricist who happened to be at Columbia with Herman, Oscar Hammerstein. Shortly afterward, Hart would be dead at the age of forty-eight.

† Herman's reply to the twentieth-anniversary questionnaire is more poignant, and almost more honest. In it, Herman admits to his alma mater that his present occupation (screenwriting) was not what he'd hoped it would be when he graduated, that he didn't think college was worthwhile, and that he didn't believe in immortality. The final question asked if he drank. After writing, "Very heavily until a year ago," he felt compelled to add: "Not at all now." He may have been on the wagon when he filled out the questionnaire, but he didn't stay there.

preoccupation in Herman's life, something that today might have been labeled an illness he could no longer control. His future held ridiculously large and risky bets on USC football games, stunning profligacy at the track, and legendary bridge games with George S. Kaufman and Irving Thalberg with stakes routinely running into four figures. But at Columbia, Herman's means were still very modest, so his gambling was at somewhat minimal levels. The money his father made as a teacher wasn't enough to keep Herman in anything but old, shoddy suits, which according to one classmate changed color "depending on whether they had been rained on or not." While the family's means, or lack of them, had always been an issue Herman thought about, it was while he was at Columbia, out from under his father's roof for the first time, that his own complicated relationship with money began to twist and deepen and coalesce into something that would eventually bring feelings of deep shame and humiliation not just to Herman but to those he loved.

For Franz and Johanna, the issue of money had been, as it was for many immigrants in turn-of-the-century New York, fairly simple: you need it to eat and put a roof over your head. But that was about as far as it went. Franz had come to America because he thought it might be easier to earn more money and a better living given his talents and gifts. The idea of altering his behavior in order to seek more money would have been as absurd to Franz as the notion that his grandchildren would someday watch people walking on the moon on a screen in their living room. Money didn't define you; it didn't make you who you were; it was just a necessity. "Pop had a real contempt for money and the things money could buy," Erna said. What mattered was "what you were inside—what you had learned that day: had you done something kind or worth doing?" But for a young man like Herman, gifted and prodigiously talented in so many ways, to be thrown into an environment like Columbia, surrounded by people of greater means and just starting to make his way in the world, money began to take on an almost holy glow. It could save you. It could lift you. It could remake your circumstances and, quite possibly, how you felt about yourself—maybe even, if you were lucky, how those around you (like your unsparing, unsentimental father) thought of you too.

The challenge, of course, was simply phrased, as Mr. Bernstein would put it in Herman's script for *Citizen Kane* decades later: "It's no trick to make an awful lot of money, if all you want to do is make a lot of money."

The question would be: *How* to make the money? One could not stoop; one could not throw away one's gifts; one had to do something worthy of being a Mankiewicz—or so, anyway, went one thread that wound through Herman's mind, the strand that had Franz embedded in it. But another, countervailing argument, was equally strong: I am smarter and funnier than anyone; I deserve whatever I can possibly get from these idiots. But the friction caused by these two strains of Herman's thought— the Franz and the anti-Franz, the "do something with integrity" versus "do whatever you want"—would create in Herman an almost unresolvable tension, which would eventually lead to a lifetime of mini–boom and bust cycles, especially in Hollywood, where he would earn enormous sums of money, live high on the hog for a time, then fritter it away, lose more than he earned in gambling and other pursuits, and have to start all over again. Simply put, Herman was terrible with money, all his life.

While at Columbia, though, Herman did what he could to earn some. He typed other people's theses, worked in a city playground one summer, and ran "a hip-pocket lending library of pornography. *Fanny Hill* cost a dollar an hour; *The Memoirs of Josephine Mutzenbacker* fifty cents." And yet for all his poverty, he still managed to squirrel away enough to gamble. Classmate Howard Dietz, who later became an executive at M-G-M and designed the trademark logo of the roaring lion (as well as being a lyricist who wrote songs like "That's Entertainment"), commented that one could often see Herman "darting into entryways for quick transactions with bookies." But the exhilaration Herman felt on such occasions went beyond the actual money. What got to Herman wasn't just the idea of trying to increase his modest stash. It was deeper and more fundamental than that.

Herman J. Mankiewicz simply did not like the rules. As one friend later said, "Show me a rule, and Herman wanted to break it." An iconoclast through and through, Herman took immense delight in thumbing his nose at authority.* But a man of excess to the last, Herman took

---

* Though he was the very symbol of authority Herman would so determinedly rebel against, it was Franz Mankiewicz who taught his children never to take authority for granted and to question it, always. Whenever one of the Mankiewicz children defended a point of view by saying they'd heard it from their teacher, he would thunder, "Is your teacher God?" Then he'd take the opposite side of the argument and make his children argue against him.

questioning of authority to an extreme degree. From the basics on how to drive a car or eat in a fancy restaurant to more fundamental (and to his livelihood crucial) lessons on how to structure a screenplay or manage money, Herman refused to accept the rules that society presented him. While such iconoclasm can of course lead to originality and daring (it's hard to imagine the screenplay for *Citizen Kane* emerging from a two-day screenplay seminar), it also leads to a painful isolation from the world and fosters a curious condition; the feeling that the iconoclast is in some fundamental way better than the society whose rules he shuns and mocks goes hand in hand with the feeling that there is something essentially fraudulent and dishonest about one's participation in society at all. The rules may be for losers and suckers, but at least those dumb clucks know where they belong. It's awfully hard to succeed when you don't buy into the game you're playing.

And so, Herman at Columbia did things in his own, possibly delightful way, even if not following life's basic rules became as restrictive and confining as following the rules would have been. Thus in addition to the drinking and gambling, he would "push his food on his fork with his fingers, would belch, would use words forbidden then." Really, the main thing that could be said of Herman at Columbia is that he absolutely relished the persona he was constructing. He loved shocking people, and he did it all day, every day—and long into the night. Known by his friends and roommates as prodigious in all things—eating, drinking, gambling, belching, farting—Herman in college enjoyed a seemingly bottomless well of appetites.

GOMA HAD PICTURES EVERYWHERE. THE SIDE OF HER REFRIGERATOR was practically a shrine to dead relatives, and the coffee tables and bureaus were all topped with slippery pieces of glass that squatted on top of black-and-white photographs. Everywhere you looked—up from the breakfast table where you'd have your grapefruit, precut by Marta the maid with a serrated knife, or down the small carpeted hallway toward Goma's room, between the framed Oscar nominations Herman had received for *Citizen Kane* and *Pride of the Yankees*, and certainly in the living room, you'd see photographs. Various Mankiewiczes, Aaronsons,[*] and other relatives and

---

* Goma's real name at birth was Sara Aaronson.

friends, though I never knew most of their names.

One arresting picture was of a young boy in short pants, standing on a New York City stoop in wintertime in the snow. The boy is smiling and wears a black cap, with dirty blond hair peeking out from under it, and his expression conveys an impish delight in the world. As a young boy, I remember being inordinately pleased once when a great-aunt said the picture reminded her of me. But as much as I saw the physical resemblance, and thrilled to it—*I looked like Herman! The great Herman who was so funny and wrote the best movie of all time!?*—I also sensed something else in the picture that was slightly alien to me. Herman looked tough. He looked strong. He looked like the oldest.

Portrait of Herman as a young man, c. 1916

No matter how wayward Herman's behavior, his years at Columbia were far from dissolute. Though he became known as "Mank the Tank," he was no cartoon drunk; he was an immensely productive student. Here, especially when one considers that alcoholism is taking hold, the portrait of Herman Mankiewicz begins to evolve. The two-dimensional improviser, the quick wit, the man of enormous appetites was in fact much more. For one thing, you don't get accepted into Columbia at the age of thirteen just by being naturally gifted and talented. But more than that, he was almost phenomenally prodigious while there. In addition to his efforts on *The Jester,* he also worked for the school newspaper, the *Columbia Daily Spectator,* where he edited a humor column titled "The Off Hour" and also contributed political doggerel.* For two years he was a member of Deutscher Verein, the German club, and for three years a member of the campus poetry society, Boar's Head. He also excelled in the classroom, graduating with honors in both English and German, taking a number of classes with John Erskine, a legendary teacher who had

---

* A skeptic of America's involvement in foreign wars who felt the US was being manipulated into the Great War by Great Britain, Herman wrote: "If England was what England seems/And not the England of our dreams/But only putty, brass, and paint . . . /'Ow quick we'd chuck her./Well, who says she ain't?"

written popular novels like *The Private Life of Helen of Troy* and *Penelope's Man: The Homing Instinct.*[*]

But for Herman, success in the classroom always took a back seat to his extracurricular activities. The real focus of his energies and passion was the stage. At Columbia, Herman Mankiewicz found his calling as a dramatic writer. And his devotion would demand far more than mere improvisation.

The Varsity Show at Columbia was miles from your typical college production. Inaugurated in 1894 as a fundraiser for the school's athletic teams, it had become such an entrenched tradition that even after it severed its fundraising connection, it maintained the name and continued as an annual event. Until 1907 it was performed in Carnegie Hall, then moved to the grand ballroom of the old Waldorf Astoria. And while the show was always an occasion for frivolity and fun for the audience, it was taken absolutely seriously by the performers and writers, offering them, as Richard Rodgers later said, "something no other school in the country could supply: an almost professional production."

By 1915, the show was so successful it was no longer being written by students; although many undergraduates still dutifully submitted scripts, it had been four years since anyone but a teacher or professor's script had been chosen as the basis for that year's production. In the fall of 1915, undaunted, Herman submitted his musical for acceptance to the Varsity Show selection committee.

Titled *The Peace Pirates,* his show lampooned Henry Ford's ill-fated mission earlier that year to stop World War I. Ford had assembled a bizarre crew of clergymen, politicians, pacifists, and businessmen and chartered a Norwegian ocean liner for a trip to Europe where Ford hoped to draw the Great War to a close. It didn't work. His coalition argued and fought among itself, and the war kept right on raging. In *The Peace Pirates,* the ocean liner is torpedoed by a German U-boat, stranding the delegates on a deserted island.

By January, Herman got the news, surprising and sweet: *The Peace Pirates* had defeated at least a dozen other hopefuls, among them at least three full professors. Herman Mankiewicz's first play swung into production.

The premise of *The Peace Pirates* reveals a penchant for irreverence and demonstrates an early willingness to take a swipe at titans—in fact,

---

[*] Erskine seemed to be everybody's favorite, and sure enough, when Joe came along to Columbia eleven years later, he made sure to take Erskine as well.

Herman was as unhesitant about attacking Henry Ford as he was his father, or as he would be two and a half decades later with William Randolph Hearst. Throughout, the libretto is the work of a precocious wordsmith with clear and obvious preoccupations, as with the show's opening, a musical homage to drinking, or later a song of a waiter lamenting his lot:

> *People may say a waiter's life is free from worry and care,*
> *Taking the tips of every man who reads the bill-of-fare;*
> *But I want to tell you now—you may know it anyhow—*
> *This life is not at all desired, because we get tired—*

CHORUS

> *Of food, food, food.*
> *I'm sick of the sight of food.*
> *They take a seat and they eat and eat;*
> *It seems they never conclude.*
> *Wait, wait, wait,*
> *We bring them plate after plate.*
> *So pity the waiter, his life is imbued*
> *With food, food, food.*

Herman was tickled by the sight of a phalanx of tuxedoed waiters kicking on, arm in arm behind the main waiter, doing a cancan while singing the chorus, though impatient when the actors had difficulty in rehearsal getting the word "imbued" to scan properly to land the rhyme with "conclude." Herman found most of the student actors so loud and self-concerned that after a time he could barely stand to be in the rehearsal hall.

Better, to Herman, was the love ditty he'd written for the central couple in the show, whose chorus was itself deceptively simple and charming:

> *If I were you and you were I,*
> *I could not live without me;*
> *If you were I and I were you,*
> *Why, I'd be just crazy 'bout me.*
> *I'd like me for my winning smile,*
> *I'd be near me all the while;*
> *If I'd be my wife,*

I'd be happy for life,
If I were you.

Beyond the cleverness of the wordplay, there is a kind of knowing narcissism in the song, a charisma that one may choose to like or dislike, but is undeniable. Despite its tossed-off quality, the song reveals a writer in growing command of his craft.

The show opened on April 12, 1916, to rave reviews. Of course the *Columbia Daily Spectator* praised the show, but more impressively, the *New York Times* gave it a glowing notice, calling the Mankiewicz script "particularly clever."

Herman Mankiewicz was triumphant at last. For the first time he had a success—the roar of crowds, the handshakes and claps on the back from strangers, a rave review in the *New York Times* for an essentially professional musical: in a roundabout kind of way, a smash hit on Broadway. He had harnessed his long-praised talents into something the world could look at and admire. A career with seemingly limitless promise spread out in front of him.

There is no record of how Franz Mankiewicz reacted to this singular event.

FOR JOE, THE NEXT YEAR, 1917, BROUGHT NOT SUCCESS BUT TRAUMA. He was eight years old when the flu epidemic that over the next two years would kill millions worldwide first hit New York City. Joe was one of the early victims, his flu spiraling into a case of double pneumonia, pleurisy, and emphysema that almost killed him. The world made little sense. He'd catch a glimpse of a worried-looking nurse or doctor, a bed curtain, the furrowed brow of Erna or his mother, but everything hurt. He felt like he was doused with flames or ice and could hardly breathe, a frightened boy with fitful dreams interrupted by the cries and smells of dying children all around him.

One of the few things Joe looked forward to was a visit from Herman, a bright spot in the seemingly endless parade of nurses and orderlies and pasty-looking doctors at a series of different hospitals. Finally, the boy was taken to Lenox Hill Hospital where, according to Joe, he "was saved by a very famous doctor, Willie Meyer." As Joe told the tale, this doctor, while on his rounds, "happened to be caught by my grin or something. He came over and talked to me and took me in hand by operating to remove a piece of my rib, which fixed me up." Erna said that in lieu of the old rib, the doctor put in a new silver rib, the treatment for emphysema in those days, though later, quixotically, Joe denied the existence of the silver rib, joking that if he did have it, he'd have put a mortgage on it years ago.*

When Joe came home from the hospital, he was surprised that there wasn't more of a welcoming committee. Years later, he told his biographer Ken Geist of his surprise that life just seemed to be going on, much as before. The sickness had done nothing to change the behavior of the family. In fact, the only person who seemed genuinely happy he was home was Erna. To her, Joe had always been like a doll really, a plaything that belonged to her and her alone. Since she'd always been unselfconsciously young for her age—she loved playing with dolls far longer than her friends did—it was easy for her to be close to her little brother. And—in spite of the eight years that separated them, Erna, at home and at hand, was much closer to Joe than anyone else in the family—whereas the eleven and a half years that separated him from Herman was sometimes an unbreachable gulf . . .

Joe slumped into his room that afternoon and lay down on his bed. He kicked off his shoes and lay in his stockinged feet on the bedspread, hands clasped behind his head for a pillow. He stared up at the ceiling and thought, hard. He had returned from the hospital expecting to be welcomed and loved, only to find instead that the whole family's focus was still on Herman, his success with the Varsity Show, his largeness, his outrageousness, the great enormous quality of Herman's that wherever he went, as Orson Welles would later say, "You felt you were in the presence of some thwarted violence, some violent magnificent creature."

For a moment, Joe found himself at a loss. What on earth could he do? Would he ever get away from it? It didn't really matter how, but he would have to—or it would kill him.

---

* It's no accident that Joe speculated it was due to his grin that he caught the famed doctor's eye. Joe believed that what saved him, ultimately, was his wit. He would craft a persona that relied on it for the rest of his life.

CHAPTER THREE

———— ♀ ————

THE NEW YORKER

I think it would be fun to run a newspaper.

—*CITIZEN KANE*

THE MYTH OF HERMAN MANKIEWICZ, PASSED DOWN FROM GENERATION
to generation of his descendants, runs as follows: there once was a celebrated bon vivant in New York City, the "Voltaire of Central Park West,"
a well-known member of the Algonquin Round Table, who, lured out
to Hollywood by the promise of easy money, squandered his talent on
screenplays for movies that were far beneath him, and soon drank himself into an early grave, hating himself for the weakness of not pursuing
a higher calling. "I don't know how it is," he once said, "that you start
doing something you don't like, and one day you wake up and you're
an old man." But however simplified this myth is, or really, whether it's
true at all, it still begs the question: What of Herman *before* Hollywood?
He didn't move out to Hollywood until 1926, and he'd graduated from
Columbia in 1917. A lot can happen in nine years.

So what happened? What was the shape of those first nine years of
Herman's professional adult life? Was there one? What had he hoped to
be doing in the 1930s if not working as a screenwriter in Hollywood? Did
he have a future mapped out for himself that he veered away from? Or
was the whole thing one grand improvisation that went horribly wrong?

Of course, it's not as if Herman knew, when this chapter of his life
ended, that he was leaving New York for good, or even that the rest of
his working life would be devoted to doing something for which he had
little or no respect. So far as Herman was concerned, he was still doing

Herman, c. 1919

it all, and living in California would just be a natural extension of the life he was building in New York—writing for the theater, contributing pieces to magazines, producing theatrical sketches, and living life as a famous wit. But even above and beyond that, there was something else Herman was doing in those early years in New York, something that wouldn't show up in the list of professional accomplishments, but something that meant more to Herman than he would ever admit, and explain the move to movies and California more than anything else. He was building a family.

TO BEGIN WITH, THE ROUND TABLE WAS A HELL OF A LOT BIGGER than Sara expected. Herman had told her about the people, of course, the intimidating names she read in columns and had heard so many stories about—Swope, Woollcott, F.P.A., Harpo Marx, Dorothy Parker, Benchley, Broun—but for some reason when she walked in, what she found most intimidating was the sheer size of the table, and the sense that came with it that she would be, as everyone was, on stage the whole time. The table must have been forty feet around, she guessed—and not only that, it looked lit by special lights. She wondered for a moment whether it was elevated, but no, she saw it was on the same level as all the other tables in the room; still, it definitely seemed set off from the rest, and not just by the velvet rope that she and Herman were ushered past as they walked in toward their seats. This would not be a meal, she realized, but a performance. Or, more than that, a competition. Part sport, part art, with the wit sharpened to knifepoint, hovering for the kill. She would, she knew instantly, be completely mute until they left.

She settled into her chair, and the hour passed in a blur and panic. The Algonquin Round Table, by the time the former Sara Aaronson attended her one and only luncheon in the early 1920s, had become a New York Institution, a place where the leading writers, critics, and theater people of the day would gather to make each other laugh—and make a kind of news doing so. The wit and spontaneous jokes flew back and forth rapidly, though Sara couldn't help feeling that much of it, though not really forced, was at least rehearsed. Spontaneous or not, though, the group and the gathering had become well-known as a center for sophistication and wit and creative brilliance. But for Sara, once she got over her anxiety over even being there, the overwhelming impression was of its mean-spirited nature. As Clare Boothe Luce, who herself refused to attend more than a handful of times, put it, the lunches were "too competitive. You couldn't say 'Pass the salt' without somebody trying to turn it into a pun or trying to top it."

What horrified Sara most was the cruelty. In one instance, it was directed at one of the least extraordinary members of the group, a public relations man she knew only as Dave. She never knew the man's last name, and he seemed a perfectly decent if somewhat plodding fellow, but for whatever reason the famed Algonquin wits seemed to have made a collective unspoken decision that afternoon to act as if he, Dave, were the funniest and most brilliant of them all. His simple request for the butter would be met with explosions of laughter, followed by, "Good God, did you hear what Dave just said?" and "Someone, for Chrissakes, write that down!" The man, Dave, was not beyond the understanding that he was being mocked, and took the whole thing in, Sara remembered, with a wan smile.

As for Herman, he was delighted to have finally persuaded his young wife to accompany him to the table, but he wasn't particularly thrilled with the results. Sara was bright, intelligent, and actually had a great and direct wit. He wanted, she later thought, "to show me off so badly, wanted me to be funny. I wasn't." But while Herman may have been disappointed in his bride, he was, very clearly, absorbed in the maw, the give-and-take of the Algonquin Round Table—the barbs and wit flying back and forth had become second nature to him, and though Sara was too intimidated to even open her mouth (until the end—at which point, upon rising, her thanking them all for the honor caused yet another explosion of inexplicable laughter and applause from the whole company, which only underscored in her own mind the rightness of the decision to remain mute until then, and her subsequent decision never to return), she was pleased and invigorated to see Herman holding his own and leading the charge. As she considered him, sitting there with a cigarette dangling from his lips, leaning forward into the table like a horseman riding low upon his mount, she swelled with pride. Yes, Herman had his faults, he was not a perfect husband, not by any stretch, but she'd known that for a while. As she looked at him, and saw him fending off barb after barb, saw the way the other men looked at him—they liked him and thought well of him, and like George S. Kaufman, who'd been his entrée into the New York world of wit and letters, they all seemed to respect his enormous gifts—she decided that she really should stop regretting her decision to marry him in the first place.

Another legend in the family, or at least the one that Goma tried to propagate, was that her relationship with Herman had been nearly perfect—for all his flaws, he was, she insisted, a faithful, loving, devoted husband. And while it's certainly true that he seemed to love her as much as he knew how, there's also no question that their relationship improved dramatically after his death. Like many widows, in later years she emphasized the positive parts of her husband and ignored not only his own foibles and faults but the very real problems that she faced in her marriage. For the truth is that Herman, from the beginning, had been a handful.

They met in February 1918, when the young New Yorker went to Washington, DC, to report for the *New York Chronicle* on a speech called "A Panorama of Ancient Judaism." While there, he caught the eye of a diminutive brown-eyed beauty; they were introduced by a mutual friend, and he walked her home that evening, talking of theater, politics, and the world. "I was absolutely in a dream world," Sara said. "I had never heard anything like such talk." Shulamith Sara Aaronson had grown up the second-oldest of five daughters and a single son to a Russian immigrant Reuben Aaronson and his wife Olga. Reuben was a Hebrew scholar who had taught math in Russia but who ended up owning a paper box factory when he moved to the United States. Eventually, the business foundered—like her future husband, Sara's father had no real business sense, but unlike Herman, he recognized the fault and did something about it: he took Sara out of high school so she could help run the business. Sara had long kept a list of her top beaus in the order of their current favor. After their first date (attending a musical comedy), she wrote Herman's name at the top and drew an *X* through the rest. One of the things that appealed most to her, she later said, was that he was a young man in a hurry.

But it's impossible to read or think deeply about the young Herman so intent on sweeping this young woman off her feet—"as if it's a race," Sara said more than once—without asking: What was he hurrying toward? Did he know?

After graduating from Columbia at the age of nineteen, Herman had joined the Army Air Service and gone off to aviation training school at Cornell, where he exhibited "zero flying aptitude," becoming repeat-

Herman: soldier, patriot,
Mankiewicz

edly and instantly airsick in flight simulators. With the war still raging in Europe, Herman had also kept corresponding with a girl he'd known while at Columbia, who he later said wrote him, "Go, my darling . . . go, and if need be, die." After enlisting in the Marine Corps, Herman finally reached France as part of the 4th Brigade, 2nd Division, AEF on November 3, 1918. Thankfully, the armistice was only eight days away; Herman saw no fighting. In the months that followed, he ended up marching across northern France, Belgium, and Luxembourg as part of a peacekeeping force. There, as he wrote back to Sara, he would entertain himself by telling the girls he met "fanciful lies about America, for example, that all American children are born with tortoise shell glasses."

Returning from Europe in June 1919 to Quantico, Virginia, for demobilization, he went directly to Washington to see Sara. On only the third time they'd met, they took a trolley to Rock Creek Park and strolled around, Herman still in his military uniform. "He was so brawny and strong and wonderful," Sara said, amazed but unconcerned by how much weight the wines of Europe had put on Herman. As soon as the two of them were alone in the park, Herman tried to kiss Sara, but she pushed him away, telling him that she would never kiss anyone unless she was going to marry him. Said Sara, "Honestly, I think I forced him to propose. I was just too pure for words."

Meanwhile, Herman kept mulling over the problem of what to do with his life. His father was pressuring him to continue his studies, but Herman knew the halls of academia could never hold him. He had been bitten by the theater bug, and he was also fascinated by politics and journalism. And through it all his restlessness wouldn't subside. Photographs of him taken in his early twenties show a young man with a sweaty hunger, an appetite for life that bordered on the gluttonous. He was sloppy, true, but young and voracious and eager, so eager to prove Franz wrong. His later claim "I'll never live up to [Pop] and I'm not going to try" notwithstanding, Herman did try. He tried to work brilliantly. He tried to make a name for himself. He tried, with bluster and virtuosity, to gain his father's approval by the sheer force of personality.

But there's a curious aspect to Herman's lifelong battle for Franz's approval, especially after he returned from Europe. Unlike many, Herman wasn't competing just against the standard his father had set down in his childhood. During much of Herman's adult life, Franz was still an active presence. For all his judgment and criticisms of his sons, Franz was very much a part of their daily lives. To the end of his life, the old man was involved in Herman's adult life—by Herman's design. Whatever it was that he was getting from Pop—even when it was dismissal—Herman craved it.

The tragedy, of course, is that Franz *was* enormously proud of his first-born son. He crowed over his accomplishments, puffing his chest up, one friend recalled, as he told of Herman's achievements at Columbia. He cared deeply about Herman, and his daughter-in-law came to rely on him for all kinds of advice. And later, when Herman and Joe were in Hollywood, succeeding in a field for which Franz had no feel and even less regard, Franz knew enough, Erna said, to be proud, and to brag about their accomplishments as best as he could understand them. One famous family tale, usually trotted out to show how unfeeling and mean Franz was, also speaks to some glimmer of pride in his sons: when they had films out in the cinemas, Franz, who of course had no time for the frivolity of movies, would pay his money to go in and watch. He'd see one of their names in the opening credits—Written by Herman J. Mankiewicz, or Produced by Joseph L. Mankiewicz, or in the case of 1932's *Million Dollar Legs*, Produced by Herman . . . , Written by Joseph . . . —two names! His sons!—and then leave the theater. He was satisfied that they were out in the world, making some kind of impact, even if it wasn't one he would ever appreciate or understand.

Under such a thumb, Herman grew up with one real goal in mind and it wasn't artistic satisfaction or mastery over his craft. No, what Herman wanted from the world was something it couldn't possibly give: love. With such an impossible goal, his professional ambition was never to attain just success or awards or even acclaim; in fact, his precise ambition is challenging to trace, but revelatory. For instance, he never said, not once that anyone could recall, "I want to write" or "I want to be a writer." Instead, the idea was *to have written*.

For Goma, the actual wedding day, Thursday, July 1, 1920, was something of a trial. An extraordinarily hot day in Washington, DC, the day began with enormous promise, the twenty-two-year-old Sara Aronson rising early in the bedroom she shared with one of her five sisters. Sara was the first of them to be married; as much pride as I had in the Mankiewicz brothers growing up, the sheer intellectual heft of the Aaronson sisters was nothing to sneeze at—each sister smarter and sharper than the last, and if intelligence wasn't enough, force and bossiness would do. Other than Goma, the ones I knew all had living husbands, each in descending order of meekness and gentleness; the women ran the show. And Herman, at least before the wedding, had certainly given every indication of playing his role to the uxorious hilt. In one of his final letters to her from Europe, he wrote how their reunion would be:

> The sun will be shining and the birds singing and I'll walk down Fairmont Street and climb the steps and ask for "Miss Sara" and [Sara's younger sister] Mattie will say, "What name, please?" and I'll tell her and she'll say, "How do you spell it?" and I'll wait twenty minutes and grumble terribly at the delay. And then my sweetheart will come down languidly to greet me. Oh, Schnutz, you will be all bathed and napped and pink dressed, won't you, darling. And shamefacedly we'll kiss right in front of everybody, won't we? We will, you know.

Fantasist that he was, it's unlikely the scene played out exactly as he imagined it, but Herman did get one detail right: the sun was shining, mercilessly, on the wedding day. In later years, Herman and Sara enjoyed talking of the wedding day's particulars: the simple Orthodox ceremony, the scorching heat in the depth of the Washington summer, the irreverent fly that buzzed around the rabbi's nose, and in particular the appalling behavior of two of Herman's closest friends from Columbia, Milt Wynn and Edwin Justus Mayer,* who had taken to drinking quite early in the day. Sara's parents had arranged for a piano player to be at the ceremony, to play a few religious songs, but at one point Milt and Eddie eased the poor man off the piano bench and began singing a song to Herman whose lyrics were something like, "Good-bye, boys, I'm through." Iconoclast though he may have been, Herman was not amused and snapped at his

---

* Mayer would go on to write a handful of Broadway plays and more than fifty screenplays, including Jack Benny's *To Be or Not to Be* and parts of *Gone with the Wind*.

friends to knock it off. As Sara said, "They were drinking like mad, these two." (In later years, the two men suggested that the real reason Herman was so incensed was because he couldn't join them in their cups.)

Herman's behavior after the wedding, both that afternoon and in the few days following, was eye-opening for Sara. An hour or so after the ceremony, as the photographer herded everyone out for formal photos, Herman encouraged Sara's little brother Meyer to perform acrobatic tricks with Milt and Eddie. For one picture, Herman had one arm around Sara, one around her sister Naomi, and he shouted, "Which one is the bride?" There was elaborate food, and the guests were ebullient, but growing up in a prim and sheltered Orthodox family, Sara was starting to realize just exactly with whom she had thrown in her lot. Herman's little brother Joe, eleven at the time, spent most of the day down in the cellar eating up all the ice cream with Sara's little sister Mattie. It was, according to Sara, "a nice, noisy wedding," but by seven or eight o'clock, she was exhausted and decided it was time for her uncle Meyer to drive the newlyweds to their hotel, where, after committing the faux pas of inviting Meyer up to see the honeymoon suite (the man politely demurred), which Herman would tease her for mercilessly in the decades to come, Sara went up to the bedroom with Herman. There, according to legend, absolutely nothing happened. Nothing, that is, aside from Sara's first experience of sleeping, or trying to, in the same room with a man who snored like a bulldozer.

The following morning, Sara and Herman had to be at the train station early to catch the train up to New York, in order for Sara to avoid traveling on the Sabbath. Though Herman was all his life irreligious and even hostile to organized religion, he was always deferential to Sara's religious wishes. Sara's family met the young couple at the station to see them off, and there was both loud gnashing of teeth and wailing—especially from Sara's next-younger sister Ruth, miserable that Sara was leaving her and getting married—and also a good deal of chiding, especially from Sara's aunts, about the previous night and what had, or had not, gone on in that hotel room now that the two were man and wife. Finally, Sara brought all the teasing to an abrupt halt when, no longer able to stand it, she shut them all up by announcing quite loudly, "Look, he slept in one bed, and I slept in another bed." With everyone properly chastened, there was an awkward silence, and the newlyweds boarded the train.

The romance continued to not blossom[*]. On the train north, Herman

---

[*] The split infinitive for effect is part of Herman Mankiewicz's legacy.

whipped out a stack of newspapers and started plowing through them. Years later Sara joked that he did so because "it was already an old marriage by that time, twenty-four hours," but at first she didn't consider it a joking matter. As he continued to ignore her for the duration of the trip, interrupting his reading once in a while to pat her hand or offer some other slight gesture of affection, her mouth began to dry. Her heart, which had stopped doing somersaults, now settled into her stomach. And when the train pulled into Penn Station, things didn't get any better. They decided to eat dinner at the counter there: their first dinner together, and their first Sabbath dinner. Because Sara kept kosher, she couldn't eat any meat, and she also didn't like fish, so her dinner consisted of Grape Nuts. Not Herman. The sensitive new husband ordered a full-course meal. What's more, on his way to the counter he bought a copy of the evening paper, which he folded lengthwise to make for convenient reading while he ate.

Now, at last, Sara permitted her self-pity to consume her. "My heavens above," she thought, "is this what being married means? No Sabbath dinner, no candles, no nothing." She felt bereft.

But then, at last, the marriage began in earnest: Sara looked at Herman and started to try to understand who he was and what made him tick. Years later, she described the scene as one that required a mirror to bring her to full realization. She looked across the counter behind the bar and saw a mirror in which she could see both Herman's reflection and her own. Thus able to get some distance on the scene, she sized up her view: a young man, twenty-two years old, with his nose stuck in his paper, slurping coffee and gobbling down steak. He was with his young wife, and she was, Sara liked to allow, a beautiful young girl, but the young man was consumed with other thoughts: he was a newspaperman and he was reading about the world, studying the news of the day, honing his intellect and learning his craft. Something stirred in Sara Mankiewicz. As she watched him read his paper so intently, she felt a new feeling: pride. Pride in what she had done, and pride in her own personal newspaperman. "You've just married the greatest guy in the world," she thought, "not just a ninny who's going to make love to you in the railroad station." Fifty years later, telling Herman's biographer Dick Meryman about that moment still brought tears to her eyes, and when she thought back, she let the silence sit there for a good long time. Finally, on the tape, you hear Meryman say, "Are you okay?" And Goma's voice is loud and authoritative: "I'm more than okay!"

And yet, Goma's insistence notwithstanding, there is something about the scene that balks at such an easy interpretation. Had she really been so at peace with the moment, would she have been flooded with such depth of feeling? Was it possible that the moment still nagged at Goma decades later? For if there was pride at Herman's disappearing into the newspaper, and into his own brilliant mind, the thoughts and ideas about the world no doubt racing full speed ahead as he pored over the agate type of the *Sun* and *World,* present too was the knowledge that for Herman Mankiewicz, connection—human connection, feelings and sympathies and the free and easy exchange of intimacies with other human animals—would never be high on the list of priorities, stated or otherwise. Faced with that knowledge, Sara Aaronson had no choice other than to make peace with it. Human connection would have to come later, if at all.

THE 1920 DEMOCRATIC CONVENTION WAS UNDER WAY IN SAN FRANcisco. Herman was aware of Sara of course, he could feel her staring at him above the *World,* he could sense how much she wanted his companionship, and he was not above, as he had done on the train, looking up at her from time to time and granting her a real, warm, genuine smile. He did love her. She was so pretty, his little Schnutzie, and he adored making her laugh more than just about anything in the world. But the importance of what he was reading was never in doubt: Franklin Roosevelt, the handsome young cousin of the former president, had just resigned his office as assistant secretary to the navy in order to pursue the vice presidency.

Herman knew that whatever was actually happening in the world, whatever was being written about or spoken about, whatever, in the end, was famous—those things were ultimately of more value than whatever Sara, or for that matter he, would have wanted in any given moment. And so he told his young wife of his frustration at not having been sent to cover the convention, and threw in some casual condemnations of the man responsible for the indignation, the editor with the strawberry nose. But as he told Sara, there was no use working himself into a lather over it. He'd just have to put his head down and go to Berlin, do the best he could there, and show them all that no one alive possessed a keener political mind.

Still, the mention of Berlin surely would have caused a shudder to run through Herman's body. His young bride was no more than two feet from him, across the table with her spoon still stuck in her Grape Nuts.

He always loved her sweet regard for the old ways, and her utterly trusting nature. Herman loved to read the newspaper, but while sometimes it would deliver information he craved, sometimes it was just newsprint to let wash over him. For now, Sara was his, and she loved him. That was enough.

SARA STOOD ON THE DECK OF THE GREAT OCEAN LINER WITH HER new husband, and she felt her whole body singing. The SS *Kroonland* was bound for Holland. From there the young couple would go to Berlin, where Herman would start a much-discussed job with the *Chicago Tribune.* They stood on deck and waved down from the throng to the wharf, where many in Sara's family—mother and father, brother, sisters, grandfather, aunts and uncles—were present, waving handkerchiefs and tossing confetti as the ship pulled out. Herman and Sara stood on the deck, waving goodbye to their family, to America. Sara was thrilled.

Looking back years later, she would admit that it was odd that Franz had accompanied them on their honeymoon in Far Rockaway, but now, she felt warm about the time they'd spent with Herman's parents, who had taken a summer rental in nearby Rockaway. The week at the beach had been practically a family vacation, with Joe, cousins, and even Eddie and Milt, the two young jokesters from the wedding, all flocking together in a cavalcade of games and picnics. And, almost presiding over the entire week: Franz himself. It's possible Herman was so much in thrall to the old man that he couldn't even conceive of striking out on his own, even at the very symbolic moment when he might have been.

Newlyweds Herman and Sara in the summer of 1920

One incident from the week at the beach did nag at Sara, though. On the way back to their hotel one evening, walking along the boardwalk listening to the waves crash on shore, Franz had lingered behind the others, for a chance to be alone with Sara. "Herman," he told her out of nowhere, "has his faults, but Herman is a very good boy." Sara looked at Franz, almost dumbfounded. Despite her disillusionment with Herman's apparent lack of interest in her on the train and at the station, she really had no idea what faults Franz was talking about. She couldn't imagine: this was her young man, her man of the world, who had taken care of all the preparations for their trip, who had made her get her visa long in advance of their leaving for Europe, and who had taken immediate control of all their money, which was no small sum. (Sara had brought to the marriage a dowry of approximately \$2,500,[*] but she wanted nothing to do with the money and was "terribly glad" to give it to him and "let him handle" it. Only later would she admit she had no idea "how quickly he would dispose of it.") But faults? Sloppy, maybe, but was sloppiness a fault?

On the boat, the two traveled in a first-class stateroom, a luxury, Sara joked, paid for "by my rich husband—with my money." And it was there, in the stateroom on the first or second night out of port, where Sara finally began to understand what Franz might have been getting at. The two had retired early, and when they got to the room, almost immediately, Herman said, "Where's that wine you got?" As wedding gifts, Sara had received a few bottles of a very sweet port wine, a Jewish wine often used for kiddush, and she'd brought a couple of bottles along.

"It's in the old trunk," she said.

"Let's get it out and have a little bit of it."

"Sure," Sara said, and she did get it out, even though she didn't really want any. Herman poured Sara a glass, then one for himself, and eventually he poured her another, as well as himself. Then another, and another. Sara looked at the man. She knew nothing about real drinking. To Sara, you drank only a little bit of wine on special occasions, or on the Sabbath, a little schnapps or wine to make the kiddush prayer. Sara had never seen anyone drink the way Herman was drinking. He was greedy, almost lascivious in his thirst.

That night, she went to bed consumed with a kind of horror that her husband had drunk an entire bottle. In the morning, the feeling grew worse; looking around the stateroom, she realized that on the sly he had also finished the entire second bottle. That morning, with her husband

---

[*] The equivalent of approximately \$30,000 in 2021.

in bed, still a sleeping log (one being loudly sawed in half), she realized she was married to a man who had finished off two bottles of wine—an incomprehensible feat to her—and understood in full what her father-in-law had been talking about.

For Sara Aaronson Mankiewicz, barely twenty-two years old, this was a defining moment. The Mankiewiczes have never been a people who listened to their intuition particularly keenly—but what must it have felt like in Sara's stomach, seeing that she had married a man of such tendencies? Above all else, Sara was a realist. She looked at him and consciously made another decision, like the one she'd made in the railroad station bar, and this one was to ignore the gnawing sense that the ship was steaming toward a collision. A man who loved to drink and postwar Germany, a place of violent excess, was not a match made in heaven. Goma considered the two bottles, looked at Herman, and went for a walk on deck, to get some air and clear her head. She looked out at the sea, the whitecaps, the foam. Above: the broad sky. Ahead: the promise of Berlin, Herman's job at the *Chicago Tribune,* and the start of their lives. She would not mention the two bottles to Herman. In fact, she would do her best not to think about them.

HERMAN MANKIEWICZ ARRIVED IN GERMANY IN THE FALL OF 1920 having told his young wife that a job with the *Chicago Tribune* awaited him in Berlin. Sure enough, after a couple of days in town helping Sara get settled in at their hotel, Herman began leaving bright and early every morning to report to work at the *Tribune* offices at the Hotel Adlon, returning home in the evening with a pocketful of paper money. The German mark was almost notoriously worthless, but money was money, and the couple was blissfully happy in those early days in Berlin. Postwar Germany had much to offer a young couple, though in truth what the city had most of all in addition to rampant inflation was galling poverty, political uncertainty, and an almost legendarily debauched culture that Herman and Sara would be front row viewers of, if not full participants in, for the next two and a half years. Their first hotel was a true fleabag in Friedrichstadt in the center of Old Berlin—a hotel that had been advertised as the only Kosher hotel around, but whose main inhabitants seemed to be cockroaches and prostitutes. Still, and despite the many "boy whores" who, rouged and powdered, appalled Herman with advances on him (which Sara found so amusing), it wasn't a bad place to make a home base while Herman scoured the city looking for work.

The *Chicago Tribune* job, of course, did not exist.

Herman pushed through the swinging doors into the lobby of the Hotel Adlon and moved toward the hotel bar, the center of the thriving expat and journalistic community in Berlin. Herman must have made his way toward it hungrily. Along the way, in the hotel's vast central hall, he would've spotted the Roman-style bust of the kaiser, whose eyes followed one around the room. The pressure was real. Herman had to find a job, and quick. The man who had promised the job for him last summer in Paris—well, it had been almost a promise, or maybe it had been enough of one to convince Herman that it wouldn't exactly be difficult to get the job—was no longer in Berlin, and Herman was now stuck enacting this ridiculous charade for Sara.

Already it had been close to two weeks, and the only work he'd been able to find was a job at a warehouse unpacking cases and crates from trucks and loading them into the warehouse of a department store. They paid in marks every evening, and Herman was waiting for the day when Sara might ask him why an American newspaper would pay in marks. He also wondered if she'd notice the calluses developing on his hands. So far, he was getting away with it, but this couldn't possibly last, and his back was killing him.

He would've sidled up to the bar, put his foot on the brass footrail that ran alongside the bottom of the banquette, and glanced around. It wasn't quite ten in the morning, the regulars wouldn't get in for another half an hour or so—soon enough the journalists would be gathering in droves at the ornate bar, to exchange ideas, kibbutz about work, and enjoy the hotel's advanced plumbing, still a rarity in postwar Berlin—but wait, was that the Sports Editor? Herman didn't give a damn about sports, but he drained his coffee, approached the man with a steady gaze, and stuck out his hand. Then Herman launched into a disquisition on the Kaiser Himself. Herman had a lot of ideas about the man, from theories on his diet to a dissection of his monetary policy blunders, and he would weave it all into something resembling a coherent argument, and more than that, a vivid tapestry that seemed to bring the man to life, the Kaiser's moustache dripping in the cold winter air outside a palace in Wannsee . . . The editor's eyes danced as he listened to Herman, the room was filling up with other journalists, and soon enough the man was ordering Herman a drink. It might not be what he'd promised Sara, but everything would work out. He'd land on his feet. He always did.

HERMAN'S JOURNALISTIC LIFE IN BERLIN PROCEEDED FROM THESE kinds of improvisations, and before long he was cobbling together actual paying work. A few weeks of haunting both the Adlon bar and then the lobby of the *Chicago Tribune* offices across the street, and he managed a meeting with *Tribune* bureau chief George Seldes,* who hired him as a part-time assistant. Then, for $15 a week, he became a stringer for *Women's Wear Daily,* writing short pieces on business and culture. Soon enough, Herman was writing theater pieces for *The New York Times* and making a decent enough living, and more than that, beginning to make a name for himself in the heady world of newspapers in the 1920s. To Herman, the life of a newspaperman was almost ideal: the pace was fast, the assignments were quick—Herman was always an extremely fast worker, when he did work—and most of all, the life itself called for a personality that Herman fell into naturally. He relished the role of the hard-bitten newsman. According to Rebecca Drucker, a part-time *New York Tribune* reporter then stationed in Berlin, Herman played the jaded journalist to perfection: "Toughness was what Herman aimed for, no question. By toughness, I mean you couldn't be caught off guard, couldn't be surprised at anything. You never sounded like an intellectual. You knew where the best food and drink could be found and what things cost and how to manipulate money. You gambled. And you could bull your way into any place, and you had no illusions."†

And because Herman knew how to talk the talk, it's not difficult to understand how, no matter what a neophyte he must have been at the Adlon, he quickly won over the Berlin crowd. His first tool was his wit, which always struck most people as both faster than anyone else's, and

---

* Seldes's own family would become quite well-known, including his brother, the journalist Gilbert, and Gilbert's daughter, the Tony Award–winning actress Marian.

† One of the curiosities in reading such reminiscences of people's experiences with the pre-Hollywood Herman in Berlin and New York is how *old* Herman Mankiewicz already seemed. It's as if they are describing a middle-aged man, not a twenty-three-year-old kid trying to figure out what to do with his life.

Herman in Germany, early 1920s, sitting to the left of
Chancellor Josef Wirth

also somehow more humane, even as lacerating as it could be. Drucker
remembered that during one of the frequent workers' strikes currently
taking place in Berlin, Herman offered anybody at the bar one thousand
marks for a good German translation of the line "It will never get well if
you picket." In addition to his wit, he had a genuine warmth of personality. Sigrid Schultz, the main secretary of the *Chicago Tribune* office in
Berlin and not Herman's biggest fan, couldn't help admitting that he was
"somebody you liked to talk to. He had a way of looking at you from
under the eyelids—a look of observing very, very closely whenever you
said anything." He listened.*

Herman also enjoyed the entrée being a reporter gave him to people
and places that had previously been denied him, and he made the most
out of his newly bestowed access. One picture from the times shows him
at a garden party hosted by Germany's chancellor, Josef Wirth. In the
picture, he is seated at table with five other people, one of them the chancellor himself, sitting directly on his right. Herman's eyes are twinkling

---

* To be clear, Herman listened well *sometimes*; that is, when he *wanted* to listen,
he would. Joe, too, would make listening a professional asset; his attentiveness to
actresses would become almost legendary. But the idea that Herman Mankiewicz
was always a great listener is not a sentiment that would have gone unchallenged
by his wife and children.

with delight, and his mouth is open as he leans toward the chancellor, a young man thrilled to be confabulating with some of the most important people in the country.

But other, more disturbing patterns started to emerge in Berlin. For one, there was his problem with deadlines. Because he was such a facile and fast writer, Herman often waited till the last minute—or even after the last minute—before turning in his pieces. For *Women's Wear*, for which he mainly wrote a variety of pieces on political, business, and cultural matters,* deadlines were Saturday, and he often missed them, sometimes disappearing when the assignments were due. On more than one occasion, Sigrid Schultz, who had helped get him the job, had to track him down, take him to the *Chicago Tribune* office, and lock him inside until he'd finished his piece.

Then there was gambling. The wagering that he'd begun in college and which would reach ruinous proportions in Hollywood was in its ascendance in Berlin. The Adlon had a luxurious bridal suite which, when available, was supplied for free to the American journalists for their poker games, at which Herman was a regular attendee, and loser. Later, when Herman was returning to the States, he appealed to his poker buddies to help fund his passage, which they generously did by pulling a small percentage from every poker pot. Once Herman was sailing safely back to America, one of the correspondents at the poker table asked all the players present whom Herman owed money to, beyond what they'd just given him. Every single man raised his hand.

Too, there was the matter of Sara. What was already clear, from the misadventure with the *Tribune* job alone, was that Herman was setting Sara up to be his policeman, a warden, someone to lie to and evade, someone to impress with big promises—not a true partner to share life's joys and sorrows with. As it was, it wasn't until years later that Herman came clean to Sara about the *Tribune* affair. Then again, Sara herself was starting to become known around Berlin, and some even speculated that, for instance, the *Women's Wear* job had come about because of pity. Though Sigrid Schultz had put in a good word on Herman's behalf, she later admitted, "I did it partly for his wife. I liked her, and I thought she

---

* The almost legendarily hedonistic culture of Berlin in the 1920s written about by Christopher Isherwood and immortalized in *Cabaret* was hardly enjoyed by Herman, who wrote that Berlin "remains unsmiling, and her night life is an insomnia cure."

had a problem with that husband." The pattern of people pitying Sara, and helping Herman as a result, had begun.

But Herman's work, when he did it and when he delivered it on time, was good and starting to get noticed. When Herman wrote his first free-lance theater pieces for *The New York Times,* along with the check for his work, he received generous praise from no less than George S. Kaufman, then the *Times's* leading drama critic. As Kaufman explained, the check was for eight dollars, "with deductions for dashes, as is the benevolent custom of the office." He then declared point-blank: "Your stuff is great. Woollcott thinks so, too. I have liked everything, uniformly, except the long piece that you wrote, and the chief reason I didn't like that is that we haven't room for long pieces."

Herman was honing his critical faculties in Berlin, though interest-ingly, while the dire political and economic situation there produced much innovation within the arts, making the city the unquestioned center of theatrical invention, Herman found much of the theater lacking. "The only real theatrical novelty of the past weeks," he wrote early on, "has been the success of the woman boxers at the Metropol Cabaret." Later, he gave a facetious nod to his boyhood home when he claimed the setting and direction of one play were "considerably inferior to what Poli's stock company in Wilkes-Barre used to provide." But beneath the gibes about Berlin's theatrical disappointments—"At the present time, the German theatre is as frankly commercial as ever the American theatre was and is, without many of the redeeming features to be found [in America]," he wrote at one point—lies a curious fact. Herman Mankiewicz, theater buff, was in Berlin as the avant-garde of German theater was coming into its own, yet he seemed not only to dismiss nearly all of it, but to seek out plays which had nothing to do with it. Why? Why was a young man so antagonistic to all that was new and potentially revolutionary in an art form he proclaimed to revere? And in a man who despised authority and thumbed his nose at convention in so many things, why did he come to hate the avant-garde with such passion? In truth, for all his gifts as a dramatist and skill as a writer, Herman always preferred the traditional to the groundbreaking, and he thought the more radical innovations of the German theater directors off-putting and pretentious. It was a harbinger of some of his objections to Orson Welles's techniques in *Citizen Kane*— and a window into a curious aspect of his personality.

There's a photograph of Herman with Jack Dempsey in Berlin— whenever a famous American came to town, Gilbert Seldes would ask

Herman to be his tour guide and, according to Sara, he "carried off the honors very nicely"—taken in front of the *Chicago Tribune* office, the name of the paper painted in its trademark font on the storefront window, the words just above the heads of Dempsey's manager, Dempsey, and, to the left of the great fighter, Herman in his suit charmingly short in the arms and legs. Next to the preternaturally strong and confident Dempsey, Herman looks every bit his age, the tough reporter replaced by a vulnerable young man somewhat adrift in life. He looks, frankly, terrified. It's no surprise that such a man, as much as he may have been attracted to anything that would threaten to upset the established order, was also profoundly conflicted about it and might in the end adopt a deeply cynical tone toward anything truly revolutionary. Let us remember, after all, that as much as Herman may have hated his father, he had invited the man on his honeymoon.

So while he continued to scramble professionally—he tried all sorts of schemes to earn additional cash: having noticed, while taking a political science course at the University of Berlin, that there were no flower carts outside, he hired a *fräulein* to tend a flower cart there; he tried to sell German war planes to someone Goma described as "an unsavory Pole"; and for a time he even got involved in the stock market and foreign currency exchange manipulations—for Herman, the two and a half years in Berlin were notable mostly for the pillars he erected for a traditional life. His marriage was thriving. When she heard Herman coming home at night, Sara would hide. He would call out, "Schnooks, where are you? Come out!" Then he'd laughingly search throughout the apartment until Sara jumped out at him. They had their first child, my uncle Don, born in January 1922, in a hospital on the edge of town. A union strike had left the place without electricity, and it was so dark and freezing that Goma slipped into bed wearing her fur coat but then, grand martyr that she was, allowed her midwife to swipe her hot water bottle to keep *her* feet warm. Herman happily handed out cigars; his one moment of anguish seemed to come when he considered the circumcision, tears streaming down his face. "Why do they have to do that to a tiny baby?"

On the whole, things in Berlin were moving in the right direction. Herman's writing was gaining notice, and though he had already started to complain to Goma that he wasn't yet writing a great American novel or hugely successful plays, there was little doubt, at least outwardly, that such successes lay in his future.

By the spring of 1922, Herman had decided that it was time to bring his young family back to New York—Berlin was no place to raise a child, and Herman and Sara had both started to miss home and family far too much—but the problem was, he didn't have enough money for the passage. The answer, at first, seemed to come strolling gracefully into the lobby of the Hotel Adlon. It may have been Herman's own first encounter with greatness.

One afternoon in May 1922, the telephone rang at the flat off Potsdamer Strasse. Herman informed Sara that he would be bringing home some guests for dinner, two people he'd met at the Hotel Adlon: the young Russian poet, Sergei Yesenin, and his wife, Isadora Duncan.

Herman (right) with Jack Dempsey (center) and Dempsey's manager, Jack Kearns (left), in Berlin, 1920s

To Herman's generation, Duncan was an almost unmatched icon, combining both personal notoriety and artistic reputation. The woman had completely revolutionized modern dance—drawing inspiration from the ancient Greeks, inaugurating a free-flowing form of dance she'd often perform barefoot and wearing a toga, sometimes not even that, a performance she proclaimed had evolved from the swaying and movement of Nature Herself. Duncan in fact was so revolutionary she didn't even consider her form of performance to be dance. "I am an *expressioniste* of beauty," she said proudly. "I use my body as my medium, just as the writer uses his words. Do not call me a dancer." Whatever she was, she was wildly successful, especially once she took her act to Europe, where she performed publicly on vast stages before thousands or privately in salons for a well-to-do few. It was while she was in Berlin that month that she and Herman crossed paths at the Adlon, and Herman almost immediately hit upon an idea on how to put their meeting to good use.

"Don't be surprised at Yesenin," Herman told Sara over the phone. "He's crazy. And he eats nothing but cucumbers and sour cream." Even so, when Herman arrived home with the two guests, Sara was baffled and astonished by their bizarre behavior. "They were both out of control," she said. The night was more than memorable. "Her conversation was all on a very high level of gaiety. She was funny, gay. There was lots of laughter. And that madman—nobody could understand. She would tell him things in English and he would pretend to understand. I'm sure he didn't understand a word. [He] laughed boisterously and started quoting Russian poetry, and she would get up and stamp her feet and do a revolutionary dance." The evening devolved into chaos soon enough, with Herman openly making fun of Duncan, the dancer far too drunk to understand, and the crazy Russian spouting his poetry and comprehending nothing anyone was saying. But by the time the night was over and Herman was placing the bizarre couple in a taxi back to the Adlon, Herman's scheme had borne fruit. He had been offered a job as Duncan's press agent. The money Herman so desperately wanted to get home was within reach.

All that was needed now was for him to manage her upcoming tour of European capitals, a task easier said than done. While Isadora Duncan may have been Herman's first exposure to genius, in some ways it was like looking in a mirror. To begin with, the woman's finances were an absolute disaster (in part because she had generously established dancing schools for impoverished children across the continent). Her attorney had sold her house in Berlin for a fraction of its value, and much of her property, furniture, and library had disappeared. What's more, a bank account in Berlin had been impounded because of her communist sympathies, and, according to a letter Herman wrote Sara, "There were some checks in Russia that Isadora 'forgot about.' It seems she gave blank checks to the director of her Moscow school with which to buy food, and he's been indelicate enough to use them."

The tour began in July in Brussels, where she had an advance sale of $12,000. Herman was there with her, and his first encounter with her actual work was something of a letdown. "The diva has danced twice," he wrote to Sara, "and she ain't so good. It's true that every one of her movements, her poses, calls to mind one's general impression of Greek art and even the faint memory of some vase or column somewhere, but on the whole there's a fleshiness and a lack of fire that makes it impossible to keep up any illusion." That she wasn't the Isadora of old could be forgiven, since she was forty-four now and overweight, but it didn't bode well for the tour. Next up was Paris, where the Trocadero had guaranteed Duncan ten concerts with a chorus of Russian children, but the Kremlin would not let the children leave Russia. Duncan's response was to cancel both the Paris concerts as well as the ones Herman was currently promoting in London and to head to Venice for a rest. By this time, Herman had lost all patience with the woman, and when he asked her for his back pay, she "threw a random handful of cash at his feet" and "railed at him for his disloyalty." Dismayed by the encounter, and somewhat disgusted by what he took to be her charlatanism, Herman returned to Berlin, no closer to getting back to New York than when he'd left.

Fortunately, the incident caused Herman to write again to George S. Kaufman, who wrote back optimistically that he looked forward to Herman's "prospective return" to New York. But the truly fateful words were these: "I think you would be a wonderful man for my job here. I'll be giving it up in about a year, I think. It doesn't pay a million dollars, but I'll do all I can if you say the word." To Herman, that vague promise—Kaufman was leaving his job, Herman would become the head theater critic for *The New York Times*—was money in the bank. This time, he shared the truth with Sara, who told him, "Herman, it isn't really a job offer, you know," but for Herman, it was close enough. The boys from the Adlon poker game offered up enough mazuma to supplement what little Herman had managed to sock away from Isadora Duncan and the previous two and a half years. It was time, at last, to return to New York.

CHAPTER FOUR

YES, *THE NEW YORKER*

You don't expect me to keep any of those promises, do you?

—*CITIZEN KANE*

THE YEARS THAT FOLLOWED LIE AT THE HEART OF THE MYSTERY. FOR if, as the fable suggested, Herman had been seduced away from the integrity and wonders of a certain-to-be-happy-life in New York City, then we would locate the man's greatness in those few years in New York, and in plumbing the depths of the dilemma he faced all those years ago, we would see the choice he made in accepting Hollywood's filthy lucre.

Of course lives don't really work that way. The choices people make may lead to different paths, but it's certainly far from clear where those paths will lead when we make them. And so to put ourselves in Herman's shoes when the fateful choice was presented to him, the important thing to remember is that at the time, it could hardly have seemed fateful.

HERMAN'S PROFESSIONAL LIFE IN NEW YORK FROM 1922 ONWARD was as scrambling and catch-as-catch-can as it had been in Berlin, with the young man darting from one freelance writing assignment to the other and trying a variety of schemes to bring in extra income. But it was on a slightly higher plane, so that rather than in *Women's Wear Daily*, his work during these next five years appeared in the *New York World*, *The New York Times*, and later, a new magazine called *The New Yorker*. Although the promised job replacing Kaufman as the chief drama critic of the *Times* never arrived (and Kaufman insisted he had never promised it, which was no doubt strictly speaking true—in fact, despite his success as a dramatist, Kaufman, to the consternation and surprise of many of his friends, held on to his day job till 1930), Herman found plenty of other outlets for his work. It was a good time to be a newspaperman in New York City. The newspapers were thriving, and the rise of mass communication had obliterated the idea of a newspaperman as a sober, dutiful reporter of facts, replaced now by the cynical, wisecracking know-it-all of whom Herman was an exemplar.

George S. Kaufman, 1928

He was also, of course, simply fascinated by the newspaper business. It was "the liveliest and most amusing of worlds," according to memoirist Stanley Walker, city editor of the *New York Herald Tribune,* "like attending some fabulous university where the humanities are studied to the accompaniment of ribald laughter, the incessant splutter of an orchestra of typewriters, the occasional clinking of glasses, and the gyrations of some of the strangest performers ever set loose by a capricious and allegedly all-wise Creator." And when, no doubt feeling guilty about having reneged on his non-promise to Herman—Kaufman, like Herman, had a way of promising things he wasn't going to deliver—Kaufman called his friend Herbert Bayard Swope, the editor of the *New York World,* Herman found a steady job. The *World,* and Swope himself, would come to have a profound impact on Herman, providing him, though of course he didn't know it, with grist for the mill that would ultimately produce *Citizen Kane.*

The *World* had been started by Joseph Pulitzer, who'd found success in creating newspapers for the common man, as adroit in taking on the titans of Wall Street as they were in reporting the grisly details of a beheading in the Bronx, and he would be emulated throughout America by publishers like the young William Randolph Hearst. Hearst openly acknowledged that serving the common man was the key to success in the newspaper publishing business, and just as this lesson was not lost on Hearst, Hearst's awareness of it was not lost on Herman. In *Citizen Kane,* after Kane's guardian Thatcher upbraids him for a series of stories he ran against a crooked railroad company, the young Charles Foster Kane responds angrily, "I'll let you in on a little secret, Mr. Thatcher, it is also my pleasure—to see to it that the decent hardworking people of this city are not robbed blind by a group of money-mad pirates because, God help them, they have no one to look after their interests." This sentiment was echoed a few scenes later when Kane tells his comrades in arms Bernstein and Leland, "I will also provide them [the people] with a fighting and tireless champion of their rights as citizens and human beings." *

As for Swope, in addition to loving the running of a newspaper ("Thinks it would be fun to run a newspaper!" the guardian Thatcher sputters in response in *Citizen Kane*), Swope became something of a mentor to Herman. Flamboyant and imposing and with a swift and encyclopedic mind, the tall, red-headed Swope impressed Herman enormously, who went so far as to flatter him by imitation. One of Swope's favorite phrases was to ask, "Where is it written that it has to be done like this?" Herman came to adopt the quotation for himself.†

Becoming something of a protégé to the older man, Herman wasn't in the least bit afraid of Swope, and the two soon became known for their raging arguments, which often ended with Swope shouting apoplectically, "You whippersnapper, what do you know?" They also became

---

* Of course, part of what makes *Citizen Kane* so brilliant is that it's impossible to tell if Kane really means what he says, or, even if he does, how the audience is supposed to feel about that. Kane's friend Jed Leland (Joseph Cotten) holds on to Kane's similarly high-minded Declaration of Principles, telling Kane with an utterly sober expression that he is going to keep the Declaration, as he has a feeling it could prove to be very important someday, "like the Declaration of Independence." Kane looks at Leland with a quizzical smile, unable to tell whether Leland is being duly and properly reverential of the great young man, or is totally mocking him. There can be little doubt that Orson Welles provided most of the sincerity these moments called for, with Herman ladling in the cynicism.

† In fact, the phrase became a standard in the Mankiewicz family, and there is something in the phrase—the elevation of a thing being written down in order to give it substance—that recalls that this family is in fact Jewish to the core, despite all protestations and evasions. Judaic culture, for over two millennia anyway, has been founded upon a dissection of the recorded word, and both Herman and Joe loved Swope's remark. One hears echoes of it in nearly all of Joe's screenplays—from *Cleopatra*'s opening narration to Kirk Douglas's desecration of the art of advertising in *A Letter to Three Wives*—and throughout his career, Joe's work is extremely literary and word-conscious (the film is about *A Letter* to the wives, after all, not a phone call).

good enough friends for Herman to exercise his wit against him: "Never Swope," Herman advised another man who failed to show Swope the proper respect, "until you are Swopen to."

Herman simply loved the milieu of newspaper work. But here the snake starts to eat its tail, because when considering the newspapermen of the 1920s—the hard-boiled cynicism, the wisecracks, the hard drinking and devil-may-care attitude that permeated the whole endeavor—it's almost impossible not to think of the wit-flying newspaper comedies of the 1930s, many of which Herman himself worked on, nearly all of which were written by the very same men who had lived the New York newspapering life in the twenties. (The list of great newspaper movies from Hollywood's golden age is a long one, extending at least from *The Front Page* in 1931—written by Ben Hecht and Charles McArthur, two of Herman's best friends—all the way through *It Happened One Night* and *His Girl Friday*, and climaxing with what many consider newspaper films' apotheosis in 1941, *Citizen Kane*.)

But for Herman, that was all in the future. For the present, Herman was a reporter and critic, a writer for newspapers, and a someone who caused George S. Kaufman to pull Sara aside at a party and inform her that Herman was an extraordinary and exceptional young man from whom he, Kaufman, expected great things. And because of Herman's quick wit and lively personality, he was also beginning to make his name—although, significantly, doing it less by his writing than by his life itself. The writer and playwright Ben Hecht, who had come to New York with his writing partner Charles MacArthur, was perhaps the first to see that Herman's wit might not be something that would ever be captured fully on paper, though he lamented it. Hecht, who labeled Herman "the Voltaire of Central Park West," said later that he "knew that no one as witty and spontaneous as Herman would ever put himself on paper. A man whose genius is on tap like free lager beer seldom makes literature out of it."

To my grandmother, the key night in Herman's cementing his reputation as a wit occurred the first night they were invited to the George S. Kaufmans for a dinner party. Such an invitation was no small thing. The Kaufmans, Beatrice and George,

Sara in New York, 1920s

were an odd couple, completely unromantic and each bound up in a series of affairs, yet in all other respects devoted as husband and wife and famous for their dinner parties. Though the invitation was something many in New York longed for, it struck terror in the heart of Sara. It was her "first real exposure to all of these . . . brilliant and wonderful and witty people and I was scared out of my wits."

When they arrived, Sara did not let Herman out of her sight. "If he'd leave my side, I'd run and get him. I really behaved like an idiot and everybody was being terribly nice trying to make me feel at home." The Kaufman dinners were convivial and lively, and the guest lists were practically a Who's Who of New York's smart set: Marc Connelly, Ben Hecht, Franklin P. Adams, Heywood Broun, and Alexander Woollcott were frequent attendees. That night, it was Herman who shone, keeping all in stitches: "[M]ost of Manky's utterances, including his deepest philosophic ones, stirred laughter. Even his enemies laughed," Hecht would say. After the elegant dinner, everyone gathered in the living room to play word games. "They were all very proficient at it and I was scared to death," Sara said. "I don't think I spoke two words." Finally, Connelly, the playwright with whom Kaufman collaborated on a few of his early successes, rose with his wife to leave. Sara turned to her husband and said, "Look, Herman, people are going home." Unfortunately, she said it louder than she'd intended, and everybody laughed uproariously. From that point on, for quite a while, Sara was referred to as "People are going home, Herman."*

For Herman, the night was a smashing success. He had held his own with the greatest wits of the day, he had performed brilliantly at the word games, and even Goma said later that he'd established that he really was "the life of every party. He was such fun, and he had such wit—after that, he was terribly much in demand. Without him it could be a deadly evening."

Spoken wit, of course, always has a curious and unfortunate you-had-to-be-there quality. But how odd that the only witticisms of Herman's that have come down from what Goma considered such a seminal evening were ones that involved deprecating his beloved wife—further evidence, if any were needed, that her reports of Herman's gifts as a husband were

---

* Sara's desire to leave didn't persuade Herman. They stayed a good while longer, and when Sara quietly beseeched him to go home, Herman responded—playfully, she insisted decades later—by telling her, "You go play over there—get a coloring book and color something."

overstated. In fact, when they did finally leave the party, Sara felt like she was being let out of a coffin. Years later she still claimed she could "get a cold chill" when she thought about that night.

But for Herman, it marked a turning point. Before this evening, young Herman was a reporter, a writer struggling with his demons, to be sure, but a man whose future would be in the field of journalism and literature—he would make his name with the written word. But hereafter, Herman Mankiewicz saw another way to make his name, and if he went for it with gusto, it wasn't just because doing the other would prove difficult—but because going *this* route was

Herman in New York, mid 1920s

going to be a hell of a lot more fun. Down this road, he would make his name not with his *written* word, but with his *spoken* word and his larger-than-life behavior that would make him a legend. Like Oscar Wilde, who famously put his talent into his work but his genius into his life, Herman would hereafter cultivate a personality that would be spoken about in almost reverent tones—as people speak of gorgeous dancers or other performers whose performances cannot be captured in any recorded way, but whose great accomplishments are necessarily ephemeral. An improvisational genius, Herman Mankiewicz had found his true calling. From now on, he would make of his *life* his greatest work of art. And if Herman had found his true calling as an improvisational actor, he was soon to find the first great theater for his performances—for soon after the evening at the Kaufmans, he became a member of the Algonquin Round Table.

SOMETIME IN THE SUMMER OF 1919, OR PERHAPS IT WAS THE EARLY autumn, a group of three, though quite possibly more, leading members of the New York literary set—or maybe they were that only in their own minds but what's the difference?—sent out private invitations to a luncheon to celebrate, or note, or at least thoroughly mock, the return of *The New York Times* theater critic Alexander Woollcott from the Great War. The invitations, which deliberately misspelled the name of the critic (who was notorious for his endless self-promotion, especially tales of his martial exploits, which often began with the phrase: "When I was in the theater of war . . ."), were sent to every editor or theater critic of note in the city and also provided an agenda of speeches to be given: all the speeches would be about the war, and all would be delivered by Woollcott himself. The luncheon would be held at the Algonquin Hotel, a converted apartment building on West Forty-fourth Street, between Fifth and Sixth Avenues—at the center of Midtown Manhattan and spitting distance from Broadway. Among those attending that first day were Dorothy Parker, then drama critic for *Vanity Fair,* Robert Benchley, managing editor at *Vanity Fair,* Heywood Broun, theater and sports writer for the *Tribune,* and Harold Ross, an old friend of Woollcott's. Despite the obvious sarcasm of the invitations, though, everyone present "acted obeisant to 'the king of drama critics'" until one moment when Arthur Samuels, editor of *Harper's Bazaar,* said, in response to Woollcott's yet again beginning a story with "When I was in the theater of war," "If you were ever in the theater of war, Aleck, it was in the last-row seat nearest the exit." When the afternoon was over and everyone rose to leave, someone said, "Why don't we do this every day?"

Herman wasn't at that first meal. And he likely wasn't at the second, or even third. But as the fame of the Round Table spread, it wasn't long before he was drawn into its orbit, for before long anyone who was anyone in New York's theatrical and journalistic circles began to show up. Soon, actors and writers, everyone from Harpo Marx to Ring Lardner, Tallulah Bankhead to Helen Hayes, began to drop by for a session at the Round Table, and soon even the non-famous were coming to the Algonquin for lunch, just to catch a glimpse of the Round Table in action. At one such afternoon, with the Round Table breaking up for the day, and Benchley, Robert Sherwood, Parker, Ross, Kaufman, and the gang all heading back to work, Herman turned to writer and Broadway publicist Murdock Pemberton and said, "There goes the greatest collection of unsalable wit in America." (Pemberton made sure that the remark found its way into newspaper columns.)

In time, the bon mots piled up like linen napkins. When someone referred to liquor as slow poison, Robert Benchley replied, "Who's in a hurry?" Once, when a passerby rubbed Marc Connelly's bald head and said that it felt just like his wife's behind, Connelly reached up, rubbed his own head, and said, "Why so it does." When Noël Coward visited the Round Table, he did so on a day when he and Edna Ferber both happened to be wearing double-breasted suits. "You almost look like a man," Coward told Ferber, to which she replied, "So do you." And then there were Dorothy Parker's legendary quips; a now-forgotten woman visited the Round Table and bragged that she'd kept her husband for seven years, to which Parker said, "Keep him long enough and he'll come back in style." When it was reported that the solemn President Coolidge had died, Parker said, "How can they tell?" She once rose suddenly from the table and said, "Excuse me, but I have to go to the bathroom." Then she added, "I really have to use the telephone, but I'm too embarrassed to say so." The word games, the play, the droll understanding that people in power were boobs . . . the Algonquin Round Table had it all.

But as with many groups of self-promoted and self-conscious artistic greats, the myth of the Round Table seems to have exceeded its members' actual accomplishments. Years later, Parker herself assessed the Round Table's whole existence rather unkindly: "The Round Table was just a lot of people telling jokes and telling each other how good they were . . ."* And given all the eating and drinking and self-mythologizing that was going on, it's fair to ask: How much work was anyone actually getting done?

HERMAN SAID THAT AT TIMES IN NEW YORK, HE FELT LIKE A JUGgler, with so many different projects all proceeding, sometimes at breakneck pace, but more often with the speed of molasses, such that he would no doubt have agreed with the archetypal producers' quip when asked what he's working on: "I have a lot of irons in the freezer." Frequently Herman would work at home on Central Park West in the mornings, where Sara, in the kitchen or with the baby in the living room, would love to hear the rhythmic clacking of the keys punching through the paper and striking the cylinder from the typewriter in the bedroom.† Usually Herman would be working on a play, like the one he and Connelly were writing together called *The Wild Man of Borneo,* which at first excited Herman with its comic potential: the play was about a medicine show faker pretending to be a great actor. He and Connelly had cooked up a number of terrific characters—the main character was a true mountebank, great

---

* "People romanticize it," Parker said. "It was no Mermaid Tavern, I promise you. These were no giants. Think of who was writing in those days—Lardner, Fitzgerald, Faulkner and Hemingway. Those were the real giants."

† She also noted the frequent long silences from the bedroom, when she assumed Herman was either grappling with a writing problem, or, more accurately, not grappling with it.

for an actor like Louis Wolheim to play on stage*—but the longer Herman toiled at it, the more it seemed like a pale imitation of other plays, not very good ones, that he'd suffer through as drama critic and then relish ripping apart when he got back to the *Times*'s offices.

Afternoons, Herman would make his way downtown, either to a newspaper office or the home of a collaborator like Marc Connelly or George S. Kaufman. For Kaufman, Herman was doing a number of things: reviewing plays and revues, and also padding Kaufman's weekly "news on the rialto" column or the "theatrical notes" *Times* column with items Herman got from friends. Too, Herman became press agent for Max Reinhardt's production of Karl Vollmöller's play *The Miracle,* and even found time to help produce, with Jed Harris, a play called *Love 'Em and Leave 'Em,* co-written by a man named John V. A. Weaver, a writer of such questionable promise his own father-in-law described him as a "used piece of soap."

So amid all the activity, and with the Algonquin and nighttime drinking bouts thrown in, it's fair to wonder what Herman's own literary output as a writer in New York really was. In truth, it's hard to determine. There were three plays in all that we know about, and a few others that would bear some kind of asterisk on the official baseball card record of Herman Mankiewicz's New York years. First, there was his helping George S. Kaufman on one of the forty-five plays the man produced in his prodigious lifetime, a play called *The Butter-and-Egg Man.* Here, a problem crops up that will recur: Goma said he virtually rewrote Kaufman's entire script from start to finish, though others said Herman merely added a few jokes. Regardless, the play was published—and produced—with Herman's name nowhere to be found, which, according to Sara anyway, disappointed Herman. In fact, more than just about anyone else, Herman actually seemed to want what Kaufman had: a life as a successful playwright and man of the theater, to be a well-respected critic and man about town. But while Herman learned what he could from Kaufman, two of Herman's weaknesses were Kaufman's greatest strengths. Kaufman would never be considered the life of the party—he was a largely silent, taciturn man who saved his humor for his work. The other remarkable thing about Kaufman was that he never stopped working. In that respect

---

* In 1941, the play would be adapted for the screen with the lead character now played by Frank Morgan, the veteran character actor whose more famous charlatan was the Wizard of Oz.

Herman was virtually the antithesis of his hero. Goma said, "There was a real compulsion against working, against writing. Much as he wanted to and loved to. If only he could postpone that evil moment." Goma took a long sigh, possibly thinking of other writers she knew who disliked the actual act. "He was like every other writer—except Ben Hecht and George Kaufman."

Despite his distaste for the actual process, Herman never stopped wanting to be a comedy playwright. While in New York, he contributed skits to revues like the *Ziegfeld Follies, George White Scandals,* and the *Little Show.* He was thrilled whenever Kaufman asked him to collaborate, and Connelly's invitation to work on *The Wild Man of Borneo* had both flattered Herman enormously and for the moment interrupted the collaboration of Connelly and Kaufman, at the time the most successful writing team on Broadway. But in the end, the script dragged on interminably, and Herman ended up leaving New York before it was ever produced.

The play with the most promise may have been a political satire called *We the People.* Herman set aside his August vacation to work on it in 1925. But where could he find the solitude the great work demanded? That summer, in Woodstock, New York, Ben Hecht and Charles MacArthur had rented a cottage with their wives, entertaining many of New York's most famed theatrical personages, including the Marx Brothers. "Then one sunny afternoon," according to Hecht, "Herman Mankiewicz appeared in the road in front of our house—as Jimmy Durante would say—unannounced. He carried two suitcases." The larger one "contained sixteen bottles of Scotch and nothing else," with which Herman "sat in a corner of an old couch for two weeks without moving" and "slowly and happily did away with his sixteen bottles," refusing to join in on "horseshoes, croquet or swimming-hole activities." Hecht reports that Herman showed up penniless because Sara refused to give him any money, knowing he would squander it on booze. "Poor Sara is an honest woman," Herman told Hecht, "and doesn't understand that liquor can be begged, borrowed or stolen by a man of firm character." At the end of two weeks' time, "a young and ravishing Sara finally arrived and carted her Herman off." Somehow, eventually, *We the People* got written. And with Kaufman's help, the play was accepted by a producer. But no production date was ever set, and Herman never saw a penny from it.

For Herman, though, while his theatrical career may have been dying a slow, honorable death, his journalistic efforts seemed to be heading in the right direction. For in February 1925, a new magazine had been born

The height of New York sophistication: Herman and Sara
with Ben and Rose Hecht at Coney Island, 1926

in New York City, one that seemed to embrace an attitude and spirit that Herman embodied. It was cynical, but also somehow humane, judgmental yet also proudly inclusive of differing opinions, worldly yet famously provincial, smart but routinely superficial—it was like the Algonquin Round Table trapped between the pages of a magazine, much like the butterfly that its dandified mascot Eustace Tilley examined through his monocle on its first cover. Yes, *The New Yorker,* and Herman would be its first drama critic.

And so the final battle began: apocalyptic if apocryphal, the war for Herman Mankiewicz's soul, between Hollywood and New York—or, more specifically, *The New Yorker.* Herman's relationship with Harold Ross, the coarse high school dropout from Colorado who ran the magazine, was notoriously tempestuous. Ross was a bit of a Western hayseed, gangly, lanky, and homely, and looked, Herman said, like a dishonest Abraham Lincoln. ("Be careful when you go to the theater," Herman would warn Ross, "don't sit in a box seat.") Salty and crude where Herman and his pals cultivated a veneer of urbane sophistication, Ross was an unlikely leader of a magazine for the smart set, causing Ben Hecht to ask, "How the hell could a man who looked like a resident of the Ozarks and talked like a saloon brawler set himself up as pilot of a sophisticated, elegant periodical?" But Ross, for all his crudity, was ideally suited to birth a magazine that would capture the aspirations of a nation full of longing for the New York of the imagination. He was a gifted editor, and Herman's work at *The New Yorker* stands out among his other journalistic work for its crispness and clarity. Herman actually learned a great deal from Ross, and according to Goma, Herman was "mad about" Ross, respected him deeply, and thought him "an enormous talent. Looking and acting like a hayseed and yet being so ultra sophisticated and knowing just exactly what he wanted that magazine to be like." Ross had an instinctive compass for where he wanted the magazine to go, and if it took the magazine a while to find its footing and shed a sophomoric attitude, it was only because Ross was having trouble imposing his vision on the rest of the staff. Goma said he "could recognize immediately something he felt was not in the style of *The New Yorker.* He set that style and made everyone else conform." As improbable as it may sound, Herman, the ultimate nonconformist, was willing to conform, at least for a while.*

Despite his battles with Ross—and some were epic, with shouts and hurled bits of clothing behind closed doors, terrifying those in the office outside—Ross, who admitted he was petrified by Herman, was able to tame him into doing some of the best work of his life. Herman's sentences, which heretofore had sometimes tended to careen terrifyingly all over the page, were now always in control, even the long ones: "Anyway, the new theatrical year allowed itself to be declared formally opened with the production at Maxine Elliott's Theater, on the night of August 3, of Vincent Lawrence's *Spring Fever,* and if the lessons of the past teach anything at all, they teach that you'll get over it all right." Or: "The Paris of *A Night in Paris* is, of course, the Paris of the man who has never been there, but, after all, there be among us cynical and jaded souls who insist that that Paris is the best Paris there is." And while the prose was more refined, there was still an incisive wit that meshed perfectly with the wry, urbane tone that *The New Yorker* sought: "If Hecuba has tears, let her prepare to shed them now. They will produce *The Morning After.* Nothing, absolutely nothing, can be done about it." He had no problem lobbing honest assessments of work he thought mediocre or bad. Of Eugene O'Neill's *Desire Under the Elms* he wrote, "It is not one of O'Neill's greatest plays but it is, fortunately, not among his worst, than which nothing is more dreadful." Of a musical comedy called *Oh! Oh! Nurse,* his prescription was merely: "Our advice is to stay at home and read a bad book." On the other hand, unlike the prevailing scorn of the Algonquinites, which tended

---

* He was unable, though, to persuade many of his Algonquin confreres to join the new venture, consoling Ross by telling him, "The half-time help of wits is no better than the full-time help of half-wits."

to permeate much of the theatrical press of the day, Herman had no problem giving credit where it was due, in particular when it concerned unquestionably great plays or performers: "Miss Barrymore as Ophelia provided this deponent with one of the greatest joys of his theatre going life." Nor was he above displaying the kind of fearsome quality that he was so well-known for in person, as when he marveled at the leading players in the "Negro musical comedy" *Lucky Sambo,* writing, "Of course, being Negroes, they probably receive about $100 a week—and this department is prepared to submit a list of six white comedians with one-tenth ability who receive over a thousand." A visit to Chicago would yield a wonderful back-handed compliment to New York when comparing the theatrical cultures of the two cities: "In New York, where the drama is controlled absolutely by the theatre landlords, the playhouses are filled with trash. In Chicago, where this is not the case, the theatergoer can choose from among Shaw and Ibsen and Goethe and Shakespeare and Molière and any other book he has in his library."

But Herman's output, ultimately, was more than mere insults and wisecracks. Even as he hewed to the institutional demands of *The New Yorker* to be arch and superior, his writing could at times be perceptive and even wise. One piece, "The Big Game," about attending a college football game out of town (between the fictional colleges Olav and Bayes), illustrates the tension between the two strains in Herman's writing. The piece begins with a self-conscious literary device: a correspondent, the night before the game, "has sat in front of his typewriter for exactly fifty minutes in stony silence, thinking, thinking, thinking." Then, inspiration strikes, and he reels off four paragraphs of sportswriter jargon: "All roads will lead to the Gump Bowl to-morrow. . . . King Football reigns supreme in New Dijon to-night . . . Both teams engaged in a light drill this afternoon and returned to their quarters for the final skull practice." But soon the piece grows beyond mere mimicry, as Herman drops the conceit of the sportswriter and describes the trains that depart the next morning from New York: "overfilled, overraccooncoated, overginned, overheated." He draws a few quick sketches of some of those onboard: "a stout little fellow in the most expensive fur coat the world has ever known . . . [another man] out of medical school one year . . . trying to grow a mustache [who will] spend most of the time en route walking through the cars, greeting as many people as he can."

The sketches deepen, most notably with a description of a "little older than average young woman" who is with an "average young man":

She has made this trip now, in mid-November, for thirteen successive years, and she is getting just the least little bit fed up on it. In particular, she knows that she is going to be very annoyed when the young man tries to explain to her the difference between a touchdown and a fullback. Some day she is going to make one of the average young men that are her lot drink the gin all at once, instead of at such long intervals that its effect wears off; and then she's going to be married; and if the average young man from then on feels that he must know how the game came out before the sport extras are on the street, let him install a radio in the parlor.

At the game, too, more bittersweet humanity sneaks into the piece: "A writhing young man is carried off the field and a greying woman shrieks." And Herman's deeper attitudes watching such a contest become clearer:

Cheer leaders have appeared and are doing their tricks. The cynic is impressed by the futility of life and endeavor. What becomes of cheerleaders, he wonders, after graduation? Are they loving husbands and kind fathers? Do their eyes ever get misty with the thoughts of the wild, old days that are no more?

At the end of the piece—the outcome of the game, of course, is of little concern ("The final whistle blows. Olav has won, or something")— Herman describes the ride back, and the tone is even more melancholy. "The young doctor has caught a cold, and is in hiding." No more is heard from the older than average young woman. "The trains roll into the stations," and he ends on a note of simplicity: "Eighty thousand Americans have had a day of outdoor sport."

This, then, was the Herman I first read as a boy in the crimson-bound volume of *The New Yorker*'s first year that Goma kept in her living room in Brentwood. He was witty, intelligent, and perceptive, and his voice was original and refined. For nearly a year he wrote a regular weekly column, reviewing two or three plays in brief and one at length. He was, Brooks Atkinson said, "saturated with the theatre." The promise of future literary success was *real*.

So what happened?

For one thing, money. At some point in 1925, a press agent told him he could make a fortune in Hollywood. The idea percolated in Herman. The movies, of course, were a thoroughly inferior art form, derided and dismissed altogether by the Algonquinites and sophisticates of all kinds, so much so that when Herman asked Ross if he could add movie reviews to his charge for the magazine, Ross said, "You don't want that. That's for women and fairies."

Still, the idea had taken hold. The press agent had urged Herman to come up with an idea for M-G-M about the Marines, and one day Herman happily told the Algonquin crowd that an idea for the movie had come to him—on the toilet. The room roared, and so did the lion. M-G-M offered Herman $500 a week to come west and work on a scenario for a few weeks. The money was nearly twice what Herman had ever been able to cobble together in his New York life.

And so, at the age of twenty-eight, he boarded a train, thoroughly expecting California to be a visit only, a one-time lark.

But he also needed the money. Gambling and drinking had continued apace in New York, as they would for the rest of his life. On his way to California, Herman stopped in Chicago, where he gave a speech on New York theater at the prestigious Book and Pencil club, got offered a job as drama critic by the *Chicago Daily News,* and promptly lost all the money he had on him, including the lecture fee, in a poker game.

California, as it was for many of the Easterners who headed there in the heady early decades of motion pictures, was a land of milk and honey. Having lived in the crowded confines of New York City for so long, Herman wrote Sara of his glee on his arrival: "Los Angeles is delightful beyond belief, with its tropical vegetation and its mad, colored, pretty bungalows." And then there was the work itself. By the time he arrived, all interest in the Marine story had vanished from the halls of M-G-M, but Herman was told to try his hand at a vehicle for the master of disguise, Lon Chaney. Without delay, Herman set to work on a melodrama called *The Road to Mandalay,* which would be advertised as "A Thrilling, Throbbing Romance of Singapore." To say that Herman enjoyed the work immensely wouldn't be quite accurate, because he barely considered it work. It was too easy. Unlike the problems posed by reviews, or the intricate plotting of a stage play, screenwriting didn't really consume much of his brain. Professionally speaking, Hollywood was a caper. The operating assumption was he'd soon get back to his real career, his work—and to New York.

"Then, suddenly, defeat! Shameful, ignominious . . ." The stentorian newsreel voice from *Citizen Kane* often bursts in when considering Herman's life, and in particular that phrase from the moment when Kane's meteoric political rise is cut short by scandal. In this case, it was no

scandal that brought an end to Herman's career in New York, merely his personality. But the news arrived as suddenly as in *Citizen Kane*: a telegram from Ross, informing him that his services at *The New Yorker* were no longer required.

There had been no last straw. It was merely the agglomeration of all the anguish Herman had caused Ross in their battles over his work, not to mention Herman's attitude of sheer condescension toward him (as well as everyone else) that finally forced Ross to cut him loose. Herman had for so long regarded everyone he met as his inferior in terms of scholarship and intellect, and here was this yokel from Colorado telling him how to write. The fact that Ross had made Herman a better writer didn't seem to factor into Herman's thinking, for his disparagement of the man had never ceased, and Ross, who had long been both terrified and affronted by Herman and his temper, had finally taken the opportunity, emboldened by the three thousand miles between them, to fire him.

Herman was outraged, and no less furious when he got back to New York a few weeks later. For three years he had been building, haphazardly but somehow ineluctably, a career in New York City. His actual literary output from 1923 to the beginning of 1926 was indeed something of a marvel—the theater reviews and occasionals for *The New Yorker,* uncredited theater writing for the *Times,* book reviews for the *Times,* as well as the demanding attempts at production and playwriting—made more remarkable when you consider his almost nightly bouts of debilitating drinking. He was a man of prodigious talent and energy—who the hell was this boob, this dude, this rube from the middle of nowhere, to fire *him*? He told his confreres at the Round Table just precisely what he would do to Ross—Herman played gleefully with the phrase "limb from limb"—but of course word spread to Ross, and so when Herman finally walked through the front doors of *The New Yorker*'s lobby on West Forty-fifth Street one fine March day in 1926, news of his presence in the building scorched through the halls, and Ross, fearing for his life, hid in a coat closet. Herman stormed in, whacked Ross's desk with his cane, and left the building.

He may as well have kept on going. Never again would Herman Mankiewicz be a celebrated young writer of promise in New York City. Never again would he ride a constant wave of impending literary success. The theater was not working out. The debts were piling up. The weather was too grubby. The boys needed food, and Sara a nicer home. Enough was enough. California, here we come.

PART TWO

———— ✿ ————

You can take Hollywood for granted like I did, or you can dismiss it with the contempt we reserve for what we don't understand. It can be understood too, but only dimly and in flashes. Not half a dozen men have ever been able to keep the whole equation of pictures in their heads.

—*THE LAST TYCOON,*
BY F. SCOTT FITZGERALD

CHAPTER FIVE

— ☥ —

HOLLYWOOD

Life, every now and then, behaves as if it had seen too many
bad movies when everything fits too well: the beginning, the
middle, and the end, from fade-in to fade-out.

—*THE BAREFOOT CONTESSA*

IN THE EARLY DAYS OF THE OLD MOVIE PALACES, THE NEMO, ON THE
corner of 110th Street and Broadway in Manhattan, was not one of the
great ones. It wasn't as large as the Roxy or as ornate as the Loew's on 175th
Street, and as for grandeur, it had very little. What it had was movies,
and lots of them. For Joe Mankiewicz, who had followed in his brother's
footsteps and entered Columbia at the age of fifteen, that was enough. In
later years, Joe would claim that his matriculation was "four years devoted
to establishing an all-time attendance record at the Nemo movie theater
and an all-time nonattendance record at a course in neoclassicism." To
Joe, sitting in the plush seats of the Nemo, listening to the piano player,
eating his peppermint stick, and staring up at the screen and watching
the films was heaven. He was, at last, in a place he felt comfortable and
safe. But there's a curious aspect to Joe's moviegoing. Not for him the
safety of losing himself in a fantasy up on the silver screen; Joe wasn't
Mia Farrow in *The Purple Rose of Cairo*, though he stared at what he saw
just as avidly as Mia Farrow's Cecilia did in the Woody Allen film about
a woman whose dreams of escape are made real when the movie star she
reveres jumps off the screen. No, Joe Mankiewicz didn't get lost in the
story, or hardly ever. He saw *Sunrise*, for instance, and marveled at how
the film re-created a dreamscape of a modern American city, but he was
never once taken in by the pantomime. He respected the movies, even
loved them for what they could do; he saw their power; and he knew,

"Ragpickers" and "pissants": Irving Thalberg,
Louis B. Mayer, and Will Hays in Hollywood, 1925

he could sense in his bones, that what the movies were giving the other people in the theater was incredibly valuable. His self-mocking claim that his education had been as much at the movies as at Columbia wasn't the idle boast of someone who loved to talk about how much class he missed. Joe Mankiewicz was *studying* the movies.

As he walked out of the theater, he would have shielded his eyes almost absentmindedly from what he knew would catch others by surprise: the daylight. Joe hadn't entered that dream-like state that so many did when they went to the movies. He hadn't lost his sense of self, his sense of place, not for a single second. He was six blocks south of the main entrance to Columbia, eight blocks south of Phi Sigma Delta, his fraternity. He walked slowly up Broadway. The sun dipped behind a cloud. The movies. He knew Pop didn't think much of them, and Herman even less—was Joe the only one to see they were going to be the most important form of communication in this century? There was so much power there. That word again: power. Herman thought the only ones who had it were the politicians, them and the robber barons, the tycoons and captains of industry, but Joe knew power came in many different forms.

If you really wanted to control things, Joe thought, you could do a lot worse than be in the movie business. Herman's first few letters back from California had been full of delightful descriptions of the foibles of the men he was working with—the "ragpickers" and "pissants," the "Jew tailors" who were setting themselves up as arbiters of actual taste—and Joe's favorite, the "blintze brains."

God, how Herman was thriving: $400 a week, with another $5,000 for every produced story, with a guarantee, he said in his letter, of four stories a year. Joe did the sums in his head, and the result was practically unfathomable—Herman J. Mankiewicz, making $40,000 in a single year? For writing the titles for silent movies he wouldn't attend even if you dragged him there in a straitjacket?

Joe might have quickened his pace, but more likely thought better of it. Young Joe Mankiewicz realized that walking fast wasn't going to get him where he wanted to go any faster than walking slowly would. He steadied his gait and crossed Broadway, walking straight toward the sun, now descending over the river to the west. Setting over a future that didn't seem so far away anymore.

BUT COLUMBIA WAS NOT ALL THAT EASY FOR JOE, FOR THE PRINCI-pal reason that he was still very much living in Herman's shadow there. Though he would rarely admit it, except to toss it off as part of a gibe, the comparisons made Joe feel small. When he joined the honors English program like Herman, he found many of his teachers still laughed, remembering *The Peace Pirates* nearly a decade before. They inquired about Herman's well-being, asking Joe to send their regards in his letters. *Herman had a play reviewed in the* Times *when he was Joe's age!* Yes, Joe had joined the Deutscher Verein as Herman had urged, but the main theater he was involved with was a play he helped produce called *Ein Knopf,* a silly little German one-act, about an absentminded professor with a button sewn on his coat to remind him to kiss his wife. This was not anything like *The Peace Pirates* performance that would bring Mama and Erna to tears, possibly even make Papa proud.

Yet Joe did make a name for himself at Columbia in his own right. He always did brilliant work, refining everything he worked on with Pop's voice in his head urging him on, telling him that if the analysis of Kant treatises he was writing for his philosophy course was anything less than perfection, he may as well throw it into the fireplace. He was dependable, orderly, and polite, dazzling and impressing teachers, not like Herman, who would allow himself to fly into arguments with his teachers when he thought they were wrong.

As he sat in his English classes at Columbia, Joe felt a familiar feeling sneak into his belly—one he'd felt at P.S. 64 and Stuyvesant. So many people, even the teachers, got lost in the plots of the novels and plays they read. How his class discussions would bore him—his fellow students lamenting the fate of Steerforth or Uncle Tom in that damn cabin. Never Joe. Joe read to understand the author's tricks. What are the best plot devices, what distinguishes the ordinary from the great? How had Dickens made Steerforth's death work on us when the character had been so heartless just a few chapters earlier? Was it Harriet Beecher Stowe's prosaic and dull voice, or something else, that caused the boy next to him to snore and drool into his notebook as the class argued about the characters? And how had Antigone's sacrifice been set up so beautifully in that play? These were Joe's concerns at Columbia, but to his literary acumen he added something else, something that Herman never possessed: a hope that his comrades would accept his brilliance easily without feeling he was condescending to them. Even as Joe knew that he could dissect a book and explain his thoughts about it more clearly than anyone else in the room, he was equally careful to measure out Mankiewiczian charm and ease. So while he explained precisely why Antigone's familial sacrifice was so arresting to a Hellenic audience, it likely would not have amazed his classmates, or bothered them, that this brilliant young classmate was destined to do great things.

HERMAN'S CONTEMPT FOR CALIFORNIA DIDN'T COME ALL AT ONCE. Like the vegetation which covered the hills he drove through on his way to work, it took some time to reach full flower. He arrived in July of 1926 and sent for Sara and the boys in September. They rented a house on upper Vine Street, Herman happily walking from the kitchen into the living room singing "We're in the money, we're in the money." What wasn't to like? The weather was ideal and virtually identical day to day, and better than that, the money was great.

Ah, yes, the money. His friend Walter Wanger was a producer at Famous Players–Lasky Corporation, one of the newer studios, and he'd arranged Herman's deal for him. Joe was right about the details of the money: the studio, which would soon change its name to Paramount, paid Herman $400 a week and $5,000 for each original story that ended up being filmed, with a minimum guarantee of four stories. For the first time in his life, Herman had real money to spend, and though he wasn't particularly organized about it, he started getting rid of the money nearly as fast as he could: fine clothing, gold golf clubs, membership in a country club, a convertible Cadillac, and a Buick were soon his.

As for the work, he continued to regard it with suspicion. One eye was still on New York, and would be for a while. Before finally packing up and heading west, his hopes for a plum job in New York had briefly soared when the *New York Times* fired their theater critic Stark Young, only to plummet when the job went to Brooks Atkinson. Now he was writing Atkinson, a natural rival if ever there was one, asking if the *Times* would take him back if he failed in California. Atkinson, not quite believing him, had said that the Gray Lady would indeed open her arms to Herman if need be. But Herman's center of gravity slowly caught up with him. California was where he was. And the movie studio was his home now.

In the first place, he was afforded more respect than he'd ever had in New York. Unlike the other writers, who were housed far from the executives in a shed-like building at the edge of the studio, Herman was given a large office in a bungalow near the administration building. And the work itself was a breeze. Responsible for all the printed titles in Paramount's films, Herman oversaw the construction of the stories and proved himself a much more adept scenarist than anyone else on the payroll. The time spent in theaters absorbing the work of other playwrights was

"We're in the money": Herman poses for a publicity photo on the set of *Laughter* (1930) with, from left, Diane Ellis, Nancy Carroll, and Fredric March.

"Is that beard supposed to be Russian? It looks like an ad for cough drops!" Poster for *The Last Command* (1928)

now put to good use. Providing the voice and understanding of a critic, especially on the story line or concept, Herman's insights often made the difference between success and failure, between a story that worked and one that didn't.

And most of all, there was the wit. For much of the life of the art form, silent movies had been devoted to melodrama, so titles were mostly simple and often florid, righteous declarations, conveying moral rectitude and judgment of the characters. Herman injected brio and style: "I've got as much chance to wash in private as a six months old baby" may not be an epigram worthy of Wilde, but to silent film audiences it moved things along in a much livelier way than earlier titles like "the fragrant mystery of your body is greater than the mystery of life." Soon, Herman's success in titling was noticed across the burgeoning industry. Director Josef von Sternberg got Herman to title *The Drag Net, Thunderbolt,* and *The Last Command,* the latter a fascinating film about a group of Russian aristocrats who are forced to flee during the Revolution and, led by a charismatic former general, find work in California; in Herman's colorful phrase, "And so the backwash of a tortured nation had carried another extra to Hollywood." Herman's titles poke fun at the pretensions of Hollywood—the movie director, needing "Russians," complains to the exiled general, "Is that beard supposed to be Russian? It looks like an ad for cough drops!"* Paramount's chief, B. P. (Ben) Schulberg, became a huge Herman supporter, and the two men were soon drinking and smoking cigars together. More than that, they were gambling.

Now that Herman was making good money, the gambling took even more serious hold. Of course he was not alone. Gambling was as common

---

* Three thousand miles away in New York, his worshipful younger brother remembered "fighting my way into the Paramount theater to be the first one to see *The Last Command.*"

in Hollywood as booze. There was everything from poker at dinner parties to pitching pennies and rolling dice in the office. On weekends, much of Hollywood would go down to Mexico to hit the casinos and racetracks just across the border. For a time, both the *Hollywood Reporter* and *Daily Variety* printed racing charts and bulletins, and illegal casinos like the Colony Club and the Clover Club sprouted off Sunset Boulevard. Like everything in Hollywood, gambling became another way to compete, though winning and losing, for Herman, wasn't so clear-cut. In fact, for Herman, it became almost a status symbol, how much he could afford to lose at a place like the Colony. Betting more than you had was part of the thrill. It was a way of showing courage. As Ben Schulberg's son Stuart said, "My father and Herman believed that the courage you showed through gambling was a badge of honor, of manhood."

Like the drinking, the gambling has been passed down through my family largely as fodder for anecdotes. His penchant for difficult bets was so well-known that *Variety* wrote in 1926, "On football wagers everybody phones, rushes and probes to find out who Mankiewicz likes—to bet the other way." Years later, he and Joe were at Santa Anita, betting on horses, and toward the end of another losing afternoon, Herman decided to put all his remaining money on a horse that was listed at 40 to 1. Joe, who had watched with mounting disbelief as Herman placed difficult bet after difficult bet, losing them all, finally asked his brother, "What the hell are you doing? Don't you know that horse is 40 to 1?" Herman looked at Joe with a curious expression. "What are you talking about? It's fifty-fifty. Either the horse wins or it doesn't."

ON CHRISTMAS EVE, 1926, HERMAN WAS DRIVING HIS BUICK CONvertible to a party in Beverly Hills. Driving past a policeman on Sunset Boulevard, Herman gleefully hoisted his hands in the air and said, "Look! No hands!" The car swerved and was demolished.

HERMAN'S EARLY DAYS IN HOLLYWOOD COULD MAKE FOR A PEPPY montage sequence in an old* biopic, the kind where about twenty minutes in the hero first enjoys the fruits of his first act's labor. Along with the money and the prestige come fun with Sara—lovemaking in both

---

* Or new.

the nineteenth- and twentieth-century meanings of the word. But if this imagined movie has any depth, alongside the gags and delicious jokes, all brimming with Herman's unique sparkle, are scattered here and there a few seeds for his third-act fall from grace: Herman, in the money at last, his nose buried deep in the *Daily Racing Form,* sits idly in his office on the Paramount lot when the studio chief comes calling to check on his next screenplay, and without looking up from his perusal of odds on the fourth race at Santa Ana says, "I've always felt that when a man stops reading, he stops learning." Herman and Sara, on a yacht with Charlie Chaplin, Pola Negri, and William Randolph Hearst, heading to Catalina Island for the weekend. Herman, trying to rent a blimp to float high across the Rose Bowl during a big USC football game, trailing a sign that reads "Send Your Boy to an Eastern College." Herman and Sara in Palm Springs for the weekend. Herman, with his gambling debts constantly piling up, confidently telling friends, "They can't fire me. I owe them too much money."

Then there was the work. Unlike the more solitary efforts of prose or even, usually, playwriting, screenwriting was a collaborative affair. Herman would hold forth in a roomful of other men—gag men and studio assistants, producers and secretaries. As Ben Hecht would later say, "Movies were seldom written. They were yelled into existence at conferences that kept going in saloons, brothels and all-night poker games." It's no wonder that Herman flourished. He was virtuosic in the room, lying low, looking out at them all from underneath his heavy-lidded eyes, curling his lips as an idea flashed through his mind and he'd bark out a new title designed to "hit the back wall of the theater." "Paris," he'd shout. "Where half the women are working women . . ." Then the celebrated Mankiewicz leer: "And half the women are working men."

The others lapped it up, and Herman was soon so prominent that he was being mentioned routinely in Louella Parsons's columns, though initially she was complaining that the studios were paying too much obeisance to "eastern scribblers like Herman J. Mankiewicz . . . who have never proved they know anything about the tricky essentials." Herman was convinced otherwise, and for the most part, the studio agreed. Everything he wanted, he got. He even told other writers how to get what *they* wanted from the studio, instructing one new arrival to complain immediately about the office he'd been given. "Tell them to repaint it! Get them to move your desk, move a couch, put a picture on the wall." The point,

Herman told the man, was to let them know you are there. "Never explain in this town," Herman said. "Deny. Always deny."

As his comfort level increased, Herman went to Paramount chief Ben Schulberg and said he wanted to bring better writers to the West Coast, too. He told Schulberg he wanted to give a yearlong contract to his friend Ben Hecht, promising that if Hecht failed to write a successful movie, Schulberg could fire them both. Soon, Herman was sending the telegram that, aside from *Citizen Kane,* may be his most enduring literary legacy—the one he sent Hecht, imploring him to come west for three hundred a week to write for Paramount. "The three hundred is peanuts," Herman added. "There are millions to be grabbed out here and your only competition is idiots. Don't let this get around."* Hecht, of course, accepted Herman's call, and soon joined his old friend at Paramount, where without much delay he wrote a film called *Underworld* for director Josef Von Sternberg. The script took Hecht all of one week to write. When the movie opened, Schulberg announced his intention to give Hecht a bonus, whereupon Herman, though the exact choreography isn't clear, intercepted it. Telling Hecht, "I just want it for a few days to get me out of a little hole," Herman swooped in and took the money.

Hecht was an understanding friend, and Schulberg an understanding gambling buddy—and boss. When Herman was having difficulty paying back the money, the three men arranged for Schulberg to grant Herman a $500-a-week raise. The money made Herman the highest-paid writer at Paramount—and it went straight to Hecht.

If Herman bristled at the success of friends like Hecht, there is no evidence of it. Indeed, he maintained a rather magnanimous view toward those he considered his equals (or even betters) throughout his life. It was the great mass—of humanity in general, not just writers—toward whom he felt nothing but scorn. But with men like Hecht, Charles MacArthur, and later F. Scott Fitzgerald and William Faulkner, other exiles from the East who were intending their stays in Hollywood to be short ones, Herman felt something akin to a brotherly regard (more brotherly, in fact,

---

* When I was growing up in New York, spending time in bookstores like Coliseum Books at Fifty-seventh Street and Broadway, I would invariably flip through books about Hollywood and check the index for mentions of Herman's name, to find, about three-quarters of the time, this telegram, with its sublime "Don't let this get around.' "

than to his actual brother). For the real work, it was always quite obvious, was not being done for the screen, but for the stage or the page. Herman continued, in those early years in Hollywood, to harbor the belief that New York was in his near future. The setbacks of his plays—his and Kaufman's *The Good Fellow* ran for only six performances on Broadway in late 1926, and *The Wild Man of Borneo* fared little better the following year—did little to diminish his feeling that he would soon wrest himself from the bland comforts of California ("a lovely place to live, if you're an orange," in Fred Allen's famous phrase) and return to the East. In the meantime, he would try to surround himself with as many of his old New York chums as possible.

For another change had come to the movie business, one that demanded more writers and also proved Herman's worth more than ever: sound. Anyone who could actually write the words that came out of the actors' mouths would be even more valuable. An accomplished theater critic and playwright with an intricate knowledge of what worked and didn't on Broadway, Herman was one of the few men in Hollywood with any experience writing dramatic dialogue. As the success of the talkies spread, Schulberg put Herman in charge of building a staff of dialogue writers and sent Herman on a two-week recruiting trip to New York, which Herman labeled the "Herman J. Mankiewicz Fresh Air Fund for Writers."

In the end, he and his screenwriting friends like Hecht and Nunnally Johnson would be instrumental in changing the course of Hollywood movies. Continuing the turn away from what they considered the sentimentalized slop of middle-American morality, Herman picked recruits in his own image: newspapermen who would overturn the romantic sentimentality that had a stranglehold on the movies. Together, they introduced loquacious and smart-talking characters. Herman and his team were growing in leaps and bounds.

The only question was: Was there anyone whom Herman would not let into the club?

GRADUATION DAY DAWNED SUNNY AND BRIGHT FOR THE COLUMBIA graduating class of 1928. As the class assembled for the ceremony, young Joe Mankiewicz stood ramrod straight, eager to get on with the business at hand. Joe admired the pageantry of graduation, the playing of "Pomp and Circumstance," the filing of the old dignitaries and alumni in their multicolored robes into the open-air auditorium at Columbia, but while he hadn't exactly hated college, to him it had been something of a chore, a necessary hurdle before beginning his life. Like Herman, he had rocketed through high school in three years, and like Herman he now stood poised to graduate from Columbia at the tender age of nineteen. Like Herman, his immediate plans after graduation called for a trip to Berlin, where he, too, hoped to find work with the *Chicago Tribune*. But while Joe, as he stood under the trees in the open air and waited for his diploma, was still planning a career in academia, he also knew that Berlin was the capital of the thriving German film industry. His interest in movies would soon have Herman helping him secure a job with the leading German film company of the day, UFA, translating the inter-titles of silent films from German to English for foreign release. Like Herman, Joe had had a solid academic career, studying in the honors program tutored by Herman's favorite teacher, John Erskine. Like Herman, Joe had concentrated his extracurriculars on the theater at Columbia, contributing to the annual Sophomore Show, sort of a Varsity Show of comedy and song-and-dance acts, as well as, like Herman, taking part in the Varsity Show itself his senior year.

There were, of course, a few crucial differences with Herman. For one thing, according to Joe, sports. Joe told his biographer Ken Geist that he'd spent a considerable amount of time playing team sports at Columbia, winning athletic honors in football, baseball, and basketball. However, Joe's senior yearbook (a yearbook, incidentally, on which Joe worked) notes that the only sport he played was freshman baseball, so it seems that here again either Joe's memory was failing him or he was stretching the truth. But if so, to what end? The Mankiewiczes have never been a particularly athletic family or cared all that much about prowess on the athletic fields. The conjecture is unavoidable: Joe's lifelong Eve Harrington–like tendency, to exaggerate and fabricate certain facts about himself so as to elevate his own importance or sense of self, was here being deployed to distinguish himself from the cheerfully unathletic Herman.[*]

But there were other differences as well. Joe had actually entered Co-

---

[*] My mother once explained why gambling was her dad's preferred pastime: "We are a family who sits rather than stands and lies down rather than sits. What we do well is talk and think. And gambling is a thing, if you're not going to play a sport—[and] I think it's fair to say that nobody in this family has ever really gone into any kind of sports in any way . . . [But] clearly you have to take some interest, so you watch it, and what is more interesting than watching it is betting on it."

lumbia as a premed major, thinking in a loose kind of way that he might want to end up as a psychiatrist. However, he was quickly discouraged by a biology course in which he was required to dissect an earthworm and disembowel a frog, an exercise that "horrified and nauseated me." But the final blow that ended his medical career was his physics class. "I got an F-minus," he said. "There is no such grade, so I went to Professor Farwell and protested. He said, 'I feel that I must distinguish between mere failure and total failure such as yours.'" Joe abandoned the sciences and switched his major to English.

Also unlike Herman, he joined a fraternity, Phi Sigma Delta. His history here is suggestive, for while the frat didn't have much of an impact on his life, it signaled in Joe a far greater willingness to conform to societal rules and roles than Herman possessed. Fraternities had reached their peak in numbers and influence at Columbia in the 1920s. Each of the thirty-six campus fraternities had its own social codes the frat brothers were expected to conform to—conventions on drinking, dress, and, of course, relations between the sexes. Joe didn't merely tolerate life in the fraternity in a way that Herman never could have, he thrived within its clear social guidelines. He learned the history of Phi Sigma Delta, absorbing the songs, chants, and traditions faster than anyone else in his pledge class, exuding a knowledgeable ease with all of it within weeks of joining. Herman scoffed at it to Joe—"Lie down with idiots, you'll wake up with your brains gone"—but Joe felt Herman was missing the point. When people liked you and trusted you, they listened to you, did what you asked, and took your advice. He realized that helping his frat brothers—whether with their homework or advice about what to say to that girl who kept talking to them on their way to French class—gave him social power and influence.

And indeed, the young women from Barnard whom Joe met at dances were all quite taken with him. By making the pretty girl laugh who caught his eye at the mixer at Low Library, enchanting her with his wit and warmth, he quickly gained her confidence. Soon enough, he would be sitting at the edge of the mess hall with that pretty girl, hearing all about how she's so tired of her roommate crying about her beau stationed overseas. Joe was never totally absorbed by their conversation; he knew with intuitive alchemical, scientific, and artistic sense exactly how long he had let her talk about her worries, making her feel understood, an investment he was sure would end in a major win: kissing under the maple grove next to her sorority when he walked her home.

Throughout Joe's rising social influence, he was powerfully aware of Herman's long shadow. Joe's best friend at Columbia was a would-be actor named Chester Eckstein. (Under Herman and Joe's influence, Eckstein would ultimately change his last name—to Erskine, to honor the much-loved teacher. "You're not going to get Eckstein in lights very easily," Herman said.) Joe and Eckstein talked endlessly of the theater, "sharing gossip," Eckstein later said, "because you feel you're in it if you talk about it." In addition, Joe and Eckstein worked together as aspiring humorists, sending twenty-five-to-fifty-word humorous sketches to magazines. One day, Joe came tearing up to the second floor of the fraternity house shouting, "They've bought it!" It was his first professional sale: a paragraph purchased by *Life* magazine for six dollars. But more significant than the sale was the author's name, as listed in the magazine when the article ran: Joe Mason. Joe explained later, "I didn't want to use my brother's name—the name of Mankiewicz, at that time, belonging to him in the world of art and letters and to my father in the world of pedagogy." It was a curious if admirable decision, not to trade on the family name, though not one that would be repeated.

While he was in college, Joe also earned extra money for college by teaching English to foreigners three nights a week, and during the summers served as a counselor to theater-starved kids at a summer camp in the Hudson Valley, a camp partly owned by the Marx Brothers. According to Joe, "That's where I had a fistfight with Zeppo when he wanted to play first base on the camp team. I was the coach, and the kids were supposed to play first base, not one of the owners of the camp. After all, the kid's parents had paid a lot of money for these activities. I told him to get off the field, and one word led to another."

All the same, even while indulging in Joe's love for theater and writing in college, Franz presumed that his youngest son's future lay in academia. Joe didn't disagree. The plan was to study at the University of Berlin, go to the Sorbonne, and finish at Oxford. Joe had been a superb student, and as he went up on stage and accepted his Columbia diploma, his teachers and his father were hoping and expecting that his future lay in the halls of academia. John Erskine was in fact even more specific than that. After the ceremony, Joe and Erskine had a long talk, and Erskine, the respected professor and author of celebrated novels, spoke of his great hope that after his European travels Joe would come back to Columbia as an instructor in English, and "by teaching, writing, and taking it more slowly, perhaps develop into a good writer."

The thought appealed to Joe. "He thought I might possibly write some plays and some books, and he was probably goddamned right." But Erskine admitted he had a trepidation about Joe's future. "He told me of his fear that I was going to follow the easy road and succumb to the blandishments of Hollywood." Joe swore up and down that he wouldn't.

Less than ten months later, on his first night in Hollywood, Joe tagged along with Herman to a party at the Santa Monica home of Jesse Lasky, the head of Paramount Pictures. Joe was in a daze. He'd spent four glorious months in Berlin, where he'd held two journalism jobs while translating titles for foreign films, a period that he later described as an "absolute intoxication of theater, excitement, glamour, and sex," leaving Berlin, he said later, only when a kindly bank teller told him to get out of town after he'd bounced a check. Following that, he'd spent three miserable months in Paris ("Everything that Paris was described as, Berlin is," Joe said), where in March of 1929, he wrote his big brother a letter so despairing that Herman fired off another telegram with huge repercussions. For this one, no real wit was required: "For Christ sake come out to Hollywood." So Joe did, with Herman arranging a job for $60 a week as a junior writer at Paramount. Joe would have to undergo a mild legal ordeal to get approved—he was still under age—but now, Herman had picked him up at the train station that afternoon and so here he was, in a borrowed suit and his one remaining good pair of shoes, attending his first Hollywood party.

Herman had been absorbed into the maw and was holding forth among a group by an unused billiards table, and Joe was alone and exhilarated: "Imagine the man who discovered Tutankhamen's tomb . . . There was Clara Bow, Gary Cooper, William Powell, Kay Francis—it was like being alone in a candy store no one's watching."

Suddenly, he recognized a familiar back. "I saw a back, and I knew that back. I couldn't place it." But when the back turned around, he saw the face, one he hadn't seen since graduation: John Erskine. Joe greeted his old teacher warmly, and asked what on earth the man was doing in California. Erskine, ten months removed from his powerful denunciation of the horrors of Hollywood's easy money, replied that he was now working at Warner Brothers.

Joe stood chatting with the man in a kind of disbelief. "At that moment, an illusion shattered that I don't think I've ever recovered from. He had just sold *The Private Life of Helen of Troy* to Warners and was out there working on the screenplay." As Joe and Erskine spoke, it dawned on him not only that people would all essentially do anything in their self-interest, that they would say anything at any time to further their goals, but that there was simply no use resisting Hollywood or what it offered.

Joe took in the scene coolly, much more cool in fact than his old professor: "It skipped his mind completely that he'd delivered that impassioned speech about not going Hollywood, and he talked to me exactly like one Hollywood pro to another."

For Joe, the journey was complete. There was no use fighting it, and every reason to embrace it wholeheartedly—Hollywood, movies, the whole damn nonacademic fun of it. He had come to where Herman was. And he would get everything he could from it, whether his brother did or not.

CHAPTER SIX

⚓

TRAPPED

Something told you to do as I say, didn't it? That instinct is worth millions. You can't buy it—cherish it, Eve. When that alarm goes off, go to your battle stations.

—*ALL ABOUT EVE*

JOE LOVED ALMOST EVERYTHING ABOUT THE STUDIO. HE LOVED watching the men roll the hand trucks with scenery down behind the back lot, he loved the sound coming from the woodshop when the carpenters were sawing wood and banging hammers into nails constructing sets, he loved (absolutely loved, in more ways than one, about which more later) the starlets, the many young ingénues who would be parading around the lot, some flitting toward the commissary for a quick bite before auditions, others headed to the costume shop for fittings, some coming from who-knows-where with flushed cheeks, and others dashing from the set, dressed absurdly in eighteenth-century peasant garb, or bedecked as mermaids, bar wenches, prostitutes, nuns, aviatrixes, or nurses. And he loved, too, the work. He loved kibbutzing with the other junior writers, even those whom he thought were clearly inferior. He knew a good idea was bound to come from anywhere, and as the youngest writer on the Paramount lot, he was hardly in a position to impose his will on anyone yet. But he also knew it was just a matter of time before he'd be able to rise through the ranks. Sixty dollars a week wasn't much to start with, but it was just a start, and he knew it wouldn't take long for him to be earning, if not Herman-type money, at least a hell of a lot more than he was now.

Joe had little trouble adapting to whatever they threw at him. For a time he was enrolled in what was called the junior writer program, devoted to teaching the younger writers from back East the rudiments of screenwriting: tricks of the trade, Joe later said, which included how to establish the jeopardy that would "carry the furniture of the film" (like opening with a wide shot of the factory that would include a sign that said "Danger: Explosives" so that you could stage a chase through the area in the eighth reel), and also rules like the "what he doesn't know," a bit of back story, say, that Jean Arthur's handsome young mechanic is, unbeknownst to her, actually the richest man in all of Australia.

"Joe loved almost everything about the studio." Here he pals around with two friends, identified on the back of the photo only as "Claude and wife," c. 1932.

Joe lapped it up. Always a good student, he learned the lessons well, and though surrounded by slightly older young men who had attended Yale and Harvard, he was the first one promoted out of the group and into a real writing job. As always, Joe, however witty and self-consciously funny as he could be, was studious and alert, and he took the craft of writing seriously. He imbibed the rules and learned them well. He knew something early on that it takes many writers years to discover—you have to know the rules in order to break them.[*]

Immediately Joe impressed the directors he was assigned to. More than just being young and handsome, with a fresh and optimistic spirit that contrasted with many of the more cynical writers from back East (including Herman), he seemed unusually secure personally, and was, unlike nearly everyone else in Hollywood, perfectly willing to admit his weaknesses as well as his strengths. When he was assigned to the movie *Skippy* under director Norman Taurog, Joe told Taurog that while he was

---

[*] By the late 1940s and early '50s, there was an unstated rule in Hollywood screenwriting circles: a good picture—a quality picture not a B movie—could never be made if it was full of voice-over. Joe Mankiewicz had learned the rule so well that he was able to obliterate it in films like *A Letter to Three Wives*, *All About Eve*, and *The Barefoot Contessa*.

confident in his dialogue, and considered it excellent and natural, Joe thought it would be wise for the director to get someone else to handle the construction of the screenplay. Taurog was amazed: "I was strongly impressed by his not trying to bluff me that he could do everything." Then, when the screenplay of *Finn and Hattie,* an adaptation of a novel by Donald Ogden Stewart, was completed, Joe went to Stewart and "very apologetically informed me he had just written the screenplay from my book, and forewarned me, 'Don't go to see it.'" The movie had dispensed with the book's satirical tone and replaced it with broad comedy in service of Leon Errol, the film's pratfalling star; Stewart would always like Joe as a result of that "voluntary apology." Such examples of modesty and honest self-effacement were rare in Hollywood, and almost unheard of in a Mankiewicz.

Joe had another advantage of course: he was Herman's brother. Everyone knew Herman; the name opened doors and greased wheels, and it had gotten Joe the job in the first place. At the time Herman was at the top of his game—Paramount's best writer, writing for films ranging from *Ladies' Man* to *Man of the World* to *Love Among the Millionaires,* he was also seen as almost an oracle on the lot. "[Herman] was the kind of guy who could pull a picture through to completion," James M. Cain testified. "Nothing could blow him down or faze him or get his nerves." But in part that may have been because of how he viewed his work: unseriously. How could he become truly disturbed by something that wasn't very important? *The Hollywood Reporter,* which along with *Variety* was one of the official trade publications of the town and reflected its mores (or lack thereof), took note of the attitude and complained of writers who "sat at the famous 'bachelor's table' in the Montmartre Restaurant—Herman Mankiewicz, the high priest. Here writers pledge themselves to a 'few more years of tripe and then something worthwhile.'" As the *Reporter* sensed, since these first writers were making the big money, they tended to view the rest of the writers with disdain, especially the green young recruits from the East Coast colleges, who arrived full of spit and polish and would happily do the labor on dialogue that ran down the right hand side of the scripts—or the construction that took up the left-hand column—while their imagined betters, or bettors, were rolling craps and playing cards.

In fact, by the time Joe arrived at Paramount, Herman's gambling was intensifying. Now that he was making big money, Herman was only too willing to raise the stakes on his poker games. As Richard Meryman later estimated, "one million dollars passed through Herman's hands and left no residue"—a staggering achievement of a sort. His career seemed better than ever, and he had big funds at his disposal. Who could complain about a life like that? As for Joe, while not overly adoring of the kid, Herman treated him with respect and affection. He'd talked him up before Joe even arrived, proudly waving the telegram Joe had sent from Albuquerque announcing his imminent arrival: "TWO HOURS LATE. HORSES EATEN BY WOLVES. GOLD SAFE HOWEVER."

Joe's rise pleased Herman enormously—and just as Joe benefited by Herman's presence at Paramount, so did Herman gain reward from Joe's being on the lot, and it was a reward that was even easier to calibrate than respect or residual affection, for Joe's boss was Ben Schulberg, his frequent gambling buddy and one of his best friends. After Joe had established himself as a dialogue whiz and an all-around writer worthy of support, Herman decided that Joe was underpaid. He stormed into Schulberg's office and demanded a raise on Joe's behalf. A good half hour of conversation later, when Schulberg acceded to Herman's demand and raised Joe's weekly salary to $125, Herman pulled his brother aside and dispensed some hard-earned wisdom. "Money in this town never lasts," Herman said. "Put twenty-five dollars a week into a savings account, and you'll be glad you did." Joe did as he was told, grateful and somewhat surprised at his brother's words.

Six months later, Herman was in a tight spot and demanded all the money in Joe's savings account.

For years, Joe had looked to Herman as his real father figure, outstripping the distant and imperious Franz. What to do, then, when your father figure turns out to be as disappointing, if in totally different ways, as your father himself? Joe had already absorbed the blows of Franz's remoteness and coldness. Now, in Hollywood, Joe would be exposed to Herman's utter unpredictability and unreliability, especially when it came to money. The hero worship that had nourished Joe, seen him through his difficult patches both in New York and Europe and brought him west, was eroding. Still, a Hollywood neophyte who owed so much of his life to Herman, he could hardly refuse him that first time. And Herman took full advantage of his position on the lot as a "god among writers," one friend of Joe's later recalled. "Joe was the kid brother all right. Herman rode him, patronized him, did everything but send him out for cigarettes."

Later, though it would never be easy, Joe would learn how to say no to Herman. Once, when Herman needed money to pay off an even larger gambling debt than usual, he told Joe to borrow on his life insurance for money. Joe refused. Herman responded by summoning Joe to a conference in the office of their mutual friend, writer Charlie Lederer. When he arrived, Herman banged a big book on a desk, startling Lederer's office mate, writer James McGuinness, then announced, "This is a trial." Then Herman turned to McGuinness and said, "Now will you kindly tell this little SOB what a brother is—that everything he has is mine."

There is of course a huge difference in how a younger brother and a little brother perceive things. To the older brother, the younger brother can range from an afterthought to a usurper . . . but since all of life predates the little pisher, how in the world does he think that anything he gets does not belong to me? Does the Earth not depend on the Sun? Of course the older brother would take without asking. It is the little brother who wouldn't dream of it. He may covet what the older brother has, but to get it will require cunning, patience, and resolve. To him, nothing is given. It will need to be earned, or taken.

"I SEE YOUR CAREER RISING IN THE EAST, LIKE THE SUN," ADDISON DeWitt declared to Miss Caswell in *All About Eve* after the young ingénue (played to halting, ignorant perfection by Marilyn Monroe) has cajoled the old producer Max Fabian (Gregory Ratoff, dyspeptic, irritable, also perfect) into getting her a drink at Margo Channing's party. Like Miss Caswell, Joe was shrewd in his advancement, and his career initially seemed to consist of nothing but rising. He became an immediate favorite of the Paramount directors like Taurog, Norman Z. McLeod, and Edward Sutherland. "Joe Mankiewicz ruins you for anyone else," Taurog said. "He never let me down." When Joe was assigned to a picture, he invariably did the job more thoroughly and intelligently than the next fellow, and he was recognized almost immediately for his skill. After collaborating on the screenplay for the adaptation of the long-running comic book *Skippy*, in 1931, Joe was nominated for an Academy Award at the age of twenty-two, though the ceremony contained an early embarrassment which revealed Joe's intense competitive streak as well as his laser-like focus on winning a golden statuette. Ever the professional, Joe soon refined the incident into a first-class anecdote. Apparently, according to Joe, the man announcing the award winner that year was an aging screenwriter named Waldemar Young, who, when he opened the envelope, said that "the choice was particularly pleasing to him because it was a friend of his—which I was, a young friend—but also because the subject matter was so American and so fresh . . . and went on describing *Skippy*. Then he announced, 'Ladies and gentlemen, the Best in Screenplay Award goes to . . .' and I stood up. 'Howard Estabrook for *Cimarron*,' and there I was, standing with egg dripping off my face." Fortunately for Joe, Estabrook was right in front of him, "so I did the big ham bit of reaching over and shaking his hand, when I actually hated the son of a bitch."

Joe had learned quickly to adapt—to shake the hands of the sons of bitches he hated. Would it have been possible for Herman to have ever tried to get away with such a move? Would he have even wanted to?

"A cloud floated right into my soup plate." Poster for *Dinner at Eight* (1933)

For Herman, movie writing was increasingly becoming something of a chore, and here's where the true tragedy of Herman's output begins to dawn. It was the golden age of Hollywood comedies, or so we all later agreed, but Herman Mankiewicz didn't value the work. His disdain is almost heartbreaking.

Consider *Dinner at Eight*, for which he was loaned out from Paramount to M-G-M. The movie sparkles from beginning to end, and it isn't just because it's based on a successful play by Edna Ferber and George S. Kaufman. Working with Frances Marion and Donald Ogden Stewart, Herman turned the play into a real movie, with scintillating lines from dazzling performers. It's almost demoralizing to watch Jean Harlow's spoiled blonde say, "Politics? Ha! You couldn't get into politics. You couldn't get in anywhere. You couldn't even get in the men's room at the Astor!" or Marie Dressler declaim, "And then I had a restful, nice luncheon . . . with four lawyers. On the eighty-eighth floor of the Watson's building. You know, the sky club. A cloud floated right into my soup plate"—and think about not only Herman's involvement in the movie, but his contempt for it.

In fact, the movie, about grasping ambition at the start of the Great Depression, has painful echoes to Herman's situation. It's the tale of an alcoholic former matinee idol on the down side of a once-brilliant acting career, portrayed with searing believability by John Barrymore. Those who know of Barrymore's own alcoholism and self-loathing will likely see the added poignancy in this man who has "outlived everything but his vanity," but what of the parallels to Herman's life? Watching Barrymore decide to end his own life, seeing him turn on the gas in his hotel room, it isn't just the waste of a character's life that's so sad. It's the implied nobility that Barrymore brings to the act—almost as if someone, somewhere, lurking behind the actor, was agreeing with the decision: life is stupid and the people in it are idiots, and genius goes unrecognized, and maybe the whole thing isn't really worth much in the end. The weariness in Barrymore's performance, the utter defeat that he seemed so willing to embrace . . . is it wrong to wonder if some of this was placed there by Herman?

Herman's derision for the work is unquestioned, and one interesting bit of evidence for his disrespect for it is that, unlike a lot of other screenwriters, Herman didn't take his work home with him. According to my uncle Frank, while you might hear Pop complaining about various sons of bitches at the studio (Frank and Don's name for Herman was the same as Herman and Joe's for Franz), you never heard him talk about the actual work: no "how do I resolve this character problem" or "how can I get the hero back to town before the dynamite goes off without his knowing the dynamite is set to explode?" Nor even, according to Frank, did he talk much about the business of Hollywood—"There was no 'Zanuck is smarter than Mayer,' or 'I'd rather work at Warner Bros. because they have a more sensitive understanding of character . . .' No. No, they were all clowns. Idiots. The inmates were running the asylum."

In fact, Frank often said, if you didn't know what Herman did for a living, you wouldn't know what he did for a living. Work, the way Herman lived, was something that was off to one side. You left in the morning, you came home in the evening, but you never talked about it. You suffered through it, you did it, but all the while you were dreaming that maybe in some alternate universe you were actually doing something you respected.

Ironically, the disregard that Herman had for the place may have been precisely what allowed my uncles Frank and Don (and later my mother) to grow up in such relative peace and normalcy compared to typical Hollywood children of celebrated parents. When you're being driven from house to house in a limousine on Halloween, as Mom remembered doing with the Selznick children every year, and the chauffeur is going up the walk to collect the candy, it can tend to be a little hard to keep your priorities straight. But if the whole damn game is considered a waste of time, if you never go to your father's movies because he thinks they're slop and vomit, and he further believes that "there weren't that many literate people in Hollywood, certainly not people with whom he could even talk," then you're liable to grow up feeling a certain distance from the place, something that prevents you from investing too much mental energy in the town and its games. Herman and Sara made a nice home on Tower Road in Beverly Hills, and Don and Frank grew up secure and happy, knowing their father was successful, and on balance a good dad, albeit distant, even diffident at times. Still, that he cared for them deeply they never doubted. And that he wanted to create a haven of his family life was also clear. It was a place he could escape the stupidity and madness of the system that was, he felt, eating him alive. And so, rather than give lavish parties attended by actors and movie stars—"What have you got to say to a movie actor, and what has he got to say to you?" Herman would ask—when he and Sara did entertain, even if famous people attended their dinners, the guests would more likely be writers and playwrights from back East than performers: men like Alexander Woollcott, Edmund Wilson, F. Scott Fitzgerald, S. J. Perelman, Jed Harris, and Bennett Cerf. Talking to Uncle Frank late in his life about his dad, you got the sense that Herman was trapped in Hollywood—utterly starving for intellectual stimulation and companionship, believing with every molecule of blood in him that he was wasting his professional life, but making far too much money to leave. Family would be, would have to be, his consolation.

Myrna Loy and Clark Gable in
Manhattan Melodrama (1934)

"An ideal dinner guest":
Joe in 1934

But how much consolation could it really have been? Can a life be filled with genuine joy if you're living in a perpetual state of rage at the people you work with, and for? If you grow up imagining that you will have tremendous success in a field that you respect and honor, having success, no matter how great, in a field you find demeaning and insulting and generating a product that is pap for the masses, who are generally slobs and fools, can't possibly be balanced out by a loving family. Because if, as Herman felt, you are every day failing to be what you might have been, surely you can't shower your family members with the kind of warmth and paternal love you'd want to. It's hard, every dimestore philosopher will tell us, to love others if you don't love yourself. So while it's easy to respect Herman for all he accomplished with one hand self-tied behind his back, fighting through his self-loathing and addictions to become for a time that "god among writers," and admirable to consider his devotion to his family, there's also something ineffably sad about his warmth toward Sara and the kids. The bittersweet twinkle in his eyes as he watched Don and Frank play their childhood games was unmistakable—love for your family is wonderful, but is it enough?

Joe, meanwhile, was relishing the life of the young man-about-town. He was handsome and much sought-after—an ideal dinner guest who didn't bring nearly the level of tension to the table that his brother did. There was little chance he would throw up on the tablecloth, or get in a violent political battle, or make a scene of any kind—he was well-behaved and well-mannered. In fact, he had so much of that newfangled "sex appeal" that William Wellman once asked Joe when he would "give up this crap about writing" and offered him a contract as an actor (Joe respectfully declined). Joe was even used in *Finn and Hattie*, as a model in a photo for a magazine ad illustrating the "It" pose, with the ad copy asking, "Do women thrill at your approach?"

In Joe's case, many did. A succession of starlets shared his bed, if not his heart.* At one point, Joe seemed poised to marry a young Brit-

---

* In the mid-1960s, watching his son Tom navigate through Hollywood's social world as a young man, Joe gave him a piece of paternal advice on dating actresses;

ish socialite, if only, Herman said, so he could name his son Napier. Later, he was linked publicly to a number of different actresses, one of whom, Frances Dee, he later told Ken Geist, did break his heart. In fact, he told Geist that he had planned on eloping with her until he learned that she had already run off with another man, actor Joel McCrea.* Joe said that

Man-about-town on a boat: Joe, mid 1930s

she was the great love of his life, though the story of their meeting one last time after she married McCrea is hard to believe. According to what one friend told Geist, Joe said he was driving his car down Coldwater Canyon, when a car pulled alongside, and there she was, Frances Dee, the beautiful dark-haired ingénue taking her car out for an afternoon drive. She "waved to him and pulled up at the side of the road . . . They looked at each other for a moment, and she suddenly reached out and embraced him passionately, kissed him, and then threw her car into gear and zoomed away." Joe must have found it a reassuring story to tell, not only to others but to himself. After all, how easy and safe for Joe to have lost the one great love of his life before he actually got married. Looked at from the vantage point of a man with three marriages under his belt, it's easy to view the story as apocryphal, Joe announcing to the world that he did in fact have a heart to break.

But Joe's relationships with actresses would continue, professionally and personally, for the next three or four decades. For while Herman had nothing but indifference for actors, Joe would remain fiercely attracted to them his entire life, a moth to the flame. Sometimes, later, talking with actresses on film sets, he would see that they were hanging on his every word not just because he was the director, but because, literally, they didn't know what to think until he told them. In a relationship with an

---

the crassness of this counsel would echo through the decades and contribute to Joe's poor reputation in my own nuclear family. "Never fuck a starlet," Joe told Tom, "when you can fuck a star."

* Joe was not too distraught to spread the story that Dee had confided in producer David O. Selznick that she had chosen McCrea over Joe when she realized that her attraction to Joe was purely physical.

actress, Joe could play several roles—devoted, adoring audience member and admirer who would happily shower her with support and love and feed her likely starved sense of self; director, there to cajole and wheedle and draw a great performance out of her; and most of all, Svengali—a near-hypnotic manipulator and overbearing mentor, there to tutor the actress and fill her presumably empty head with ideas. "You belong to me now," a steely Addison DeWitt tells Eve Harrington toward the end of *All About Eve*. And it was this role, practically as the woman's owner, that would keep ensnaring Joe, lasting through his first two marriages and exploding into personal turmoil and tragedy that would nearly derail his professional life, even as his understanding of the relationship would fuel his greatest work.

To Herman, an actress was someone who had nothing to say.

To Joe, that may have been the point.

JOE'S SUNDAY WEDDING AT TOWER ROAD MUST HAVE BROUGHT BACK memories for the groom. Joe had loved playing with Sara's little sister Mattie at Herman's wedding, and he would always remember the ice cream they'd snuck out with together on the back porch, as well as how Herman and Sara had behaved that afternoon—the way they looked at each other, held hands, even how she rolled her eyes at him when his friends had been drinking and confounding the rabbi. Now they were practically an old married couple, together almost fourteen years—Sara was in back talking to Elizabeth's mother. Mrs. Von Schermerhorn was a horrid woman, but Sara managed to talk to her almost politely, probably the one member of the family able to swallow her distaste enough to be civil. Mrs. Von Schermerhorn had withheld her approval of Elizabeth's choice in groom for some time—there were all kinds of excuses but in the end Joe felt it came down to good old-fashioned anti-Semitism. Of course, breaking past religious and cultural conventions in large part explained Joe's reason for marrying this upper-crust New York City white doily of a debutante in the first place—Herman advised Joe to tell his mother-in-law-to-be that he'd happily reattach his foreskin if that would help ease her conscience on the matter—but in the end the fact that Joe was now making good money and had moved over to M-G-M, which was, even for stuffed shirts from back East, the most prestigious of all the studios, had finally allowed Joe to overcome their opposition. So now, at last, Elizabeth Young, an actress from the East, would become his bride.

Herman served as host for the afternoon, and fortifying himself with some scotch, did a fine job of it, seeing to the guests in the Tower Road garden, making sure everyone had canapes, or drinks, or both. Herman's hair was thinning by now, and Joe, whose own mane was still lustrous and rich, couldn't fail to notice how much Herman was beginning to resemble Pop, who sat sternly in the front row of seats. Herman's twelve-year-old son Don sat next to his grandfather, though the old man didn't have much of a relationship with his grandsons. Franz didn't make it west very often, and Joe knew he should feel honored somehow that Franz had come for the wedding. But relations between Franz and Elizabeth's mother had been icy from the start, and the wedding day didn't change that.

Joe considered what the day meant. Did it mean anything? He'd gotten a squib in the *Los Angeles Times* about the wedding, and Louella Parsons had promised to write something about it. And maybe the wedding would finally calm Elizabeth down. The last few weeks had been tense. The woman was in constant need of flattery, it seemed to Joe. So like an actress, so emotionally unstable. The need was never-ending—but then again, look at her.

Joe's first wife was a beauty, with dark hair and a lovely upturned nose, and her eyes conveyed intelligence and wit, though as Joe had already learned, what was conveyed in a performance was very often something that wasn't there. At Tower Road that afternoon, Joe became bored with his wife. He wished he'd been able to get away with Herman and get a drink himself. He watched Herman that afternoon with Sara, and the way the two of them were so casually, genuinely affectionate with each other, even surrounded, as they were that afternoon, by so many Aaronsons. Joe knew Herman didn't like his wife's relatives always hovering everywhere, and he took comfort in that now, for Joe knew, as he looked across at Herman, so comfortable, so at home, so situated and right, that domestic security would never be his destiny.[*]

Someone took a photograph of this moment, ten minutes before the noontime wedding. Joe looks like he is doing everything he can not to hurry things along, as if all he wants to do is get through this ceremony, then the lunch, then get as quickly as possible to the hotel, where there

---

[*] Thankfully, he was wrong. Reader, he has a heart.

would no doubt be tears and some hours of talk, recriminations for something or other he'd done wrong, then some lovemaking, he could count on that. And then some sleep, and finally, a little more than twenty hours from now, it would be time to get back to the studio.

THE MARRIAGE LASTED THREE YEARS, TO THE DAY.

In November 1936, Joe moved out of their apartment in Beverly Hills for the Beverly Wilshire Hotel and issued a statement that despite their irreconcilable differences, the two were parting on good terms. It was pure PR hogwash, and when Elizabeth filed for divorce, she claimed that Joe treated her cruelly, was overly critical of her, and no longer loved her. For his part, Joe was never entirely sure he had ever loved her, but he was certainly less interested in being with her than he had been initially, and after the physical attraction wore off, Joe was left with an actress of limited depth who simply didn't hold his interest, and whose utility had been outlived. He couldn't be blamed. It had been a marriage of opportunism on both sides, and when he saw that she was desperately unhappy, he was more than willing to let her go, to grant her a divorce on the best terms imaginable. She was emotional and silly—the tears and the yelling and the jealousies—it all struck Joe as juvenile, and when, in the end, she testified that entire days went by without Joe speaking to his wife, he realized that of course the woman was right, but it couldn't be helped.

For her part, she ended up getting married two more times, and toward the end of her life she hardly ever thought back to her first marriage. When she did, she remembered only distance, cruelty, and criticism. Sometimes she wondered if it had been deeper than that—deeper or more shallow, she wasn't sure—she asked herself just how heartless Joe really was. In some moments, she thought maybe the coldness and the cruelty had been mere manipulation, a decision on his part to get her to go away so that he wouldn't have to confront whatever it was he didn't want to confront.

TO THE BIOGRAPHER, A MOVIE IS A TRICKY ARTIFACT, MOST PARTICularly because determining the various contributions of its makers can be so challenging. How can it be determined precisely what any one person's contribution to a film was? Even if he is a total auteur, responsible for every line of dialogue and every positioning of the camera (as for instance with a man whose dream was more than anything else simply to be in control), it can be nearly impossible to say with any real certainty what anyone's actual contribution to a film was, a feat made even trickier when considering the Hollywood movies of the 1930s and '40s, when collaboration was the norm and creative credits were frequently handed out on an ad hoc basis. And when one throws into the mix a combustible nest of egos such as Hollywood was and will always be, sorting out one person's contribution from another's can be even harder. When, furthermore, two of the people who are battling for the credit are brothers with a lifelong relationship of such tension and complexity, it makes the task borderline impossible.

The most that can be said about *Million Dollar Legs*, therefore, the single movie on which both Herman and Joe received credit, is that in its own absurd and sophomoric way it's a ridiculously delightful film—anarchic and funny and bizarre—almost surreal in its lack of narrative purpose and momentum. That Herman was listed as one of the producers and Joe as one of the writers is, more than eighty years later, truly incidental.

According to the other credited writer, Henry Myers, "Nobody but Joe Mankiewicz and I wrote a syllable of that script or created one of its ideas." But while it would be nice to believe that, *Million Dollar Legs* sticks out almost like a sonnet among the epic prose poems of Joe's other work. The film is a sixty-four-minute blitz of outrageous sight gags, wild

Jack Oakie and W. C. Fields in *Million Dollar Legs*, the only film on which both Herman and Joe received credit

verbal jokes ("Don't talk to yourself, and if you do, lie"), and zany performances from a host of old-time comics—nothing at all like the more
literate scripts Joe would come to write in later years, and even removed
from his early work for Paramount by its riotous sensibility.

In truth, the film, which recounts the attempts of American Migg
Tweeny (Jack Oakie) to get the he-man president of the mythical Klopstokia (W. C. Fields) to enter the 1932 Olympic Games and so save the
country from financial ruin, resembles nothing so much as a Marx Brothers movie without the brothers. Klopstokia is a country where all the girls
are named Angela, all the men are named George, and when someone
asks why, the only answer is "why not?" An opening title informs us that
the country's chief exports are goats and nuts, chief imports are goats and
nuts, and chief inhabitants are . . . goats and nuts.* The country is also
filled with supernaturally accomplished athletes, and when Migg Tweeny
wonders what would happen if all the athletes in the country were laid
end to end, the president's daughter answers, "They would reach 484
miles." Oakie asks, "How do you know?" "We did it once." It's modern
and nutty and takes itself about as seriously as a piece of toffee. It also
pokes fun at the very idea of its being a movie, with a self-consciousness
that few movies of the time had.

In all of this, there is the whiff of Herman. And, according to Goma at
least, he wrote the whole thing himself. Certainly, as producer, Herman
would have guided the creation of the script, or at least goaded Joe into
writing what he wanted. But it is well to consider a few other things before
giving the senior Mankiewicz brother too much credit for its creation.
First is the presence of Jack Oakie in the lead role. By that point in Oakie's
career, Joe had written three other movies starring Oakie, all of which
took advantage of Oakie's skill as a comic actor (or overactor—Oakie,
a delightfully thick slice of vaudevillian ham, specialized in the double
take). Joe knew what Oakie was best at on screen—and so knew how to
write the kind of nonsense dialogue that Oakie excelled at, and to give
other lines to other players to take best advantage of Oakie's wild, open-
faced reactions. Our man Joe Mankiewicz, it's fair to say, had studied Jack
Oakie and what made him work.[†]

---

* Even Henry Myers admitted Herman wrote the opening titles after an early preview of the film bewildered audiences.

† In fact, though Joe called him a "dreadful person," he also worked well with the
  film's other big vaudeville star, W. C. Fields. Writing part of the Fields movie *If I*

He had also, of course, been studying Herman. Following him to Hollywood, becoming a screenwriter, Joe had been emulating Herman professionally for years (and would soon be doing it personally as well, or trying to, with his marriage to Elizabeth Young), and he knew that being unruly, authority-defying, and full-of-a-low-regard-for-the-form in which he was writing were all essential ingredients of his brother's personality. When he was assigned to *Million Dollar Legs,* therefore, and started to consider what the picture called for, it is likely that consciously or

"General dementia": The Marx Brothers at their peak, c. 1931

not Joe began to ape his brother's personality in its creation. So perhaps the script for *Million Dollar Legs* was Joe writing as Herman, drawing on a wealth of emotional and logical information to make a classic Mankie-wiczian farce.*

Finally, though, there is Herman, whose own battles with anarchy were already well under way. The year before *Million Dollar Legs,* Herman had been assigned to ride herd on the Marx Brothers themselves, who had finally come to Hollywood to try to extend their brilliance at vaudeville and on the Broadway stage to the movies. As the producer of their first film, *Monkey Business,* Herman's job was to make sure those brothers brought their famous chaotic humor and wit to the screen, within the confines of a Hollywood movie. And he had succeeded, brilliantly—the brothers were instant Hollywood stars.

But Herman hardly enjoyed the process. As he told the two writ-

---

Had a Million, Joe had coined Fields's stock phrase "my little chickadee," which so delighted the generally bitter Fields that according to Joe he bought the saying from Joe for fifty bucks.

* More than anything, what this particular biographer-descendant takes from the film is that here is something both men made and enjoyed. Watching the film is the closest we will ever get to watching the two brothers play.

"This is an ordeal by fire. Make sure you wear asbestos pants." Herman clowns with the Marx Brothers, here dressed with a Groucho mustache and a Harpo wig, next to Harpo in Hun outfit.

ers assigned to the project, the Marx Brothers themselves, though good friends of his socially, were "mercurial, devious, and ungrateful. I hate to depress you, but you'll rue the day you ever took the assignment. This is an ordeal by fire. Make sure you wear asbestos pants." For five months, Herman presided over writing sessions in his office with the writers and the brothers themselves, who like Herman had trouble staying focused. The work sessions frequently deteriorated into "bedlams of shouted ideas, insults, trade-offs, and general dementia"—not to mention gambling and drinking. What the brothers needed wasn't so much a producer as a policeman.

Still, it worked. And after the success of *Monkey Business*, Herman was assigned to produce their follow-up, *Horse Feathers*. That film, too, was successful, though Groucho, never known for generosity of spirit, especially when it came to people who were *not* his brothers, would later say that Herman's contributions were less than exemplary, given that he was so often away gambling with Ben Schulberg, or drinking. In fact, Groucho said that as brilliant and talented as Herman was, he was generally useless after lunch.

But Herman's problems with the Marx Brothers were not all his own making. He was deeply concerned about Groucho's tendency to use jokes from the script to humor his friends. Time and time again, Herman would hear Groucho trying out the lines on friends and complain to the comedian that repeating the jokes that way would only lead to staleness on film. Others made the same complaint, and they were right—both *Monkey Business* and *Horse Feathers* can suffer from an over-rehearsed quality that doesn't mar some of their later films like *Duck Soup*. Herman, as spontaneous a wit as ever lived, recoiled from, and was even pained by, the fusty quality that permeated some of the Marx Brothers' films.

Still, Herman couldn't hold too much against Groucho. For Herman, Groucho was the key to the brothers' success—he valued his intelligence and comic mind, while the others he thought were mediocre at best. In particular, Herman felt Chico's talents were limited to an Italian accent, and while he came to like and appreciate Harpo's mute performances, Herman also felt that Harpo took himself far too seriously. At one point during the creation of the script of *Monkey Business,* Harpo said that he wanted to read the whole script because, as he told Herman, "I want to find out what my character is." With a somewhat sour expression, Herman looked at him and said, "You're a middle-aged Jew who picks up spit because he thinks it's a quarter." That, Harpo told friends, "punctured his pretensions forever." It also demonstrated Herman's real-world weariness and his utter disregard for the Hollywood fantasy-game he was playing. He didn't believe it, he didn't support it, yet he seemed to be stuck in it—a success in all ways except the ones that mattered most, and to all people except the one person who mattered most. He was sinking deeper into a self-loathing morass from which it would be a monumental challenge to extricate himself, though he would have opportunities.

Given his work with the Marx Brothers, it's difficult to imagine that Herman's influence had absolutely nothing to do with the creative chaos of *Million Dollar Legs.* But, not for the first time, Herman's contribution was made better by the devotion and commitment of others on the project; had Herman alone been responsible for *Million Dollar Legs,* it's doubtful that the spirit of inspired anarchy, even if it echoed Herman's own sensibilities so accurately, could have been so successfully sustained throughout the sixty-four minutes. Herman's own disdain for what he was doing was essential to his wit. One exchange in *Million Dollar Legs* shines with impertinence toward the work itself, and its provenance. When the Klopstokian athletes have arrived in Los Angeles for the Olympic Games, one says, "It never rains in Los Angeles," only to be told, "Only money, only money." But to shepherd something through all the way to greatness, you need more than disdain for the whole enterprise; you need true believers. The longer the two brothers stayed in Hollywood, the more it became clear that the one who did believe was Joe.

For a time in the early '30s, they could easily have been confused for a happy pair of siblings, having the time of their lives as they rose in a flourishing new industry. Joe loved the bonhomie of the town, and for years he remained proud of the figure his brother cut. "My brother was one of the all-time popular dinner guests," he said, a Hollywood celebrity in his own right. "He was a guarantee that the party would not suddenly die . . . Even if he got drunk and individually insulted every guest, that would make your dinner party the conversation piece the following day." At one dinner party, Herman roared in late, to find that he had missed the entrance and exit of John Gilbert, the movie star whose career and life were spiraling downward after the advent of sound. Gilbert had apparently stormed in, boisterously drunk, and placed his gun in front of him on the dinner table, sending the entire party into a tizzy from which they still hadn't recovered. "Oh, come on!" Herman bellowed, "How much can a gun eat?" Joe's pride in Herman was real, and in later years he liked to portray the two of them almost as partners in crime in those early days. "We used to take people on together and tear them apart," he said. "We had wonderful times."

But the differences between them were always apparent. Marian Spitzer, a screenwriter who knew both men, said Joe "seemed like a nice, bright, modest, sweet, more respectable version of his brother." John Lee Mahin, another writer who knew them both, said Joe was "a cool customer. He's tougher than Herman. He's smarter about himself. More regimented, more controlled." But as Joe became better known, it was clear his reserve and caution would prevent him from becoming the kind of grandly popular figure Herman was. "Nobody seems to like him," Mahin said. Where Herman was expansive and emotional, Joe was reserved and withholding. Even he admitted he would take on "the color of my environment without absorbing it." But if Joe was recessive, Herman never was. After Joe's Academy Award nomination, he'd wanted a raise from Paramount but was unsure of how to go about it. Herman solved the problem the way any younger brother would want an older brother to: he thundered into Paramount chief Ben Schulberg's office and threatened to quit if Joe didn't get another raise. Of course, because it was Herman, Schulberg called his bluff and let him leave the studio. For a few very terrifying days, neither Mankiewicz had a job; then, at last, Herman's agent got both brothers raises, and all was well. For Joe, it was another lesson that Herman and money were not to be linked. He had already discovered that his brother, who borrowed money from just about everyone, had a reputation as one of the softest touches in the business, never denying anyone any money if they needed it for any reason. In part, this was because Herman simply didn't understand money; as Dr. Hacker put it, Herman's relationship to money was an "infantile regression. He had no relation to money . . . It didn't mean anything if he had it, it didn't mean anything if he didn't have it." So he would borrow, and loan, without reason. But with Joe, it was different. Herman continued to see Joe as a kind of extension of him, and so Joe's earnings, whatever they were, were Herman's too. As a result, Joe said he grew "terrified of Herman. I never felt I could call on him for help. Everybody else in the world could." He was losing the one true ally he ever had.

Worse than that, in the thirties, Joe was always struggling, despite his success, to get out from under his brother's long shadow. If Herman was a god among writers, Joe was not. "Even people who knew him," one friend later recalled, "when they bumped into him around the studio, would say, 'Hello, Herm—I mean Joe.'" It got so bad that one day Joe realized what would be engraved on his tombstone: "Here lies Herm—I mean Joe—Mankiewicz."

FOR HERMAN, THE YEAR AFTER *MILLION DOLLAR LEGS* SAW AN attempt, not the first and not the last, to break the Hollywood mold, to do something meaningful and lasting and real. Continually disappointed with the work he was being asked to do, Herman strained to write something of deeper importance, something that would last, that might even have a genuine impact on the world. In the back of his mind, therefore, as he went about his business, whether that business was gambling, riding herd on the Marx Brothers, driving to and from the studio, or working on scripts or outlines for films he felt were beneath his talents—he began casting about for ideas that might make him feel like he was contributing something of value to the world. In 1933, with Europe in the grip of a rising tide of fascism and intolerance, Herman hit on an idea that excited him at last—a film that would target the biggest idiot of them all: Adolf Hitler.

While much of the Hollywood output of that year was filled with lighter fare like *Gold Diggers of 1933, King Kong,* and *42nd Street*—pictures that would take audiences' minds off the rise of the fascist menace in Europe and the Great Depression that still held half the globe in its grip—Herman determined to take another route. In January 1933, Hitler had become chancellor of Germany; the following month, the Reichstag was engulfed in flames and civil liberties in Germany were halted; and by March 1933, Hitler was dictator. Here is a horrible, dangerous, evil anti-Semite. So: How to fight this man?

Herman's response was in some ways to take a practical, two-pronged approach. He knew that the Hollywood studios would be loath to risk the big business they did in Germany by producing an original picture that attacked head-on the head of the German government. So rather than start from scratch, Herman determined that he had better write a stage play first, a property that the studios could then develop into a movie—which would shield the studios, Herman felt, from any suggestion from the German government that they had commissioned the work. Second, the play—and resulting film—would be a satire, and so not be directly about Germany or Hitler at all. Herman's strategy here was less than subtle; he set his play in a fictional Transylvania and changed the dictator's name from Adolf Hitler all the way to Adolf Mitler.[*]

Herman worked on the play and discussed it with his friend, Sam Jaffe, then a producer at RKO, and when Herman had completed a draft, Jaffe optioned the property from Herman for a small price[†] without even considering producing the play on stage first; the two of them then hired a screenwriter, Lynn Root, to adapt it for the movies. The result, "The Mad Dog of Europe," tells the story of two families, the Mendelssohns and the Schmidts, who live in Transylvania in the years following the Great War. The Mendelssohns are a Jewish family of war heroes who lost sons in battle and revere the Transylvanian homeland. The Schmidts, not Jewish, are good friends with the Mendelssohns and equally patriotic.

The film script tracks the changing nature of the friendship between the families as the Nazis and Mitler rise to power. Herman's story demonstrates that, at first, everyone laughed at Mitler, a small whiny man who could barely hold a job as a housepainter, but then, when Transylvania lost the war, he was able to weasel his way into power through loud, obstreperous speeches in beer halls and gain influence, and the public went along with him like flunkies following a studio boss. The character of Heinrich Schmidt, son of Herr Schmidt, embodies this change in the public. Originally a dear friend of the Mendelssohn clan, Heinrich finds himself changed by the war, becoming disillusioned, ultimately condemning the entire notion of compassion and the idea that Transylvania could attain glory again through anything other than the use of might: "Brotherly love! Humanity! Where have they brought us? If Transylvania doesn't think of her future she'll never have any." Like many "good Germans," Heinrich becomes angry and bitter, claiming "the good Transylvanian heart" has destroyed the country; the nation, he declares, should "be

---

[*] Seven years later, Chaplin used a similar strategy in making *The Great Dictator*, about the Tomanian dictator Adenoid Hynkel.

[†] One thousand dollars for eighteen months.

hard and strong and ruthless . . . crush [their] enemies, inside and out." Heinrich happily becomes a Nazi and develops a deep love and respect for Mitler, even standing next to him in "awed silence" as Mitler finishes his memoirs in prison.

Remarkably, and presciently, Herman's story dramatized one of the most disturbing aspects of a fascist's appeal to the public, namely the way the public forgets. Early on, Professor Mendelssohn, patriarch of the Mendelssohn clan, is treated with respect by all; people compliment his son Johann's war efforts and mention how their city "is proud of Johann." But after Mitler has gained power, this same group of people "turn their backs on [him] and whisper among themselves." The Transylvanian people forget themselves and happily follow an idiot so long as the trains run on time, and they turn on those who have earned their respect through diligence and hard work.

More disturbing, and probably more damning to the project's ultimate prospects, Herman didn't shy away from the overt racism and anti-Semitism of the Nazi regime. The hatred that Hitler, the Nazi Party, and the public at large felt for the Jews is unconcealed. The script contains graphic dialogue depicting characters' revulsion for the Jews: Mitler calls Heinrich "a Jew lover" and Heinrich labels Jews "enemies of Transylvania—parasites feeding on Transylvania's blood." When the Jews of Transylvania march down the street bearing placards that read "I am a Jew," according to the screenplay, "Mud and filth [are] thrown at them by children and brutish looking adults . . . Stores padlocked. Windows bearing scrawled signs, 'Don't buy here—Jew!' . . . Children throwing stones through windows." The horror is not hinted at or hidden under layers of sarcasm or satire; the scenes are explicit. The truth is ugly, but Herman wanted us to see it.

He also wanted people to see through Hitler's tactics in his rise to power; the script demonstrates, without much subtlety, how Hitler convinced people to join the Nazi cause in Germany—by saying exactly what the group of people he was speaking to wanted to hear. So Mitler/Hitler gives each group a different scapegoat to blame for their struggles. He tells workmen that capitalism is the enemy, and to capitalists, he says labor and communism are to blame. Trying to get across "the illegitimacy of the movement," how it's all a sham, and that the German people need to wake up, Herman says through the character of Heinrich's brother Fritz that the Nazis "don't even make sense. No thinking person would listen to them."

The problem, of course, is that it wasn't clear the Nazis actually needed "thinking people," any more than Hollywood needed "thinking people" to see its movies. Unthinking people—idiots—have an equal say, and sometimes they make up the larger share of the movie-going public, or the voting public, or the public that follows dictators of all kinds, political or cultural. In trying to make a bigger statement on humanity, the script falls into something of a trap, reading as moral instruction as much as entertainment. Desperate as he was to change things—in the world, in his own life—Herman and his screenwriter made a pitiful if noble attempt to call for people to embrace kindness again, compassion, love, and respect. As the character of the Countess states to a group of women, "We are all one in our hopes and in our griefs. Our sons are her sons, my sisters." How noble a thought—we are all one—and yet how innocent, too, how doomed. Heinrich's moral descent is underscored when Professor Mendelssohn's daughter Ilsa tells him, "You've thrown away loyalty and love and honor."

Of course, Herman was torn as to what would really happen in the real world. A democrat with a big *D*, Herman had long revered the idea of Democracy, and even began the film with an on-screen ode to its glories:

> This picture is produced in the interests of Democracy, an ideal which has inspired the noblest deeds of Man. It has been the goal towards which nations have aspired—one after the other having asserted a determination to overthrow tyrants and erect a government "of the people, by the people, for the people." Today the greater part of the civilized world has reached this stage of enlightenment.

Of course, Herman couldn't let it go at that—he was still hoping this would be some kind of comedy—and so to the introduction was added a sarcastic coda:

> THE INCIDENTS AND CHARACTERS IN THIS PICTURE ARE OF COURSE FICTITIOUS. IT IS OBVIOUSLY ABSURD TO ASK ANYONE TO BELIEVE THEY COULD HAPPEN IN THIS ENLIGHTENED DAY AND AGE.

The film's story curiously reverses the normal pattern in Herman's work, in terms of its attitude toward the family. Herman's complicated feelings toward his own parents are hardly reflected in the portrayal of the parents in the film: the script's parents are treated as heroes, people who see through Mitler and his tactics, martyrs who sacrifice their own lives rather than give up their belief in humanity. They are the voice of reason, harbingers of truth. At one point, Herr Schmidt says that his Nazi son lacks wisdom and that the country "is threatened from the inside" by Nazis. Refusing to follow the Nazis blindly, he supports his friends the Mendelssohns. Similarly, it is the Franz stand-in himself, Professor Mendelssohn, who is given one of the script's most passionate defenses of Jewishness:

> We Jews are good enough to die on the battlefield but not good enough to live in the Fatherland. You call us traitors—you're following the greatest traitor the world has ever seen. Your Mitler— your leader! Promising everything, then throwing you Jews to kill so you won't notice he can't keep his promises. Every time he opens his mouth, he lies!

Of course, a lot of good it does the professor: At the close of his speech, the Nazis shoot him, and he falls across the body of his dead son like Jesus, arms spread in the form of a crucifix. Likewise, Schmidt is also killed for his beliefs. Speaking to his son as *he* lies dying, he says:

> My son, I implore you . . . if you have a spark of humanity left, consider what you're doing. Consider the millions of innocent men, women, and children whose lives you are destroying . . . who are even now cursing the name of Mitler and all of his officers.

It is worth noting that both these fathers—noble, heroic, but utterly doomed—are killed, and that Professor Mendelssohn's wife, unable to cope with life without her husband, kills herself. Further, consider the fate of the two German brothers in the story, Fritz and Heinrich; Fritz, popular but doomed, who never joins the Nazi cause, while young Heinrich becomes a key member of the Nazi party, until his redemption at the story's end. The unconscious desire is clear and even a little pat: Is it fair to suggest that Herman felt he himself would never succumb to the fascism of Hollywood group-think, while Joe would for a time yield to Hollywood temptations but ultimately turn his back on the town? In

1933, in the wake of their joint success in Klopstokia, it's possible that Herman was already feeling like Joe was a "collaborator" and that he would need to be taken down a peg soon enough. But despite Heinrich/Joe's conversion at the conclusion of the story, he is the one who is killed, in a noble sacrifice to save the life of Fritz/Herman, who escapes to safety.

Regardless, the project itself was troubled from the start. While Herman and Sam Jaffe desperately wanted the script brought to the screen, the film faced intense resistance from Hollywood. As Herman knew, there was a huge market in Germany for American films, and it had only grown since Herman's stay in Berlin the previous decade. In addition to not wanting to jeopardize their German business, the studio owners had always been skittish about their Jewishness, and putting forth any such staunchly anti-anti-Semitic film would only remind the movie-going public of the non-Christian nature of the men who ran the business. Assimilation was and would remain the cardinal rule for the men who had once been furriers, hat makers, and upholsterers. And so most Hollywood honchos rejected "The Mad Dog of Europe" in favor of maintaining the cooperative relationship they had with the German government, in which no films would condemn the Nazi Party, even as filmmakers and artists fled the Third Reich for Hollywood in droves. So as men like Fritz Lang left Nazi Germany to find work in Hollywood, the Hollywood establishment refused to produce films that could be considered anti-German. In particular, Georg Gyssling, the German consul in Los Angeles and a Nazi, threatened the Hays Office that if "The Mad Dog of Europe" were made, his government might ban all American films from showing in Germany.

Herman didn't give up easily, even after Sam Jaffe, seeing the writing on the wall, sold the rights to the production to the agent Al Rosen. While Rosen continued his efforts to get financing for the picture, the Nazis upped the ante, threatening that if the film were produced, actual harm would come to the Jews in Germany. Rosen tried to convince executives in Hollywood to provide independent monetary support for the project and set up an independent studio to produce the film outside the studio system, but he found no takers. Finally, Joseph Breen, the moralizing Catholic who ran the voluntary Motion Picture Production Code under which the studios operated, weighed in. Breen declared: "Because of the large number of Jews active in the motion picture industry in this country, the charge is certain to be made that the Jews, as a class, are behind an anti-Hitler picture and using the entertainment screen for their own personal propaganda purposes. The entire industry, because of this, is likely to be indicted for the action of a mere handful."

The movie was doomed. Louis B. Mayer, the head of M-G-M, laid it all out explicitly: "We have a terrific income in Germany, and as far as I'm concerned, this picture will never be made."

Herman never got over the irony: His attempt to reveal the truth about Nazi Germany was stopped by the Nazis in the United States, a land of supposed freedom and democracy. It was too dispiriting for words.

———— ✢ ————

CHAPTER SEVEN

MONKEYBITCH

Joe Mank—pictures smell of rotten bananas.

—FROM THE NOTEBOOKS OF
F. SCOTT FITZGERALD

IT WAS GENERALLY ACCEPTED AMONG A CERTAIN PART OF THE LITERARY set in Los Angeles's burgeoning cultural scene in the late 1930s that Joe Mankiewicz didn't measure up. His work was good, excellent in fact, but there was a strain running through later comments from people who worked with him during that period, and it was what generally gave rise to the idea that Joe may have been the inspiration for Sammy Glick, the monomaniacally ambitious hero of Budd Schulberg's lacerating satire of the town, *What Makes Sammy Run?* And Joe was keenly aware of his reputation. In fact, until *All About Eve,* he worried that his lasting legacy in Hollywood would be as the man who had dared to fire the great F. Scott Fitzgerald—that "Joe Mank" would forever represent all that was unsophisticated and antithetical to Art in Hollywood. Yet curious ironies always lie at the heart of the clash between art and commerce, and certainly between Fitzgerald and Joe. The hero of Fitzgerald's final, unfinished novel, *The Last Tycoon,* was Monroe Stahr, the head of production at a studio not unlike M-G-M, where Fitzgerald famously spent his final fruitless years. Fitzgerald's time in Hollywood was, like many East Coast writers, Joe's brother among them, extraordinarily frustrating, and unlike many who came to loathe the town and its conventions, Fitzgerald never made his peace with the place. Partly this was because unlike men like Herman, Fitzgerald actually seemed to *believe* in the movies. His Monroe Stahr was based on Irving Thalberg, the brilliant head of production at M-G-M, who despite having fired Fitzgerald managed to earn the writer's respect and admiration. Where Herman derided nearly everyone who worked for the studios, Fitzgerald saw that Thalberg had a kind of genius for understanding what it was that made movies work— and Fitzgerald, in his encounters in Hollywood, was vitally anxious to make his work there *work*. While of course he needed Hollywood's money and wouldn't have been there without it, he wasn't just in it for a quick buck—he wanted his movies to last, to be great. To Herman, who hosted Fitzgerald more than once at Tower Road and in fact counted "Scotty" as one of the few literate men he could talk to in the entire boob-filled movie colony, Fitzgerald's attitude, while charming, was utterly naïve and, at least in Herman's mind, doomed to fail. The forces aligned against a writer with that kind of integrity, Herman felt, were too great. The enemy in California, Herman had come to see, was not just the system itself, but the group of people who manipulated it and ran it. The studio chiefs. The producers. The people with no real class or taste. Boobs. Clucks. Idiots. The people, in other words, like his brother Joe.

The ultimate irony is that after Irving Thalberg's untimely death at the age of thirty-six, the man many assumed would be groomed to be his eventual replacement at M-G-M—the stand-in for the stand-in for Monroe Stahr, Fitzgerald's great hero, one of the few brilliant individuals capable of holding the "whole equation in his head"—was none other than the man whom Fitzgerald came to despise so much that behind his back he had taken to calling him Monkeybitch.

In 1934, after Joe had written a succession of pictures for M-G-M and was itching to move to the director's chair, Louis B. Mayer told him that he had to produce before he could direct: "Young man, you must learn to crawl before you can walk." For Joe, crawling was an apt metaphor for producing,

Joe loved golf. And pipes.

And his dogs.

and decades later he would still say it was the best description of producing he had ever heard. It held none of the glamour or ultimate artistic power of directing, and very little of the creative joy he could sometimes associate with writing. Instead, it was a painstaking, slow process to produce a film from start to finish, make sure that all the necessary things were done to ensure its successful completion. The task also involved more groveling and supplication than even Joe sometimes felt able to swallow. But produce he did, and in the next eight years, Joe's record at M-G-M was remarkable. Included among his productions were *A Christmas Carol, The Shopworn Angel, The Adventures of Huckleberry Finn, Strange Cargo, The Philadelphia Story,* and *Woman of the Year.*

But perhaps no production was more storied than *Three Comrades,* and the tale of its making is a perfect parable for Joe in Hollywood—how he was misunderstood, how he applied his talents, and how he was derided, ultimately, for doing his job so well. The film was, in Joe's own mind, a rather silly little "women's picture" set in the wild years after World War I in Europe. For the first draft of the screenplay Joe sought for the job a man he felt was uniquely qualified to write a movie set during the Jazz Age, seeing as how he'd coined the term and all.

By the time Joe called F. Scott Fitzgerald onto *Three Comrades,* the shine was definitely off the one-time wunderkind of American letters. Deep into his tempestuous marriage with the flighty (or manic-depressive) wife Zelda, this was Fitzgerald's third go-around in Hollywood. The first, in 1927, had been an eight-week stay courtesy of M-G-M, full of wacky Scott-and-Zelda-show-up-at-a-party-on-all-fours-barking-like-dogs kind of shenanigans, and which did little to convince the Hollywood machers that the man would be able to convert his mastery of the novel into effective screenwriting. The second, while Scott applied himself more vigorously, had also flamed out with a failed screenplay, this one for an adaptation of a novel called *Red-Headed Woman* which Thalberg himself had called off. Now, in this third go-round, Fitzgerald, desperate for success, was happy to be engaged by M-G-M for $1,000 a week. And *Three*

Comrades, at least initially, seemed a good fit for his talents—the story of three young men in World War I who become enchanted by a young woman, a consumptive who would be played by Margaret Sullavan. A doomed love affair set in the 1920s might be just the thing for Fitzgerald, and Joe was hopeful that the writer would be a good match.

But from the opening pages of his first draft, Joe sensed that maybe Fitzgerald wasn't the right man. He recoiled at some of Fitzgerald's scene settings, which, to be fair, are a little much: "She seems to carry light and music with her," Fitzgerald's description of Sullavan's character reads. "One should almost hear the music of the 'Doll Dance' whenever she comes into the scene—and she moves through the chaos of the time with charm and brightness, even when there are only sad things to say."

In the end, though, it wasn't descriptive writing like this that bothered Joe so much—as florid and overdone as it may have been, the worst that could be said for it, really, was that it was irrelevant to the process of making a movie—it was the dialogue. Here, Joe was on firmer ground. To a novelist, a line of dialogue from one lover to the other like "I don't think about anything—except about us and the sun and the holiday and the sea" may make all the sense in the world. But to Joe's ears, the line was virtually unplayable, and coming from an actor's mouth was almost a guarantee to spur mocking laughter from an audience.

As for Fitzgerald, the heartbreaking thing is that he cared so much. He handed in his script to Joe in early January 1938, just a few weeks before shooting was to begin—and within a week, Fitzgerald was reading an entirely new script, churned out by Joe and the team of junior writers whom he now commanded at M-G-M. Reading the two scripts side by side, it isn't at all clear that one is better than the other—if anything, Joe's version can seem more pretentious. But it's also, quite obviously, more of a movie. It *moves*. Dialogue crackles, sometimes with forced wit—but always with a kind of directness and power—that "playing to the back wall" rule that Joe had come to understand, and which Fitzgerald, alas, did not.

In horror at the resulting script, the novelist wrote the producer a scathing letter. "You are simply tired of the best scenes because you've read them too much . . . You are or have been a good writer, but this is a job you will be ashamed of before it's over. The little fluttering life of what's left of my lines won't save the picture . . . Recognizable characters they simply are not, and cutting the worst lines here and there isn't going

Joan Crawford and Clark Gable
in *Strange Cargo* (1940)

to restore what you've destroyed. It's all so inconsistent." But consistency of tone, of character—these were secondary in Hollywood, not nearly as important as action and story. Joe saw that Fitzgerald, despite his almost pathetic protestations in the letter ("For nineteen years . . . I've written best-selling entertainment, and my dialogue is supposedly right up at the top"), simply didn't have the knack for screenwriting.

In later years, Joe defended himself:

> I personally have been attacked as if I spat on the American flag because it happened once that I rewrote some dialogue by F Scott Fitzgerald. But indeed it needed it! The actors, among them Margaret Sullavan,* absolutely could not read the lines. It was very literary dialogue, novelistic dialogue that lacked all the qualities required for screen dialogue. The latter must be spoken. Scott Fitzgerald wrote very bad spoken dialogue.

The irony is that so many who did have the knack for screenwriting would have given anything to be able to do what Fitzgerald could do—what self-loathing screenwriter from the 1930s wouldn't have traded his entire output to have written *The Great Gatsby*?—but Fitzgerald was too blinded with fury to see the truth.

---

* It's worth noting that Joe named an actress in the picture and not Robert Taylor, Franchot Tone, or Robert Young, the three comrades of the title.

When Fitzgerald finally saw the movie a few months later, his companion Sheilah Graham recalled that he was "miserable." "That S.O.B.," he growled when he came home from the theater, and furiously, helplessly, as if he had to lash out at something, he punched the wall, hard. "My God, doesn't he know what he's done?"

What he had done was make a movie. When Fitzgerald had been in the depths of his rage at Joe, he'd even allowed himself one vain wish, which seems to get to the heart of the problem for many of the New York writers who came west, including Herman. "My only hope," he'd written Joe, "is that you will have a moment of clear thinking. That you'll ask some intelligent and disinterested person to look at the two scripts . . . I am utterly miserable at seeing months of work and thought negated in one hasty week." What Fitzgerald utterly misunderstood, or couldn't bring himself to act on anyway, was where the power in the relationship actually lay. Fitzgerald was a screenwriter—the old joke about the Polish starlet sleeping with the screenwriter made sense precisely because writers were so low on the Hollywood food chain—they were "schmucks with Underwoods," in Jack Warner's famous phrase—and if the movies could somehow have been made without them, the studios would have been a far happier place. While Scott understood that intellectually, in his heart he was an artist who had, in *Gatsby,* in *This Side of Paradise,* in *Tender Is the Night,* shown himself capable of painting a rich world full of human beings of complex emotions, of passion, of settings with music and color and light—and here was Fitzgerald who understood the power of the medium so well, whose hero Stahr in *The Last Tycoon* was in some ways his greatest creation since Gatsby precisely because he understood this powerful new mechanism for art and commerce so thoroughly—here was Fitzgerald *understanding* all this, having proven his own genius time and time again in the novel, and so he didn't see himself as *stooping* to screenwriting so much as being the first artist in a line of artists who would be making movies . . . And it was he,

Ernst Lubitsch with Joe, early '40s

F. Scott Fitzgerald! Surely a man as cultured as Joe Mankiewicz would see that and let some reason and wisdom and smarts prevail.

The plaintive end of Scott's letter to Joe is painful to read not just because the man is so obviously doomed to lose, but because even at the end, he seemed to grasp so little how the game was played: "Oh, Joe, can't producers ever be wrong? I'm a good writer—honest. I thought you were going to play fair."

Where is it written that Hollywood ever had, or ever will have, anything to do with fair?

THE HIGHLIGHT OF THE WORKDAY, FOR HERMAN, WAS LUNCH. HIS life had fallen into a predictable routine. The morning would consist of a hearty breakfast, usually something with ham or sausage washed down with black coffee, then a slightly late arrival at the studio. There'd be some work on a script—maybe a newspaper picture for Luise Rainer (or was it Constance Bennett? One year they wanted to make Constance Bennett a star, so what Herman liked to call his "employer's discourteous demands on my time" had expanded to include a trifling newspaper picture, *After Office Hours*, though he'd found it fun to write for Gable, actually)—but usually, there would be another writer assigned to do it with him, and as Herman liked to say, "nothing puts me to sleep faster than my collaborator's typewriter," so no use killing yourself if they get some other "stout little fellow" to work on it too. In addition to the writing, morning held the distraction of phone calls; M-G-M wasn't known as the country club for nothing. Herman would pick up the telephone and make a bunch of calls. The one to Sara right as he arrived, of course, asking how the day had gone. ("Herman, you just left," she'd say. "Give me one thing," he'd plead. "Surely something must have happened." His desire to avoid work was never more impressive than when he had work to do—a disease that Herman and other Mankiewiczes used to call *Schreibfaulheit,* literally "writing laziness," though John Houseman would call it "neurotic inertia.") And then calls to various friends or other studio executives, often trying to find work for friends, or getting caught up on political matters, raging about some new cockamamie scheme of the writers to unionize.*

---

* Generally a supporter of labor unions, Herman felt, according to a fellow writer, that "the writers had a good thing going" and he "didn't want to rock the boat."

So, all in all, for a morning at M-G-M, not an awful one. And now here we are: Romanoff's at last, and lunch.

Herman would slide into the table kept for him opposite the bar, and hold forth. It was the central table in the entire restaurant, the prestige table, Herman knew. He could have been back in New York at the Algonquin; most of the club's members had pretty much all moved west by now. The wit here wasn't as celebrated, far from the Broadway press agents and newspaper reporters, but the barbs, from Herman anyway, were just as fast and furious. Herman would vent on any number of topics, from another screenwriter's work ("that man should never be allowed alone in a room with a typewriter") to his own work habits ("a loafer is a loafer is a loafer") to the peccadilloes of Hollywood types ("If people don't sit at Chaplin's feet, he goes out and stands where they are sitting"). Herman would expound deliciously, the food wolfed down and the drinks flowing naturally and easily, at least in the beginning.

Sometimes, the object of Herman's humor was the restaurant's owner, a man everyone called Mike who claimed to be a fallen Russian prince named Mychal Andreyavitch Dmitry Romanoff. Nearly everyone thought the man absurd, knowing he was an imposter and probably from Hoboken, but Herman would go further: "This man here," he told the gathering once, "everyone knows he's no goddamn prince." He gripped Romanoff's arm. "That's why we eat here. But what the hell do you think we'd do if we found out your secret, Mike?" For a moment, the man looked scared. "Secret?" "Yes," Herman exploded. "You actually *are* a prince! You pose as a foolish imposter pretending to be a prince, but in reality—you *are* one! If we find that out, Mike, your cover as a total fraud will be blown, you'll lose all face in this town, and no one will ever eat here again!"

The room rocked with laughter as Herman spun out his counterfantasy, poking fun at the man, all done with that telltale combination of warmth and hostility. Romanoff's was a central watering hole for half of Hollywood, and the only question was, would Herman be able to stop drinking enough to get back to the studio at all in the afternoon? As director Gottfried Reinhardt said, "Between the fourth drink and the twelfth drink, Herman was the most brilliant man you will ever listen to in your entire life. If you got him at the right time, with the right amount

---

They were getting paid huge money to do something that wasn't really writing; why jeopardize that?

of lubrication, it was dazzling." But frequently, as the afternoon wore on, the hostility would start to win out. Herman's sweating would grow more profuse, and even as the room started to empty out, Herman would keep drinking, with predictable results. As Reinhardt said, "After about the twelfth or fifteenth drink, he was incoherent."

Soon enough, the afternoon would be over. The laughter would die away, the drinks would be sipped more slowly, and now Sara would be standing by the table. She had missed her afternoon call from Herman, and when three o'clock came she'd made a few calls of her own, to the places where she might find him. Her investigation wouldn't get very far—everyone protected Herman, no one would ever say a thing—and so she'd get in the car and drive to Romanoff's. She'd stand over Herman and say his name quietly. He'd look up and nod, give his little two-finger salute to the table, gather his hat, and follow her out to the car without a word.

Herman's adolescent behavior met its match in Sara's maternal nature. Had Herman married a different kind of woman, there's little doubt the marriage would have ended in divorce—few women really want to be chasing after their husbands all afternoon, retrieving them when their impulsive behavior has finally petered out. But because Herman's appetites were so strong—the man was a stranger to impulse control—he needed tending as much as any wayward child. The sad truth was that, despite his protestations, Herman didn't consider Sara an equal partner in an adult relationship—because it was hard for him to have any kind of belief in himself as an adult.

But what kind of woman puts up with this kind of treatment?

Her nickname in Hollywood was "poor Sara," and of course it had been Herman who gave her the designation. (A friend once asked him how Sara was doing, and he said, "Who?" "Your wife, Sara." "Oh, you mean 'poor Sara'!") Indeed, poor Sara suffered mightily and thoroughly at his hands. The drinking and the gambling were bad enough, but then, lately, there'd been the women. More and more, Herman had been having lunch with other women. They gobbled him up like pudding. He was flirtatious, appreciative, flattering, cuddly, enchanting, sweet, and warm. What wasn't to like? Before long, gossip bloomed, usually about secretaries or actresses like Miriam Hopkins or Nancy Carroll, sometimes the wife of a studio executive who spent more time in the commissary than seemed right. Most deliciously, the family friend and movie star Margaret Sullavan had, according to her own therapist, "permitted the world to think that Herman had an affair with her, which was not even true—he never came close to her." Herman was, in the therapist's mind, "scared stiff." But for his part, Herman saw no need to discourage any gossip. People were talking about him and beautiful women; why should that be stopped?

But while the Hollywood stories were just stories, there had been one actual moment of crisis, a turning point in Sara and Herman's marriage that was so dramatic and sensitive that even though she told Richard Meryman about it when he interviewed her for her husband's biography in 1972, by the time he was finished with his book a few years later, the story did not appear . . . [*]

In the early thirties, the family had taken a trip to England, and in London, Herman had worked with a typist who came to the house every afternoon. According to Sara, the woman was "a real frumpy English secretary" who had become an object of humor to both Herman and Sara for her smell; after she left in the evenings, Sara would throw open the windows of the living room to rid the house of the odor. Finally, the family reached the end of its stay; Sara and Don were going on to Switzerland, and Herman was taking Frank back to the United States. But on their last night in London, Sara had been up packing and tending to the boys when she noticed there was no typing noise coming from the living room. "No typewriter, nothing, but I could see down the hall there was a light in the living room. My heart was pounding . . ." When she got to the living room, Sara found the woman and Herman in a clinch. A "ghastly" look came over the woman's face and Sara, rising to the drama of the moment, told the secretary, "Out. Get your things and get out."

Herman was mortified: "Humble, humiliated, and terribly, terribly sad, sorry and everything else." Sara refused his entreaties, naturally. "I wouldn't let him touch me, wouldn't go near him," and she slept in a separate room that night. The next morning, the family took a train to Dover to catch the boat for the continent: "He was with Don, giving Don the last instructions and trying terribly to catch my eye, and I was sick with hurt, it was the most miserable time I can ever remember." Finally, at the dock, Herman held her and implored her not to go away feeling as she did, that he could explain, that he was sorry and miserable. But

---

[*] While she had no contractual rights to what Meryman put in his book, it's entirely possible that after the interview she asked him not to include the story. He has now passed away, so we can't be sure. But Goma was scary, and he was a very kind man.

Sara refused to bend, boarded the boat, and left without a word. For the next few days she refused to phone Herman or accept his calls or flowers or answer any of his many apologetic cables. Finally, one night when Don was sick in bed with a cold at their hotel in Switzerland, Sara was downstairs having drinks (accepting the flirtatious attentions of a young man, which, she said, made her feel "a little more secure and wanted") when a call came in:

> A steward announced there was a call for Mrs. Mankiewicz from the SS Berengaria* and it was Herman and he said "Schnooks, I will jump overboard unless you tell me that you are going to forgive me. I can't live this way, I'll die. I can't think of anything else. I'm absolutely at my wit's end. Please tell me that you love me."

For Sara, it was a watershed. She decided that torturing Herman further wasn't going to help matters. She had loved Herman for years, and she felt that his heart was large. She knew how much he needed love, how much he had craved it as a child and hadn't gotten it. "Herman," she said at last, "I love you." Decades later, she remembered cherishing what came next: "[R]econciliations were the most wonderful times of our married life." She said that after that phone call, their relationship was reinvigorated, and that there was "something almost virginal about our relationship again."† She remembered how fascinating Herman could be, how much she loved his famous laugh, how hard he could make her laugh. As for Herman, she said he seemed to appreciate her more after that. "To this day," she said years later, "I start to tremble about it." Telling Richard Meryman, "I'm saying some terrible things, I never told a person in the world," she said Herman would "act amorous" and ask her, sometimes, to dance for him at night.

So now, years later, back in Hollywood, Sara was mostly untroubled by rumors and gossip. Rather than disparaging any potential rivals, Sara insisted, "I was smart about those things." With hallmark self-possession and utter lack of self-doubt, she said: "I immediately made those women my friends. It was the best thing I could have done." By befriending

---

* The boat taking Herman and Frank back to the United States, the *Berengaria,* was nicknamed the 'bargain area' for its inexpensive crossings.

† Still, in a letter to him once he was back in the United States, though she thanked him profusely for the call, she also called it "needlessly extravagant."

anyone who might be a rival, Sara turned the women into her allies, that much less likely to cheat on her with her own husband, but equally important, she made the women less attractive to Herman. After all, if a thing isn't done in secret, it can hardly be worth doing.

And so Sara carried on, mothering Herman as best she could, protecting him, and also serving all too often as his kind of warden. Years later everyone would say how much they loved poor Sara, and yet also how sorry they felt for her. For there were times she didn't find Herman at Romanoff's. Often he would return home drunk and uncontrollable, madly bellowing about this or that, and Sara would try to find the root of the trouble. The next day, she'd go to the studio and attempt to extend the deadline for whatever he was working on, or when his issues were paying back debts, Sara would go to Louis Mayer (then the highest-salaried man in America), who would listen patiently to Herman's problems and eventually decide to pay off the debts, more as a favor to Goma than anything else—the money of course would be deducted from Herman's salary.

What made it all worthwhile, for Sara, was the verve with which Herman lived his life, and what surrounded it. Sara loved their life together and couldn't conceive of anything else; she loved having the Marx Brothers over for dinner, their goosing her when her back was turned or throwing her about like a rag doll from Chico to Harpo and back again. She loved hearing Herman deal with Don and Frank, even when he was being a little too harsh and Franz-like for his own good; Herman hated to see the boys waste any time, and once told Don when he was lying on the floor listening to a baseball game on the radio, "I can't think of anything sillier than listening to a ball game you can't see." Don, who'd inherited more than a little of his father's wit, had a ready retort: "I can. Listening to a ball game that you can see." Most of all, maybe, Sara loved Herman's hands, the thick thumbs and round solid stubs of fingers, and the sound his hands made as he rubbed them together as he read the morning paper.

So as frustrating as it must have been to be Herman Mankiewicz's wife, and as much as Sara was pitied in her day, there was an unquestioningness to Herman's love and devotion that made everything else usually fall away. Time and again, those who spoke to Richard Meryman about Herman's wit, those savage barbs he aimed in one direction or another, said there was only one exception to his withering sarcasm: he never once directed it at Sara. He could be exasperated with her, God knows, and funny about her, and he could be afraid of her, and deep down, he undoubtedly hated her from time to time (if you can't hate spinach, surely you can hate your wife), but he never got seriously angry with her in public, or made her the target of his cruelest humor.[*]

By then, though, Herman had mellowed somewhat. The cause of that was easy to trace, for in addition to Sara and the boys he now had another consideration to occupy him at Tower Road: at last, a daughter. My mother Johanna was born on October 2, 1937, and to Herman, who had grown up with boys (Erna/Erma notwithstanding), who enjoyed his own two sons enormously, whose every waking moment was dominated by his relationships with men, competing with other men—the primal relationship with his father writ small and large across all his relationships—the softening effect of having a young girl to care for cannot be underestimated. To a person, all of Herman's friends and colleagues said the same thing: he loved having a baby girl. Someone he could love without reservation, complication, or competition. His wonder at her was constant; "I might, with more chance of success," he wrote Don at Columbia, "try to put into words a picture of a moonbeam."[†] According to Goma, "He never got over the miracle of having her."

But if it was a miracle, it was also a miracle with an expiration date, at least in my mother's mind later on. Her memories of her father were deeply colored by his early death when she was only fifteen, and so in all her recollections there is a deeply bittersweet tone, a melancholic view, a sense that, as with so many things Mankiewiczian, this will not end well. We can laugh and tell funny stories, we can admire our accomplishments, we can take great pleasure in our families and even, in rare instances,

---

[*] One of the only times he did speak out angrily against her was when she was trying to protect the boys from having to fight in World War II. As an ex-Marine and an unquestioning patriot who loved the United States and what it stood for (its politicians notwithstanding), Herman recoiled when informed that Sara had tried to call to find the boys a softer job than actually seeing battle. He thundered at her, "This man is trying to kill everyone in the world, and you think our boys should let others do the job? No!" Perhaps amazed by seeing his volcanic temper hurled in full force in her direction for once, she backed down. The boys went and served with distinction, with Frank, at the age of twenty-two, fighting in the Battle of the Bulge.

[†] The letter went on: "If you care to believe the story your Ma will tell you that Johanna has said 'Choo-choo' and 'I've been wondering when you were going to take me east to see my grandparents, my brother at Columbia, and the scenic beauties in and around the nation's capital itself'—it's perfectly all right with me. I won't even say flatly that Johanna didn't say those things. All I can say is that I didn't hear them."

Johanna Mankiewicz, born October 2, 1937

in those intimate moments when true connection is achieved. But fate will have the last laugh.

My mother's own early death was of course a repeat of that primal pattern, not just for me, but across the family. Most relevantly, her early death both robbed this book of one of its most important voices—and also set this book in motion. It's doubtful that the two titanic figures of Herman and Joe would have loomed quite so large to me had she lived, for if she hadn't died young, there would have been far less mystery about them both. Any questions would presumably have been answered by Mom herself, speaking to me directly, not through the decades from the tapes from Dick Meryman's reel-to-reel recorder.

Here, then, in either book—the one where Johanna Mankiewicz lived, or this one, where random chance would strike her down at thirty six— would come a section on her first memories. The pony rides at friends' houses in Beverly Hills, Brooke Hayward's house or at the Fondas', where young Jane and Peter were playmates. The visits to the studio to see her

"A picture of a moonbeam": Uncle Don with his baby sister, my mother Johanna, late 1930s

Uncle Frank with Mom, late 1930s

Herman and Johanna, c. 1939

father, and touring the gigantic sets, and seeing a memorable water tank with model boats the size of small dolphins. Being summoned into her father's bedroom late at night when he got home from the studio, being asked to sit on his bed and tell her all about her day, and all the serious and not so serious questions he would ask her, all with a genuine interest and concern for her welfare.

And then the tricks: the scares he would throw into her dates when they would bring her home from an evening, his deep voice booming from inside the house while she and the boy were lingering too long at the door: "What the hell's going on out there? Get in here! It's time to go to sleep!" The embarrassing mornings when he'd drive her to school still in his bathrobe. The way he would come to her junior high school basketball games and sit and cheer loudly, almost indiscriminately, in the stands, both thrilling and mortifying. The time he attended her gymnastics meet and sat in the bleachers with a portable radio blaring, because the Kentucky Derby was being run that day and a considerable amount of money was at stake. The pressure he put on her, in his own self-aware way, for he knew the cost and so tried not to be unduly judgmental. The way he looked at her, always, his eyes filled not just with love but a kind of astonishment, that she existed and always would. His smell in those late-night sessions in his room, the curious mixture of camphor oil and alcohol and a velvety cream he so often rubbed into his achy limbs. And most of all, the gentle kisses he would ask for, on his eyelids right before she left his room at night, little butterfly kisses he called them, that filled him with such gentle hope and her with such tender affection and pride.

"If you listed all the things that would make a good father," Mom said, "he wouldn't in any way qualify." Mom told this to Richard Meryman in 1973, more than two decades after her father had died. "And yet," she continued, "if you knew him, and you knew that he loved you . . . that he was . . . then your father was the greatest thing in the whole world."

Listening to the tapes now, you can practically hear her shake her head, as if she knows this description is inadequate. Indeed, her sympathy for her father's biographers was deep:

So that's what you can't get to. The heart of this man was . . . it was unfathomable. He was just the most—and that doesn't come through just through the facts, it doesn't come through in the stories, it doesn't come through in anything. There's no way of showing that. He was the most loving, generous, loyal . . . you know, you say this. . . . So we all forgave him.

The stories, then, Mom's memories of her father, may be suffused with loss and melancholy, but the depth of her love for him is profound. At least by the time she recorded the interviews, she had started to understand some uncomplicated truths about her father. For all the absence and loss the memories contain, Herman's real legacy, beyond the movies, beyond the self-loathing, beyond the funny stories and the "white wine came up with the fish,"* was actually far simpler: values, compassion, love, family, and the importance of forgiveness.

JOE'S LEGACY, AT LEAST FOR HIS OWN YOUNGER DAUGHTER ALEXAN-dra, would in some ways be similar—the stated values that Herman and Joe stood for and expressed were quite alike: the importance of work, of education, of family, of being a literate citizen of the world. But there were crucial differences. For one thing, Joe survived to tell the tale. Other, subtler differences appear as well . . .

In the 1970s, a few years after he had directed what would be his final movie, *Sleuth,* Joe found himself spending more time in Europe. It made sense; his third wife, Rosemary, was from England, and their daughter, my cousin Alex,† went to school in London for a time. To Alex, her life,

---

* Perhaps Herman's most famous witticism came about after he threw up, loudly and boisterously, in the rest room at a Hollywood dinner party thrown by the elegant producer Arthur Hornblow Jr. "Don't worry, Arthur," Herman reassured the host on his return. "The white wine came up with the fish." To Herman aficionados, finding this casually brilliant wisecrack become a crucial plot point in the movie *Mank,* delivered in William Randolph Hearst's palatial San Simeon dining hall at the end of a climactic speech in which the movie's Herman (Gary Oldman) clumsily attempts to destroy Hearst in front of his mistress and guests before disgorging himself of a sickening stream of vomit, was like seeing a delicate Michelangelo sketch placed atop the pedestal of the *David.*

† Technically, Alex and I, though virtually the same age, are first cousins once removed, since she is the daughter of my great-uncle.

which to an outsider like a cousin hearing about it in New York might have seemed glamorous or star-studded, was normal; her father feted at film festivals, her grandmother and aunt living in Spain, trips to Monte Carlo and Greece, companions like Christopher Plummer or James Mason or the Burtons of course, Richard and Elizabeth, whose world-famous romance Joe once jokingly took credit for, having directed them together in the notorious *Cleopatra.* Best of all, at least to cousins whose lives seemed monochromatic by comparison, were the visits Alex had paid to the set of *Sleuth,* where Laurence Olivier taught her how to sneer.

But amid all the European memories, one stands out, though it was far from glittering. Alex was on an airplane headed for Zurich with Mum and Dad, where they would be meeting again a man she'd come to know as "Cousin Eric," but this time, Mum and Dad decided to tell her the truth: Eric Reynal was in fact her brother. He was born when Joe had been married before.

The information must have been confounding. Alex knew Dad had been married before. The woman's name had been Rosa, and she was Chris and Tom's Mom, the lady who had died—but she was never spoken of. Like many things one was told as a child, it was not talked about. Now, on the airplane, the bare facts were laid out clearly and cleanly: this was not the mother of Chris and Tom, her considerably older brothers; there had been a third wife, even earlier—a woman named Elizabeth Young, an actress. Elizabeth and Joe had had a son in the 1930s, named Eric, who had gone to good schools and had become an international banker and been adopted by a man named Eugene Reynal who had been married to Elizabeth for a time.

Alex took the information in. She knew there were things you simply did not discuss. Unlike Herman's side of the family, one didn't fight back, or question what was presented. The process was merely "quiet absorption" of new information: "Right. Okay. Noted." The simple white lie, told until she was old enough to grasp the real information, faded away. In its place now was nothing dark or sinister but actually something a little amusing, because soon enough Alex would be returning to school having acquired a new brother. She may even have been quietly tickled by how she might answer any questions that could come up from inquiring school mates: "How did that happen? Surely your Mum is a little old to have a new child!"

But what did Joe think? How had he managed it? As he sat in the first-class cabin on that TWA flight, twisting his body to speak across the aisle to Alexandra, what was the feeling in his chest? And what had it been all those years earlier, in the late thirties, after the divorce had gone through and the boy had been removed from his life?

To Joe Mankiewicz, it really wasn't that complicated. His first marriage was like many of the unpleasant things that happened to him—it was something to be put in a box and stored away somewhere safe, where you never had to look at it. Certainly not something to be taken out and considered. As for the boy, well, Joe paid Elizabeth a considerable amount of alimony and child support, for fifty

Alex on the set of *Sleuth* with Laurence Olivier, c. 1972

months anyway, but even after that, after Elizabeth remarried and asked Joe to allow her new husband, Eric's stepfather, to adopt Eric and change his last name to his own, even after that, even after Joe realized that this other man would be "Dad" and he would be "Joe," he made sure, even if he didn't go as far as Franz, who urged him to forget the boy entirely and focus on his work—the work is what lasts, the work is what matters, Franz wrote Joe in a letter that reverberated through the decades—but Joe would do his best to see that the boy led a good life. Beyond that . . . He wouldn't think of it. The boy was fine, would be fine. Joe told himself that and didn't bother to see if he was shuddering anywhere down deep as he did so.

HERMAN WAS TIRED. HE FELT SOMETIMES AS IF HE WERE A MAN IN a dusty western town, waiting for a train. The train wasn't coming, there were no other patrons at the depot, and no one could give him any information. He started to worry the train wasn't coming at all. Maybe he'd come on the wrong day. It's possible the train was due tomorrow. Or, worse, he'd missed it entirely; it had come yesterday and would never come again. Still, he kept waiting. Deep into the 1930s he continued to try to convince himself that the train was just out of sight, coming soon.

Of course, by now the list of people he'd alienated was almost as long

Alex knew him as "Cousin Eric."
Joe swims with his first son, Eric, in the 1970s.

as the people he'd worked with, and much longer than those whom he just hadn't gotten around to yet. After Paramount and a productive stretch at M-G-M in the mid 1930s, there really wasn't much work for him in the late '30s, and certainly nothing to excite him, or to cause him to pry himself from Romanoff's or the Brown Derby any earlier after lunch. The wit was still there, and the talent was never in doubt, but more and more, the young writers weren't hanging on every word when he came to the commissary. And his old pals weren't quite as willing to put up with him anymore.

Still, the spark remained. He retained genuine literary aspirations, still sent occasional pieces to *The New Yorker*. He had long filled his notebooks with ideas for plays, including a John Dillinger–inspired portrait of a gangster called "The Tree Will Grow," though he'd abandoned it after the first act. In 1936, he actually went back to New York, allegedly for a two-week trip to research a film he was doing for M-G-M with the incongruous title "Princess of Pasha"—but in reality he wanted to test the waters for a possible return. He made the rounds of many old friends, and even more old haunts, and one afternoon found his way to the "21" Club, where he could be heard muttering, "Oh to be back in Hollywood wishing I was back in New York." More soberly, there had been one final play—a form of honest writing, Herman felt. The play was *The Meal Ticket*, a comedy about a vaudeville family on the brink of big success in Hollywood when the eighteen-year-old daughter falls in love with a doctor and runs away with him. The play was financed by John Hay

Whitney, and when it opened to awful reviews and closed in less than a week, it extinguished, seemingly for good, Herman's dreams of Broadway.

The movies were as dreary as ever. One that held his interest for less than two weeks was a quick job for M-G-M, a rewrite of a movie musical based on a series of children's books he was quite familiar with. Herman had read L. Frank Baum's Oz books aloud to both Don and Frank when they were younger, and he'd enjoyed their whimsy, and also what Herman considered a very real anti-fascist sentiment hidden underneath the talking pumpkins and the like. For the rest of their lives, Don and Frank remembered the intense and admiring conversations their father had with them about the books. Still, despite his affection for the books, or maybe because of it, Herman didn't believe they could translate into film and wrote the head boys at M-G-M a long memo dictating precisely why it was a bad idea to try to make a film of *The Wonderful Wizard of Oz*. Herman, though, was unable to alter the course of history, and the movie proceeded, though he dreaded the project. Within three days of being placed on the picture, he turned in a seventeen-page treatment. Five days later, Herman handed in the first fifty-six pages of the script, and though he felt he'd helped flesh out the characters in Kansas, he'd also added a redundant Pekingese named Adolphus Ajax Rittenstaufen III to compete with Toto. Finally, relief came at last—two other writers were assigned to the film, and Herman moved on.

One section from Herman's work on the film bears closer scrutiny, though. In the pages he wrote, Herman rather casually decreed that when Dorothy finally lands in Oz after the cyclone has ripped her house from the Kansas plains, the film should switch from black-and-white to color. That one moment, a simple yet utterly transcendent moment of cinema, sticks out among Herman's work, not merely for the fact that it is wordless and in some ways as much an idea one might have attributed to a director as a writer, but because of where in Herman it seemed to come from.[*]

At the time, Herman was aware that his life had settled into a kind of monotony and routine which was joltingly in need of new energy. The routinized existence of studio, drinking, gambling, and family—it was like a black-and-white montage sequence without end. It needed color. The question for Herman was, would the color ever arrive? Would his

---

[*] It's also notable because, "Rosebud" aside, it may be the most famous moment in Herman's (if not all) cinematic history.

moment ever come? And if it did, if some cyclone managed to lift him out of the doldrums, if that whirling tornado arrived to whisk him away from that dusty train depot and plop him down in a new place with mystical creatures and he actually crossed the threshold into a brave new colorful land, what would he be stepping into?

And: would he have to wipe his feet on the curb after he did so?

PART THREE

It's like she was studyin' you, like you were a play or a book or a set of blueprints. How you walk, talk, think, eat, sleep.

—JOSEPH L. MANKIEWICZ,
ALL ABOUT EVE

CHAPTER EIGHT

————— ⚳ —————

AMERICAN

You know, Mr. Bernstein, if I hadn't been very rich, I might
have been a really great man.

—*CITIZEN KANE*

TO TOLSTOY'S CREDO THAT ALL HAPPY FAMILIES ARE ALIKE AND EACH
unhappy family is unalike in its own way, Hollywood has added a corol-
lary, namely that each family has its own movie. Not necessarily a favorite
movie, but a movie that has infused the family—it goes beyond like or
dislike, the film has become practically a religious totem for the members
of the family, almost a sacred text. For some it's *Casablanca*; others point
to *Star Wars* or *The Godfather*; friends of mine insist their families swear by
The Shawshank Redemption, quote it constantly, refer to it when beloved
pets pass away.

For anyone associated with the name Mankiewicz, that text is *Citizen
Kane*. Not that it's such a great film—though it is—but more that the
movie itself, in plot, script, shots, dialogue, music, and everything else
associated with its making is simply a part of the air we breathe. Thus it
is that this grandson of the man listed as co-screenwriter of the film issues
a warning: if it's possible that you have read this far without ever seeing
it, it's hard to imagine that this chapter will be in the least bit interesting,
much less enjoyable, not to mention understandable, without a rudi-
mentary knowledge of the movie. There will be no pop quizzes, no trick
questions on the year that Kane's mother entrusted him to Mr. Thatcher,
no fill-in-the-blanks on the lyrics to "Dear Old Charlie Kane," no essays
requiring you to compare and contrast the men of the *Inquirer* with the

"Sing Sing, Gettys! Sing Sing!" Orson Welles
and Ray Collins in *Citizen Kane*

men of the *Chronicle.** But having seen the film at least once would probably help. The movie, simply put, is a part of my flesh, and so is its history.

The fact is, *Citizen Kane* was made through such an odd combination of bizarre events, megalomaniacal personalities, strange coincidences,
and unique sets of circumstances that in the end it has all come to seem
inevitable. Of course, many films are made this way, through trial and
error and crazy happenstance, those that are awful but make a lot of
money, those that are great and largely forgotten, and those that are in
the mass of middle mediocrity. The challenge for the biographer, much
less the grandson, is to try to determine how it actually felt at the time,
because as surely as biographers can say things like "meeting Welles was
Herman's last chance—almost certainly it was now or never," it is equally
certain that if indeed it felt that way to Herman (and I'm quite sure that
it did, just because pretty much everything did), I'm equally certain that
if, say, *My Dear Miss Aldrich*, a 1937 M-G-M movie which Herman seems
to have written all by his lonesome with no John Houseman to hold his
hand or Orson Welles to come along and confuse the issue of credit and

---

* Itself a trick question of course; the men are one and the same.

control, had become a legendary, talked-about movie, then people would have come to think that for Herman, getting the go-ahead on writing *that* story, of a newspaper baron who dies and leaves his wealth and publishing empire to his only living relative who turns out to be an old maid schoolteacher from Nebraska, *that assignment* was surely the pinnacle, the one final moment where Herman J. Mankiewicz could seize the gold ring and show himself and everyone else what he really had in him. We would all be looking for clues of Herman's life in the fact that Miss Aldrich (Maureen O'Sullivan) was from the Midwest—it was all about Wilkes-Barre, we might say—and we would see that Martha Aldrich's initials were M.A.—'*Ma!*'—and we would assume, no, we would *know*, that she was therefore based on Herman's mother, Johanna, a woman so much on Herman's mind in that magical year of 1937 that he named his daughter after her. We would see in Miss Aldrich's decision to become a journalist herself, to demonstrate to the arrogant chauvinist managing editor (Walter Pidgeon) that a woman can be just as good as a man, an analogue for Herman's attitude toward his own domineering father, to show him that becoming a writer was a viable career and that he could succeed on his own terms—and of course if we were so inclined, we could see in the inevitable romance and pairing of the old maid and the managing editor Herman's ultimate fantasy that he would somehow earn his father's love and bring peace at last to his own conflicted self.

There is evidence, in other words, for anything, wherever we look, if we want to look hard enough to find it. And it's not that those things are necessarily wrong—almost by definition, anything a writer writes comes from himself, whether it's a wild fantasy that seems to have no bearing on his actual life or something more closely aligned with his quotidian biographical details (*Rosebud was Herman's bike!*)—but that it gets us no closer to understanding what it was actually like for Herman, himself, for real, to be working on the movie that became a masterpiece and the thing for which, both in and outside the family, he would be best remembered.

IT WAS A STUPID IDEA FROM THE START. WHY IN THE WORLD HERman agreed to go east with Tommy Phipps in the fall of 1939 he really didn't know. And now look at him: lying pinned underneath Phipps's Buick convertible, his leg throbbing with pain, Phipps moaning deliriously next to him. Idiot. He and Phipps both, but Phipps more, stupid heartsick kid whose endless dissections of the brief note he'd received when his girlfriend broke up with him had no doubt taken his mind from his principal task of driving. "What did she mean when she wrote 'Take good care of yourself always Ethel'? Why was there no punctuation? What did she mean by 'take good care'? Why hadn't she just said 'take care'? And what of this bewildering 'always'?" If nothing else, the accident had shut Phipps up at last. The kid had broken his collarbone and was unconscious.

Of course, Herman *did* know why he'd decided to go. M-G-M had finally fired him for good, for one thing. Had it only been a few days ago that, having been given a final warning, he'd been gambling with the boys in the commissary? He knew he shouldn't have been, Mayer had told him just the day before when he'd given him an advance on his weekly salary—but it was for such small stakes! He could still see Mayer glaring at him from across the room, spotting the final indiscretion. Herman had simply collected his hat and coat and left. Gone straight back to the office, taken his usual box of stationery and pencils and quit the lot, getting official word the next day never to return. He doubted any studio would hire him at this point.

Now, just a few short days later, with "Beer Barrel Polka" playing endlessly on Phipps's car radio, Herman found himself in too much pain to cry, though he did tell the cops who finally came, "If you can't give me something, shoot me." By the time the ambulance arrived and he was in a stretcher on the way back to Los Angeles from whatever godforsaken part of New Mexico they'd made it to, any thought of rescue from anything in the east—that was what this road trip had been, him and Phipps hoping to make it across the country in less than a week—those thoughts had vanished for good. There wasn't going to be another play. Pop couldn't help. There was no magazine piece to do for Ross, nothing he could even send off to the *Hollywood Reporter.* His debts were monumental. There were too many creditors to count, and he'd long since lost track of how many thousands of dollars he owed. Joe said he'd help, though of course not with any actual money; still, Joe and Sam Jaffe were trying to coordinate the debts and maybe talk a few folks into cutting Herman a break on some of them, though Herman wondered why Jaffe, his agent now, wasn't paying ten percent of the debt.

The truth is, Herman had boxed himself into a corner, and it wasn't entirely clear that this time he'd find a way out. Sara had moved the family out of Tower Road again—he wasn't sure how many times they'd had to rent the place out and move into a smaller place, but now they'd be hard-pressed even to find the rent for that one unless Herman found some work somewhere. In the ambulance, he waxed philosophical. Something always seemed to come along, but sometimes that something was just a culvert post to smash Tommy Phipps's goddamn Buick.

People whizzed through his mind, possible saviors, or just employers. Dore Schary. Harry Cohn. Charles Lederer, for some reason, Marion Davies's nephew. Lederer had been a friend for a while, back when Herman and Sara had been frequent guests of Hearst and Marion at San Simeon. Now Lederer was working at Fox. He might be able to pull a string or two. Herman thought of others, men at the racetrack, people with deep pockets, a haberdasher who had laughed his head off once as Herman entertained him while being fitted for a suit. But how the hell would he find the guy? Then there was that lunch he'd had a year or so back with that big overgrown monkey Orson Welles at "21" in New York. Brilliant and dynamic, Welles was undeniably charming, and he knew Welles had liked him too. He'd heard from Cukor that Houseman said that Welles told him that he and Herman had both probably left the lunch feeling like they were the two smartest, most brilliant men in the entire Western Hemisphere. Sonofabitch was right, too. He had, and they were.

WELLES DID COME ALONG IN THE END, OF COURSE. THE BOY WONder had come out to Hollywood a few months earlier, with a huge contract from RKO giving him carte blanche for four movies. In a town notorious for the venomous envy it inspires in others, the twenty-four-year-old Welles was setting world records. He was more than detested and despised, and most likely feared. The guy had such contemptible arrogance, saying that a movie studio was the biggest toy train set any boy ever had. As if! As if years of hard work, of craftsmanship and study and patient devotion to the art and science of making motion pictures was as simple as playing with a toy train set. It was a discipline, even Herman knew that by now. A crazy damn idiotic business, but if you didn't take it seriously, it would eat you alive.

The whole town had its knives out for Orson Welles. And it was kind of delicious, watching the boy wonder struggle, fail, fall on his face. RKO had promised to do whatever he wanted, but when *Heart of Darkness*, which Welles had already done for radio and was his first choice to be a movie, proved to be too expensive, RKO dropped it like a hot potato, and the town did a jig. Welles started a thriller, *The Smiler with a Knife*, but the attempt seemed half-hearted, and the columnists were ripping into Welles with regularity now.

In here, at last, he turned to Herman, flat on his back in Cedars of Lebanon Hospital. Orson was one of Herman's many visitors, and the one who rescued him from a feeling that the game had passed him by.* At first Welles just needed help with a few radio scripts—Welles and his Mercury Theatre were still doing radio shows, and Orson paid $200 a pop. Herman cranked out as many as he could in the hospital, drinking them up, even if they were uncredited. To anyone who might have wandered into the room and seen a man with his left leg in a cast and hoisted up in traction—it was broken in three places—the wheezy cough, his packet of cigarettes on the bedside table further evidence of the man's utter disregard for his health—Herman looked like he was ready to be sent out to pasture, the renowned Hollywood screenwriter so down on his luck he was writing uncredited radio scripts.

But in the photographs taken of Herman in this bed during this time—and there are quite a few—it is impossible to ignore the glint in the man's eye. Something had happened, and it is no accident that for the first time in his adult life he was letting his moustache grow. The moustache was not just an emulation of Franz, though it was certainly that—and it wasn't just the laziness of personal hygiene that comes after an accident. No, the moustache was Herman finally saying, fine, here I am, world. I'll work with this kid, because he's exciting and the whole town hates him too and who knows what'll come of it but damn if it isn't more interesting than the swill I've been churning out for over a decade.

In time, Herman and Welles, who visited Cedars of Lebanon often and among other things mesmerized my poor grandmother—people forget what a colossally handsome man the young Orson Welles was, but Sara never did, and to read her interview transcripts about the neck massages Welles gave her while she reclined on Herman's hospital bed is to go to a place no grandson should ever go—the two men began talking about a movie. Where the idea precisely came from is always impossible to discern, and evidence abounds on both sides of the eternal debate over who contributed what to the final script of *Citizen Kane*. Both Welles and

---

* A group of writers from M-G-M who brought Herman a silver cigarette box engraved with the words "From Manky's pals" did not help; Herman wept when the men left the room, convinced it was like a man receiving a gold watch upon retirement.

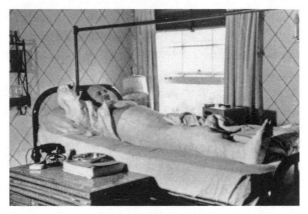

Herman in bed after the crack-up in
New Mexico, 1939

Herman had independently been interested in telling the story of the life of a great man using multiple narrators, and each had their own interests in power and journalism. Herman knew about as much about politics and William Randolph Hearst as any man alive, and he invented the Rosebud gimmick as a way in to the screenplay; as for young Welles, as an actor he was a protean figure capable of conveying immense strength and power in a possibly fallen, possibly tragic, but definitely magnetic hero.

So does it matter who wrote what?

The challenge, all these years later, is that of course it does. If it doesn't matter to a well-adjusted, mystical spiritual being who is trying to live her life in accordance with the truest values of life on this planet, it does matter to the biographer, and it matters to the grandson. Who said "Kane" first matters, and who suggested Hearst as the model matters, and who said "Rosebud" matters, and who came up with "a white dress she had on" and where the breakfast table scene came from, and whose idea was the newsreel, and who contributed the scene about the unfinished review of the mistress's performance, and who put the dreidel in the nursery, and who "Is Pop governor yet?" and on and on and on.* It matters, of course it does, because if we're all going to be judged by what we leave behind, and who came closest to bringing home the missing three points, if the

---

* Orson, Herman, Herman, Herman, Orson, unclear, Herman (though Welles added the brilliant touch of Kane finishing the thing), Herman, Herman, and on and on and yes the score, in this rigged unfinished game gives Herman a lead of six to two (or six to three if you give them both credit for the review).

whole damn thing is a competition, then we play to win, and the only way to win is to beat the other guy, to beat him down into submission until he cries uncle, or great-uncle, and gives up and admits of our overpowering genius.

But in the beginning, Herman is forty-two years old and desperate for work, and all of a sudden he's discussing a possible film script with one of the most exciting personalities to come along in years. He couldn't give a rat's ass, at this point, who was going to be getting what credit. At this stage, the assumption is, it's a one-man show—Welles's brilliant PR machine demanded it, really, that he write, direct, produce, and star in whatever movies he was going to make, just as with the radio shows, like the *War of the Worlds* trick the previous fall that had landed him on the cover of *Time* when he managed to work half the country into a conniption fit because Martians had landed in New Jersey. Herman knew that Welles took credit for everything—the Mercury Theatre was his creation, no one knew about John Houseman, toiling away to keep the great young actor's ego and wilder impulses in check, and fewer still had heard of any of the Mercury Theatre's actors—Joseph Cotten or Agnes Moorehead or Everett Sloane or any of the other professionals who had pushed the Mercury to such heights. Everyone at Mercury was aware of the fundamental fact—and Hell, it was hard to be angry at the guy about it, he had such an inclusiveness of spirit—that it was "The Orson Welles Show." The rest of them—Herman included, now—were just supposed to bask in the Sun King's glory.

At the beginning, given where Herman was coming from, that was okay. Herman was feeling depleted and low when he first met Welles— the self-confidence and cheek of the young man who had invaded the New York City theatrical and journalistic worlds over a decade and a half earlier had been replaced by a wariness bordering on depression. Herman simply didn't feel very good about himself or what he brought to any situation anymore, so when he met Welles, as much as he loved entertaining the young genius with his still undimmed wit (and even affectionately bossed the younger man around at times, making him adjust his bedpan at the hospital) and as much as he may have projected a world-weary "Aren't we the two smartest fellows around, and won't we show these morons just exactly how it's done?" he was also nervous that somehow he would manage to blow this opportunity as he had so many in the past. So he took, maybe for the first time in his career, what the defense

"Herman was able to do the great work at last": John
Houseman, Rita Alexander, and Herman in Victorville,
California, 1940

Orson Welles paying a visit to Victorville, where Rita
Alexander tends to Herman, and John Houseman watches

offered—he didn't push it when it came to credit or money. He was happy
just to be in the game again.

As he and Welles had their conversations, a movie idea began to burble
and grow, and then, most crucially, they hatched the plan for the delivery
of the script. Welles seems to have realized at some point along in here
that Mank was too invaluable to the project to let him do half-assed or

in any way unsupervised work, and so it was that one morning in early February of 1940, Herman and Houseman crammed into a Pontiac with secretary Rita Alexander and went out to the Kemper Campbell Ranch, a vacation retreat in Victorville, California, on the edge of the Mojave Desert, eighty miles from Los Angeles. It was there, for the next twelve weeks, that Houseman did whatever it was that Houseman did—organizing and editing the notes Herman and Welles had taken before they'd come to Victorville, keeping Herman from drinking (too much, anyway; there was a canteen not far from the ranch that they often drove down to in the early evening), talking endlessly with Herman about the script, and, according to Welles at least, stoking the fires that Herman would inevitably keep banked toward any authority figure, in this case Welles himself, probably planting the seeds for what would grow into the credit battle that would eventually consume so much needless energy—and Rita Alexander contributed her patience, good spirit,* and unflagging ability not to bother Herman, to stay interested in the story: But how is it going to come out? she would ask him at the end of every night's dictation, and Herman, lips turning up in that characteristic leer, would say, My dear Mrs. Alexander, I'm making it up as I go along—and Herman was able to do the great work at last.

And it is great work. For all its cleverness and wit that can tend to obscure rather than illuminate what lies underneath, for all the sparkling dialogue sitting on its surface, for however much Pauline Kael may have damned it with faint praise by calling it a "shallow masterpiece"†—that screenplay stands as the bedrock of what with a handful of other films are utter breakthroughs in the medium, and as such it can only have come from someone—not Welles—who had mastered the form. And Herman took the form he'd been practicing, even if it was with one hand behind his back, maybe holding a bottle or a pair of dice, and he broke it wide open. As *Moby-Dick* was to the novel and *Sgt. Pepper* to the rock album, so *Citizen Kane* was to the movies—a piece of work that demonstrated anew the possibilities of the form itself, a work so astonishing that everything that came afterward had to stand, if not in the thing's shadow, at least in

---

* And her surname—to Susan Alexander Kane.

† To be sure, Pauline Kael loved the film, and loved B movies, but it's sometimes hard not to feel that her conviction that the film is the perfect B movie was a backhanded compliment.

some relation to it, with an understanding of just how much the game had been changed as a result.

Among the script's many joys is in its unapologetically contradictory presentation of Charles Foster Kane. Unlike most movie characters, Kane comes across as a real, breathing human, sometimes ruthless, sometimes droll, sometimes, as he himself puts it to Thatcher, "a dangerous scoundrel." In fact, Kane undersells the multiplicity of his roles when he tells his guardian, "The trouble is, Mr. Thatcher, you don't realize you're talking to two people." He is far more than two people; he is virtually unknowable, an infinity of complexity and unpredictability, as are we all, at least according to Herman's script. The screenplay—or the screenwriter, Herman—trusts the audience will understand, that they will recognize themselves in his portraits of complicated, messy, irrational creatures. "A fellow will remember things you wouldn't think he'd remember," Bernstein tells Thompson before losing himself in thought, remembering a girl on a ferry he would never see again. Who was she? What did she represent? Where did it go, and would Bernstein ever get it back? Loss suffuses the screenplay—to begin with, we've lost Charles Foster Kane, and again and again, the script shows us people aching for things, or people, who are no longer there: memories, youth, vitality. We can never quite have what we want. And those rare instances of grace—Bernstein's memory of the girl on the ferry, or, equally tenderly, Kane and Susan Alexander's meeting, her suffering from a painful toothache and laughing at him as he attempts to cheer her up, and the wonder that overtakes him as he realizes she has no idea who he is—those moments are to be cherished; they cannot sustain, but they are all we have. They swirl through our lives, ungraspable and fleeting, like snowflakes drifting in a globe that is about to smash on the floor.

And somewhere in there Herman started to realize what he'd accomplished. This was not, after all, *My Dear Miss Aldrich*. This was *American*.

"I am, have been, and will be, only one thing—an American."
—CHARLES FOSTER KANE

The script Herman and Houseman returned from Victorville with was called *American,* and in an era when a long film script could sometimes run to 150 pages, it was 325 pages long. It was unwieldy, overwritten, and unfinished. But inside it, one can see nearly all the scenes

"Jo-Jo the Dog-Faced Boy":
Herman and Orson Welles, c. 1940

and characters that eventually made their way to the screen, and the thing's overall revolutionary structure and shape, the time shifting recalibrations and resettings of the same scenes, is already intact. The script is a masterful mess, moving forward with urgency and momentum, so much so that even people who have seen *Citizen Kane* dozens of times can be surprised, when watching, at what happens next, which flashback or flash-forward follows which. The movie feels constantly both unexpected and inevitable. And while there are a few blind alleys, what seem like mistakes to a reader who knows the finished work—Kane having a lover of Susan Alexander's killed, Kane's mourning the death of his son, the attempted assassination of a president that is blamed on Kane—it is easy to read *American,* see the great man die in a huge abandoned mansion with the word "Rosebud"* slipping from his lips and setting the whole plot in motion, and think: okay, it's all there.

And yet, of course, it isn't. It simply wasn't done yet, and the artist who helped find the figure at the center of the limestone that was shipped back from Victorville, the visionary that drove that part of the making of the screenplay, was most assuredly not Herman Mankiewicz. Not that Orson Welles shaped the final thing alone. The collaborative nature of filmmaking, even with a boy genius like Orson around, meant that no one person supplied the precision conveyed in the progression of the original screenplay of *American* to the final shooting script of *Citizen Kane.* And Herman played a huge role, though not immediately. After handing in his second draft of *American* in early May, he did some uncredited work on a film for M-G-M—word of his work with Welles, and his exemplary conduct

---

* In addition to its overtones in Herman's life and the fact that it was modeled on a memorably traumatic moment with his own father, the word itself was a deliberate thumb in the eye of another authority figure, for it was rumored to be William Randolph Hearst's pet name for Marion Davies's private parts.

at Victorville, had brought him another chance from the studio—but he returned to the Mercury payroll in late June,* and from then through the end of July, when the principal photography began, he was responsible for cutting and trimming, shaving the script. And, at least outwardly, there was no rancor at all between the two men. Many unofficial cast gatherings were held at Herman's house on Tower Road, where the cast would read aloud parts of the script (these rehearsals were unofficial, in order to circumvent a studio rule that forbade uncompensated rehearsing), Herman with a notebook and pencil, jotting down notes and ideas as everyone shouted them out. But there was no doubt as to who was in charge of the final product. It was Orson Welles's show now, and no one doubted it.†

Which brings us to the battle for credit. Herman, of course, knew what his contract said. Everyone who worked at Mercury had the same contract, which stipulated quite clearly that "All material composed, submitted, added or interpolated by you . . . under this employment agreement, are now and shall forever be the property of Mercury Productions, Inc., who, for this purpose, shall be deemed the author and creator thereof." However, the issue of authorship was not quite the same as that of screenplay credit. While Mercury had rarely if ever given a writing credit for their radio broadcasts, and when they did the majority were given to Welles, Hollywood had its own customs, and here the irony was that Herman, who had long been opposed to screenwriters unionizing in any way, was ultimately saved from having his name appear *nowhere* on the film by the existence of the Hollywood guilds. When it became clear that Welles and RKO intended to give Welles sole screenplay credit, Herman began to make noise. A lot of noise. He and Houseman had taken to calling Welles "Jo-Jo the Dog-Faced Boy," and Herman had also joked about the boy wonder's "decision to make the first full-length revolution-

---

* Technically, all the people who worked on *Citizen Kane* were employed by the Mercury Theatre company, which was paid by RKO.

† The vastness of Welles's ego is hard to overstate. Decades later, in the late 1970s, my cousin John, Don's son, was eating at Lucy's El Adobe, a Mexican restaurant across the street from the Paramount lot. John was sitting in the front booth, right next to the cashier's station, when he realized that "Orson Welles was sitting in the next booth, holding forth with some enraptured film students, voice booming, almost a caricature of himself." When the students were paying the check, John says, "Welles stood behind them, right next to me, for a long time. I thought about it, and finally introduced myself. 'Mr. Welles? I'm John Mankiewicz. You worked with my grandfather.' He looked down at me for a moment, and said, 'Did I?' "

ary 'motion-picture completely without film!' " But there was something more serious at work.

Herman had made, not for the first or last time, a bad deal. Desperately needing the money and the work, he had quite clearly understood that he wouldn't be getting credit for the film—but it was a decision that rankled. Rita Alexander told Richard Meryman that at some point in Victorville, Herman remarked casually that it was too bad he wouldn't be getting any credit because the script was actually going to be pretty good. (The secretary, unfamiliar with the depths of Herman's self-defeating ways, was shocked that he had agreed not to be credited on-screen.)

And Herman, once he had turned his mind on a target, was fierce and single-minded in his attacks. As the rushes started to come in and word of the footage's qualities began to spread, Herman knew the movie was going to be something to be genuinely proud of, that it would be a highlight of everyone's career. He also knew that the town loathed the young would-be genius, and the industry's hatred for Welles would only be magnified if people thought he was trying to deny credit to one of their own. The irony in Herman appealing to Hollywood to be thought of as one of their own cannot have been lost on him. So it was that the *Hollywood Reporter* gleefully claimed on October 3, 1940, that "the writer credit won't be solo for Welles, if Herman Mankiewicz can keep talking." He could, and it wasn't.

Whatever Welles's true feelings about the matter—and in later years his magnanimity in acknowledging my grandfather's "contributions to the screenplay" almost define condescension: "I didn't come in," he told Richard Meryman, "like some more talented writer and save Mankiewicz from disaster."* Orson Welles now perpetrated a gesture that was both generous and indicative of just how much he had himself contributed to the making of the film, and the making of its central character. He decided to grant Herman coauthorship and so end the battle for good, and also to put Herman's name first. Thus the final credit reads:

ORIGINAL SCREENPLAY
HERMAN J. MANKIEWICZ
ORSON WELLES

Granting Herman this credit did several things. First, and most important, it was probably more than fair. Herman laid down the basic struc-

---

* Gee, thanks, Orson.

ture and shape of the film and had written if not, as he later claimed to Alexander Woollcott, 99 percent of the dialogue, or, as he later testified in court,[*] 98 percent, at least 51 percent of the film. So it made sense for his name to go first. But it also made sense for Welles's name to be included, for too many of the film's literary inventions—let alone his countless directorial flourishes—were his. But also, most crucially and strategically, Welles's public magnanimity prevented Herman from taking the ultimate step, and there's no evidence that he ever really considered it at the time, though in later years it may have haunted him that he hadn't—namely, to actually try to gain sole credit for the screenplay.

Interestingly, the move echoes a change Welles had insisted on in the screenplay itself, and which Herman fought him strenuously over. One of Herman's cherished stories from his days as a newspaperman in New York was of passing out after writing one sentence of a review of an execrable performance delivered by magnate Samuel Insull's wife in a performance of *The School for Scandal,* and it struck him as wonderful grist for the *Citizen Kane* mill, a perfect way to show how Kane's friend Jedediah Leland would respond to the impossible task of having to review Susan Alexander's operatic debut in Chicago. Welles, too, loved it—and then added to it, with something that Herman felt would destroy the scene: Kane sitting down at the typewriter to complete the immolating review. "Why would he do such a thing?" Herman argued. No one would finish such a review! It made no sense! But in fact Kane's completing the nasty review of Susan's performance gives more insight into the depth of Kane's character—Charles Foster Kane always had to prove he was better than everyone else   and by finishing the review, he demonstrated that in fact he wasn't deluded about Susan's talent, he knew better than anyone what she really was—but of course he also knew that he had to fire Jedediah. He had his cake and his review too—Charles Foster Kane, and Orson Welles as well, in putting Herman's name first on the credits. It was masterful.

HERMAN, ON THE OTHER HAND, HAD HARDLY BEEN MASTERFUL IN coping with the success now in his grasp. With news of the movie's revolutionary merits spreading through Hollywood, it soon became clear that only one man stood in the way of the film's triumphant release: William

---

[*] In 1944, there was a lawsuit in which RKO was accused of plagiarizing a book that was found in Herman's library, *Imperial Hearst,* by W. A. Swanberg.

Randolph Hearst, the man on whom Charles Foster Kane was more or less loosely based. Embarassed and outraged by what he was sure would be a wildly unflattering portrait (and reportedly incensed by the film's treatment of Marion Davies, who was in fact a gifted comic actress and nothing at all like the untalented opera singer Susan Alexander Kane), Hearst did everything in his considerable power to bury the film, igniting a campaign against the film in his papers, and even offering RKO one million dollars to burn the film without ever displaying it to the public. But well before the public had its chance to see the movie, Herman had made his move. Perhaps because he couldn't tolerate the good fortune that was now so close, he had inexplicably sent the script of the film to his pal Charlie Lederer, Marion Davies's nephew, before shooting began. It's possible that Herman was merely trying to demonstrate to Lederer—and by extension Davies and Hearst—that they had nothing to worry about, for the script had fictionalized so very much. But it's also possible it was an act both of braggadocio—*look how good this damn thing is!*—and uncontrollable self-destructiveness; indeed, when Lederer returned the script (without comment), it was covered with pencil markings that had all the hallmark of Hearst lawyers pointing out possible beachheads for lawsuits.

Luckily, Hearst's campaign to destroy the film failed, RKO stood firm, and the movie's release went on as planned. Herman's self-destructiveness had, for the moment at least, been defeated.

In later years, Herman's children adopted a curious metaphor to describe their father's greatest success. His years in the newspaper business, and in particular his time spent observing William Randolph Hearst, they said, was like a nickel Herman had been carrying around in his pocket for years. With *Citizen Kane,* finally, Pop had spent the nickel.

ON THE NIGHT OF THURSDAY, FEBRUARY 26, 1942, HOLLYWOOD WAS in a state of high alert. Three nights before, on Monday night, the Japanese submarine *I-17* had surfaced less than a half mile from shore not far from Santa Barbara, just ninety miles up the coast from Los Angeles, and fired seventeen shells at some oil tanks behind the beach. News of the attack triggered reports of an impending Japanese "invasion" throughout the state, and the following night, air raid sirens pierced the air throughout Los Angeles County. Thousands of air raid wardens scampered into position, and finally, just after three in the morning, the 37th Coast Artillery Brigade began firing 12.8-pound anti-aircraft shells into the air at reported Japanese airplanes. For nearly an hour, the sound of the guns rocked Los Angeles, and by the time the all clear sounded, guns had hurled 1,440 rounds of ammunition into the night sky. Nearly ten tons of shrapnel and unexploded ammunition rained back on the city. Now, on Thursday, on a small island in Los Angeles Harbor called Terminal Island, the FBI began rounding up and arresting the first Japanese-Americans and sending them to internment camps.[*]

So as the Academy Awards ceremony got under way in the Biltmore Hotel that night, few could be blamed for having their minds elsewhere. And fewer still could blame those who, for one reason or another, stayed away that night. Orson Welles, whose *Citizen Kane* had been nominated for nine awards including Best Picture, Best Actor, and Best Director for Welles alone, as well as for screenplay, was in Rio de Janeiro, working on a film for the war effort called *Carnival*. But missing from the ceremony, as well, was Herman Mankiewicz. Part of the reason Herman gave for avoiding the awards banquet was the same reason he gave for getting into *Kane* in the first place: his busted leg. He had finally gotten his cast off a few months earlier and celebrated with an impromptu party at Hollywood's famed Chasen's, at which, of course, he had slipped and rebroken his leg. Now, hobbling on his left leg, Herman, convinced he was going to lose, knew that he would not respond well to a defeat and so decided to skip the ceremony. "He did not want to be humiliated," Goma said. "He thought he'd get mad and do something drastic when he didn't win."[†] So he stayed home and listened on the radio in his bathrobe and slippers, though he made a show of pretending to nod off periodically in his chair as the ceremony dragged on. As expected, despite all the nominations, it was not *Citizen Kane*'s night. The voters were all Hollywood insiders and they weren't about to reward Welles for his efforts. *Kane* lost out in virtually every major award—save one.

When they announced the winner of Best Screenplay as "Herman J.

---

[*] The "Great Lost Angeles Air Raid," as the incident came to be known, later served as the inspiration for Steven Spielberg's 1979 film *1941*.

[†] Another possible reason for staying home: by now, Herman had had over four decades of never measuring up to his father's expectations. When we consider what happened after that night—Herman's inability to leverage *Citizen Kane*'s success into a sustained, thriving career—it's hard to avoid the conjecture that Herman stayed away from the Oscar ceremonies not because he was afraid to lose, but because he was afraid to win.

Mankiewicz..." Herman jumped out of his chair, grabbed Sara, and danced a limping jig. Screams and cheers for Hollywood's resident loser-genius filled the Biltmore ballroom, and Herman and Sara could hear "Where is he? Mank! Mank!" from the radio as they hobbled around Herman's bedroom. A few blocks away, Sara's sister Mattie let out a yelp and grabbed her cousin Olga, and the two women, still in their nightgowns, drove straight to Tower Road for a spontaneous celebration: everyone jumping around, and the phone ringing, and even little Johanna, just four, twirling and sashaying . . . In a flash it hit Herman what he would have said had he attended the ceremony: "I am very happy to accept this award in Mr. Welles's absence, because the script was written in Mr. Welles's absence."

Somehow, maybe because the industry hated Orson Welles so much, Herman had become a sentimental favorite, and despite his many pec-

A letter from Moss Hart congratulating Herman on
Citizen Kane, April 11, 1941

cadilloes, he had become something of a beloved figure in Hollywood. Now, at last, the town was his. If he so wanted, he could begin afresh, with new confidence gained from the triumph of *Citizen Kane,* and to conquer the field as never before. The town wanted it. It seemed that everyone was joining in.

Not everyone, of course. Across town, listening on his radio, was an M-G-M producer with an uncanny physical resemblance to the screenwriter. The producer had also decided not to attend the ceremony, though several of the pictures he'd worked on had been nominated for various awards. Still, he felt a strong connection to the ceremony, and to *Citizen Kane* in particular. For one thing, he would later tell interviewers that he had been the source for one of the movie's great inventions, for he had owned a sled called Rosebud in his youth and he was sure Herman had gotten the idea from *him.* But he really didn't want to go to the ceremony because, like Herman, he didn't want to be humiliated.

Now, when the moment came and his brother's name was announced, Joe looked over at his wife, who was listening with him, and said, "I don't think I'll ever win an Oscar." He stood up from his chair, went to the wet bar, and poured himself a drink, just because it was something to do. Years later, long after the moment had served as inspiration for his own greatest work and the coveted Oscar had been transformed in *All About Eve* into the fictional Sarah Siddons Award, Joe could still remember the awful feeling in his stomach, and the thought that went with it: "He's got the Oscar, and I'm a producer at Metro, goddamn it!"

————— ⚘ —————

FRATRICIDE

Stop behaving as if fear were something to be ashamed of. Stop being such a pompous know-it-all!

—*PEOPLE WILL TALK*

JOE MANKIEWICZ HAD ANOTHER REASON TO AVOID THE 1942 ACADEMY Awards ceremony—namely, the 1941 ceremony. Joe had attended that banquet with full confidence, proud that one of his productions had been nominated for no fewer than six awards. True, he was still itching to direct, but with *The Philadelphia Story,* Joe had had a tremendous success—his first blowout hit for Metro, grossing $1.3 million for the company—and on the night of the ceremony, he'd soaked up the night's glamour. While he hadn't really expected to win the top prize—he knew the town had fallen in love with *The Grapes of Wrath,* and on the off-chance John Ford's homage to the simple people suffering in the Dust Bowl didn't win, everyone loved this roly-poly Alfred Hitchcock now, and Joe told friends not to be surprised if Hitch's *Rebecca* took the cake—what he hadn't counted on was an actual snub in the speeches. For in the end, his film had taken home two prizes, one of which was for Best Screenplay, by Donald Ogden Stewart, who had, in accepting the award, tossed off a thank-you that cut Joe to the quick. The line had been a throwaway really, what Stewart told the crowd gathered at the Biltmore that evening, and was clearly a joke: "I have no one to thank but myself"—everyone knew the movie had been based on a play by Philip Barry (the film won not for Best Original Screenplay but for Best Adapted Screenplay). But to Joe, smiling through his clenched pipe as the laughs ricocheted around the ballroom, the line stung. Did no one know what he had done? Dammit

Joe at an awards ceremony in Hollywood, c. 1940

to hell, there wouldn't be any movie at all without Joe. Would he never get to direct?!

By that point, it had already been six years—six years of playing the game and doing it well, producing the crowd-pleasers Mayer expected, and making 'em laugh. But it still wasn't enough. Joe's drive for excellence had come practically with his first words, with Pop's demand for perfection, and while he had nothing to be ashamed of from his years as a producer, producing no less than twenty movies for M-G-M, the whole thing still galled him. And here was Stewart, an alleged friend, and all but forgotten was that Metro had Joe's unrelenting ambition to thank for the acquisition of *The Philadelphia Story* in the first place. When Philip Barry's production starring Katharine Hepburn as the witty but chilly heiress, Tracy Lord, beautiful but seemingly as unfeeling as stone, became the biggest Broadway hit of 1939, Joe had known instantly that he had to produce the movie version.

Hepburn, who had famously been deemed "box office poison" in a survey of movie exhibitors in 1938 after several unsuccessful films,[*] had cleverly acquired the rights to the film, enabling her to recreate Lord on the silver screen, a role that turned her career around. But her lover at the

---

[*] These films included *Bringing Up Baby,* a box-office disappointment on its release in February 1938, but which is now regarded, at least by this non-relative of anyone associated with its making, as one of the three or four funniest movies of all time.

time, no less a tycoon than Howard Hughes, had thrown a stumbling block into any agreement, requiring that all screen versions of the play have two men with significant star power acting opposite Hepburn. Unfortunately, the play had only one substantial male part that would attract a star—an antagonistic reporter with small town origins who ultimately falls in love with Lord.

At first, Louis Mayer was wary. He didn't trust Hepburn to carry a picture any more than any of the other moguls in town did, and he didn't see how the play could possibly yield a second male star. But he believed in Joe, and in the end, trusted that his young producer, one of the most brilliant minds in Hollywood, was a consistent hard worker who always surpassed expectations. If anyone could, Joe could create a logical solution and an acceptable trial script, and get the rights for the movie.

For weeks Joe puzzled it over, trying to decide how to change Barry's script to create another male part worthy of a star . . . The brother? The father? The staunch, dull fiancé? Change the photographer accompanying the writer to a male part? No, that made no sense—there's a love story there, a triangle with the photographer, and he didn't want to get into some fool homo thing . . . the problem was this damn brother.

And suddenly, there it was. The dream of so many younger siblings, not least of all Joe. The remedy was simple: get rid of the brother.

By removing Tracy Lord's brother from the movie, Joe could enlarge the part of her former husband who would ultimately win her back into one that a larger star could play, a role the debonair and eternally sophisticated Cary Grant would eventually land. He gave the ex-husband C. K. Dexter Haven many of the brother's old lines, and now, with a killer test script in tow, Hughes relented, and *The Philadelphia Story* was M-G-M's, and Joe's, to make.

Although Joe handed the script job to Donald Odgen Stewart, his influence on the final movie is felt everywhere. Having built the new story on a kind of fratricide, Joe further helped establish the dynamic between Hepburn and Grant's characters by writing the film's prologue in which Grant's goal is made clear: knock the untouchable heiress down a few pegs. The prologue is a silent sequence, completely Joe's idea, in which C. K. Dexter Haven (Grant) leaves his wife, Tracy Lord (Hepburn). He walks out of the house, carrying his bags, while Hepburn follows with his golf clubs, which she promptly dumps at his feet. She takes one club out and breaks it over her knee. Grant is about to smack her, but instead shoves her backward through the front door, creating a classic comedic tableau to begin the movie.

The plot of the play was instantly appealing to Joe. The movie, post-prologue, begins on the day prior to Tracy's second marriage to an up-wardly mobile dull man—played by the stalwart journeyman actor John Howard, who the audience instantly knows is no match for the poised and clever Hepburn. When Hepburn realizes two invitees pretending to be her absent brother's friends are actually gate-crashing reporters, she decides, with an almost Mankiewiczian thrill, that she'll outsmart them. She puts on a show—masquerading around the house, creating caricatures of an upper-class snob, animatedly speaking French with her sister Dinah, deftly weaving insults and jabs into pleasantries, making the undercover reporters from *Spy* magazine (James Stewart's and Ruth Hussey's characters) squirm. Mocking the two, watching them writhe under her scrutiny, Hepburn is almost an amalgamation of Herman and Joe, smarter than anyone, proud and cold and dominant. Of course, the Mankiewiczes were no Main Line Philadelphia members of the Social Register themselves, but they did always claim the innate high status of intellectuals and could enjoy the victory of brainpower over lesser folk.

The focus on the psychological state of the statuesque Hepburn charac-ter also appealed to Joe. When Tracy reveals to journalist Macaulay Con-nor (Stewart) that she divorced C. K. Dexter Haven because he drank, Haven complains that Tracy is not of this world as "she finds human imperfection unforgivable," going on to say, "When I discovered that my relationship to her was to be not that of a loving husband and a good companion . . . but that of a high priest to a virgin goddess, then my drinks grew deeper and more frequent, that's all." Not for the last time, it would be the female character who would be more like Joe, for while Haven admits his vulnerability in talking about the causes of his drinking and wins audiences over with his easy, self-loathing, even Herman-like charm, the remote and less revealing Tracy has built walls around herself, much like Joe. Joe's statement "I don't think I've ever told the truth or confided in myself the way external people do" would not sound foreign on Tracy Lord's lips.

But masculinity would assert itself, of course—neither Joe nor the Hollywood machine would dare give complete autonomy to the woman over the man. Ultimately, it would be the man—the ex-husband in this case—who would position himself as the director of the final scene. Min-

Ruth Hussey, Jimmy Stewart, Cary Grant,
and Katharine Hepburn in *The Philadelphia Story* (1940)

utes before her wedding ceremony is to begin, Tracy Lord and her dull-
ard of a fiancé split. Dexter then suggests that Tracy speak to the crowd
assembled for her wedding, and she repeats these words as he dictates,
in which she and the audience learn simultaneously that they are to be
remarried: "Two years ago, you were invited to a wedding in this house.
I eloped to Maryland, which was very bad manners. But I'd like to make
it up to you now by going through with it as originally planned." A
woman, reciting, puppet-like, the words her ex-husband puts into her
mouth could well be expected to offer some little expression of unease,
but in the world of Hollywood movies—and especially a film based on
a play by a man, rewritten into a script by another man, and overseen
by a producer who's a Mankiewicz, the woman doesn't stand a chance,
no matter that George Cukor, a "woman's director" (Hollywoodese for
"gay"), was directing. "You know how I feel?" Tracy asks Dexter after she's
finished being the dummy in this ventriloquism act. "Like a human, like
a human being." It wouldn't be the last time that Joe would embrace a
woman's happy marriage as central to her own self-conception.

But while *The Philadelphia Story* ended on a note of equality among
the sexes, the finale of Joe's next film with Katharine Hepburn, *Woman
of the Year,* would be downright reactionary. Produced the following year,
it would be the first movie to pair the legendary screen team of Hepburn
and Spencer Tracy. It was Joe's idea to put the two together—he said later
that he felt Spencer Tracy would be a perfect match for Hepburn's stub-

born streak, and he was justly proud of teaming the two stars for the first time. For years afterward, Joe loved to tell the story of their first meeting outside the studio commissary, after which Hepburn, clipped and aristocratic, watched Tracy walking away and told Joe, "He's a little short for me, isn't he?" "Don't worry, Joe said, "he'll cut you down to size."

Significantly, rather than a "woman's director," "man's man" George Stevens directed, from a script attributed to Michael Kanin and Ring Lardner Jr. Hepburn's Tess Harding is a self-confident, world-renowned journalist, humanitarian, and women's rights activist, accomplishments that earn her the prize "Woman of the Year." During the film, Harding feuds with the more conventional sports journalist Craig (Tracy) before finally, inevitably, their sparkling banter reveals that they love each other, and they marry. But then, Craig is left to wither in the shadow of a woman who feels good about herself. Although Tess Harding is in many ways unlike heiress Tracy Lord, both are presented as superior, haughty creatures, in whose comeuppance an audience will take great pleasure. Tess's sin is one she shares with Joe Mankiewicz: arrogance. As she says, "I like knowing more about what goes on than most people."

Just as Cary Grant suffered under his "goddess," Spencer Tracy endures the humiliations of a man with a more accomplished wife. He submits to the comic interruptions of a large crowd wanting to discuss war news on his wedding night. He quite literally wears the apron in the family, making his wife eggs for breakfast. But, finally married, before he heads off for work, leaving her alone for the day in their new house, he remarks, "The outstanding woman of the year isn't really a woman at all." To allow the comic reversal a restoration of traditional gender requires, the movie then offers a denouement, but the original one cooked up by Kanin and Lardner hadn't done the trick. In it, to get back in her husband's good graces after a quarrel, Harding researches and writes an article about boxing and puts his byline on it, and the two reconcile at a boxing match. The first preview audience of the film was cool to the ending, and something else was required.

Joe's solution, entirely his own, was the final breakfast scene, when to win her husband back, Harding attempts to transform herself into a docile, traditional wife and fails miserably. Her attempt to make him breakfast is both comic and unintentionally ludicrous—waffles explode as she watches helplessly, crying. When her husband comes in, she tells him she will become a true wife and give up journalism. The movie ends with seeming domestic bliss between the pair—though achieved only through reducing a highly successful and powerful woman to tears, making breakfast for her man—her aspirations diminished from the hope of exposing the horrors of Nazi occupation to the hope of pleasing her husband.[*]

Where did it come from, this final humiliation of Katharine Hepburn? Joe proudly told Ken Geist that he wrote the scene in anticipation of the response women audience members might have to Hepburn's perfection throughout the first 85 percent of the film.[†] Her humiliation, he figured, would make her more palatable. "The average American housewife," he declaimed, "seated next to her husband staring for two hours at this paragon of beauty, intelligence, wit, accomplishment, and everything else, cannot help but wonder if her husband isn't comparing her very unfavorably with this goddess he sees on the screen . . . Now they can turn to their schmuck husbands and say, 'She may know Batista, but she can't make a cup of coffee, you silly bastard.'"

Upon receiving Joe's new ending, Hepburn had a similar reaction to a modern viewer. She called the breakfast scene "the worst bunch of shit I've ever read." Kanin and Lardner, too, were displeased and rewrote some of the final scene's dialogue, though to little effect: "Some of the worst

---

[*] The film's retrograde sexual politics were somewhat mortifying to me when I first saw it, at a revival house during college; hardly the thing with which to impress a date in the 1980s.

[†] There are a full thirteen minutes of her failing at using kitchen appliances.

Hepburn and Tracy in *Woman of the Year* (1942)

lines we rewrote," Lardner said, "but we couldn't fix it, we couldn't change it fundamentally."* It is unsurprising that decades later, the movie less focused on creating a groveling, humiliated Hepburn, *The Philadelphia Story,* is still hailed as a classic, while *Woman of the Year* has faded from all but the most devoted cineastes' lists.†

Still, for the moment, the film proved another success for Joe and the studio, landing on many critics' top ten lists and cementing Joe's status as the go-to producer on the Metro lot. But inwardly, Joe continued to seethe. Herman's Oscar had only poured more salt in the wounds. Because as Joe, finally, dutifully, put in a call to Tower Road the night of Herman's *Citizen Kane* triumph, hearing the domesticated bliss warbling in the background through the phone wires as the gathered crowd tried to summon Herman to the phone to talk to his kid brother—who was calling, after all, to congratulate the big macher—Joe heard again that his brother had, now, not just ultimate professional success with the Oscar, but something approaching a happy home life. Joe knew instinctively that it would be a while before he could ever attain that—his plan for being in decent relationships seemed modeled on the men and women in the two Hepburn pictures: the woman is wonderful and damn near independent, is in fact nearly the intellectual equal of the man; the man and woman spar for a few reels, falling in and out of love; finally, enough is enough and the man tells the woman what to do; the woman does it; there's a happy embrace; fade out.

It was bullshit, Joe knew, but it would have to do—for now.

---

* Once again, the Academy Awards provided Joe with a dramatic moment: at the 1943 ceremony, Lardner and Kanin picked up the Oscar for Best Original Screenplay, and Joe stood up to shake their hands as they passed him on the way to the stage. They snubbed him.

† The ending is hardly the only thing that mars the film—its characters are far more broadly drawn than in *The Philadelphia Story* and generally less appealing, even down to the grating Greek refugee boy Tess wants to adopt.

CHAPTER NINE

A NEW HEART

Maybe I wasn't his friend. But if I wasn't, he never had one.

—*CITIZEN KANE*

TO THOSE OF US WHO NEVER LIVED THROUGH IT, THERE WAS ALWAYS
an irresistible allure and glamour to the age of coast-to-coast train travel,
though how much old black-and-white movies contributed to the
romance is anyone's guess. The trains had wonderfully evocative names,
like the *Super Chief,* the *20th Century Limited,* and *El Capitan*—and there
were the Pullman porters who paced the halls and cleaned your shoes (and
just about everything else) overnight, and the dining car, where likely as
not you'd find yourself seated next to a spy or a beautiful blonde, or best
of all both in one, and you'd strike up an innocuous conversation as you
ticked off the menu with the well-sharpened pencil so thoughtfully provided by the train. Of course, in reality, these trips were likely as mundane
as a Greyhound bus trip from the Port Authority to New London (if
perhaps less uncomfortable) and no doubt the movies and the people who
remember them in books have romanticized them all out of proportion.
For just ask yourself: What is it like to sit in a cramped compartment for
three days and two nights with your brother who hates you on board a
train carrying the dead body of your father back East?

Such was the romance that greeted Herman and Joe in December
1941. The country was freshly at war. Herman had brought whiskey. Joe
had brought his armor. Herman drank, drank some more, then decided
to drink, before finally pulling himself together and doing some serious
drinking. There was no reason *not* to drink. For Joe, the trip was an

unrelenting nightmare. Herman was dismissive, antagonistic, and in the end cruel. For brothers, it's never entirely right to use the word "unprovoked"—Joe had provoked Herman by being born—but as far as Joe was concerned, Herman's attack had come without reason and from out of nowhere, an emotional Pearl Harbor that left him reeling. "You're a lousy goddamn writer," Herman blasted, and Joe shriveled; Joe wasn't even writing much anymore, he was a producer, why was Herman even bringing it up? Also painful were the attacks on Joe's character: "The only reason you're still around is you kiss so much goddamn ass. Jesus Christ, doesn't your stomach turn kissing so much goddamn ass?"

It was the writing jibes that stung most. Witless, stupid, unoriginal. Each word another dart aimed right for where Joe was most tender and sensitive. Consciously or not, Herman was echoing Franz's withering style. Joe's work, he thundered, had no originality, no spark, no spirit. Joe was not only not talented, but he was such a goddamn know-it-all. What a combination! To be so lacking in talent and so full of oneself! Jesus, if Herman didn't know better, he'd think Joe was a Protestant schoolmarm.

To tell Herman that he'd had too much to drink never did any good, and it certainly didn't help Joe on the train. If anything, it only turned up the flame. Herman, when he got going, could be vicious and relentless, like a heavyweight boxer circling his opponent, flicking, jabbing, each blow landing solidly, and somehow giving Herman more strength, to keep going, keep looking for that knockout punch. But really all he was looking for was any sign that Joe had feelings at all. Herman was so wide open, such an open book when it came to his emotions, his face so easy to read—he had no poker face at all, it was part of what accounted for his terrible luck at games of chance—when he was happy you knew it, when he was miserable you knew it, and when he was angry everyone in the room knew it—and now, the whole damn car on the *Chief* could hear them as the train rumbled east. . . .

But Joe had his armor up, and there was no touching him. He sat there, taking Herman's hits, one after the other—nodding, wincing a little, a kind of half smile to suggest to Herman, "Yes, this is all very smart, but in the morning you're going to have a splitting headache and I'll be the one to bring you bicarbonate of soda, and you'll let loose a colossal belch and we'll forget all about this, only I'll still have a job at Metro and you'll still be you, determined to destroy yourself." For more than an hour Herman erupted, the whiskey fueling the rocket of his rage—and then, when Joe finally thought it was over, that the worst had come and gone, an

Franz in California, c. 1940

innocuous remark started it all up again, and finally Herman brought out the biggest gun he had: Franz, the looming Lear whose shriveled body lay in a pine box four cars behind them in the *Super Chief,* hurtling toward New York City at 90 miles per hour.

At the age of sixty-nine, Franz had finally retired the previous month: November of 1941. For years Franz had come West in the summers, to teach and plan for a possible retirement. He had taken trips up to Puget Sound and imagined what kind of house he might build with the little bit of money he had put away, a small one to be sure, but with a study lined with books, to look out over the sea. He and Johanna had arrived on a Saturday and were staying in a small apartment by the marina. Herman and Sara had gone over Saturday night and had a peaceful visit. The next morning, as they were dressing to go see him again, the phone rang. Franz had been up early and was out walking to buy some fruit when he'd collapsed on the street. Herman and Sara got to the apartment in time to ride with him to the hospital in the ambulance. Herman kept gently teasing his father: "Some fine thing, you come here to California, this beautiful country, and what do you do, you fall down and get sick the first day. Utterly ridiculous the way you're carrying on here, give us all a bad name." Franz smiled, seeming to appreciate his son's humor. Sara, looking at her stricken father-in-law, was wordless with fear.

That afternoon, tests, blood taken. And then, that night, as they were leaving the hospital, Herman asked his father, "Papa, what can I bring you tomorrow? What would you like to have?"

Eyes rheumy behind thick lenses, Franz looked at his oldest son. Could anyone doubt the depth of love the man had for Herman? Did Herman really doubt it? Of course Franz never said it; one didn't say such things. He had never told Herman—or Joe or Erna for that matter—that he loved them. He had been exacting and severe, a disciplinarian who expected the best of everyone at all times, who demanded that people behave their best, do their finest work, work their hardest, no matter what. And now he saw Herman's supple face, lined with worry and genuine concern, the oldest son who could never do enough to break down the walls of his reserve. He saw Herman's pain and anguish, a boy hanging on his father's every breath, and Franz answered the only way he could: "A new heart."

The following morning he was in a coma. Herman was a wreck. He sat beside his father's bedside that whole day, and the next, day after day, weeping. Franz would never come out of his coma, and Herman was there every day. He didn't go to work all that week—"It didn't take much to keep him from working," Goma admitted—and he sat talking quietly to his unconscious father, stroking his father's hand gently, sometimes just calling to him, "Papa, Papa. Pop." An eight-day-long vigil.

Joe came to the hospital once, didn't stay long. He saw there was nothing to be done and made to leave. Herman told him, "If only we had six more months." Joe, practical and sensible, knew six months wouldn't make a difference. He's going to have to go eventually, he told Herman as he grabbed his hat and headed back to the studio. Somehow, Joe had already made peace with the fact of their father's death, long before. He had cut ties years ago—he couldn't even remember when, and he knew he wouldn't be further hurt when Franz was finally gone.

Now, on the train, Herman ripped into Joe for being unfeeling, cold, heartless—what kind of an artist could create anything truly original if he doesn't even mourn his own father? Herman bellowed and blew, the storm of Joe's childhood coming back to him full on, but now Herman was both men rolled into one, Herman and Franz both, and that titanic powerful storm was sweeping through Joe, a cold wind howling, and this time there was no closet in which to hide, no harbor, no peace anywhere on this train rocketing east.

But, curiously, Joe found that he didn't need it. As the two brothers battled it out, it is well to return to the classic movie trope of cross-country train trips, with their close-ups of locomotive engines pumping madly, smoke billowing, and crisscrossing train tracks. For so long, Herman had been in front—larger, beloved, more successful in so many ways . . . but Joe had been gaining steadily. Now, on the *Chief*, carrying their dead father's body east for burial, had Joe passed Herman at last?

Joe looked at Herman, and he felt the unwitting power of being unharmed by his brother's colossal temper. He saw that Herman was just being himself, raging, angry, alcoholic, out of control, a complicated system of neuroses and complexes that Joe knew had predated Joe and would continue regardless of what he did or didn't do. Joe was frequently in awe of this magnificent creature: like a whale thrashing in the waves, with half a dozen harpoons in him but refusing to go down, blood spouting everywhere—a gorgeous, natural, beautiful thing—a force all its own, something to behold the same way you would appreciate an actress like Bette Davis in full emotional tilt. Joe heard Herman telling him now what Franz had evidently told him—that Herman was the talented one, that Herman should be making more money, and what on earth did they pay Joe all that money for? Pop at least respected me, but you . . . Herman's voice was trailing off, the alcohol thickening his tongue and the wit curdling in on itself, there were no punch lines anymore, just blind blows, most of which were missing.

Joe knew that there were no knockouts in this fight, for even if Herman landed a punch, Joe kept bouncing up, and he knew, and this knowledge became the steel of his armor, that he would actually one day make something of *this,* this creature, this gorgeous lovely Herman, and his own cold resolution to outlast him no matter what. Things could get awfully bumpy, this emotional turbulence that would swirl around you, even if you were the cause of all the Sturm und Drang. In such a situation, the only thing to do was to fasten your seat belts.

In some ways, Joe knew he was still training for the big fight. He didn't know when the fight would come, but he knew he'd win, and he knew that he was training all the time—at the studio, and, more and more especially, at home. With Rosa.

VIENNA'S JOSEFSTADT THEATER IS ONE OF EUROPE'S GRANDEST AND greatest old theaters, having been in continuous use since 1788. Ludwig van Beethoven, Richard Wagner, and Johann Strauss conducted there, and famous directors and actors, from Otto Preminger and Max Reinhardt to Klaus Maria Brandauer, have done acclaimed work on its stage. In the 1930s, one of the theater's leading lights was a gifted and volatile actress named Rosa Stradner.* Stradner was a stunning-looking woman and notoriously mercurial. According to one of her Viennese friends, Austrian director Walter Reisch, she was "beautiful beyond description . . . the Viennese equivalent of Ava Gardner, a femme fatale or dangerous woman with syndromes, which were part of the chemistry of her own life." In time, she would become Joe's second wife, and though her career would wither in the United States, her star shone so brightly on the

* Rosa was sometimes credited as Rose Stradner, but in the family, and to her colleagues, she was always known as Rosa.

Viennese stage that even a few years after her suicide, her special qualities would be remarked upon to one of her two sons.

Tom Mankiewicz, Joe and Rosa's second son, loved to tell a gloriously awkward story about the time he was at a Hollywood party in the early 1960s and came across Oskar Werner, the acclaimed Austrian actor then becoming well known in America for *Jules and Jim, Ship of Fools,* and *The Spy Who Came in from the Cold.* At the party, Werner was drunk, and he took exception to someone calling him German. According to Tom, Werner "snapped at this guy, 'I'm not German, I'm Austrian.' There was a big silence, and me being a big kissy face twenty-three-year-old kid, I said, 'You have to understand, to call an Austrian a German is a little bit like calling an Irishman an Englishman, they don't appreciate it.'" Oskar Werner was delighted, and asked Tom how he knew so much about Austrian resentments. Tom said that his mother had been Austrian, an actress in fact. Werner asked her name, and when Tom told him, Werner's eyes lit up. "The Josefstadt theater, 1935." Tom nodded proudly. Werner smiled thoughtfully, then said, "When I first masturbated, it was to a picture of your mother."

The room went silent. Tom stared at the man. "If you live fifty lives, no one is ever going to tell you that. The only thing I could say," he told me forty years later, "was thank you."

SUCH WAS THE FATE OF ROSA STRADNER, BY ALL ACCOUNTS AN accomplished and talented stage actress who, discovered by Louis B. Mayer's talent scouts and brought to Hollywood as a possible foreign star in the manner of Hedy Lamarr, essentially became Joe Mankiewicz's frustrated hausfrau, a woman with not much of a career, few friends, no outlet for her substantial emotional undercurrents, a love of alcohol, and a husband who, despite his considerable and public embrace of psychoanalysis as a tool for understanding what makes humans tick, seems to have had a tin ear for his wife's distress.

They were married in 1940. Joe, of course, was quite the ladies' man, and during the years leading up to World War II, he had made it a special habit of squiring the leading German-speaking actresses around the studio when they came to try their hand in Hollywood. His list of affairs was long: at various times he was linked with stars from Myrna Loy to Linda Darnell to Judy Garland. But Rosa was the one he married, and despite what her firstborn Chris may say, it's not just because he got the woman pregnant. No, there was something else at work, and it had to do with Joe's own need for control. Here was a talented and well-bred Catholic actress from Austria—how impressive indeed to land her. She was cultured and refined, everything Joe aspired to be; indeed, her decorous refinement represented everything Franz wanted for his sons, so she was exactly what Joe would want to own and possess. What's more, her professional time in Hollywood was, unlike those of the other starlets he spent time with, frustrated from the start, as she was tossed into not-great films like *The Last Gangster* and *Blind Alley,* where her accent lay in that netherworld between Garboesque allure and Teutonic flatness.

Rosa would not be meeting Joe, ever, on equal footing. She would not, could not compete with him. What could be better?

Joe never wanted to meet anyone on a level playing field, especially women. Them, he was glad to woo, to charm, to persuade that he understood. And he wasn't entirely wrong. Even a strong woman like Joan Crawford, who admitted that for a time she was madly in love with Joe, said, "I don't know of any woman who knew him at all who wasn't in love with him. At one time or another, all the ladies at M-G-M were in love with him." But while Joe had been able to imbue Crawford and so many of the others with a kind of confidence that they otherwise may have lacked—Joe's "crooked little smile that was absolutely irresistible to any woman . . . gave me such a feeling of security I felt I could do anything in the world once I got on that stage"—for Rosa, he could only try, and fail, to keep her confidence up. Yet because of her cultured background, he also

sensed that in some deep way she was worthy of him, as the others were not. For someone like Joe who didn't really want to be known, someone with what Addison DeWitt later called "an inability to love or be loved" and who told Ken Geist that he became so "adept at participating in almost everything without becoming part of anything," it was a perfect marriage.

But what did marriage mean to the Joe Mankiewicz of the early 1940s? Think of Joe's depiction of Katharine Hepburn as the successful journalist diminished to a groveling hausfrau—

Joe with his boys, Chris (left) and Tom (right), c. 1944

not too far from the domestic situation he created for himself. Rosa Stradner's exotic talent, discovered by Mayer, had been whisked off to Hollywood without protection. When the roles dried up and her emotional health wavered, she was happy to blame Joe for ending her career and subjugating her to a subservient wifely role. While life on the stage and screen had made her feel alive, Rosa was stifled by Joe's expectations—to be the perfect hostess to the never-ending stream of Hollywood types who Joe brought home, and to take care of babies Chris and Tom. As Joe never wanted to consider anyone, especially a woman, his equal, the lopsided domestic dynamic he portrayed on screen and in his marriage was his ideal.

In the meantime, Rosa was never alone in being the object of Joe's attention and desires. At the studio, the process by which Joe came to know actresses—convincing them to speak at length about their own lives, encouraging them to share details with him about their relationships with their mothers—often came with an agenda. According to Lyle Wheeler, an art director who worked with Joe on many projects at Fox, Joe definitely thought he would get more out of his leading ladies if they were in love with their producer. Again and again, in his many romantic affairs, women succumbed to Joe's charms, as a wise man/psychoanalyst, confessor/lover. Sometimes subtly, sometimes more crudely, Joe undermined these self-confident women (as Tracy's character does Hepburn's), making them feel weak, insecure, and vulnerable. This may have been key to his technique in wooing women. Giving women the feeling that only he can help them get through the traumatic elements of their life (elements that he himself has forced them to confront) was likely at least in part, as Chris suggests, a manipulative scheme to win them over romantically. It "was his way of getting girls in the sack," Chris said. "It was manipulation, an intellectual game."

The game was a dark one, and ultimately unwinnable: Joe's desire to prevail, to get the script, the Oscar, to have the power, and to prove that he could beat anyone in town was matched by an insatiable desire to be adored by his actresses, for them to want him, to need him. As he tried to distinguish himself from his brilliant, sloppy, irresponsible, and raging brother, he built a façade of near invulnerability, someone who could advise the beautiful women who needed him, hear their worries, and comfort them.

For Rosa, then, the nightmare of her life was to oscillate back and forth between being condescended to—looked after, maybe even with a

"The pain is invisible": Rosa, Joe, and the boys,
early 1940s

gentle touch, but there was no mistaking Joe's superiority as he tended her needs with such an ostentatious uxoriousness—and being cheated on. This kind, misplaced swan from the Vienna stage, emotional and lost to begin with, was being driven slowly mad by a man who pretended to care for her—hell, he did care for her—but continued to philander and so drive her into paroxysms of jealousy.

So it was that Rosa Stradner, living with Joe, became classified as mentally ill. She went to sanatoriums. She fought with Joe, bitterly. She threw things at him. He ducked, and the items hit the wall. He tried to soothe her, all soft tones and honeyed phrases. She yelled. He yelled back. She threw more. He clenched his pipe in his mouth and walked out—would go for long drives, to this or that starlet's house, for affairs that were far more than mere flings. "It was not a *thing*," Joe said indignantly when Ken Geist used the word to describe one such relationship with actress Linda Darnell. "I don't have *things*!" On the tape, you hear a pause, then a silence and the draw on his pipe as he tries to get his mind off the unpleasant Rosa. Linda, he finally says, was a "marvelous girl with very terrifying personal problems." The attraction to unbalanced women was constant. Rosa. Darnell. Crawford.

Then of course there was Judy Garland.

When you're Judy Garland, say, and at age three, you're shoved onto a stage into a spotlight to sing "Jingle Bells," and from that moment on, you're told and told and told by everyone—from audiences that cheer you in that spotlight when you sing, to a draconian mother who drills the unshakable conviction into you (you'll carry it with you until you die)—that only in that spotlight, singing as loud as you can . . . were you even acceptable to society, much less attractive in any way at all—how the hell can you possibly, for the rest of your life, *know who you really are?*

—JOE MANKIEWICZ, 1972

Joe's affair with Judy Garland blossomed at a curious moment in his domestic life. Rosa had just been committed to the Menninger Clinic in Topeka, Kansas, for the first time. She was sent there for nine months of treatment after a particularly hellish battle with Joe had left her in a near-catatonic state. So Joe was, in a sense, looking for a new "case," and in late 1942, twenty-year-old Judy Garland was a willing and available patient. She was also temporarily unattached because her year-and-a-half marriage to musician David Rose was ending. Joe said, "I'd never met someone like Judy at the time. I'm not talking about her talent. She was the most remarkably bright, gay, happy, helpless, and engaging girl I'd ever met."

But Judy was different from the starlets who typically shared his bed. "You can write down everything Lana Turner ever thought and felt and meant," he said years later, "and then put the pencil down," he said. "That's it, a closed book. But I don't think anybody's going to close the book on Judy Garland." He was particularly fascinated by her psychological condi-

Gene Kelly and Judy Garland in *The Pirate*

tion, why she clung to her lovers like a safety net, and why at twenty years old she still consulted her mother and M-G-M studio chief Louis B. Mayer about every element of her life, down to what color lipstick to put on in the morning.

Since the moment "Baby" had stepped on stage at age three with her two older sisters, Jimmie and Mary Jane, Garland had been instructed that all that mattered was her performance on stage. Ethel Marion Milne, Judy's mother, whose life's ambition was to make her daughter a star, was overbearing and severe, sometimes locking Baby in closets to force obedience. Constantly pushing her daughter to exhaustion with a brutal regimen of dance and voice classes, auditions, and performances, Ethel gave Judy pep pills for the day and counteracted them with sleeping pills at night.

When Judy was signed by Metro at age thirteen, Ethel finally met her match, Mayer, who was just as eager to mold Judy into a star. Calling her "my little hunchback," Mayer felt Judy Garland's body was the property of M-G-M, contributing to her overall feeling that she was an ugly duckling. Battles were fought over every French fry and spoonful of ice cream, ending ultimately in Judy adding diet pills to her drug cocktail. By the time Joe met her, the barrage of criticism had crushed her self-esteem. "Until M-G-M I had enjoyed being myself," she said later. "I had been judged by my talent, but in the movies beauty was the standard of judgment— and definitely I didn't have it." Her abuse by the studio has been well documented. Between 1939 and 1943, she was a virtual indentured servant to M-G-M, making ten pictures in all. On the rare occasions that she was not completely done in from exhaustion at the end of the day and ventured out on the L.A. club scene, a publicist from Metro, stationed at all major clubs, would ridicule her, worried that one too many sightings in clubs would tarnish Judy's virginal, girl-next-door image.

Horror mingled with fascination for Joe as Judy regaled him with tales over late-night drinks about the years of anguish at the hands of M-G-M and her mother. Judy had grown up on Lot One, she explained, and Joe realized everyone still treated her like that thirteen-year-old girl who had first come on the set. Joe knew Mayer was trapping Judy in roles of girl-next-door teenage fluff, one-dimensional characters not worthy of her talent. Don't take every shitty role offered to you, he urged. She needed a protector from her mother and the studio, someone who didn't care about her money—and Joe was happy to play the part.

Joe knew she was harboring unconscious hostility toward Mayer and mother, so he brought Judy to the same Dr. Menninger who had treated his wife. Menninger would become the first in a long line of trained psychiatric professionals to meet with Judy Garland, and he would not be the last to suggest that Ms. Garland had serious problems. But Menninger's prescription was unrealistic, though not at first to Joe's ears: The good doctor advised that Judy should be in treatment for at least a year, away from Hollywood. With Mayer's need to keep her star burning as brightly as possible,

Judy Garland in the 1940s

such a treatment was of course impossible, and Mayer told Joe so. Joe didn't miss a beat. He devised another plan, and so soon Judy, now fully trusting Joe to understand her needs, was getting out of bed an hour early each day, before work required her presence at the studio, so that she could sit instead on the couch of none other than Dr. Ernst Simmel, the same renowned Freudian whom Herman had seen. There, in the deepest Freudian psychoanalysis the town could muster, she would, Joe hoped, pour out her anguish and come to understand her demons, and also, perhaps, become aware of her immense gratitude for the man who was making it happen.

That man, of course, was not Louis B. Mayer.

The truth is, Mayer was a difficult man to work for, and Joe had done it long enough.* That the final straw would come was never really in doubt. Joe's decision to introduce Judy to psychoanalysis provided it at last. Like all the early moguls, Mayer had downplayed his religious and cultural identity ("hide the Jew" in him, in one mogul's colorful phrase) in order to gain mass acceptance for his movies, and so he had become a full-throated proponent of Mom, baseball, and apple pie. Psychoanalysis,

---

* In later years, Joe used to joke that Mayer was such a monster that he was sympathetic to the Nazis and agreed with them about everything—except one issue; but even on that one issue, Joe said, "Mayer was willing to negotiate."

Dr. Freud's "Jew religion," which by stressing the Oedipal tendencies of young boys and the Electra complex of young girls, seemed to be undercutting or at least muddying the clarity and goodness of one's central relationship with one's mother, was not to be trusted.

And Mayer had an ally: Ethel didn't like the "Jew therapy" either. She insisted that Mayer step in and remove psychoanalysis—and Joe—from Judy's life, and Mayer was only too happy to oblige. Since Judy had begun sessions with Simmel, Ethel had felt her influence slipping away. Asserting her own independence, questioning authority, Judy was changing and Ethel was alarmed. Mayer was not happy that anyone was rattling his big moneymaker, and undermining the sacred role of mother.

Finally, Joe and Mayer had a showdown in Mayer's office on the M-G-M lot. Mayer, who had always been suspicious of Joe, insisting on calling him "Harvard" in story conferences,* told Joe in no uncertain terms to stay away from Judy Garland. He then gave a long, impassioned homily about the importance and divinity of mothers. Mothers were holy, Mayer told Joe, and Judy Garland had to leave analysis immediately. Matching the mogul's clichés, Joe told Mayer that the studio wasn't big enough for the two of them and stormed out of the meeting.

That the final straw for Joe was Mayer's insistence on the holiness of the matriarchal role is illuminating. Like Herman, Joe rarely talked about his mother. To the Mankiewicz boys, it's as if their mother didn't exist. One can imagine Dr. Fred Hacker, Joe's own long-time psychoanalyst and eventually a family friend to many Mankiewiczes, waxing about how curious it was that it was Mayer's bringing up the importance of Mother that tipped Joe over the edge. The mother was inescapable, the root, primal. Joe would dispute it—she meant nothing, it was always Pop. Of course, as Hacker no doubt pointed out to Joe, in leaving Mayer, he was also defying his own current father figure.

For Joe, escaping M-G-M and Mayer was the final step—what he called the end of his "black period" and the beginning of a kind of professional adulthood, of making his own way at last, starting down the path that would eventually lead to the director's chair. Herman wouldn't help him get there. Joe would do it on his own. He would live or die on his own merits, and on what he was able to do for whatever studio he ended up with. As for his heart, he had plans for that little instrument.

The heart, though, has plans of its own. We can anticipate what it will

---

* Joe said it was the only college Mayer had heard of.

do, but we can never truly know. So while we may think that Mama is a fool and an illiterate, we may be surprised by the surge of irrational hatred that courses through us when our stubby little hydrant of a boss brings her up in an argument, forcing us, despite our intentions, to speak in hot temper even when we had not planned to.

Young Judy, of course, didn't know that Joe's defiance of Mayer was in part the surface of an internal struggle over feelings about his own parents. Instead, Judy saw Joe's choice to quit M-G-M as the ultimate declaration of love and devotion. He was her hero, and this was her kind of love. The ideal man in her eyes, Joe was a standard by which she would measure all later lovers. She confided in her sister that she couldn't imagine ever meeting a man as brilliant, kind, and attentive.

For his part, Joe did care about Judy deeply. He would never stop fighting to get her the help she needed and the parts she deserved. But his feelings did not match Judy's, not by a long shot. Speaking to Garland's biographer Gerald Clarke, he explained the nurturing kind of love he felt for her: "I was in love—and I know this is a terrible analogy—the way you love an animal, a pet." But while she was hearing wedding bells, Joe was hearing something else: the impending return of Rosa, who was coming home from the clinic in Topeka. After months of mostly furtive meetings, Joe broke the news to Judy that their affair had to come to an end. At the time, Judy took it well—like a champion, Joe thought. It was as if she'd both been expecting it, and, more terrifyingly, that she didn't really believe it.

As for Rosa, the homecoming was hardly what anyone would have wanted. There were, almost immediately, more tears, more fights, and eventually one frightening scene in a bungalow when Tom saw his mother go after his father with an actual carving knife. Even the aftermaths were scary, Rosa walking into Tom's room the morning after the storm had passed, sitting on the boy's bed and saying, glassy-eyed and blank, "I'm sorry, Tom. I'm so, so sorry." And then, allowing herself to collapse into tears, and crying with her boy, shuddering the whole time.

She was desperately ill, and no one knew how to help the poor woman. But can it have helped to be married to a man like Joe? Someone who sought control in everything he did, who was horror-struck at the thought that anyone knew how sick his wife was, even as he also played for whatever sympathy he could get? He would sit there, stoically, as she ran off at the mouth, cursing him for having ruined her career, for forcing her into the airless role of housewife, when she'd had such a promising future as an actress; pipe in mouth, Joe would listen and nod and then, when the steam had finally run down, would launch into a calm psychoanalytic disquisition on what was ailing her. Mad woman indeed. In his view, though, she simply had a desperate need to create drama. She had grown up in a family with a rich military background, but where the men and boys were the center of the action; only on the stage could Rosa claim an equal share of the attention. Now, with her career stalled, taking a back seat to being mother to Chris and Tom and playing the less than satisfying fulltime role of Mrs. Joseph Mankiewicz, she sought drama wherever and however she could find it.

For Joe, it was the thunder and the storm yet again—what he was drawn to, irresistibly. A great storm, a howling wind, with him always at the cyclone's calm eye, watching the rage swirl, and even seeming to gain strength from it. Was it possible that he could find a way to orchestrate such a storm, gain control of it too, and in so doing master all the turmoil that had churned around him at the start? There was certainly room to try.

Another storm soon clamored for his notice. Judy Garland had not given up easily. She telephoned "the most wonderful man she ever met" one afternoon in late 1943 or early 1944, and announced in that breathless way that Joe and audiences found so thrilling, that she was pregnant with his child. Joe took it ruefully. A pregnancy was largely wishful thinking, but he knew that she knew that it would get his attention, far more than love letters, flowers, or phone calls. Joe was convinced that the pregnancy was a ruse—more because of the way she told him rather than any physical impossibility—but he felt he could not call her out on the lie without injuring her fragile ego, so he agreed to join Judy on a secret trip to New York. There, in a doctor's office on Sixth Avenue, an abortion would be performed, once the pregnancy was clearly established. First, the hesitant ex-lovers waited in an East Side apartment for the results of a pregnancy test. To no one's surprise, the test results came back negative. Joe recalled that after that, "a little happy, a little sad," the two of them went back to Grand Central and boarded a train back to Los Angeles.

Although Joe urged Judy to move on, he was the love of her life, and to Joe's frustration, she wouldn't let him forget it. For the next decade or more, she was often asked to sing at Hollywood parties, and if Joe happened to attend, her song of choice was always Harold Arlen's "Happiness is a Thing Called Joe," which she sang at the piano with every eye on her. For Joe, it was a mix of embarrassment and pride to be the subject of her singing. Judy Garland, after all, was a brilliant and well-practiced performer, and she knew how to look pointedly at Joe while singing but with enough subtlety that no one else would notice. He urged her to stop, but she would laugh in coy refusal, her eyes glittering in triumph.

While Joe found her neediness annoying, and never again reciprocated her feelings, speaking to Clarke decades after her death he could not deny that what he had with Judy was special: "I've had my share of affairs with women," he said. "But they only exist as affairs with women. Every year, as I grow older, the memory . . . grows dimmer and dimmer. That isn't the case with Judy. I remember her as I would remember an emotion, a mood, an emotional experience that is now an event."

> Of all the females that inhabit the society of theater folk, the one for whom I have always felt the greatest compassion is she for whom, in that society, only one role is available: that of "wife to _____."
>
> —JOSEPH L. MANKIEWICZ, 1972

JOE LANDED AT FOX AFTER LEAVING M-G-M, AND HIS FIRST DECISION there was fascinating. As his first picture to produce, he chose *The Keys of the Kingdom,* based on a novel by A. J. Cronin. Immediately, he rewrote Nunnally Johnson's script,[*] about a humble Catholic priest, Father Chisholm (Gregory Peck), who withstands all manner of adversity and cruelty in serving thirty-five years as a missionary in a small Chinese village. Hoping for the same kind of lightning that had struck with other high-class literary adaptations set in foreign locales such as *How Green Was My Valley* or *Goodbye, Mr. Chips,* the studio intended the movie to make great use of the foreign setting. And to take fullest advantage of the exoticism the movie called for, Joe decided to cast, in the small but pivotal role of the stern European Mother Superior who disapproves of our hero, an actress he

"Wife to ____." Rosa Stradner in *The Keys of the Kingdom* (1944)

---

* The arbitrators at the Screen Writers Guild ruled it a cocredit.

knew well who had begun her career on the Viennese stage: one Rosa Stradner.

Of course, it was not easy to cast his wife in the part. Though she had retained her striking beauty, the studio had hesitations—in part because the male star of the film, Gregory Peck, was young and largely untested, with only the as-yet-unreleased film *Days of Glory* under his belt. At the start of shooting, even after Rosa was cast, Ingrid Bergman, a bona fide box office draw coming off the hits *Casablanca* and *For Whom the Bell Tolls* and studio head Darryl Zanuck's first choice for the role, became available. In a stunning act of chauvinism, Zanuck told Joe he'd give Rosa a two-picture deal if she stepped aside.* According to Nunnally Johnson, Joe got down on his hands and knees and pleaded with the studio to keep Rosa, and though Joe denied making such a dramatic appeal, there's no doubt he needed Rosa to make the film. In the first place, it would get her out of the house and working again, away from the role of housewife she felt so confined and restricted by. Whether this particular role would actually serve to launch Rosa into the upper firmament of film stars was another story. In the end, the Bergman deal collapsed, perhaps because the role in question was small, largely unsympathetic, and quite curious indeed.

That the one role Joe Mankiewicz ever wrote for his wife was that of a haughty and superior Catholic nun (literally, a Mother Superior), who treats the hero of the picture with thinly disguised contempt on meeting him, is interesting enough. But more curious is how the relationship developed between our hero Father Chisholm, a man who "failed in all things, except an understanding of his fellow man," and the imperious Austrian-born nun, Maria-Veronica.† For while at first the Mother Superior, arriving at the Chinese village with two other nuns a day ahead of schedule and catching the priest unaware and in shirtsleeves, is disappointed in everything he does, toward the end of the movie, after witnessing his near-saintly response to mistreatment by others, in addition to physical heroism in defending his beloved church, she has a complete change of heart. On the eve of her departure from China after her difficult stay, she approaches the priest in his church and tells him she needs to tell him something, and it isn't easy for her to say. Peck nods gently, encouraging her to unburden her heart, which she does, abjectly:

---

* There is no record of Zanuck speaking to Rosa herself about this possibility.

† Joe changed the nationality, which had been Bavarian in the book, for Rosa.

From our first meeting . . . I have behaved shamefully and sinfully toward you. I want you to know that I am most bitterly sorry for my conduct. Believe me, no apology was ever more abject than mine . . . nor has anyone ever been less worthy of forgiveness.

Joe's wish fulfillment is working overtime here, putting words into his wife's mouth that he must have dearly loved to hear her say off-screen. For her confession wasn't just about her cruelty and coldness, but for her contempt for the man she had lived with side by side, whose virtues only made her own seem puny:

I was born into arrogance, Father, and taught contempt for those who were not. How could I hope to live by the word of God which is the same for all men? From the beginning, your presence tortured me. I knew that yours was a true humility and that mine was a duty. I resented your deep and honest compassion because mine was difficult and filled with doubt and pain.

Gregory Peck, Joe's stand-in here, has little to do but gently accept this most submissive apology, to bask in the compliment and tell her she needn't apologize. "You know," he says piously, "we're all children to God, and with His help, we'll work and mature." Fade out . . . on the scene, and on Joe's hopes for how his marriage would resolve itself.

Instead, after the picture was completed, but just six weeks before it was released to the public, a small item appeared in the *Los Angeles Times* of November 3, 1944, stating that Joe and Rosa had mutually agreed to separate, with Joe moving out of their home in Pacific Palisades and taking an apartment in Beverly Hills. The separation didn't last, and though there's no record of when or how the reconciliation was achieved, Joe maintained that though several analysts told him through the years he should leave the marriage, he felt he owed "an allegiance" to Chris and Tom to stay and try to make it work. So by the time *Keys of the Kingdom* opened in December, Joe and Rosa were arm in arm at the premiere. Of the boys, neither would remember this particular separation, and Chris would always claim he saw almost nothing of his actual mother in the role she played in the film.

And so the miseries continued, for Joe and for Rosa, who would sob openly at dinner parties, yell and scream and race upstairs to shriek at the children, or complain about some guest or other molesting her, with Joe sometimes sitting quietly, sometimes trying to calm her, always dazed and despairing. Clearly, Joe needed these dramatic scenes too, and people who knew the couple sensed it. According to composer Johnny Green, "They wouldn't have lasted if there wasn't some need." The fights were nearly constant, and often played out for an audience of friends and intimates. "Rosa would sit there sobbing while Joe walked out of the room, losing his temper: 'You see! How can a man live like this?'"

But Joe *could* live like that, and he did, though it was also clear that he dreamed for it to be over. If only Rosa would submit to him, she would find the happiness and peace she had been seeking all these years. As he'd had Mother Superior tell Father Chisholm in her apology, with a serene look overtaking Rosa's beautiful face, "How strange that the moment of my greatest humiliation should bring with it the only peace I've ever truly known."

But life off-screen, as Joe well knew, was not make-believe.

CHAPTER TEN

SHIPS IN THE NIGHT

If you'd only see her . . . You're her whole life—you must have
spotted her by now, she's always there.

—*ALL ABOUT EVE*

A MAN IS IN HIS EARLY FORTIES, HAVING SUFFERED THROUGH A VIRTUAL
lifetime of feeling that he has not fulfilled his potential, squandered his
talents on projects that are beneath him. Then, finally, with Herculean
effort, and through a fortuitous set of circumstances, he finds himself
summoning from the depths of his
experience and his soul The Great
Work, a piece that plumbs his deep
knowledge of American politics
and journalism and takes advantage of his special gifts as a wit. He
is rewarded for this work with his
industry's highest award, and in the
succeeding years the stature of this
work will only grow.

Why does this man not revive?
Why does his life continue on its
slow, gradual, even graceful downward spiral? Where is the restart
that he so desperately needed, and
that by God he'd now earned? Why
didn't it come?

For a moment, it appeared that

"Why did he not revive?"
Herman and his Oscar

New York's Mayor Fiorello La Guardia with Herman at
Yankee Stadium, shortly after *The Pride of the Yankees*

it might have. The calls that ricocheted around the Biltmore Hotel ballroom for Herman on the night of the 1942 Oscars continued to echo for
a few months. Looking at the bare facts of his career, the grandson-fan
can see that Herman soon earned another choice assignment—*The Pride
of the Yankees,* in the year following *Kane*—which, while not the groundbreaking film *Kane* was, is about as good a sports biopic as one could hope
for in Hollywood's golden age, with a wealth of powerful moments. To
his many baseball-loving descendants, these lines would be quoted and
requoted with glee: Lou Gehrig's German immigrant parents, who had
for so long held up to young Lou his (fictional) Uncle Otto as a paragon
whose career as an engineer should be emulated, rather than pursuing this
baseball nonsense, shouting out "Otto Schmotto" when Gehrig slams a
key home run; Gehrig telling Billy, the prototypical dying kid in a hospital, "I'll hit two homers for you if you hit one for me"; Lou telling the doctor who tells him he's dying of an unpronounceable disease (amyotrophic
lateral sclerosis, or ALS, soon to be known as Lou Gehrig's disease), "Well,
Doc, if I've learned one thing, it's that all the arguing in the world can't
change the decision of the umpire"; and finally, of course, what Herman
and his coconspirator on the screenplay Jo Swerling took from Gehrig's
actual speech on his retirement from baseball, though they moved it from
the beginning of Gehrig's speech to the end: "Today, I consider myself the
luckiest man on the face of the earth."* The taut screenplay earned Her-

---

* To my cousins and me, these were right up there with "Frankly, my dear, I don't
  give a damn."

man his second straight Academy Award nomination. (Again, he would not attend the ceremonies, and this time his pessimism would prove founded, for the film lost out to *Mrs. Miniver* in the adapted screenplay category). He was getting full-time work from the studios again—Fox, Columbia, Universal. So—what happened?

First of all, alcohol. After *Kane*, Herman tried for a time to repeat what had worked in Victorville: no drinking (or not much—he and Houseman, remember, would head down to that desert canteen for a nightly drink), and more discipline and devotion to the work. But he'd never respected the work in the first place, and it wasn't *Kane* anymore—the people making the movies weren't interested in breaking new forms, or tackling great subjects, or tearing down iconic figures like William Randolph Hearst. They didn't want Herman's greatest expressions on journalism, politics, human psychology, or even memory ("a white dress she had on"). They wanted formula, dependability, hits. And so, as it happened, shortly after Franz's death, Herman began to drink again, heavily. Welles's dismissal of the Rosebud technique—"dollar book Freud"—comes to mind, for it's as if Herman's self-destructiveness simply wouldn't allow him to conquer the demons of the past. And without Franz to resist, to rebel against, and to measure his failure against, it's as if Herman didn't know where to turn. Without the sand in the oyster, how could he possibly make any more pearls, even if they were only cast before swine?

In addition, *Citizen Kane* laid a curious kind of curse on Herman. Kane's success had come with a man, Welles, who was himself so antagonistic to the Hollywood system that it had been a natural pairing for Herman, and the two men had enjoyed having their cake and eating it too—making the ultimate "movie movie" while at the same time thumbing their noses at Hollywood conventions. There was no way to repeat it, and Herman knew it would be fruitless to try, especially since after Kane and Welles he would be returning to a system that had less use of his particular genius.

So while some of the movies ended up being entertaining enough (*The Pride of the Yankees* would be joined in this class by the compellingly strange noir *Christmas Holiday* and the Jack Oakie vehicle *Rise and Shine*, based on a Thurber short story), they were anything but entertaining experiences for Herman. And the drinking didn't help. It certainly didn't help his relationship with the producer of *The Pride of the Yankees*, the maddening and prolific Sam Goldwyn. While Herman could be very funny when talking about working for Goldwyn—the ex-haberdasher-now-mogul wanted the game shortened to two strikes and three balls, Herman claimed, because baseball dragged: "Can we do that, Mank? Make it strike two, you're out!"—he was humiliated in the actual writing process. Unbeknownst to Herman, Goldwyn at one point hired another writer to write a parallel script, then when he spotted Herman inebriated one afternoon, summoned Herman into his office to read the script, showing him what a real screenwriter could do without drinking. Herman glanced through the other man's pages, then said: "He should drink."

In truth, Goldwyn proved so impossible to work with on *The Pride of the Yankees*—with an irritating combination of stubborn ignorance about baseball and bizarre attention to the movie's every single detail—that he practically drove any teetotalers on the set to the bottle. M-G-M veteran director Sam Wood, who was known for controlling his temper and proudly never yelled on set, could not hold back his criticism of Goldwyn in a note to Herman: "I dismiss Goldwyn as a loathsome person, something you would expect to find under damp logs when you roll them over. If he had been where he belongs, making button holes, we would have had a better picture." Working with Goldwyn only deepened Herman's frustration that with nearly everyone around him playing the Hollywood game, he could no longer hope to find many people to work with who even wanted to turn the system on its head.

For Herman, the years after *Kane* were a succession of those kinds of experiences—he wasn't the young whippersnapper anymore, and the competition was no longer idiots, but ambitious young Sammy Glicks who were less willing to sit with the aging self-loathing screenwriter in the commissary and hang on his every word about how stupid and corrupt everything was. Now, when they saw him coming, it was "Ho-ho, here comes crazy Mank," or, even worse, they'd slide out of the way.

The little matter of his younger brother becoming an even more powerful and successful man in the town surely did not help. Joe, now, lived in a bigger house, drove nicer cars, and had his phone calls returned. He was the rich uncle who gave his niece and nephews their biggest Christmas present, the one they would save for the last to open—"because it would always be something marvelous," according to my mother. The antagonism toward Joe grew. The totality with which Joe had accepted the rules of the Hollywood game, the thoroughly bankrupt values he had embraced . . . In the 1930s, when Herman signed a big contract at M-G-M, Sara had written Herman a letter instructing him how to treat the little *pisher:*

"Did you show that big producer Joe and his wife your contract and was he properly impressed and depressed? Please be very superior and important with him." Now that the roles were so obviously reversed, there was little to do but try to wring pleasure out of Joe's perceived moral failings, and his inability to get close to people. "Just once," Herman said, "I'd like to meet somebody at Joe's birthday party I'd seen the year before." The characters had solidified in nearly everyone's mind: Joe was cold and isolated, Herman a big-hearted mess. "Joe was a man of principles, a fighter for causes," Erna said, "but you could sit for an

"Young man, you must learn to crawl before you can walk": Joe Mankiewicz, c. 1940s

entire evening and be practically in tears, and he wouldn't notice. If there was something bothering you and you walked into a room where Herman was sitting reading, after three or four minutes he would look up and say, 'What's the matter, kid?'"

But as his drinking and gambling swelled, Herman's situation became ever more unstable. With increased debts came increased risks to try to earn money back. The family silver was pawned. The house was mortgaged more than once to pay off bookies. The good doctor Hacker analyzed it all as "a surrender gesture, an attempt to play forever the role of an infant, a total falling-apart, an inability to handle himself, total reliance on other people, particularly his wife, a real return to the womb," and even Herman recognized the horrors his behavior inflicted on those around him. The toll his misbehavior took on his wife and children made him miserable. He quoted a favorite playwright to make his point: "Like Shaw said, 'Parents should be a warning to their children, not an example.' Nobody can deny I've been a good bad example." Even toward Joe, Herman understood the role he was playing: "I've been an influence on Joe's life," he said, "but it's been mostly negative." After one particularly hellish evening when Joe had been witness to one of Herman's more bellicose drunken performances at a producer's dinner party—vomiting, insulting the producer, calling the producer's wife names—Joe asked

Herman, "How can you do this? It's so embarrassing to the people who invited you." Herman responded: "Who invited me? I crashed the party."

Many of the other so-called "best" Herman Mankiewicz stories come from this period, though a drumbeat of misery plays under all of them: Herman, fired for drinking at Universal and replaced by a man named Dwight Taylor, marching soberly into an executive's office a week later and getting his job back by asking, "Don't you think Herman Mankiewicz drunk is still better than Dwight Taylor sober?" Herman, telling a friend that with the help of psychoanalysis, he had finally determined that he wasn't a drunk: "It is not Herman Mankiewicz who is drinking. It is the little boy in me!" Most famously, the encounter with the head of Columbia, Harry Cohn, when Cohn was explaining to a roomful of executives and writers that he knew a movie was lousy when his ass twitched during the screening. Herman leered at Cohn, and the story goes that one man even whispered, "Don't say it, Mank," but it was impossible for Herman to resist. "What makes you think," Herman asked after an impudent pause, "that you have the monitor ass for the entire world? Where is it written that your ass is wired to all other asses?"* (He was fired the next day.)

There was no escaping the dreadful fact that he liked the work even less than ever. The movies included the creaky melodramatic romance *The Enchanted Cottage,* the costume spectacular *The Spanish Main,* and so many others for which he received, thankfully, no credit† that he ended up telling Joseph Cotten, "My contract says I have to come to work and write so many hours a day. But it doesn't say I have to admit what I'm writing." John Houseman summed up Herman's predicament: "When you can earn twenty-five hundred dollars a week making jokes, and working two or three hours a day in the studio and having long lunches and getting drunk or making more jokes, why would you go to an attic and beat

---

* As with many famed witticisms, there is no actual record of how it was first said, and I've seen this particular remark phrased in at least half a dozen ways. While it is often cited as "Imagine—the whole world wired to Harry Cohn's ass," it's likely Herman avoided the acting that phrasing required and opted instead for the familiar Mankiewiczian trope invoking writing.

† My other grandfather, Frank Davis, once apologized to Herman for having rewritten him on a picture for RKO called *Fighting Father Dunne,* and Herman said, "Frank, that's great. You write me out of it, then you get someone else to write you out of it."

your brains out doing something you're afraid you might not be able to do?"

Herman was in fact still submitting occasional satirical pieces to magazines, but most went unpublished, and he was so stung by the impersonal rejection letters he received from *The New Yorker* that he wrote his old adversary Harold Ross a funny if heartbreaking letter stating, "Somebody is getting your mail before it reaches you and attempting to ruin you by returning all worthwhile contributions." Thereafter, the rejection letters came from Ross himself, including one which stated

Herman in the 1940s, when it was all about lunch

baldly why Herman was trying too hard: "It is overweighted because you are in California, wasting the best years of your life."

Herman, of course, disagreed. The best years had already been wasted.

JOE'S ESCAPE FROM LOUIS B. MAYER WORKED OUT BEAUTIFULLY. AS his contract still had nearly two years to run, it was left to Mayer to decide what to do. In those days, the studios would assign contracts to other studios when situations like this occurred, and Joe was worried he would get sent to Warner's where he would likely never get a chance to direct his own pictures. Instead, Mayer—feeling guilty, or just unknowingly—did Joe the greatest favor he possibly could have by sending him to 20th Century–Fox. There, Joe negotiated a deal that not only gave him a slight raise but in which the studio promised him that he would be given a chance to direct at last.

Sitting in a director's chair for the first time did not provide Joe an epiphany. It didn't announce to him anything he hadn't already known. This was where he had wanted to be for some time—the director controlled everything in a picture—and now that he'd finally gotten here, it felt right and inevitable and just plain decent. He'd worked hard for it, and he wasn't going to squander the opportunity.

And so in the late forties Joe Mankiewicz, sober and dutiful, directed his first five movies, learning a little more each time. Careful and precise, unafraid to admit what he didn't know about directing, Joe was wise and smart on these films—taking baby steps in each one to better himself and his directing technique, and deliberately choosing scripts others had written so as to focus on learning his new craft. On his first film, *Dragonwyck,* he learned much about camera placement from his cameraman, Arthur Miller, who told Joe just to place the camera where he would want it to be in a theater* and also said to him, "I have all these other directors' experience at your disposal—for Chrissake take advantage of it;" on his second film, the mystery *Somewhere in the Night,* Joe knew that suspenseful night and fog sequences would require expert editing and so asked the editor, James Clark, to be on set as much as possible to ensure he got the proper coverage; on *The Late George Apley,* Joe, worried that his films were becoming too stagey, fell so much in love with crane shots that he received word from his producer Darryl Zanuck: "you've earned your wings, you can come down now." Through it all, he was learning, studying, and working to understand his hard-earned role. And the movies themselves, while no masterpieces, are models of a kind of '40s studio efficiency, but with enough traces of wit to suggest that more than a mere studio hack was at the helm. Many of the performances—both from those, like Walter Huston and Vincent Price in *Dragonwyck,* who were used to acting with spirit, as well as some, like Nancy Guild in *Somewhere in the Night* or Vanessa Brown in *The Late George Apley,* who were not—glow with life.

For while the technical side would never come easily to Joe, directing actors would prove much easier. It was there he shone from the start. For one thing, Joe had a genius for finessing those around him into doing what he wanted. He was affable, gentle, persuading, and always so erudite and intelligent that his actors felt listened to and understood. He spoke with them at length, especially the actresses, about their own lives and—that favorite word of Joe's—their "neuroses." They came to feel so known by him that it was no surprise that more than a few of them did end up in love with him. At his office on the lot, he kept a drawer full of gold pencils, all given to him by actresses. Gene Tierney fell under Joe's

---

* Miller took pity on Joe, who had looked through the wrong end of the viewfinder on his first day on the set, and gave Joe a somewhat sneaky strategy for dealing with cameramen. He told Joe to choose a spot for the camera but not tell his cameraman, instead asking them where *they* thought it should go. If they agreed with Joe, so much the better. If not, Joe was instructed to say, "Yes, that's what I was thinking too" and so preserve his authority and directorial control.

Gene Tierney in *Dragonwyck* (1946)

spell and as a result was able to deliver, in *The Ghost and Mrs. Muir,* the most sensitive work of her career, as a believably repressed and intelligent woman who finds herself in love with the ghost of a salty sea captain (Rex Harrison, preening, obnoxious, brilliant). When seen today, the performances are nuanced, human, and full of a kind of relaxed compassion rare in studio films of the era. While Joe would later tell Ken Geist that in this first batch of films he was concentrating upon learning the craft of directing and the technical side of the job, it's also true that the performances throughout are almost uniformly excellent.

At last, on *Escape,* his fifth picture for Fox, as they were setting up for a shot, Joe let Rex Harrison in on a little secret. Harrison was a gifted stage actor who was doing his best to tone down his natural ham for the camera, and Joe was helping enormously, as he also had in *The Ghost and Mrs. Muir.* Indeed, Joe considered Harrison such a great instrument capable of speaking intelligent and erudite dialogue that he would end up modestly referring to the actor as his very own "Stradivarius" and cast him several times over the next three decades (most notably in *Cleopatra* and *The Honey Pot*), something of an alter ego for Joe. Now, looking at the technicians on the Dartmoor stage set in England where *Escape* was filmed, he pulled Harrison off to the side. "I suppose," he confided, "that this shall be the last film I shall ever direct unless I have written it myself." It was said almost casually, the way he liked to talk to actors, keeping them comfortable and in his orbit. But Harrison understood immediately that Joe was dead set on directing his own stories from now on.

Joe may have been the inspiration for Sammy Glick, the hero of Budd Schulberg's lacerating satire of Hollywood, *What Makes Sammy Run?*

The question was: what stories did Joe have to tell?

First up was one that took full advantage of Joe's love of women, flashbacks, and voice-over. Yet Joe's role in creating the film *A Letter to Three Wives* was far from certain at the outset. After Zanuck purchased the short story "One of Our Hearts" by John Klempner, a *Cosmopolitan* story that the author later expanded into what Joe called an unnecessarily dull and long novel, Joe got to work to create an acceptable treatment. He pored over his treatment late into the night, listening to the British rain after long days of work on *Escape*. But his first draft did not meet Zanuck's expectations, and Joe was crushed; the story had so much potential, and he was certain he could turn it into something great.

In fact, Zanuck and Joe had long held each other in mutual wary contempt, so it is hardly a surprise that Zanuck favored another producer's treatment and gave him the go ahead to make the film. To Zanuck's chagrin, that producer, Sol C. Siegel, then turned around and selected Joe to write and direct the picture. Zanuck's protestation over the choice was memorable: "For Chrissake, that arrogant bastard. I can't get along with him now, after four flops. If he gets a hit with this, he'll be unlivable!" Siegel replied, "I'll take my chances."

Joe had to admit that Zanuck's intuition was brilliant when taking a first look at a script or a picture, and he was sheepishly appreciative when Zanuck wisely diagnosed that the problem to Joe's overly long original script "*A Letter to Four Wives*" was "you've got one wife too many." But by and large, Joe was wary of giving Zanuck too much time with an editor's pen—the longer Zanuck had to analyze a film, Joe felt, the higher the chance he would cut from peak to peak of action. Joe liked words; Zanuck tolerated them. Yet Joe would always shake the hands of sons of bitches he hated, and so the two made their peace.

LIKE MANY ACTRESSES BEFORE AND AFTER HER, LINDA DARNELL, who played Lora Mae, the most captivating of the three wives, was swept away by Joe. He was funny, perceptive, handsome, attentive, and took her seriously in a way that her husband, the cinematographer J. Peverell "Pev" Marley, never managed to. Like Garland, Darnell had a terrible relationship with her mother and would empty her heart out to Joe at private lunches in his dressing room. Intrigued by her neuroses, Joe readily dispensed his psychoanalytic advice, which she consumed eagerly along with her baked pears. As he did with many of his actors, Joe helped cultivate her talent, leading to a subtle and sophisticated performance that made people respond to her for the first time as a serious actress. *Time* wrote of her performance: "Miss Darnell, who can be a temptress without even trying, has never shown so strikingly that she can be an actress as well."

The fact is, Joe fleshed out the anxieties of his female characters with a sensitivity far ahead of his time. The movie begins with all three wives confronting their fear of being replaced by another woman after they get a letter from friend Addie Ross saying, "I've run off with one of your husbands." Addie Ross's voice (Celeste Holm: delicious, never seen) was soft, insistent, and even mildly threatening—but at the same time richly sympathetic as it kicked off the plot. The story was divided into thirds, using Joe's signature flashbacks to tell the stories of three women's fears, which went far beyond infidelity, abandonment, and betrayal to the core social

Jeanne Crain, Ann Sothern, and Linda Darnell in
A Letter to Three Wives

Joe directs Linda Darnell in *A Letter to Three Wives,* 1948

anxieties women felt about rising in the middle class after World War II, with mobility eased by economic and social change. Unlike many films of the time, Joe elevates women's fears to the level of public discourse—advocating they be taken seriously. Joe's social awareness was undeniable: all three of the movie "wives" must negotiate tensions between private and public lives in ways that were fascinating and germane to movie audiences of the late '40s.

First, he tells the story of a country girl Deborah (Jeanne Crain), who, when she sheds her service uniform, is suddenly on unequal terrain with her wealthy suburbanite husband (Jeffrey Lynn). The story of a wartime union bridging social divides may feel familiar to a modern audience but was novel at the time. As an outsider worried she won't be accepted by her husband's friends, Deborah feels she has reverted to "a caterpillar while her husband remains a butterfly."

Unfortunately, Deborah's somewhat overlong speeches aren't helped by Jeanne Crain, who Joe felt brought little life to the role. And to Joe's dismay Jeffrey Lynn was hardly better as her husband. Joe was furious that Zanuck had foisted these two Fox contract actors on him, thus weakening the first part of the film. What was the point of "creative freedom" if Zanuck could throw bad actors into the mix? Joe had flaws on the technical side of directing but he could get great performances out of *his* actors! For the first time, Joe started mentioning to friends the idea of having his own production company, without execs like Zanuck who could shoot him in the foot.

The second wife, Lora Mae, played by Darnell, is a poor young woman who defies her smitten yet boorish wealthy boss (Paul Douglas), refusing to go to bed with him without a ring on her finger. The sexual frankness of the segment is unshocking but everywhere apparent, and as the plot unfolds, Darnell tames her brutish boss expertly, forcing him to act gallantly time and time again, until he finally laments, "You win, I'll marry you."[*] In fact, Joe turns the caricature of the gold digger on its head, suggesting Lora Mae is not selfishly marrying up, but envisioning a better life for her mother as well. Moreover, Lora Mae's psychological complexity is deepened when she worries later that her aggressiveness in courtship had been excessive—and Darnell's own combination of strength and vulnerability makes the sequence affecting and believable in a way that went beyond usual melodramas.

So too the third wife, Rita Phipps (Ann Sothern), departing from the one-dimensional characterization so familiar to moviegoers of the time, is a thoughtful portrait of a woman who struggles with maintaining a home and a family while holding down a job that requires her to work late into the night. This tension comes to a head when she forgets her husband's birthday, only to be reminded when Addie sends a birthday present.[†] As for Rita's husband George, Kirk Douglas brings the movie to rip-roaring cynical life when he attacks the mores of the day. A forerunner of Joe's more famous cinematic mouthpiece Addison DeWitt, George gave Joe the delightful opportunity to take shots at soap operas and advertising. As Franz's son, and Herman's brother, Joe had nothing but disdain for radio soap operas that he felt diminished the intelligence of its listeners, and advertisements that incited fear in consumers. Writing for a radio soap opera, Rita holds a dinner party and invites her producer, who insists they listen to two hours of radio instead of eating dinner. At the end of the night, George, bursting with contempt, finally, blurts out Joe's opinion of the industry:

---

[*] The line is the comic climax to a terrific scene, as Douglas's frustration mounts throughout, a train rattling ever closer to Darnell's house until he seizes her for an almost simian kiss as the train noise crescendoes.

[†] Joe would repeat the gesture, to even greater effect, when Eve remembers Bill Sampson's birthday in *All About Eve*.

The purpose of radio writing, as far as I can see, is to prove to the masses that a deodorant can bring happiness, a mouthwash guarantee success, and a laxative attract romance. "Don't think," says the radio, "and we'll pay you for it." Can't spell cat? Too bad. "But a yacht and a million dollars to the gentleman for being in our audience tonight." "Worry," says the radio. "Will your best friends not tell you? Will you lose your teeth? Will your cigarettes give you cancer? Will your body function after you're 35? If you don't use our product, you'll lose your husband, your job, and die! Use our product and we'll make you rich, we'll make you famous!"

The scene crackles not just because of Douglas's comic delivery, but because of the reaction shots of the producer and her husband, and Sothern's mix of exasperation and sympathy as her husband's fury surges. It's expertly written, yes, but more than that, as they've said in Hollywood story conferences for nearly a century, it *works*. The scene is tight and fun and funny, and each reaction shot builds on the previous one. Joe was getting the hang of directing, of telling a story in pictures as well as words.

The success of the film emboldened Joe, though it also threw his difficult personal life into relief. That he was now deep in a marriage that pleased neither participant was clear, but the irony was, he now had proof that his interest in the female psyche was paying off professionally. As he turned his attention to his next script, he had acquired his favorite themes and techniques. Women would be front and center, and voice-overs would help drive the story. While Celeste Holm would return, the rest of the cast would be new. The pieces were coming into place—the complex neuroses of the female characters, a few male characters to try to help the poor females, and somewhere off to the side, *of* the action but not *in* the action, a charismatic and nasty man dripping with bile, self-loathing, and contempt for much of the world he occupied . . .

Joe was ready for *Eve.*

CHAPTER ELEVEN

EVE

Nice speech, Eve. But I wouldn't worry too much about your heart. You can always put that award where your heart ought to be.

—*ALL ABOUT EVE*

HERMAN SAT IN THE JAIL CELL. HE WAS STONE COLD SOBER NOW—IT'S amazing how a car accident and a scuffle with the police had the power to clarify the mind almost instantaneously—but then again, he didn't really think he'd had all that much to drink. Now, he alternated between reliving the events of the evening, and seeing, with almost crystal clarity, how it would all play out. The future and the past were having a meeting in the present, and the present was a six-by-eight cell in the Los Angeles County jail.

He'd had a few drinks at Romanoff's, but probably not more than three. Four, tops. Then he'd driven up Benedict Canyon Drive toward home, and the next thing he knew he'd hit Lee Gershwin's car. Lee, wife of Ira, "the wrong Gershwin," had been in her little station wagon with her maid and her secretary. Mrs. Gershwin ended up with a nasty case of dashboard knees and a mean cut on her forehead, but the details were still a little fuzzy. Had she been driving? Why the hell was she driving? What was the point of having a secretary and a maid if neither of them could drive you places and prevent your car from being drifted into by a man with a lot on his mind?

That was hardly the worst of it. For in a life filled with self-inflicted wounds, this one, however accidental, was surely the finest example: the crash had happened right outside the large Benedict Canyon home belonging to Marion Davies, or more legally speaking, to William Randolph Hearst. The old man kept the house strictly for Marion's use. At the time of the crash, as Herman and the Gershwin party were trying to sort things out, with Herman apologizing and limping around the two cars and Mrs. Gershwin near a state of shock, Hearst happened to be on the estate playing cards with a publishing crony of his, William Curley, publisher of *The New York Journal-American*, whom he sent out to investigate. When he got back, Curley told the Chief he wasn't going to believe it. That the coauthor of *Citizen Kane* was now in Hearst's total power was delicious, a dessert too good for the Chief to pass up. By the time the Beverly Hills Police arrived on the scene, so too had the Hearst papers. As a result, the whole world, or so it seemed to Herman, would now know of his inability to walk a straight line.

Herman had argued bitterly with the cop administering the test—the man was an incompetent, and the line between the two cones he'd set up was almost criminally close to a white traffic line that was already painted on the ground—on which line did the officer want one to walk?—but all of Herman's arguing had done more harm than good, he knew that; he saw the man scribbling away in his notebook, who knows what kind of dark character assassination was going on in there—and then of course the indignity of being put in the back of the black-and-white, and hustled off to the jail for fingerprinting.

The rest was practically preordained. The Hearst press would delight in the story, flogging it day after day, releasing new sordid details—Mrs. Gershwin's injuries would multiply, grow more serious—how had the woman even survived? Before he knew what had happened, Herman would find himself promoted in the minds of his accusers from a middle-aged, flat-footed writer into Cary Grant, who, with a tank, had just drunkenly plowed into a baby carriage occupied by the Dionne quintuplets.

There'd be a trial, of course. Herman would be mortified by having to call character witnesses—he'd even summon Orson Welles, the big monkey would enjoy that—and in the end Herman and his lawyer Jerry Geisler (the same man who got Bugsy Siegel off, Herman would point out, "so we have hopes") would argue that the reason Herman failed the drunk test was *not* because he was drunk but because his left leg, ever since the crash in New Mexico, was now permanently shorter than the right. Dramatically, and with great Claudette Colbert style, Herman would hike his garment up from his left leg to display his shapely gam to the jury and convince them of the utter impossibility of his ever putting one foot directly in front of the other. Nothing quite like a hairless spindly limb to influence a jury of one's peers.

Herman didn't know quite how, but as he sat in the jail cell he was confident that this great public issue ("on which no Hearst paper would take no stand," he could practically hear *Citizen Kane*'s faux narration intone), would in the end blow over. And he was right. The trial would end with a hung jury, and Mrs. Gershwin, who originally sought more than $50,000 in damages from Herman, settled for a little more than $3,000. Herman himself would bellow out to Prince Mike as he left Romanoff's, "Call Mrs. Gershwin and tell her to stay the hell off the street for the next twenty minutes. Herman Mankiewicz is on his way home."

But now, as he sat in the cell waiting to be let out on bail, nothing struck him as particularly funny. He was tired, exhausted to his bones. His hair hurt. He felt as if it was an effort to keep his face from sliding off his skull.

And he realized quite simply and suddenly that he couldn't go on. It was nothing drastic, there would be no pills, no locking himself in the room over the garage and putting a single bullet into his brain—where would he find a gun, for one thing—not only that, he hated guns, what kind of message would that send to the boys, or Johanna for goodness sake, that their father, an avowed lifelong pacifist, decided to end it all by going out and purchasing a revolver at a gun shop in Encino . . . No, there'd be nothing dramatic, and God knows he would be happy to stay around as long as he possibly could, he wanted to see how it was all going to come out—whom would Don marry? His oldest son was still only twenty, and it would be years before Herman would become a father-in-law—but he was haunted by the growing certainty that he wouldn't be around at the end of this picture. What would happen to Don? To Frank? To say nothing of Johanna, she had years and years ahead of her. . . . He wanted to cry, but he couldn't. He knew he'd be lucky to last another five years, maybe ten, before the liver or the heart or the kidneys, whatever combination of organs that needed to be pumping and working to keep Herman Mankiewicz alive, gave out and he was left only with ambition and desire and rage, the cocktail that had kept him going, but which now seemed to be a watery recipe for nothing but a terminally diluted life.

IN 1971, THE AUTHOR GARY CAREY DROVE UP TO POUND RIDGE, NEW York, to interview the eminent director Joseph L. Mankiewicz for a book they were collaborating on, *More About All About Eve*. Carey thought to begin the process by asking Joe about the spark for his most celebrated film, presumably when he first read the short story on which the film was based, "The Wisdom of Eve," by Mary Orr. But Joe demurred. The story was valuable, of course, and had sparked Joe's imagination, but really, the germination of *All About Eve* had come much earlier. Joe had been fascinated by the outsized personalities who demanded to be the center of attention for decades. Whether in theater, on screen, or in life, Joe had always been drawn to dramatic characters. He told Carey, in only a slight exaggeration, "I often wonder why serious students of the human psyche look to anything but theatre-folk for most of the answers they seek." Joe was passionately interested in acting, in actresses, and in what he called "the quirks and frailties, the needs and talents of the performing personality." When Carey asked him about Mary Orr, Joe talked instead, for more than an hour, about the theater. The theater, he insisted, was why he created *Eve*.

Of course, Joe didn't create his masterpiece all by himself, and film's collaborative nature sometimes challenges easy interpretations. For just as Orson Welles didn't hurl a lightning bolt and create *Citizen Kane* out of nothing—he needed, in addition to Herman's talents and those of his cinematographer Gregg Toland and his actors and his editor Robert Wise, studio executives and technicians, craftsmen and artists of all kinds to create *his* masterpiece—so too did none of Joe Mankiewicz's films come only from a single source. To assume that Joe's films were *his,* therefore, revealing his world view in a deep way, is both true but also overblown, a case of retrospect serving to smooth and make clearer what was not obvious then and what may not even be true at all. In the case of Joe's greatest film, it would also obscure the contributions not just of its cast and crew, but the work of Mary Orr in the first place, and Darryl Zanuck, the film's producer, who helped shape and whittle the script down into manageable form, and whose valuable presence in Joe's work life is best seen by what happened to Joe's movies when Zanuck was no longer a part of them.

Nonetheless: *All About Eve*.

It stands like a Colossus among Joe's other movies. All of the archness in his other work which so often kept audiences at a remove now worked in his favor, beautifully; indeed, the movie is all about archness. There are defenders and even lovers of *The Ghost and Mrs. Muir, A Letter to Three Wives; Suddenly, Last Summer; 5 Fingers, No Way Out, Cleopatra, Sleuth,* even *The Barefoot Contessa*. The list goes on and it's impressive, but above all there is *Eve*: *Yes, Eve. You all know all about Eve . . . what can there be to know that you don't know . . . ?* The lines are so quotable: *It's about time the piano realized it has not written the concerto!* The characters so delicious: *What a story, everything but the bloodhounds snappin' at her rear end.* The script so full of acid-tongued wit: *Remind me to tell you about the time I looked into the heart of an artichoke.* It is above all such a thoroughly entertaining movie from start to finish—a movie about performance, about acting, about actors, about theater, about show business itself—and Joe never came close to equaling it. The reason for that, I think, is that both the film's central dynamic—between the lovable, maddening elder and the scheming, ambitious usurper—and its setting were so central to the essence of Joseph L. Mankiewicz.

As Herman longed for politics and journalism, Joe idealized theater.[*] He had fallen in love early, and his time in Hollywood had only strengthened his desire to fulfill what John Erskine had predicted for him all those years ago: to write a great play someday, the equal of Shaw or Wilde if not Shakespeare himself. For there it is again in *All About Eve*, evidence that Hollywood and movies are not the equal to live theater: the condescension with which the film world is viewed in the world of the movie itself, the assumption, in fact, that any intelligent person would prefer the theater to the movies. When Eve Harrington asks the young theater director Bill Sampson why he intends to go to Hollywood, he responds with a lengthy and defensive diatribe about the theater, beginning with a spin on a classic Mankiewiczian formulation, "What book of rules says the theater exists only within some ugly buildings crowded into one square mile of New York City?" The theater, Sampson goes on a little pompously ("Listen, junior, and learn," he tells Eve), encompasses all kinds of performances, from opera to magic to minstrel to Donald Duck and everything in between—so movies themselves, bastard art form that it might seem, is part of the great Theater world as well. "Wherever there's magic and make-believe and an audience, there's theater . . . It may not be your theater, but it's theater of somebody, somewhere." But coming from an artist like Sampson, not to mention Joe Mankiewicz, there's something slightly disingenuous about this common man pose. The fact is,

---

[*] Just as Joe described *Citizen Kane* as "an absolutely perfect marriage of writer and material, as it combined the political and sociological aspects that Herman knew better than almost anybody," *All About Eve* was a perfect marriage for Joe and his own theatrical "aspects."

Joe in June of 1950, not
long before the release of
All About Eve

Bill is clearly going to Hollywood for the money (despite maintaining that 80 percent of it will go to taxes) and a few lines later, he collapses back in his chair and says resignedly, "It's only a one-picture deal." He hasn't been proclaiming the glories and democratic virtues of all kinds of theater because he believes it; in fact, trying to break free of the New York theater world, he's been mocking its pretensions. Whereas the New York theater people only want the allegedly high art and the Hollywood movie people just want money, Sampson is hoping they are two sides of the same coin, a heady mixture of glamour and prestige and applause that can ruin you no matter which town you're in. Sampson is merely trying to convince himself that Hollywood won't ruin him.

But who had Hollywood ruined?

By now, Joe's older brother carried with him so much venom and hate toward the place where both of them made their lives, that it would have been impossible, even if Joe had never idolized Herman, for Joe not to have noticed it, regardless of how much of it may have rubbed off on the younger brother. But more than that, it was impossible for any son of an educated man who cared about history, language, literature, and politics not to end up thinking that the largely uneducated boorish men who ran the town were beneath them. Joe Mankiewicz, like Herman, Ben Hecht, Faulkner, Fitzgerald, and Fritz Lang and probably 97 percent of all the émigrés to Hollywood in this time, felt that he was better than the town. Joe called Hollywood "professionally and socially inbred and self-preoccupied—a weird mixture of goldmining camp and ivory ghetto." But what made Joe different, and the reason he was able to thrive there, was that he knew it was all a game. He never took any of it that seriously—he worked hard, God knows, he wrote to the best of his abilities, and he resolved to make the best movies he could within the confines of the system, but, maybe because of Herman, he knew the game's limitations, and as much as he pushed against them, he knew you had to play with the ball the big boys had thrown you, or they'd toss the ball to someone else. In his later years, Joe took to calling himself the old-est whore on the beat, but from the start of his directing career, he knew he wasn't in it for love.

Joe's attitude can be found in Bill Sampson's conflicted resignation as he slumps back and says, "It's just a one-picture deal." It's crap he's going out there for, and he knows it, but dammit, why is it only one picture?

If Joe scorned Hollywood and the movies, he idealized New York and the theater, and so brought forth what Celeste Holm called his "love letter to Thespis," which may have been possible only due to the inconvenient fact that Joe didn't have any actual professional experience in the theater. So he was able to take his purest feelings about art and pour them into the theatrical world of the movie, and take his contempt for the business side of the film industry and pour that into the Hollywood of the movie. Consider the unseen film star who arrives late to Margo's party, dumps her sable on the bed, then leaves early, significantly, as Birdie points out, "with half the men in the joint." The simple equation: Hollywood equals prosti-tution. The theater, New York, Art with a capital A—these were what Joe valued and loved, and in the film these virtues are embodied by Margo Channing, Bette Davis's magnificent creature—"a great star, a true star, she never was or will be anything less"—the one whom Eve Harrington sets her cold eyes upon. The gorgeous, thrashing whale, "something made of music and fire." So Joe had his theme. Mary Orr's story had lit the spark, but it had been lying there in wait for decades, ever since Joe had first hid in the closet listening to Herman and Franz rage.*

To write the script, Joe faced a challenge not unique to him, or Her-man, or millions of other writers: namely, he disliked writing. But know-ing this, he always isolated himself when he had a script to write, found his own private Victorville. In the case of *All About Eve,* after Zanuck had acquired the project for him,† and he'd worked on a long treatment while also overseeing the preproduction and production of *No Way Out,* he went off, alone, to the San Ysidro Ranch in Santa Barbara to write the script. Though he was in the midst of at least one affair at the time (and

---

* Joe had also been struck by the "strangely unenduring gratification" he felt on winning the Directors Guild Award in May 1949 for *A Letter to Three Wives,* and he'd already been considering a film centered on the idea of an award before he was first shown Orr's story.

† Fox bought Orr's short story "The Wisdom of Eve," which had run in *Cosmopolitan* in May 1946, for $5,000.

still saw Garland occasionally), Joe was insistent that the writing during this phase be done in isolation, and so just as Herman had restricted his alcohol intake while at Victorville, Joe kept pretty much to himself while at San Ysidro. The ranch, which Joe's great-nephew John later called "the place where God goes on vacation," was sun-dappled and full of orange groves. There Joe poured it all out in his first draft. In the battle that rages between Margo and Eve, even or maybe especially when Margo is initially unaware of what Eve is after and is so patronizingly dismissive of her, Joe was writing out his version of the epic, endless battle between Art and Commerce, between New York and Hollywood, between Cain and Abel, Herman and Joe. Everything that Joe had in him, that he truly cared about, from the depths of his soul—not the pedantry of *People Will Talk,* not the political posturing of *No Way Out,* not the domestic infighting and soap opera of *A Letter to Three Wives*—but what Joe had been thinking about his entire life, ever since he was a boy. His nickel. How could he make it? How could he beat Herman?

Pedantic, irritating, holier-than-thou, preachy, a talkative goddamn know-it-all—Joe Mankiewicz was all these things and more, and this made its way into his scripts—but he was also a little brother who, no matter how much he wanted to defeat his older brother, loved the guy. So it is that the starring role in *All About Eve*—in Joe's entire oeuvre—is not Eve Harrington but Margo Channing. And Eve, Joe's stand-in in the battle of the two? She gets her comeuppance in the end, Joe made sure of that—a shallow, hollow life of awards and no meaningful relationships, and destined, quite clearly, to be the victim of another Eve herself in the film's Phoebe, who weasels her way into Eve's hotel suite and life (being 'helpful' by picking up shards of broken glass) as surely as Eve wheedled her way into Margo's life. As Phoebe holds up Eve's Sarah Siddons Award in the film's final shot and bows to an invisible, unheard, adoring crowd, she is determined to take from Eve whatever she is able, and the film's final irony is bitter indeed: Eve Harrington wins, but she will not last.* Indeed, just as Eve is a kind of lesser, carbon copy version of Margo, Phoebe is a still more diluted version of Eve Harrington. The clothes and look may be similar, but underneath the carapace, the talent ebbs with each successive iteration.

Joe knew, and he felt that Eve knew as well, that there was simply no

---

* As Joe later put it, Phoebe "will become another Eve," and the mirror reflects "that the world is full of Eves, and that they will be with us always."

filling the hole at the center of her being; he told Carey that at the end of the film Eve was confronted "by an acute awareness that in fact, ever since the beginning, she has been servicing a bottomless pit." Only applause seemed to do the trick, of making her feel like a human being. As Eve tells the gathering at Margo's party:

> Why, if there's nothing else—there's applause. It's like—like waves of love coming over the footlights and wrapping you up. Imagine . . . To know, every night, that different hundreds of people love you . . . they smile, their eyes shine—you've pleased them, they want you, you belong. Just that alone is worth anything.

The love of applause and desperate need for approval is clear from the moment Margo catches Eve backstage, standing and bowing into a mirror, hearing that same adoring unseen crowd so familiar to megalomaniacs everywhere, just as Phoebe does at the end of the film. It's also why Eve lashed out at Addison in the hotel room, giving voice, as Joe later said, "to the emptiness she was and had always been: "I had to say something, *be somebody*." The action of the movie is driven by that one fact: Eve Harrington—Gertrude Slesczynski, after all—felt like nobody.

As for Margo, sure, at times she's annoying and self-dramatizing, but she is also, the film makes clear, somebody, and somebody who cares about other people. Bette Davis gives a sensitive, warm, and deeply intelligent performance,[*] which makes clear that it is in fact Margo's vulnerability toward people (she misreads Eve and so "develop[s] a big protective feeling for her—a lamb loose in our big stone jungle") that allows Eve to come in and nearly take everything from Margo that is rightfully Margo's. But the film—Joe—won't give Eve any lasting satisfaction—won't give her even the satisfaction that Eve in Mary Orr's original short story got, in stealing Karen Richards's husband away from her. No, the film's Eve is left with nothing but a hollow victory, an award where her heart should be. Most crucially, Eve is awarded at the end of the movie with a trip to Hollywood. And, as Phoebe remarks, looking at the trunks Eve has packed,

---

[*] On the first day of an abbreviated rehearsal schedule (Bette Davis had replaced Claudette Colbert in the role after Colbert suffered a slipped disk), Davis's voice was unusually husky, and she apologized to Joe, as she was just getting over a cold; Joe smiled and told her to keep the deep voice. Davis later said that by giving her the role, "Mankiewicz resurrected me from the dead."

she might be staying for a long time. In Joe's view, what he often called the "cesspool" of Hollywood was the best, if not only, place for someone who possessed, like Addison DeWitt and like Eve herself, "a contempt for humanity, an inability to love or be loved, insatiable ambition—and talent." And so he sends his Eve there.

And Margo? While her fate is less anti-woman than many commentators have taken it to be—Margo makes clear that she's not giving up acting altogether to be with Bill Sampson, but just the part of Cora, a part she is too young for anyway—Margo Channing is not about to be anyone's hausfrau, though some have seen it that way. "Bill's thirty-two," she says early on of her lover. "He looks thirty-two. He looked it five years ago, he'll look it twenty years from now. I hate men." Now, at the end of the movie, she knows that the eight-year age difference between them "will stretch as the years go on," and certainly she worries about the life she is about to embark on out of the spotlight, but even so, she is certainly far more fulfilled, having won Bill Sampson at last (or at least having allowed herself to be happy with the idea of becoming Mrs. Bill Sampson), no matter that he, like many of Joe's male characters, could easily be described as a pompous, self-righteous ass, than she was when she was more entirely self-concerned. She ends happy, victorious, and triumphant. And in fact whenever Margo Channing disappears from the picture, the movie suffers for it.*

And Joe knew it. He knew that Margo won. He was thrilled that she won, and he claimed later in life that he despised Eve. "You gather I don't like Eve?" he asked Gary Carey in *More About All About Eve*. "You're right. I've been there." But if Eve, for Joe, was the part of himself that he despised, then Margo was the part of Herman that he loved, the idealized Herman: confident, brave, funny, raging, self-loathing, brilliant. It's as if by letting Herman win in the end, Joe was fantasizing that he himself was still the adoring younger brother, giving Herman the good life they both wanted, doing whatever he could to save the man.

But one thing Joe could not do was change who he was, at least not yet. Which is why in the end the character he most identified with in *All About Eve* was neither Eve nor Margo but Addison DeWitt, the acerbic,

---

* Interestingly, though the film today can seem dominated by Bette Davis's powerful and charismatic performance, before the film came out, Joe's identification with Eve was so strong that he was convinced that the film was going to make a huge star out of Anne Baxter.

almost gleefully venomous critic played with relish by George Sanders.[*] It is Addison whose suave and sophisticated voice provides the opening narration of the film, setting Joe's scene with droll confidence, Addison who introduces himself with a pompous self-regard that is funny, self-aware, and echoes Joe's own: "To those of you who do not read, attend the Theater, listen to uncensored radio programs or know anything of the world in which we live—it is perhaps necessary to introduce myself." Yet a few moments later, DeWitt acknowledges that though he plays a critical role in the life of the theater, it is as "ants are to a picnic, as the boll weevil to a cotton field." As full of obvious self-love as DeWitt is, he also doesn't like himself very much.

By making him our guide, Joe makes Addison, at least initially, a sympathetic figure, the one who gives the audience their privileged information regarding the other characters, especially since he doesn't take part in much of the action of the film, at least in its first half. Addison is like our secret friend every time he shows up. His asides are deliciously arrogant, and in contrast to the other male characters—Joe freely admitted he found writing for men "damned limited . . . predictable, conforming" and he was hardly helped by Gary Merrill or Hugh Marlowe as the stalwart leading men anchoring the film like pillars of gray flannel rock—he delighted in Addison DeWitt. While it's clear that no one else in the movie likes the guy, rare is the audience member who doesn't revel in the villainous Addison DeWitt.

Of course, being Joe's surrogate, Addison admits he's unlovable. In the New Haven hotel room prior to Eve's opening, after DeWitt exposes the litany of Eve's lies, he tells her how alike the two of them are, these Joe stand-ins: "You're an improbable person, Eve, and so am I. We have that in common . . . We deserve each other." The bond between Eve and Addison at the end of the movie is fixed fast by their mutual need, if not outright contempt—it is nothing approaching love, and as Addison says, "that I should want you at all suddenly strikes me as the height of improbability."

---

[*] Sanders's own curious life story contains depths at which a footnote can only hint. Born in Russia to British parents, he left the country during the Russian Revolution, became an actor known for playing cads (so much so that his memoir was titled *Memoirs of a Professional Cad,* though he later proposed *A Dreadful Man* for his biography), married Zsa Zsa Gabor among three other wives, and left one of the world's most maddeningly inconclusive suicide notes when he killed himself at the age of sixty-five: *Dear World, I am leaving because I am bored. I feel I have lived long enough. I am leaving you with your worries in this sweet cesspool. Good luck.*

"That I should want you at all suddenly strikes me as
the height of improbability": George Sanders and
Anne Baxter in *All About Eve*

What also makes it improbable, of course, is that Addison is an effete
dandy, as queer as the day is long, and no more sexually attracted to Eve
than he is to that boll weevil. It's curiously remarkable that it took a man
as flamingly devoted to his own heterosexuality as Joe Mankiewicz to create two such iconic gay characters, closeted though Addison and Eve may
be. Indeed, Eve is an almost passionately asexual figure, in thrall not to
sex or romance but to power and ambition. Still, can anyone doubt that
if the film were made today, we'd get more than just the whiff Joe gives us
of Eve's lesbianism (walking up the stairs arm in arm with her roommate;
Eve's short mannish hair throughout, especially when she slips off her wig
like a female impersonator in the film's final scene; her quick attachment
to Phoebe; the lack of any serious romantic heat between Eve and any of
the male characters, notwithstanding the almost play-acted sexual longing she displays toward Lloyd Richards), or that Addison would not hail
from what one critic, referring to Clifton Webb's character in Otto Preminger's *Laura,* calls "the Waldo Lydecker School," whose closeted members' relationships with women are proprietary rather than romantic?[*] As
such, Margo Channing's neuroses, her fear of aging, her sexual rage at

---

[*] Today's Addison would likely be a gay, theater-mad blogger: a different movie
indeed.

the possibility of being passed over for a younger version of herself,* her professional anxieties, her drunken self-pity, and much of what makes Margo Channing so fascinating as a character comes from Joe's understanding of how women operate. He was, in the end, more fascinated by women than men—as he said, "male behavior is so elementary that All About Adam could be done as a short."

And yet . . . And yet there remains the problem of Rosa. Chris Mankie-wicz maintains that some of the dialogue in the party scene in *All About Eve* ("Cut! Print it! What happens in the next reel? Do I get dragged off

"What happens in the next reel? Do I get dragged off screaming to the snake pit?" Bette Davis and Gary Merrill in *All About Eve*

screaming to the snake pit?") was practically a transcript of what he heard growing up with his parents, whose battles never seemed to stop. But whatever went on between the two of them was far more serious than the battles between Margo and Bill. As Chris said, "Because when the lights are out and I'm lying in bed and I can hear them screaming at each other through the walls, I know what's really going on."

What was really going on was Joe's philandering. For there's the crucial difference between real life and *All About Eve*—the real-life Margo Channing's fears about Bill Sampson's alleged infidelities are presented as pure paranoia, whereas in real life, Rosa's fears were justified.† In fact, from the very beginning of his knowing Rosa, Joe was philandering. As Joe is getting Rosa pregnant with Chris and deciding to marry her, he is having affairs. As Tom is being born two years later and Joe is beginning his

---

* The Eve-as-younger-Margo theme would have been more explicit had Claudette Colbert, whom Joe originally cast in the role of Margo Channing, not suffered her ruptured disk and been forced to withdraw from the production less than ten days before shooting began—Colbert and Anne Baxter are almost freakishly similar in appearance, whereas the sui generis Bette Davis looks nothing like Baxter.

† Chris: "Although in *Eve,* Bill Sampson is not fucking Eve Harrington and is supposedly fair to Margo, in our story, he *is* fucking her. In real life Dad is fucking the Eve Harrington all the time!"

Joe with Bette Davis, Anne Baxter,
and Celeste Holm on the set of *All About Eve* (1950)

years-long affair with Judy Garland, he is telling Rosa he is not having any
affairs, and she is ending up in a sanatorium. In Chris's mind, his mother
was never truly crazy, but was being convinced that she was going crazy
by Joe's constant lying. Was that craziness, or a picture-perfect example
of gaslighting? While Rosa had serious mental illness, it's impossible not
to feel that Joe's lies contributed to her demise. "She came at him with
knives," my mother said years later, "but boy was she provoked!"

But for all of Joe's faults—and he admitted them freely later in life,
never claiming to have been a faithful husband to Rosa—I think he
wished it could have been otherwise. Whatever went on behind closed
doors between them, the happy ending between Bill and Margo was, to
some extent, clearly another wish fulfillment on Joe's part. "Heaven help
me," Joe had Margo Channing say, "I love a psychotic." Joe loved Rosa,
and he wanted, dreadfully, things to have been different between them.
He wanted a wife whose work he valued, the way Bill valued Margo's—
and who was a success in her own right, not just the hausfrau who "could
play the Eva Braun character and maybe one or two other roles" and
pose at movie premieres for happy domestic pictures that belied her inse-
curity and misery. Still, however much Joe may have wished it, he was
unequipped to make it so. Though Rosa's work in their one collaboration
had received generally positive reviews, *The Keys of the Kingdom* had led
to no more movie roles. Her film career was over. She had returned to
her miserable gilded cage in the role of Mrs. Mankiewicz, and Joe and

Rosa had continued to battle on, Joe continued to philander, and Chris and Tom continued to grow up in an atmosphere of almost unbearable domestic tension if not downright abuse that magnified *All About Eve*'s party scene—to quote Lloyd Richards, "the general atmosphere [was] very Macbethish."

IN LATER YEARS, JOE WAS PROUDLY RETROGRADE WHEN IT CAME TO assessing and analyzing the work of artists. He told Gary Carey that "the offstage or offscreen moral and/or political propensities of creative talents should not be applicable to a judgment of their work." What's more, he seemed to delight in taking a perversely antipsychological stance with regard to the roots of his own films. So while he admitted that *All About Eve* had its genesis in his lifelong love of theater, he completely denied and in fact scoffed at the idea that his greatest film had anything at all to do with his feelings about his brother. In fact, he loved to state instead, almost gleefully missing the point, "Herman had nothing to do with *All About Eve*, and I had nothing to do with *Citizen Kane*." Given Joe's reverence for psychoanalysis, his staunchly incurious attitude toward the genesis of his own films is strange indeed. As my mother told Ken Geist, "He's very versed in psychiatry, and you'd think . . . but it doesn't get to him."*

ON THE NIGHT OF MARCH 29, 1951, HOLLYWOOD GATHERED TO PAY tribute to itself. *All About Eve* had been nominated for a record fourteen Academy Awards, breaking the mark set by *Gone with the Wind* eleven years earlier. In Beverly Hills, Herman Mankiewicz no longer even listened to the ceremony on the radio. He wasn't well, and with no ability to affect the outcome, what could be gained by hearing his brother reap more plaudits? He took some satisfaction from the fact that his younger brother's big successes always came from adaptations, that "Joe the genius"

---

* It is one of the chief regrets of this book that I was never able to ask Joe about his feelings for Herman, and how much they had influenced, consciously or not, the writing of *All About Eve*. Instead, I asked Rosemary, his devoted third wife and widow, who gave me the answer he himself probably would have given, though her answer was probably far shorter. In fact, she used only one word for the theory that *All About Eve* had anything to do with Joe's and Herman's relationship: "Absurd."

was never rewarded for original work, but overall, it was a hell of a lot easier to find other things to think about. Joe told friends with a sensible display of sympathy that it must have been hard for Herman watching his rise as Herman continued his one-way ticket to the bottom. In the ballroom, as Joe made his way through the crowd, one old-timer, a studio executive Joe had worked with years earlier, mistook him for Herman,[*] but Joe merely smiled and moved deeper into the throng of well-wishers, sensing that behind him the man's companions were clarifying the confusion and telling the man the sad truth about Joe's big brother: Herman had been in and out of work for a while, and the few scripts that came his way—like *The Pride of St. Louis,* a biopic of the St. Louis Cardinals baseball star Dizzy Dean and a pale attempt to duplicate the success of *The Pride of the Yankees*—had not been notable.

Back in Beverly Hills, Herman fussed. The annual ceremony, according to his daughter years later, was never anything the family paid attention to. There was no ritual, no sitting around the radio together, not even the enchanting American tradition of mocking Oscar participants together. For Herman, the night of Joe's greatest triumph was spent much like any other: reading. To the end, Herman was a voracious reader, and when it wasn't politics or biography, he often as not kept a large pile of unread manuscripts and galleys sent to him by friends. In early 1951, that pile would have included Budd Schulberg's *Disenchanted.* Budd had sent it to him more than a year earlier for his opinion when it was still in galleys, then a few months later the hardcover, which sat unopened and undigested for months. Budd wanted Herman to adapt it into a screenplay, and Herman's reluctance could be found in the fact the book was still unopened. In Herman's view, Schulberg had done his best work already—*What Makes Sammy Run?* was a damn good summation of everything that was wrong with the town, and its Sammy Glick was a beautiful embodiment of all of its most horrible characters rolled up into one hugely unsympathetic, grasping ball of ambition, who reminded more than one Hollywood reader of Joe. But now here was this book, *Disenchanted,* making its way up the best-seller lists, which seemed, from an unread perspective anyway, to be a vain attempt on Budd's part at stepping in the same river twice; this one about a young screenwriter's relationship with a novelist whose own career had, like F. Scott Fitzgerald,

---

[*] Joe, in repayment, will neglect to remember the man's name when he tells and retells the anecdote in future years.

the character on whom the book's Manley Halliday was based, seen far better days. Herman's reluctance to read the book may also have stemmed from its intersection with his own life. The book's main theme, in the end, was about confronting one's own bitter disappointment and admitting that the great successes one had attained in the past couldn't be repeated at will, no matter how hard one tried. . . .

The project that had most sparked Herman's interest, and which had him holding out the most hope during the entire post-*Kane* era, with his health, career, and faith in the industry all in serious decline, was called "*Woman on the Rock*," an original script that fictionalized the life story of evangelist Aimee Semple McPherson. Herman's script had been years in the writing, rewriting, and revisions, and he was at times certain it would be a worthy successor to *Kane*, a searing indictment of religious hypocrisy in America. It would prove to Welles, to Joe, to the whole damn town, that he was still the master who fundamentally changed the rules of the game. This movie would also, not incidentally, serve as the tide that lifted him up from a sludge of medical and unpayable debts.

It's not hard to understand why the story of McPherson's rise and fall was so tantalizing to Herman. Just as Hearst spewed sensationalized garbage to millions of American newspaper readers, so too a few decades later, McPherson sent what were often called "slap-stick sermons" into the ears of millions of Americans every Sunday. As a pioneer megachurch evangelist, she whipped crowds of thousands into frenzies at her Angelus Temple in Los Angeles by speaking in tongues, not to mention giving sight to the blind and healing the crippled.

Reading about the lifetime of nonsense McPherson ladled out to audiences eager to gobble it up, Herman couldn't fail to think of his little brother. Scooping up accolades left and right for churning out crowd-pleasers and being such a kow-towing sycophant . . . this is who gets rewarded for success in this country? Writing the script gave Herman the chance to unleash his anger against an enormous charlatan. Herman regained the twinkle in his eye, thinking of giving Joe and the industry the lecture of a lifetime: "You see what's wrong with this country? Look at the kind of crap that rises to the top!"

McPherson's life had taken one particularly bizarre turn that became the focus of Herman's script. On the morning of May 18, 1926, she did not arrive to preach at the Angelus Temple. Word spread, though no one knew whether it could be believed: she had drowned during a swim earlier that day. The Coast Guard patrolled up and down the coast, and deep-sea divers plunged into the water. No expense was spared in the resulting search. A month later, dazed and disoriented, Aimee Semple McPherson reappeared in a small Mexican town south of the Arizona border, and in a bedside interview painted a dramatic picture of her past month. She had escaped kidnappers who had drugged her and smuggled her over the border, holding her for ransom for weeks in a corrugated tin shack. It was a riveting story to be sure, but almost no one believed it.

Soon, other stories emerged. Witnesses reported spotting McPherson in Northern California during the time she was supposedly bound and gagged, and worse, a married engineer who helped broadcast her radio program had disappeared at the same time. The headlines, gossip, and rumors continued until a judge decided there was enough evidence to proceed with charges of conspiracy and obstruction of justice. But soon, witnesses recanted their stories, and others began to seem less reliable; charges were dropped. Controversy over the apparent fraud went unresolved. To Herman, it was all too juicy to ignore. He based the structure of his script with *Kane* forefront in his mind—using as the main plot device a newspaper reporter researching a retrospective story on the evangelist. As Hearst had become Kane, McPherson became Ruth Church, an alluring, dissolute dame.

When Herman first completed the script, all those who'd shrugged him off like the plague in the previous few years, not taking or returning his calls, were now seeking him out. Everyone, it seemed, wanted to get their hands on the project. Directors William Wyler, Otto Preminger, and Joseph Losey were interested; so were actresses Evelyn Keyes and Mercedes McCambridge. Whether she'd read it or not, Hollywood gossip columnist Hedda Hopper declared it "one of the hottest scripts of the year" and said "every top star in town is drooling."

Sitting there determined not to listen to the Oscars broadcast at which *All About Eve* would be crowned, it must have been difficult for Herman to avoid thinking about what had happened next, and to wonder if he had done the right thing. First, Joseph Breen, who administered the Motion Picture Production Code and who had been the one to strike the dagger through the heart of "*The Mad Dog of Europe,*" brought this project to a screeching halt as well. The man who Herman delighted in calling "a devout Catholic layman and fathead," known for forcing even Betty Boop into a housewife's skirt, had pronounced that the script was in clear violation of the code, as it "cast ridicule" on evangelistic activities and portrayed religion as "a racket." As there was no clear alternative path forward, Herman made changes Breen's staff recommended, softening the piece's hostility toward organized religion.

But it rankled. The script, already overlong even in Herman's eyes, had gotten even longer. But that was no excuse for what Herman did next. Was it just more showing off? Pure ego that drove him to do what he did, or, as Dr. Hacker would have suggested—and Sara would have agreed, had she known what he did because of course he'd hidden it from her—another act of self-sabotage and self-destruction for the ages?

The project's death blow came thusly by Herman's own hand: he sent a copy of the script to McPherson's daughter, Roberta Semple Salter, heir to her mother's ministry.

How did he imagine she would respond? While Herman probably understood the risk he was taking, as a gambler he would have loved the thrill and danger in sending the script. But more than that, in Herman's brilliant, expansive, loving mind, it's possible he assumed—"you don't like spinach, you hate your parents"—that any daughter would in fact be *thrilled* to see that others knew how awful her parent was. Wouldn't Herman have welcomed a script "The Imperious Professor, or 'What Happened to the Three Points?': The Franz Mankiewicz Story"? If he looked deep into his own motivations and his own miserable childhood, the ways he had suffered at the hands of a man whom so many looked up to and respected—even Jimmy Cagney thought his father a whale of a fellow—Herman must have thought that the child in such a situation would respond with sympathy—*at last, someone sees the agony I endured!*—rather than with a strongly worded attorney's letter threatening to sue for libel and invasion of privacy. Perhaps instead of all interest in the film quickly fading, as no production company or studio would want to embroil themselves in a lawsuit, Herman would be welcomed with open arms, and he might even find a new friend in Roberta Semple Salter. The project lost all momentum. The studios and production companies moved on to other projects. Even Orson Welles, whom Herman sent the script to in a last-ditch effort to resuscitate the corpse, had no interest. Herman was left, a few months later, to readjust for the thousandth time his position in the wing back chair near the radio he refused to turn on and so hear his brother's name called, again, as it had been at the previous year's ceremony, not just once but twice. Disenchanted, indeed.

———⚜———

THE BEST DIRECTOR AWARD, JOE INSISTED, HAD BEEN SOMETHING of a surprise. How else could he explain his behavior when the award was announced? He had been backstage, chatting with fellow nominee Billy Wilder. (Earlier in the evening, Wilder had won for Best Original Screenplay for *Sunset Boulevard,* as Joe had won for Best Adapted Screenplay for *Eve.*) According to Wilder, Joe had been laying it on thick with fulsome praise, and what an honor it was just to be with Billy, to even be considered on the same par with him. "Then all of a sudden they announced [Joe] as the winner of the Best Director award, and he pushed me aside and rushed on the stage as if I were a stagehand. Suddenly his compliments cut off instantaneously, and with a cold glance at me as if to say 'who are you,' he just took off." No "thanks, Billy, I gotta go now," it was a cut as clean as a razor blade, and Joe was off to collect his prize. It was, Wilder said, "pure ambition."

Wilder said he'd never seen anything like it. Had he not seen the picture for which Joe was being honored?

In later years, when Joe talked of the movie, and not just of Eve, but Phoebe, the young actress who enters Eve's hotel room in the final scene, he would discuss the characters whose ruthless ambition is so terrifying as if they were utterly foreign to his own nature. But the fact that the portrait of ruthless ambition is so exact and precise, even today giving audiences chills, suggests that Joe must have sensed that it came from him. He may not have had the personal vanity of Phoebe, wearing a tiara and gazing lovingly at her own reflection, again and again in an eternity of mirrors as she holds up the coveted award, but Joe Mankiewicz knew narcissism and its discontents. As Phoebe prepares to help Eve, tired and drained after her triumph earlier in the evening, and worn out from the exhausting and ruthless climb to the top, Joe was reflecting on him and Herman as well. To the vanquished Margo Channing Joe had given the happy and fantastical ending he may have actually wished for Herman, a happy retirement from the game and a peace of mind that had always eluded his beloved and feared older brother. But to Eve, to himself, he had given no peace at all, only the sense that the game would never end, that there would always be more champions coming after him, determined to wrest away what he had gained.

When Joe considered Herman at all now, it was with pity and concern, mostly. He knew Herman hadn't escaped to that life he'd prescribed for Margo at the end of *All About Eve,* happily married and with a "home— not just a house I'm afraid to stay in." Herman wasn't in a house he

"Had he not seen the picture for which Joe was
being honored?" Joe and Billy Wilder, c. 1951

was afraid to stay in—that was Joe, really—but his home was far from
comfortable. No, when Joe pictured Herman now, the big brother was a
shrunken figure back at Tower Road, rattling around the big old house
with Sara, the boys off for good, into their adult lives, and though Herman fiercely loved young Johanna, who was growing up so beautifully
(but also so strangely—the gloom and doom in the house was hard to
escape, Joe assumed), Herman's miasma had totally engulfed him now.
It made Joe sad. Sara had told friends of a wretched moment not long
before. She'd come across Herman in slippers and robe, in the middle of
the night, sitting on the couch in his office, holding his dressing gown
across his spindly knees and crying. He looked up at Sara with tear-filled
eyes. For a while he didn't speak, maybe because he wasn't able to, or
because the truth struck him as too cliché, too absurd, too basic a thought
to express aloud. Finally he'd gotten the words out, a simple sentence: "I
miss the boys."

It wasn't just the boys, of course—it was their childhoods, and his own,
the youth and vigor of his own earlier days forever vanished, the young
man tootling around Hollywood in his DeSoto, careening carelessly into
accidents but rebounding so beautifully, the screenwriter barking at others in story conferences and bringing the room into helpless states of
laughter, the wiseacre with Kaufman back in New York, the tongue-tied
press agent with Isadora Duncan, the uncertain reporter standing next to
Jack Dempsey in those trousers so painfully short, the glowering young
doughboy just back from the Great War, ready to conquer the world, take

a bride, make a fortune, and show these idiots there was no one ever quite like him. Herman missed that boy most of all.

WHEN JOHANNA GREW UP, SHE WROTE A NOVEL, *LIFE SIGNS*. AND in that novel, the heroine has a dream in which she visits the Hollywood home of her childhood. She floats through the house, seeing it like a single long shot from a film—panning past the library, bookshelves everywhere, through the dining room, candles burning, a pyramid of fresh fruit, and then up the back stairs to her father's office. It's all wrong in the dream, no one should be there, she nearly always came home to an empty house after school, with her mother off shopping, getting her hair done, or with friends, and her father at the studio, but in the dream, it's as if there is a presence in the house, drawing her on—the wind stirring the papers in her father's office, cigar ashes everywhere—then through her own child-hood bedroom, past the little girl's bed, ruffled and flowered, into her mother's bedroom, the white bed, the chaise lounge, and then, at last she stops outside her father's room. She knocks but does not enter. She stands there, motionless. And from within she hears a voice. "It won't be long," her father says from the other side of the door. An ambulance is coming. "Sit with me," he whispers. "Don't let me be alone."

In the novel, the character wakes from the dream with a start, to find that her father is dead, life has moved on, it is years later and she is in her own bed, next to her sleeping husband. She is not going to go in and relive those memories, sit with her father, and whisper quietly so her mother doesn't hear them, tell him about her day and who said what to whom.

And my mother is not with her father and mother, but with her husband, my father. It is the summer of 1971, and she is writing this novel in a summer home we have taken on Long Island. She is plumbing her childhood memories, and it can be painful and unpleasant, but waking in her bed, she knows that she is no longer there, in an airless house on Tower Road, lured on by a barely living father who will cast such an enormous shadow.

Will she ever escape it? She will have risen beautifully in the years after Tower Road, graduating with glowing marks from Westlake School for Girls, then Wellesley, where classmates and professors alike will seem to compete to see who loved her most—then a stellar career at Time-Life, breaking hearts throughout the building and becoming the first woman on the masthead at *Time* magazine—Johanna Mankiewicz Davis, though after a few weeks she will insist that the magazine drop the "Mankiewicz" from her name.

But still she is shadowed, and so are all the Mankiewiczes, by what Herman's voice has said: "It won't be long."

It cannot last, this dream. Nothing can.

PART FOUR

———————— ✿ ————————

Life was about to be very different, had already started to be; she would have to learn to take happiness in stride, along with the other. She was neither doomed, nor saved. There was love in her, and anger, the same as everyone else. She would get back to essentials, her husband, her children; she might try some poetry, dream on paper. She was special, she was ordinary; like her father, unlike him, like her mother, unlike her, she was whoever she chose, she would belong to herself.

—*LIFE SIGNS,*
JOHANNA DAVIS

CHAPTER TWELVE

———— ✿ ————

NO WAY OUT

There is a man / a certain man
And for the poor you may be sure / That he'll do all he can!
Who is this one? / This favorite son?
Just by his action / Has the Traction magnates on the run?
Who loves to smoke? / Enjoys a joke?
Who wouldn't get upset / If he were really broke?
With wealth and fame / He's still the same
I'll bet you five you're not alive / If you don't know his name.

—*CITIZEN KANE*

ON AUGUST 28, 1963, MARTIN LUTHER KING JR. LED THE MARCH ON Washington and delivered his stirring oration on the steps of the Lincoln Memorial, looking out over the nearly half a million who had gathered to protest on behalf of the civil rights movement. That same day presented, for celebrated movie director Joe Mankiewicz, a chance to take part in a curious television program called *Hollywood Roundtable*. A special-event colloquy hosted by David Schoenbrun, the show presented a conversation with six Hollywood celebrities talking about the movement and giving "their own personally held views on Negro Rights." Sitting across from Charlton Heston, Sidney Poitier, and Harry Belafonte and next to Marlon Brando and James Baldwin, Joe kept his pipe firmly in his mouth and spoke of the "urgency of human rights in America now." The Hollywood celebrities were each earnest, well-meaning, and achingly sincere. Brando talked about his wish that the day's march had brought the world "one step closer to understanding the human heart." Heston admitted with a movie star's practiced pang that until recently all he'd done about civil rights was talk about it at cocktail parties, and while Baldwin expressed his belief that "the first step [toward progress] probably has to be somewhere in the American conscience," it was in many ways Joe Mankiewicz who took the lead on behalf of the Hollywood liberals. "The time has come," Joe concluded as the others nodded in agreement, "to stop dreaming this dream and wake up to it."

By now, Joe was more than a decade removed from Hollywood, but his place in the industry was secure, and more than that, his persona had now morphed into something far larger than that of a mere moviemaker. By 1963, Joe Mankiewicz had become a Conscience Personified, a far cry from the grasping, striving, Sammy Glick–like figure that Herman and his pals had derided. Though hale and hearty in his early fifties, Joe now was almost an éminence grise, a figure of renown and respect. His reputation had transformed not just through his actual work in movies, but by his bull-dogged insistence upon changing the way the industry saw him. He had willed the change into being, bent perception to his desire. The crucible had come during his now-legendary tenure as head of the Screen Director's Guild,* and while it hadn't exactly been "I Have A Dream," few in Hollywood had ever forgotten Joe's leadership on behalf of an oppressed minority. For a man who took great pride in his commitment to social justice, his guidance of the Guild through a long and perilous fight against forces of intransigence and intolerance may have been his finest hour. He had cared, he had fought, and he had helped people. In the New York years that followed Herman's death, in fact, the episode was something Joe delighted in being talked about . . .

IN APRIL 1950, JOE HAD BEEN ELECTED PRESIDENT OF THE SCREEN Director's Guild. He was pleased to gain the post and so represent his confreres in the challenging battles for better studio conditions, increased wages, and the all-important issue of residuals in the fledgling television industry. But it soon became clear that his control was nominal—Cecil B. DeMille, one of the founding fathers of the film industry, was the real force controlling the Guild. The sixty-nine-year-old DeMille was exasperating, imperious, and a die-hard Republican red-baiter. At the time, Joe was a Republican too—he called himself a "Pennsylvania Republican"†—

---

* The guild is known today known as the Directors Guild of America.

† In 1940, he claimed later, his vote for Republican Wendell Willkie over Franklin D. Roosevelt had gotten him summarily ejected from a Hollywood party at the house of Edwin Knopf, brother to a well-known publisher.

and ordinarily, serving as figurehead to an angry, out-of-touch old-timer might not have bothered Joe. But this was no ordinary time. The Red Scare was gathering steam, and while Joe tolerated DeMille's other peccadilloes, he didn't feel he could sit idly by as DeMille made it his personal mission to expel Communists from Hollywood. The battle was waged over loyalty oaths, which would require that a member declare that he had never joined the Communist Party, though of course it was perfectly legal to have done so. One studio head had happily told DeMille that such an action would have a steamroller effect; all other guilds and unions in Hollywood would soon go along. With the House UnAmerican Activities Committee already sending a group of moviemakers, the "Unfriendly Ten," to jail for refusing to cooperate and name names, there was rampant fear that an industry-wide blacklist was inevitable, and many were all for it, among them Hedda Hopper, who added her feeling that "those who aren't loyal should be put in concentration camps before it's too late." Anti-Communist fervor in California was rampant, intensified by the volatile U.S. Senate race then being waged to unseat Helen Gahagan Douglas, a woman whose opponent, Whittier's own Richard M. Nixon, had labeled the "pink lady" because of her sympathy for left-wing causes. Many in Hollywood were holding their breath wondering who was next, and DeMille was posing as a man offering a simple solution: Who wouldn't sign a loyalty oath other than someone who was disloyal to this great country that had given all of them so much?

Joe and many others in Hollywood didn't see it that way. You didn't have to be a Communist or even much of a Communist sympathizer to understand that there was a slippery slope from loyalty oaths to outright fascism, and that the movement begun by Senator Joe McCarthy and his terrifying, if almost cartoonlike declarations that "I have here in my hand a list of names . . ." could be a step toward the kind of authoritarianism that the country had just defeated in World War II. Of course DeMille knew that Joe was opposed to the loyalty oath—like many in Hollywood, Joe had publicly rejected the idea. At that point in his life and career, Joe was not particularly political, even calling himself "the least politically minded person in the world," but he did care about doing what he could for those he was in a position to help, from the beauties he met on set to promising young writers who reminded him of himself. And he was horrified by the witch hunt he saw brewing in Hollywood, calling those hunted "as much [a minority] as the Negro and the Jew . . . being slandered, libeled, persecuted, and threatened with extinction."*

The drama's next act came in the summer of 1950, as Joe and Rosa sailed home from a vacation in France after completing the filming of *All About Eve*. With Joe beyond telephone reach, DeMille seized the opportunity and called an emergency meeting of the Guild. There he crafted his mandatory non-communist oath, and, using an open ballot system, he and his pals were able to bully enough people into voting in favor of its creation.

When Joe landed in New York and learned what had happened, he was furious. He blasted the idea that the meeting had been held because of a so-called "emergency" and said that using an open ballot system was a brazen scare tactic. But worst of all, when Joe got back to Hollywood and convened his own meeting of the Guild's board, he learned that DeMille and one of his chief allies, Frank Capra, were introducing a new bylaw—one that would require the Guild to send producers a list of directors who refused to sign the oath—essentially, in Joe's view, a blacklist. Capra resisted the use of the word blacklist, pointing out that producers could still hire anyone they wished. Joe found that idea absurd: " 'This guy's un-American but you can hire him . . .'—that's a blacklist!" Still, a lot of Hollywood's top directors weren't convinced. John Ford told Joe, "I will not stand for any blacklist, but why shouldn't a man stand up and be counted?" "Because," Joe thundered, "nobody appointed DeMille to do the counting!" Like a chess master, Joe seemed to be thinking several steps ahead: he agreed to sign the oath as an officer of the board, but he refused to sign it as a member, putting that year's Oscar-winning director on his own Guild's blacklist. Then he volunteered to step down from the board, knowing DeMille and his cronies would look awful if they accepted the resignation. With all of Hollywood caught up on the ongoing battle, the next day's *Daily Variety* blared "Mankiewicz Will Not Sign Oath."

With the news buzzing through town (the story was so widespread that Chris and Tom, all of eight and ten, were called "Commies" by fellow students at the El Rodeo School in Beverly Hills, and they tearfully

---

* Technically, Joe was himself Jewish, though to the end of his life he disliked being lumped together with a group he had no part in choosing. As Alex puts it, "He couldn't brook *anyone* not having a choice as to who they were, beyond the unavoidable ones like sex and skin color," which may account for why he addressed issues of race and gender so boldly in some of his films.

asked their father why he wasn't signing), DeMille upped the ante. First he screened several of Joe's films, looking for Communist propaganda, but having apparently failed to find any evidence of pinko-ness, he convened a secret meeting of board members on the Paramount lot. This time, however, not all the board members were invited; against the rules in the Guild's own bylaws, DeMille and his cronies invited only sixteen members of the board, including Frank Capra and Leo McCarey, but deliberately excluding any known Joe-supporters like Fred Zinnemann, Nicholas Ray, and Robert Wise. The "council of sixteen" drafted an anonymous ballot to recall Joe from the presidency, the entire text of which stated: "This is a ballot to recall Joe Mankiewicz. Sign here [box] yes." The ballot was then mimeographed—with dozens of copies flying off the mimeograph machines in the Paramount basement that evening. But DeMille and his pals were careful. They needed only 60 percent of the Guild's directors to win a recall, and they didn't want any of Joe's friends to tip him off, so Vernon Keays, the executive secretary of the Guild, combed through the list of the Guild's directors and excluded those who might tell Joe of the attempted coup. Then messengers on motorcycles stormed off into the night with 160 envelopes to see what could be done.

It was the night of October 11, 1951. Joe was in a screening room across town at Fox when the phone rang. It was Herman, with a gleeful question: "What do you have in common with Andrew Johnson?" Then, not waiting for a reply: "You're being impeached, my boy!" Joe was stunned, and Herman told him, "Did you know, for Christ's sake, there's a fucking recall action on against you? Johnny Farrow said some guy just drove up on a motorcycle to his house to get him to sign the petition."

The next night, *All About Eve* opened to rapturous reviews at the Roxy in New York City. But Joe wasn't there. Instead he was at Chasen's in Hollywood, fighting for his professional life. He had summoned to the restaurant, in addition to his lawyer, Martin Gang, many of his friends and supporters, including some of the most prominent industry directors, including the four most recent Best Director Oscar winners before Joe (Billy Wilder, William Wyler, Elia Kazan, and John Huston). Gang started the meeting by emphasizing the severity DeMille's recall action posed—if it was successful, Joe's career was over. Gang suggested a legal order to halt the spread and counting of the ballots, and a petition for a general meeting of the members to inform everyone of Joe's position on these events.

The next ten days were a flurry of activity—secret meetings, phone calls, impassioned righteousness on all sides. Joe's friends worked around the clock calling directors to urge them not to sign, and the recall vote itself soon seemed likely to fail. Gang filed a complaint in Superior Court, claiming he had enough evidence from interviews he and George Stevens had conducted at the Guild office to "blow DeMille right out of the water." At the next board meeting, where its members were intending to determine how voting would take place at the membership meeting the following Sunday, DeMille offered an olive branch: he would drop the recall if Joe would perform "an act of contrition," perhaps a written declaration that Joe could write and give to Louella Parsons or Hedda Hopper, "who can read this to the American people . . . that you are sorry for what you have done." Joe was characteristically aghast: "Oh hell, you can stuff your act of contrition." Frank Capra suggested that the board give Joe a unanimous vote of confidence, and the entire board agreed. But DeMille refused to stop the recall, and finally Capra had had enough. Like Jimmy Stewart looking down at his hand after shaking hands with Mr. Potter in *It's a Wonderful Life,* Capra finally turned on DeMille and resigned from the Guild's board of directors.

The stage was set. The next night, October 22, 1950, several hundred members of the Guild gathered at the Crystal Room of the Beverly Hills Hotel for what one would later call the most tumultuous meeting in Hollywood history and what Joe would say was the most dramatic evening of his life. Joe drove to the meeting with Elia Kazan, who had just finished filming *A Streetcar Named Desire,* but as they pulled up outside the hotel, Kazan turned to Joe with a sheepish look on his face. He told Joe that he couldn't attend the meeting. DeMille knew about Kazan's Communist Party membership, he explained, and he would no doubt use it, and anything else he could, against Joe. With that, the men shook hands, and Joe went inside alone.

The ballroom was packed. Joe called the meeting to order and began with a speech that was quiet and calm, primarily a recital of the facts as he saw them, outlining the events leading up to the meeting and refuting the accusations of the recall committee. Cleverly, he never used the word "I" but rather said "Mankiewicz" throughout the speech, and with the exception of one reference to DeMille, never referred to a board member by name. He ended with an attack on the "Politburo quality" of the recall ballot, and when he was finished received a standing ovation.

Then DeMille took the stage. He began quite artfully, as he acknowledged that Joe had no connection to communism, and insisted that the board acted democratically. But then he turned to Joe's supporters. In an attempt to appear reasonable, DeMille admitted his fault in this debacle, that the Guild "could have avoided this laundering of rather soiled linen tonight," and suggested that the ballots be destroyed. But he couldn't leave it at that. He criticized Joe for refusing to sign the joint statement drafted by the recall committee and suggested that if Joe stayed in office his left-wing backers would take over the Guild.

What followed was a barrage of more talk and counter-talk, criticism and grandstanding worthy of one of the "socially responsible" films of the period. John Huston declaimed that many of Joe's admirers were "in uniform when you [DeMille] were wrapping yourself in the flag." George Stevens read from a report he had made on the secrecy of the whole recall movement: "He would just have been smeared and out . . . quick, overnight, or in 36 hours, if you please." One of DeMille's allies, Leo McCarey, tried to defend the action by saying, "Everybody was moving pretty fast, and it was a fire, and maybe we used the wrong nozzle." Joe saw an opening and fired back: "But I am the only one that got wet!" Still, DeMille would not yield, continuing to refer to several directors' alleged susceptibility to Communism, and then, misreading his audience for perhaps the final time, he adapted a vaguely Jewish accent and read the names of "Mr. Villy Vyler . . . Mr. Fleddie Zinnemann . . ." as well as a list of the Communist organizations they were affiliated with. He was met with a torrent of hissing and booing.

The tide turned, at last. Wyler rose in his own defense and said that the next time someone questioned his loyalty to his country, he would "kick hell out of him. I don't care how old he is or how big." Fritz Lang, the German director who had escaped the Nazis to come to Hollywood in the 1930s, said, "Mr. DeMille, do you know this is the first time since I'm in America that I'm afraid, because I have an accent?" Finally, after midnight, John Ford raised his hand. When he got up to speak, Joe knew that the members of the Guild would lean whichever way Ford did.

The director, wearing his customary eye patch, surveyed the room slowly, then spoke like a character from one of his movies: "My name is John Ford. I am a director of Westerns . . . I am one of the founders of this Guild . . . I would like to state that I have been on Mr. Mankiewicz's side of the fight all through it." Then he turned to DeMille. "I admire you," Ford told him, "but I don't like you, and I don't like a thing you stand for."

The room was buzzing. "I have been sick and tired and ashamed of this whole goddamned thing," Ford continued. "I don't care which side it is. If they intend to break up the Guild, goddamn it, they have pretty much done it tonight." Ford said that seeing "the two blackest Republicans I know, Joseph Mankiewicz and C. B. DeMille, [feuding] over Communism is getting laughable to me," and he closed by calling for the resignation of the entire board. "Let's turn the guild over to the Polack [Joe], and go home," Ford pleaded. "Tomorrow, let's go back and make movies." This produced thunderous applause. At 2:20 a.m., the meeting adjourned, with DeMille trudging from the hall, disgraced but defiant, and Joe getting handshakes and hearty slaps on the back from well-wishers and friends.

It was over.

Joe Mankiewicz was vindicated. The awards were safe. The reputation was safe. He had commandeered a challenging situation and made it all come out okay. Everything was in place. He had proven to the world that he was a good man. It was time to get out.

CHAPTER THIRTEEN

———— ♔ ————

HOORAY FOR THE BULLDOG

And then, last week, as it must to all men, death came to
Charles Foster Kane.

—*CITIZEN KANE*

HER HUSBAND'S FUNERAL HAD BEEN EARLIER THAT DAY, AND SARA WAS
tired. None of it had gone the way one would have liked. To begin with,
there'd been that awful rabbi, a kind man, sweet and well-meaning but
so, well, dumb, who had asked her, "Would you care to view the body?"
She looked at the man sternly: "Do you mean would I like to *see my husband*?" And the body . . . Don had been sent back to the house the night
before to select a suit, but he'd accidentally picked out one of his own,
which didn't fit Herman all that well. At least he wore the tie Sara had
picked out, the pink one Johanna had given him the year he'd won the
Academy Award, on which she had hand-painted a big gold Oscar. Herman had beamed with pride, wearing it to lunches, parties, everywhere.
He adored that tie and Sara knew he would have been happy to be buried
in something Johanna made.

After the funeral, there'd been a gathering back at the house. Close
friends, family, and more people even than the gathering the night before,
which had also gone on much too late—eleven or twelve o'clock before
people got the hint that Sara needed to rest and they should all get out.
Joe and Rosa had flown in from New York with the boys, and they were
all staying at Sara's house. Friends kept coming and going, the house
seeming to breathe with people paying their respects.

Finally, it was over, and she'd come upstairs to her little bedroom to
sleep. But not long after she'd climbed into bed she heard noises, the

unmistakable muffled noise of an argument from Joe and Rosa's room. Yelling, quarreling, a shrillness, then the lower rumble. Then the slam of the front door; Joe leaving the house, and the starting up of his car, and the roar of the automobile speeding away. For a moment, peace. Sara exhaled. Why in the world, she wondered, had the two of them left Los Angeles if all their problems had simply followed along to New York?

Then, incredibly, the door opened, and Rosa came in. Her eyes were swollen and she reeked of liquor, and she climbed into Sara's bed with her. She nestled close, hugged Sara and told her how wonderful Herman was, and how much she was going to miss him. Her hot breath wafted over Sara like a perfume of unhappiness. Joe, Rosa was telling Sara, is a miserable man, but Herman . . . Herman, she said through her tears, he was the great one. Sara got out of bed and put on a robe, and for what seemed like hours Rosa complained and cried and sobbed out her misery, how horrid Joe is, how awful, how much she hates herself and wishes she were dead, and how great Herman was, how lucky Sara was to have him.

The last three years were a blur now, all the stays in the hospital, all the tests and poking and prodding, Herman losing so much weight from the uremia that ultimately took his life that by the final months he looked almost as old as he felt, his cheeks hollow, his eyes deep set, the twinkle now so rare. Not that the wit was ever gone. Those final few days in the hospital, he'd been in top form—when Joe told Herman that he'd gotten their sister Erna a job in Rome coaching some local actors, someone asked, "In what?" and Herman answered, "Italian, of course." There were jokes, and tears, and papers, so many legal documents for Herman to sign, loans that needed to be underwritten, and Herman took to saying that he was preparing to go meet his co-maker, referring to the loans he now always needed cosigned. Joe invariably did the honors. Sara had left the two brothers alone for a while those last few days. When she'd come back to the room, they'd both seemed fine, and what went on she never knew, though it was probably in there that Herman made Joe promise to look after Johanna, and Joe said of course he would, he'd pay for Josie's college and get her a trip to Europe afterward too, he'd see to that. Joe had told Sara all of this, and he never gave her any indication to doubt him.

And their final moments. Sara, feeling flush and happy after a rare midday visit to a beauty salon for a facial, returned and leaned in to kiss Herman and before she knew what was happening, she was kissing his face all over, this marvelous, wonderful, infuriating man to whom she'd devoted her life, and he kissed her back, nibbling, the two of them necking like teenagers in front of the nurse. The next day, Sara blushed when Herman told her in front of the same nurse, "Hey, that was some love scene we played last night." He smiled at her, and she knew that no matter what, he wanted her, even as he faded.

His strength, though, never seemed to leave him, not completely, for even after he'd fallen into his final coma, Sara leaned in close to try to rouse him. "Herman," she'd call, hoping he'd regain consciousness, but he'd lift his arms and fight her, push her away, as if, she said later, whatever he was doing, wherever he was going, he didn't want to be interrupted. . . .

When the news finally came, Sara had not been in the room. Herman had been covered with an oxygen tent by then—"where I couldn't get at him," she said later—and the breaths became more labored and difficult before stopping altogether—and Frank's wife Holly saw Sara in the hallway moments later, literally shaking her fist at the heavens, furious, exhausted, and ready to collapse.

Now, five days later, Sara sat on the edge of her chaise lounge, watching her drunken, crazy Austrian sister-in-law, having requisitioned her bed, mope and wail about the sorry state of her marriage and curse the day that Joe had ever come into her life. Finally the thought flashed through Goma's exhausted mind like an arrow fired from a quiver of sanity: "What the hell am I doing comforting this woman when *I* am the one who just buried my husband?"

The next morning came a final astonishment. Rosa's plane back East left at ten, but she was still upstairs in her room when Joe marched downstairs, telling Sara that Rosa had to catch this flight. Sara was doubtful— *you didn't see her last night, she had a rough night, I'm not sure she's going to make it.* They were at Sara's breakfast table, picking at scones, and then Rosa sailed down, bright and cheerful, dressed in a tailored suit and a beautiful hat—"an absolute vision of beauty and health," Sara said. Rosa downed a quick glass of orange juice, kissed Joe goodbye as if nothing had happened the night before, and left the house to go catch her plane.

Sara wondered who these people were. How in the world did they function?

JOE KNEW WHAT IT WAS. A CERTAIN CLASS OF PEOPLE, LIKE HIS sister-in-law, would have called Rosa some kind of Jekyll-and-Hyde character. She could be so kind to the kids, look after the house, be a damn good housewife when she put her mind to it—it was no effort at all for her to pose for those pictures for *Look* magazine, all of them playing cards, the boys in their matching plaid bathrobes. Not that the four of them would have played cards together *in a million years*; but the picture certainly looked convincing. Rosa was the model of domestic solidity, and damn if she didn't keep the house running smoothly. She was good with the servants, had that domineering Austrian presence, knew when to be curt with them, when to let things slide. It was a fine home. Or at least it would've been, Joe thought, if they'd never had to deal with Rosa's other side. Joe called it "eight o'clock, curtain." It was regular as clockwork, she slipped into those moods at night, when it was time for the curtain to go up on some performance somewhere—without her.

Joe told Tom years later that one of his favorite moments in his brother's masterpiece was when Susan Alexander Kane is prowling around that big mansion and asks Kane what time it is in New York.

             KANE
Half past eleven.

             SUSAN
At night?

             KANE
Yes. The bulldog's just gone to press.

             SUSAN
Hurray for the bulldog! . . . Half
past eleven. The shows have just let
out. People are going to night clubs
and restaurants. Of course, we're
different! We live in a palace—at the
end of the world.

It's not that Joe had trapped Rosa in the same kind of gilded cage Charles Foster Kane had put Susan Alexander Kane in, but Rosa certainly felt Joe had taken her away from what she loved. Of course that was unfair. Hadn't he supported all her efforts to get into the Hollywood game? Hadn't he pushed for her to be cast in *The Keys of the Kingdom*?

Wasn't Nunnally Johnson running all over town telling people Joe said that his marriage was doomed if Rosa didn't get the part? Then there was the nightmare of Boston. Rosa had finally gotten a part in a play by Edna Ferber and George S. Kaufman. The play—bearing the ironic title *Bravo!*—was headed to Broadway, and Rosa prayed it would reignite her career. The rehearsals, or so Joe had been told, had gone well—then Joe showed up in Boston to watch a performance, one of the final previews before the show moved to New York. He didn't think it was half bad, and Rosa was good, affecting even. Afterwards, they'd gone to a party in the hotel suite of one of the show's producers, and as soon as Joe entered he felt a chill. Not that Joe expected them to ask him for notes (though he had a few), but what accounted for the damn cold shoulder? Just because he was a Hollywood guy didn't mean he didn't understand the theater. It took until the following morning, when the producer told Rosa's agent that Ms. Stradner was being replaced and wouldn't be accompanying the play to New York, that Joe understood their reticence to seek his counsel. "As you know, it can never be the play at fault," Joe said later. "The director has to be replaced, or the actors."

Since then, there'd been very little talk of comebacks or theater, or practically anything that would get the woman out of the house. And so, every night, long about the time that imagined curtain was rising on some performance in the alternate life Rosa lived in, in whatever neurotic hemisphere she took comfort in, with whatever alcohol she could find, Rosa would start to steep in the juice of her own misery, and the temper would flare. Joe would give as good as he got—Joe's agent and confidant Robbie Lantz called the arguments the two of them enacted "murderous fights"—but in Joe's mind, a man could only take so much. Though he refused to admit his part in the tango—a dance he loved so much he'd later feature it in *The Barefoot Contessa,* and which, of course, it takes two to perform—he did agree that with the general atmosphere becoming so "Macbethish," it was frequently impossible to stay home; he had to get away, get some air, some food, some intimacy and understanding in another pair of arms. . . .

Joe wasn't happy about it, not at all. He knew that nearly every night, Rosa would go in and talk Chris's ear off, crying and telling him what a lousy damn husband Joe was, seeking advice from a goddamn kid, ten or twelve or whatever he was now—and Tom was even worse, the poor kid had asthma and would have to go into the bathroom and suck on oxygen from a metal tank, trying to calm himself down, made so unhappy by his mother's inappropriate and frankly crazy behavior—but honestly now, with all the Guild business Joe had to tend to, and the normal helping of studio politics, not to mention his actual work, trying to write and direct these pictures that were, leave us not forget, putting food on their plates, what more could he do?

What he could do, what he had done, once he'd achieved the level of success he'd reached after *Eve* cleaned up at the Oscars, was get the hell out of Hollywood. He and Herman had each talked about forty as being the age to get out of Dodge, and here Joe was, only two years late, and it was time to go. Robbie Lantz said the final straw was an incident where someone tossed a rock through the dining room window, and the only response from one of the boys was "Get the butler to deal with it." Whatever it was, Joe was happy to make his escape. In September 1951, less than a year removed from his great triumph at the Guild and six months after he'd cleaned up at the Oscars, he negotiated an end to his contract with Fox, the family packed its belongings, and a Mankiewicz returned to New York at last.* Herman viewed it all ruefully, knowing that it was too late for him, but he was glad that Joe was getting out of town. For Herman, Hollywood had become home, he would die here, he'd known that.

So here Joe was, in March 1953, back for Herman's goddamn funeral, and it was like he'd never left. Sara was still giving him those damn looks, and Rosa was still causing agony, and New York was no better on that score, and in some ways worse, what with the closeness of Broadway, the theater world almost mocking him with its proximity. And the move had begun with that damn fire, from which Joe wasn't sure he'd ever recover— there had been two Bekins moving vans taking all the family belongings East, one full of clothes, toys, and the stuff of domestic life, the other full of Joe's work. And of course that was the one that had toppled over on a lonely stretch of highway in Iowa of all places, skidding across the highway, slamming into a pylon, and bursting into flames. Three whole file cabinets' worth of Joe's scripts and notes had been incinerated, gone for good—twenty years of Joe's life, vanished up into the Midwestern sky. Worse than that were the notes Joe had taken over the years for unproduced projects—screenplays and plays, dammit, plays he intended to write when he was in New York. What survived? A few pictures, some leather-bound editions of his favorite books, and, oh yes, the Oscars. No

---

* For Joe, it felt like now or never: "I said to myself, 'If you don't get out now, you'll never get out,' and nobody can say 'Oh, he's leaving because he can't get a job.'"

one would ever believe him that he wished it had been the other way around.

In the years that followed, friends and relatives, cousins and nephews and nieces would look at those Oscars—placed, no matter the home, in a prominent spot, four proud sentries guarding an entire life and reputation—and marvel at how they gleamed. No Oscars in the history of the world, Frank's son Josh would say later, had ever been so beautifully taken care of.

Herman's Oscar on the other hand, would grow dark from misuse, neglect, and lack of care. Resting for years on Goma's mantel on 5th Anita Drive in Brentwood, it had the look of an ancient totem from a long-vanished tribe, a symbol of a forgotten time.

CHAPTER FOURTEEN

⚜

MAN-ABOUT-TOWN

It is senseless to insist that theatrical folk in New York, Hollywood and London are no different from the good people of Des Moines, Chillicothe and Liverpool. By and large, we are concentrated gatherings of neurotics, egomaniacs, emotional misfits, and precocious children.

—*ALL ABOUT EVE*

THE CITY WAS HOT THE DAY OF HIS NIECE'S FUNERAL. JOE SAT IN A rumpled light summer suit and looked across the aisle to the pew of his sister-in-law, Sara, who would now, in addition to being the world's most pitied widow, add another title: poor Sara, who lost her goddamn daughter to a tragic death at the age of thirty-six. Joe craned his neck around and looked at the mourners and his stomach tightened. What kind of world does this to a woman in the prime of her life? What kind of pitiable goddamn God could there possibly be if this was how He was going to treat one of the few good ones to come along? Josie had her faults, God knows, but would it have been too much to ask for it to have been someone else slammed by that goddamn taxicab? . . .

Rosemary* squeezed his hand and tilted her head in the direction of Peter and the boys, now walking in. His nephew-in-law and the two boys, Timmy and Nicky, walking down the center aisle of this vast unair-conditioned chapel, with all eyes on them in their ill-fitting suits and waffle-sized ties. But the boys looked okay. They looked like they would probably be able to survive this damn thing as well as anyone—boys had a way of doing that, didn't they? The whole day, Joe told Rosemary later, he had found himself thinking of his own boys, not too distant in ages

---

* Joe's third wife was named Rosemary; his second was named Rosa, or Rose; yes, this was confusing.

when they first moved to New York than Josie's kids here, and how they had to survive so much, and while he knew Chris hadn't exactly pulled out of it yet, he would, just give him time, and he knew Josie's boys would be okay too . . . So funny, that there were all these sets of brothers. . . .

AND SO, THERE THEY WERE, TWENTY-THREE YEARS EARLIER—NOT in midsummer 1974 when Herman's daughter Johanna died in a freakish car accident on the streets of Greenwich Village, but autumn 1951, with the Joe Mankiewiczes happily settling into an eleven-room apartment on Park Avenue and the boys sent off to private schools: Tom to St. Bernard's, Chris to Collegiate. From the start, it seemed that the boys, like many sets of brothers two years apart,* had fallen into different grooves: Chris the sloppy underachieving mess, Tom in the do-goody, hard-working scholar role. In later years, in other ways, consciously or not, the boys' relationship would come to echo that of their father and uncle, with several people suggesting a Herman–Joe dynamic in their ultimate paths. Tom, the younger, became, like his father, a successful Hollywood screenwriter, working on several James Bond movies, the first two Superman movies, and creating and running the popular *Hart to Hart* television series, while Chris, by many people's reckoning (especially his own) the more brilliant intellect, had foundered in job after job, angering bosses with his disdain for the niceties of human interaction and completely unable to swallow the "Hollywood bullshit."

As children, Tom's and Chris's estrangement was less pronounced than it would be in later years, but they were never great companions; they read different books, had different interests and friends, and, most seriously, viewed their father and mother in very different ways. While both boys were fascinated by movies, it was Tom who seemed to idolize his dad, and as soon as he was able, he could be found on Joe's sets. Chris was moodier and took after his mother; he distrusted his father with every ounce of his being; his deep and pronounced love and knowledge of classical music came from Rosa. But in a family steeped in movies, there was almost nothing a boy could do with a devotion to classical music. Though in later years both his father and brother would make a show of bemoaning that

---

* The difference between Chris and Tom was twenty months, not too far off from Don and Frank's twenty-six months, or the twenty-two months between Tim and me.

Chris had never found his true calling and become, perhaps, some kind of musicologist, at the time Joe mocked Chris mercilessly for the way he swung his arms around pretending to conduct. One relative remembers a typical diatribe Joe hurled at the adolescent Chris in front of guests: "You think you're Leonard Bernstein just because you throw your arms around like that, you don't know the first goddamn thing about it."

The brutality of the comment . . . It was as if Joe were determined to stick it to his sons, the way Franz had to him and Herman. And while Joe could certainly hide behind the fact that he was as unforgiving of himself as he was of his two sons, that he never softened his own self-criticism (the movies he'd made were bad, he routinely told friends in New York, they were beneath him; he'd wasted his talents; he should be writing a play . . .), it didn't make it any easier to be on the receiving end of such cruelty. To harangue one's sons and detail their faults was simply par for the Mankiewiczian course. Interestingly, Chris sensed something else at work, a kind of autocratic gene that all family members are born with that endows one with an imagined special insight into the way people should be living their lives. Chris's favorite title of any Joe Mankiewicz movie was *House of Strangers.** "It's funny," he told me years later, "that a family of writers has such great difficulty communicating with each other. The problem in our family is, everybody wants to tell everybody what they want to tell them, and nobody wants to listen."

In Chris's mind, one of Joe's biggest faults—and Chris was a fan of listing them—was that he never listened: not to his sons and certainly not to Rosa. Because while being yanked out of California was obviously a shock to both boys' systems, New York didn't bring any real change in their lives in one crucial way: their mother was still unstable. Ill, sick, crazy, angry—however the problem was defined, it was no easier to live with in New York than it had been in Hollywood, and now, for the first time, perhaps because the apartment was so vast, Joe and Rosa took separate

---

* Joe routinely derided his 1949 film starring Edward G. Robinson, a neo-noir about an Italian-American family whose members all seem motivated not by love but by hate, but it holds up pretty well. Once you get past the hammy mid-century Italian accents ("I do-a what-a I think-a is right!"), the acting is excellent, anchored by Robinson's controlling, vicious father whose rages and legally questionable business practices have poisoned his four sons. Now that *The Godfather* and *The Sopranos* routinely top lists of the greatest screen achievements of the last half century, *House of Strangers,* about the dissolution of an Italian-American family in the wake of criminal charges against the patriarch, seems ripe for a critical renaissance.

bedrooms. But the boys shared a bedroom, meaning it was even more natural both for Rosa to be alone and for
her to come to their room and berate
the boys. Classically, each later felt that
he was the one most often targeted by
his mother's rages. She would rant and
yell, and it was impossible to do anything but sit and take it, no matter that
it made everyone miserable and usually
exacerbated Tom's asthma to the point
where even after his mother finally left
the room and the boys would be alone
in the dark, he would be wheezing so
loudly he'd keep Chris awake. Chris

Joe at the top of his game

would ask him to please let him get some sleep, and Tom would go into
the bathroom and lie down on the floor, seeing his reflection in the mirror
on the back of the bathroom door. Deeply unsettled by her desperation,
Tom sensed his relationship with his mother growing increasingly bizarre,
highlighted by her strange proclivity for predicting precisely how, and
with whom, her youngest boy would lose his virginity.

In some families, these two brothers might have become closer than
words, bonded by growing up in the same foxhole—but not these particular grandsons of Franz Mankiewicz, who instead became competitors
and combatants. Chris and Tom would eye each other suspiciously at the
breakfast table, seeing who could sit closer to Dad, and which of them
could get him to look up from his paper, on those days when he was
even home for breakfast—now that he was running an actual production
company, he had less time, or so he would insist, for things like breakfast,
lunch, or dinner—and catch the old man's eye for a moment, perhaps tell
him something funny that had happened at school, or maybe a witticism
that had been thought of overnight, an idea that had been polished like a
gem, to take to the King in the hopes of becoming the favorite.

The contrast between Joe's personal life and professional life could not
have been starker. For here was Joe at the top of the heap at last, cresting
on the wave of his greatest success: friends with the smart set, free to do
as he pleased in the great city that represented the opposite of everything
he hated, and continuing to write and direct literate entertainment for the
masses. Of course it may sometimes have been too literate; his first film

after *All About Eve* was the aptly named *People Will Talk,* a speechifying movie starring Cary Grant as the brilliant Dr. Praetorious, a gynecologist who expounds at length on the virtues of psychiatry, one of Joe's great interests. Interestingly, the woman in the movie, a pregnant widow who falls for Dr. Praetorious, was played by Jeanne Crain, for whom Joe had developed a strange antipathy, though he'd also cast her in *A Letter to Three Wives.* (When asked about the curious coincidence of her playing women named Deborah in both movies, Joe said, "I don't like the name Deborah, and I don't like Jeanne Crain.")* Watching the film today, you are struck by how unlikely a pair Grant and Crain are, how patronizing he is, and how much the film seems to accept and even approve of the doctor's pomposity. It is Joe's own attitude toward women projected on a screen, unmediated by any Eve–Margo dynamic and without the luscious scorn of Addison DeWitt to leaven the proceedings. Dr. Praetorious claims to be fascinated by women—he's a gynecologist, after all—but Joe cast an actress he loathed in the lead role, and Crain and Grant's ultimately getting together feels much more like the demands of genre than any true meeting of the characters. As Chris says, "If your conception of conversation is, you're on and you get to say everything, and everybody else is simply supposed to listen and basically applaud, laugh or whatever . . ." The movie feels lopsided and inauthentic. Joe's difficulty in getting close to people had worked when it came to painting a portrait, as in *Eve,* of people who are admittedly damaged and neurotic and belong to a class of people—show people—who revel in their own hang-ups. But a movie like *People Will Talk* doesn't have the built-in excuse of being a portrait of characters who can't connect. Instead, it shows people not connecting, but thinking they are—haranguing each other with arguments, righteousness, and a sense of aggrievedness, as if the whole world somehow owes them the chance to speak and be heard. It's not a bad goal, really, but as he

---

* Why Joe had such an aversion to the actress is hard to discern, as is why he continued to cast her if he disliked her so much; originally he'd cast Anne Baxter to play the role in *People Will Talk,* but Baxter, ironically, had to give up the role when she became pregnant. "I could only rarely escape the feeling that Jeanne was a visitor to the set," Joe said of Crain, who had been raised in a Catholic home in Santa Barbara and had been an ice skater before becoming an actress, and who fought fervently for Republican causes in Orange County. Joe found her "very pleasant, very shy, and very devout," and it's likely that this sane creature just never responded to Joe in any way. "She was one of the few whose presence among the theater-folk I have never fully understood."

Cary Grant and Jeanne Crain in *People Will Talk* (1951)

talked about his father in later years, Chris loved to quote the old Whistler line: "Conversation is going to be difficult if others insist on talking."

There's a peculiar irony at work in Joe's personal challenge in opening up to people and, more important, allowing others to open up to him, namely that he'd built his professional life and reputation in large part on being so very good at listening. But there's a huge difference between being a good professional listener, and listening well in real life. When Joe talked with his actors (or more germanely, his actresses), there was a goal: to draw out a performance to help make a great movie. He was masterful with actors and actresses—and, maybe because it was all make-believe, he was also able to reveal more of himself when dealing with them, the wit and warmth that he so often kept hidden. The story of his first meeting with Thelma Ritter is enlightening: After seeing the actress in a tiny part in *Miracle on 34th Street,* Joe realized he'd spotted "an almost extinct species in our theatrical ecology: the great character comedienne." He went to New York to interview her. "I walk in nervous," she said, "and besides I'd cut my finger and it's all done up in bandages so it sticks out like a barber pole. Joe looks at me, looks at the finger, and says 'Did you have it wrapped for a gift?' So of course, I fell in love with him."* Joe's piercing blue eyes and understanding expression instantly relaxed his actresses.

---

* The affection was mutual: Joe wrote the part Birdie Coonan in *All About Eve* for Ritter, and said that she was "that rare performing talent which the writer and/or director must treasure as a fiddler would a Stradivarius."

With them, he could calculate, cajole, and manipulate to get what he needed. But when he was at home, with his family, his children, his wife, there was no such goal. The goal was merely to live a good life, which at that point wasn't something Joe put much stock in.

The value, always, was in the work. And so it was, even more than it had been in Los Angeles, for the Mankiewiczes of Park Avenue. Joe had come to New York with hopes of writing a few plays, and only making films that he wanted to make. He had his chance now to be his own man, and from 1951 onward, he seized it with both hands. He formed a production company, Figaro, named for the happy schemer of opera and literature as well as the French newspaper—and built his professional life into a structure in which he could operate with impunity and absolute power. There were challenges, of course—he had to raise money and sometimes go hat in hand to wealthy patrons who made him feel almost as powerless as he had with Mayer in Hollywood—but for the most part, he was running his own show. He brought on Robbie Lantz, his former agent in Hollywood, to help oversee the company, which in time became something like a second family, another one where he didn't really have to listen to anyone.

But Joe's creative output in the years after his decision to move to New York yields a few serious questions: First, what of theater? Why did he never try it? Although he did stage a serious, well-regarded interpretation of the opera *La Bohème* at the Metropolitan Opera in 1952, he never succeeded in writing a play. Why? His own explanation, offered decades later, was glib but revealing: "It's as if the theater were the one woman I wanted to go to bed with and she's gonna turn me down." So he never really asked.

And in film, another question: Why did Joe all but abandon the social comedies, the literate and satirical pieces that had made his reputation? His best films had mirrored and sometimes skewered society wittily and intelligently; why stop? Instead, with his almost unparalleled level of success granting him the ability to write his own ticket, Joe funneled his cinematic energies in the 1950s into an almost dizzying array of genres. He wrote and directed thrillers, musicals, and even Shakespeare over the span of a few years—5 *Fingers, Guys and Dolls,* and *Julius Caesar* among them—and in a man who was so closed off personally, it is important to look at these films to try to discern what was going on inside their maker, for the vitality and sheer number of them suggest that it was here that his heart really lay in the 1950s. True, without a strong producer to check his impulses, Joe often ended up indulging himself with longer and talkier scripts. But while it would be churlish to suggest that this second family's offspring were as dear to him as his own children, there is no denying the care Joe gave his work during this time. Despite the genre switching, the attention paid off. The films, though none are classics on the order of *All About Eve,* are good, solid professional entertainments.

Joe's final contract film for Fox, the last he would make with Zanuck before being free to go out on his own, foreshadowed his need for independence. In *5 Fingers,* an entertaining spy caper after Hitchcock, James Mason stars as the central spy character, a valet to the British ambassador to Ankara who sells top secret allied files to Nazis. Joe's smart dialogue hooks up beautifully with Mason's British cynicism. As a charming, conscious social climber, unsuspected by the embassy, Mason expertly masks his cold ambition in a way that is reminiscent of *Eve.* And just as with *Eve,* Joe could channel into the character that part of him he claimed he despised—his drive to beat everyone to the finish line at any cost. It works beautifully, anchored by a charismatic and chilly performance from Mason. Joe deserves credit for bringing it out of him, and for directing some of the best action sequences of his career in the film.*

For his next project, Joe went to the source: Shakespeare. Having been offered a deal to go back to M-G-M, Joe first recoiled at the thought of reteaming with Mayer, but in the end, the prospect of tackling one of the Bard's most fearsome and cold assessments of ambition proved irresistible. With *Julius Caesar,* Joe could explore ambition and its attendant risks, of self-destruction and the corrosion of the soul. Conservative in his dramaturgy as always, Joe left the original text intact save a few minor excisions, but the risk this time was in the casting. Here, notwithstanding James Mason's excellent Brutus, Joe made the decision that makes the movie still worth watching—he chose Marlon Brando to play Marc Antony. Later, Joe recalled that when he first asked the method hero to tackle one of Shakespeare's toughest roles, Brando had only muttered, "Oh, my God," and made no other comment for weeks. But finally, Joe was summoned to Brando's apartment, "a filthy pad on Fifty-seventh Street that bore the remnants of many broads." There, where Brando kept live possums, the actor played Joe his early practice tapes and began to forge an alliance; in

---

* Twenty years later, Mason said that the film was in fact Joe's last good one, maintaining of Joe-without-Zanuck: "I personally have not seen a Mankiewicz film that appeared to be well directed since then."

Louis Calhern, Marlon Brando, and Greer Garson
in *Julius Caesar*

the end, Joe got Brando to perform an Antony that both made sense to 1950s audiences and captured the essential complexities in the character. Brando enjoyed working with Joe and for decades afterwards repeated a favorite story from the shoot: of the time a day player, not knowing a particular scene was ready to be shot, had snuck away to relieve himself. For a full twenty minutes, with Joe stewing up on a crane, the cast, led by Brando, Deborah Kerr, and John Gielgud, made pee-pee jokes. Finally, the day player returned, apologized profusely, and the cast settled down from their punning hijinks. With everyone waiting for Joe to call action, he did nothing for a moment, then took the pipe out of his mouth, looked down imperiously, and said, "You don't have nearly the talent, young man, to keep this company waiting twenty minutes." According to Brando, "We all snapped to, straightened up like a bunch of school kids . . . Joe had just taken his set back."

Defying expectations—and the mockery of comics who were sure he would make a hash of the Bard—Brando received an Academy Award nomination and generally glowing reviews; *New York Times* critic Bosley Crowther called Antony's oration over Caesar's body "brilliant" and "electrifying." Although the location and action sequences were marred by budgetary constraints, the movie was a solid success, and Joe was proud that he had brought Shakespeare back to Hollywood, where he had been declared unfit for the screen ever since Max Reinhardt's disastrous *A Midsummer Night's Dream* in 1935, with Mickey Rooney as an ingratiating Puck.*

The first independent project Joe undertook was *The Barefoot Contessa,* perhaps the "quintessential Joe Mankiewicz" movie. All the trademark signs are there: the use of flashbacks, a focus on women's psychology, and even a Joe stand-in who eviscerates Hollywood. Trying to balance entertainment and didacticism, the screenplay showed unusual sensitivity toward women as Joe explored the crushing difficulties actresses face as the object of male fantasies. He also used the film to deride the superficiality and destructiveness of the upper-echelon "international set." But because Joe combines cultural criticism with tragedy rather than comedy (and because Humphrey Bogart, for all his gifts, was no George Sanders), the commentary comes across as far more heavy-handed than in *Eve,* and the film's reputation as preachy beyond belief, "with an astonishing lack of subtlety and aesthetic judgment," is hard to defend. Joe self-deprecatingly referred to it as an unknown film years later and acknowledged that he hadn't entirely settled on what the movie should have been, but what's curious is his explanation: "It was almost a good film but there were too many stories; I was angry at too many things."

"Angry at too many things" would make a fitting subtitle for this period of Joe's life. Like many successful men, the fact that he'd built a successful career (and family, at least for public consumption) did not soothe the savage breast. For Joe, making *The Barefoot Contessa,* which purported to show how so many different men abused and exploited a poor helpless girl from nowhere while one man alone saw the ruin but failed to stop it from happening, proved another fatal step in the long parade to ruin that he and Rosa were leading. In fact, the film's ending, with

Joe on the set of the Roman Forum, *Julius Caesar,* early 1950s

---

* Even the generally better received *Romeo and Juliet* in 1936, directed by George Cukor and starring Norma Shearer and the forty-three-year-old Leslie Howard as the star-crossed teenage lovers, had flopped at the box office.

Humphrey Bogart with Joe on the set of
The Barefoot Contessa, 1954

the successful writer-director (Bogart) mourning the unstable actress's tragic death, would prove prophetic.

Joe had brought his own fragile and insecure Rosa to Rome with him while he made the picture. (He'd also brought along Tom, while Chris stayed home in New York to finish eighth grade.) The fighting between Rosa and Joe was intense in Rome, made more so by Joe's bizarre decision to also bring to Rome—to help take care of Tom—Rosa's mother, Gross.* From the moment Gross got off the plane from Austria the two women were at each other's throats. For Tom, the experience provided not just a distorted insight into women and their mothers—"they hate each other worse than if they'd actually once been lovers"—but one of his early exposures to life on a film set, because to help Tom escape his battling mother and grandmother, Joe brought the boy to work with him almost every day. There, in a cavernous building at Rome's famed film studio Cinecittà one morning, while technicians moved lights around on a vineyard set, Humphrey Bogart spotted eleven-year-old Tom Mankiewicz. "Are you cold?" Bogart asked young Tom; Tom nodded. Bogart poured the young boy a thimble full of scotch, which Tom all but inhaled. A half hour later, the conversation repeated itself, with the same results. When a few moments later Joe saw Tom weaving around the faux vineyard, he confronted Bogart: "He's drunk. It has to be you, you prick."

That's the last thing Joe needed. Bogey apologized, sort of: it wouldn't

---

* Short for the German *Grossmutti* (grandmother).

happen again, but anyway, what was the big deal? Everyone out here drank, or probably everyone. . . . Not Joe, which Bogey knew, but the problems of drunks in the movie business was not in any way special to the Mankiewicz family. Joe had found himself thinking more and more of Herman on this picture, though his biggest concern was with Ava Gardner. Joe was having a lot of trouble with her. He was failing her, he could sense it. He was known for getting such great performances out of women—he'd gotten a "good luck" note from Bette Davis on the first day of shooting the movie; she

Humphrey Bogart with Rosemary Matthews (later Mankiewicz) during *The Barefoot Contessa*, Rome, 1954

remembered; she knew—but somehow he wasn't reaching Ava Gardner. She wouldn't fuck him, but that didn't matter—no one on *Eve* did either—he simply wasn't doing what he was supposed to be doing: providing her with the safety and security she needed. He hadn't realized how nervous and sensitive she really was till they'd started. In Joe's view, Ava Gardner was the dame who'd landed Sinatra, so why was she acting like some kind of gawky, insecure fourteen-year-old? When she walks into that vineyard, she should be throwing her chest out and puffing around like the greatest gift to man, knowing that every man in the theater is hungry to rip off that blouse, throw her down in the grapes, and take her.* Instead, she slinks, and imitates confidence. The camera was catching it, and Joe knew it.

But Joe's problems with his leading lady, who seemed to be pulling

---

* Around this time, Joe took his niece Johanna to Romanoff's for a sixteenth-birthday lunch and explained how women should enter a room: "He said, 'Now the kind of woman I want you to be is a woman, shoulders back, proud of your body.'" My mother paused in recollection. "He was really kind of a pig, a chauvinist . . . 'Always walk into room as if you are better than anyone in it.' Which is not my idea of how to walk into a room. My idea," she said, "is to slouch in . . . But Joe said, 'There is no woman I have ever slept with who couldn't walk into this restaurant right now and I wouldn't be proud and pleased to see her.'" The anecdote is perhaps not the definition of "avuncular."

Ava Gardner in *The Barefoot Contessa* (1954)

away from him as the production went along, paled next to the problems he was having back at the apartment with Rosa, where night after night, life was a nightmare. Bringing Rosa's mother to Rome had hardly been conducive to domestic tranquility, as Tom described vividly: "Mother yelling, Gross yelling back, then dropping to her knees, making the sign of the cross and praying loudly in German to God and Jesus while I put an oxygen mask over my mouth from a tank that sat at my bedside." With Joe worn out from working fourteen-hour days and frequently having to call in doctors, one of whom once had to administer an adrenaline shot straight into young Tom's heart, it's no wonder Tom later characterized the whole experience as "a true horror movie."

Joe's next film was a musical, his first and last. Having always idealized New York and theater, with *Guys and Dolls,* he'd be able to combine them again, this time not in an original script about those who practiced it but an adaptation of the popular Tony Award–winning musical based on Damon Runyan's stories of small-time hustlers in Times Square. Many in Hollywood were surprised that Joe intended to leave weightier topics behind to do the film, but our old friend, producer Sam Goldwyn, now seventy-two years old, had secured the rights to the property and wanted the best director in Hollywood, so Joe came on board.

Goldwyn also wanted Marlon Brando, fresh off the heels of *On the Waterfront* and now the world's biggest box office star, to play the lead Sky Masterson. As unlikely as Brando may have been in a toga declaiming Shakespeare, he seemed even less fit to play the lead in a light musical comedy, and at first he turned it down. The actor changed his mind after Joe wired him: "Understand you're apprehensive because you've never done a musical comedy. You have nothing repeat nothing to worry about. Because neither have I. Love, Joe."

Ultimately, Brando might have wished he had stuck to his guns. The movie lacks the verve of the stage musical, and Joe found filming musical numbers very different from filming dialogue. He'd never much cared where to place the camera—he saw the medium

Marlon Brando, *Guys and Dolls*

as essentially an extension of live theater and didn't want his camerawork to interfere, a strategy which for the most part had served him well. As a result, *Guys and Dolls* is unevenly directed, with the bold Technicolor sets almost doing battle with the staginess of Joe's camera placement. The cast, as always in a Joe Mankiewicz movie, does well, though for all his charm Brando sometimes has trouble with the music. But Sinatra made a fantastically raffish Nathan Detroit. Though the singer had coveted the role of Sky Masterson, when he got the second lead, he insisted the

Joe on the set of *Guys and Dolls*, 1955

producers add more songs to his role, remaining quietly contemptuous of Brando, once telling Joe, "When Mumbles is through rehearsing, I'll come out of my trailer." Joe does give some wit to the dialogue and draws some attention away from Brando's singing by expanding and deepening the Sky Masterson–Sarah Brown love story with psychological dimension. It feels, in a way it rarely does in stage productions, that somehow Sky has truly learned something and grown up during the course of the film—he is in fact now the equal of his bride. A fantasy, to be sure, but Joe's work in the film shows he could still stir emotions about love and marriage, no matter his and Rosa's travails.

Joe's films of this period were rounded out by almost the antithesis of *Guys and Dolls: The Quiet American.* Joe had tried social conscience on film before—with *No Way Out* in 1950, the film he shot in between a *A*

Joe in a Saigon temple during the filming of *The Quiet American*

Letter to Three Wives and *All About Eve,* a melodrama about a black doctor who treats a white gangster and his brother after a gun battle. (When the gangster dies, the gangster's brother blames the doctor and targets him with his gang, leading to race riots.) The attack on racism in the film is, for its time, fairly serious, and Sidney Poitier gives a calm, steady performance that would soon make him the first bankable African-American star, for which he would forever be grateful to Joe.* But now, seven years later, in *The Quiet American,* Joe tackled an even more controversial and complicated subject.

---

* Poitier testified to Joe's enormous skill in getting him, an inexperienced newcomer, to "unact." Again and again, in interviews and tributes decades later, Poitier would say some version of "Joe Mankiewicz is totally responsible for whatever success I had in motion pictures." For in addition to casting him in his first major role in *No Way Out,* Joe saw to it that Zoltan Korda considered Poitier for the lead role in his screen version of *Cry, the Beloved Country* the following year. Taken together, the two pictures made Poitier a star.

Based on Graham Greene's political novel, *The Quiet American* openly questioned whether there was a satisfying alternative to colonialism in Vietnam. As always, Joe got terrific performances from his actors, one of whom, Audie Murphy, as the self-confident and brave American of the title, was hardly an actor at all (the United States' most decorated soldier in World War II, Murphy was famously

Joe with Audie Murphy and Michael Redgrave on the set of *The Quiet American*, 1957

wooden and unemotive on screen) and admitted later that without Joe's guidance, he would have been utterly at sea. Michael Redgrave, too, gives a passionate performance, but the film as a whole is typical of Joe's work during this period: not all that suspenseful as a thriller, if smarter than most; more comic than most dramas, but not wildly dramatic, and with not quite enough action to keep audiences from restlessness. Yet the film is so well observed that after seeing it Jean-Luc Godard wrote that Joe was "the most intelligent man in all contemporary cinema."

In fact, the film is remarkable for its subject matter alone. Few directors would have dared tackle such a subject, especially so soon after the blacklist had seemed to stamp out the very idea of dissent. And while Joe diluted the more aggressive attacks on American policy in Greene's novel, he still effectively communicated something discerning about the West's early involvement in Vietnam—even casting the heroic Murphy in the title role was a subtle stroke, as if to underscore the damage that was coming. It's impossible to watch now, after the devastating effect of the Vietnam War, without seeing Joe for the first time as not just angry, but prescient. The movie seems to sense that self-interest guided all Western states' endeavors in Vietnam, and clearly predicts that the path will lead to ruin. Courageous movies on controversial subjects tend to come in waves in Hollywood—a few years earlier, *No Way Out* had followed on the heels of Billy Wilder's *The Lost Weekend,* about alcoholism, William Wyler's *The Best Years of our Lives,* about the problems facing World War II vets, and Elia Kazan's *Gentleman's Agreement,* which took on anti-Semitism. But the

Chris, my mom's friend Anne Adler, Tom,
cousin Myra Fox, Joe, and Josie, c. 1958

mid-1950s was not really a time for political statements in Hollywood—in many ways one of the most interesting things about the film is that it was made at all.

The question remains: Why do Joe's movies of the 1950s zig and zag both in tone and style? It's possible that, having broken free of the studio system, he was testing the limits of his autonomy and avidly pursuing his interests. But partly, like a bird that has lived so long inside the cage that it doesn't know how to fly when the doors are finally opened, Joe needed something to chafe against. Herman was gone. Franz was gone. (Even Zanuck was gone.) It's possible Joe didn't quite know what he stood for when his prime antagonists were out of the picture.* But there's almost a desperation in Joe's rooting around for subject matters in these years—as if he would do anything, including making a movie halfway around the world in Vietnam, to avoid confronting what was happening at home. Perhaps it was too painful to try another "way we live now" film.

Joe Mankiewicz, film director, was by now a popular man-about-town: he and Rosa were entertaining far more in New York than they had in Hollywood and were falling in with exactly the kinds of people—editors, authors, Governor Averell Harriman—that Joe had wanted to be with. But the life wasn't adding up. He'd stopped psychoanalysis when

---

* Another echo of his older brother: "Mank," Orson Welles once declared of Herman, "always needed a villain."

he arrived in New York, preferring a fresh start, but the unease he felt every morning as he got out of bed, usually alone in his own room, with Rosa in hers across the hall, spoke to something greater than just midlife malaise. Joe had only to look at his own hands to see that there was an imbalance in his life; he was developing psoriasis, and though it would be years before he had to wear delicate white gloves on film sets to control and cover the malady, his hands had taken to itching rather severely. As Joe confided to friends, it was all very psychosomatic.

JOE WASN'T THE ONLY MANKIEWICZ DRIVING HARD TO SUCCEED IN the '50s. With Herman gone, his teenage daughter Johanna was working herself into a frenzy of accomplishment, and one early triumph even found its way into the press. With the entire tenth grade math class at the exclusive Westlake School for Girls stumped by a geometry problem, she remembered that her grandfather, of whom she had only dim memories, had been a friend of Albert Einstein's in New York. So she wrote the famous scientist at Princeton asking for help with the problem. Four days later, the mail brought a reply from Einstein: a simple diagram, not giving the answer directly but showing the young girl how to solve it. When the incident, aided by a press agent friend of Sara's, became national news, a wire photo of my mother standing holding a small chalkboard with a diagram of two circles was splashed across the front page of newspapers across the country, captioned: "When Johanna took the answer back to school, it turned out her teacher knew the solution all the time, if only Johanna had asked. Here, she copies the Doctor's answer on the blackboard."

In the picture, my mother's blond hair looks as if it took an hour to put into place, parted almost violently on the right side, the flip perfect around her ear as she looks back at us over her shoulder. Her face is open and young, but she does not look particularly lively or fun. She looks determined. Achievement, clearly, is everything to this young woman, it has been drilled into her from an early age, and she knows that success will come naturally to one so gifted who works so hard. Achievement, success, competition . . .

Visiting Herman for what would prove to be one of the last times in the hospital, she had felt she needed to teach him something. At fifteen, she sensed her father hadn't long to live. There had been too many visits, too many hospitals, and now it was painful; his cheeks too sunken

Mom showing Einstein
a thing or two

and his eyes too hollow. And so, not for the first or last time, my mother lied. She told her father, quite out of nowhere, that she had been nominated for student body president. She saw her father's face light up with pride. "Wonderful! You're sure to win." My mother let it sit a moment before providing what she knew would be the hammer: "I turned it down." Herman was crestfallen. In truth, she had made the whole thing up. "I just wanted to prove to him," she told Dick Meryman years later, "that achievements—being best—didn't mean so much." On the tape, you can hear her take a drag from a cigarette before admitting, "Needless to say, it is not my most cherished memory."

But whatever point she'd tried to impart to her dying father, Johanna Mankiewicz continued to blaze a trail of success academically, graduating from high school at the age of sixteen and heading off to Wellesley to complete her education—courtesy of Uncle Joe, who was happy to have her on the East Coast. He'd received great reports from Sara and others in California on her progress, but still he worried every time he saw her. Was she getting maybe a little plump? Were the hausfrau genes too strong in her? What kind of man would she marry? Would she be a writer? He assumed so, but the few stories and school papers he read seemed pedestrian, half-baked. What would Herman have thought? Joe thought often about his final meeting with Herman at the hospital. Underneath a drawing of my mother's he'd pinned to the wall above his bed, Herman had begged Joe to make sure Johanna was able to go to college. At first Joe told his big brother that he would get well, stop being dramatic, but Herman persisted, and Joe promised. They had talked briefly about business and family, and Herman told Joe at one point, "You know, I never had a bad steak in my life. Some were better, and some were worse, but I never had a bad one." Later Joe said that he never felt closer to Herman than in that hospital room. It was as if all the jealousies and family conflicts had faded away and they were just two brothers, born of the same parents, two men, sharing a goodbye. "It was the first time," Joe said, "I ever felt he was listening to me." For someone who idolized his older brother growing up, to have come so far, and seen his brother fall so far, was practically overwhelming to Joe. "I came closer to loving Herman than at any time in my life."

A Lautrec poster clutched in her hand, her "Adlai For Me" button pinned to her Bermuda shorts, and her extensive collection of Freud's works in her suitcase, Josie will invade Wellesley next fall. Her memories of her eight years at Westlake will be many—memories of frenzied work on Vox, of endless notes from Miss Bradlow, of R.O.T.C. practice at noon on the Senior Lawn, of long, happy hours on the sports field. However strong her attachment to Westlake, she has with great difficulty, reconciled herself to spending the next four years within walking distance of Harvard and M.I.T.

JOHANNA MANKIEWICZ
editor-in-chief of vox puellarum

28

Johanna Mankiewicz's senior page in her Westlake yearbook

SO HERE IT IS, FIVE YEARS later, Johanna has finished college, Joe has done his duty there, and Joe and Rosa are fighting again. It is a whopper of a fight. They are at the house they have rented for the summer in Mount Kisco, which they are keeping straight to the end of October. A beautiful house, a lovely spot for entertaining, and the Cerfs had come to dinner, but it was not a good evening, in fact a very bad one, Rosa had made her misery quite clear . . . That horrible hour before dinner, which Joe always felt was the worst— right after work has ended and before dinner; that's why the cavemen invented theater, to keep their minds off their troubles at that time of day, gathering around the fire to ward off evil spirits—but Rosa had carried it over into dinner, and long after the Cerfs had left the house, she'd kept it up, and worse, with threats and recriminations, and *I can't take it anymore, and all the kind of goddamn* terrifying theatrics that Joe had been putting up with for more than a decade and a half. Finally, Joe was the one who couldn't take it anymore. He drove back to New York on his own.

In the morning, Joe woke up in their big Park Avenue apartment alone. The boys were off at school now—Chris at Columbia, Tom at Exeter—and it was Saturday so the housekeeper wasn't in yet, and Joe went to his study to try to work, but it was no use. There was a mound of Figaro business Joe had to tend to and they had an audit coming up—turns out running a production company isn't nearly as much fun as directing movies—and worse than that, he had to think of what to write next. The theater was a nightmare—Joe was trying to write a play, but it wasn't working. The play was called *Jefferson Selleck,* an adaptation of a novel about a frustrated middle-aged husband, but it was coming slowly. He knew the joke that was going around—George S. Kaufman lay deathly ill in his hospital bed, but he told Moss Hart, "Don't worry, I won't die until Joe Mankiewicz has a play on Broadway."

But dammit, he couldn't concentrate now. He'd called Mount Kisco first thing and there'd been no answer. That in itself wasn't too much cause for alarm—Rosa never liked answering the phone. But now it was mid-morning, and she still wasn't answering. Neither was the caretaker, though likely he was out and about pruning trees or some such. But Rosa . . .

Joe was lonely, and scared. He needed to hear a voice that would accept him. He needed an unchallenging partner. So he called his niece. Josie would come with him upstate.

At that point in his life, it must have seemed perfectly natural to Joe to keep calling his niece until he finally got through to her, perfectly natural to ask her to come over to the apartment. Perfectly natural, to call the caretaker in Mount Kisco once Mom had reached him, and hear from the caretaker that nothing was wrong, Mrs. Mankiewicz was sleeping. Perfectly natural to tell my mother that didn't seem right and suggest they drive upstate and check on her.

Joe closed the car door and walked up the path toward the front door to the house. There was no pipe in his mouth—Joe never liked to drive and smoke at the same time. On the drive up, he'd made polite conversation, to keep it light, to focus on her, her new job at *Time,* the shopping, the boyfriends, the friends of hers he'd met, asking after them, what they were doing in their own post-college lives . . . and he'd talked to her about the upcoming Tennessee Williams movie he was planning. Later, Josie would tell him how much she liked the movie, and the play it had been based on, such a combination of tension, sexual ambiguity, and drama . . .

The feeling inside the house, my mother later said, was normal: still but not too still. So perhaps, as with the morning phone calls, Joe's next move felt perfectly normal to him too: he said he would look in the kitchen and asked his twenty-one-year-old niece to go upstairs and check the bedroom.

Was it all, as Chris would contend, an orchestration? Did Joe know to a moral certainty that his wife was dead up there?[*]

---

* "I put it you, your honor, my Lords," Chris says decades later, lapsing into an imitation of a nineteenth-century British barrister, "that someone who was genuinely concerned about his wife would have jumped into a car, or hired a car, or in some way gotten his ass up to Mount Kisco to find out what was wrong with her.

My mother certainly came to feel Joe knew, though in later years, she also developed a kind of sympathy for him, telling Ken Geist in 1973 that she found Joe "desperately insecure." He needed adulation, she said, and the fanciness of the Park Avenue apartment was part of that: fingerbowls with dinner, leaving "your order with the maid and then she brings you the egg the way you want it in the morning and pulls the drapes;" it was all part of Joe's need to control things and orchestrate things because he was so terrified of life itself. He could deal with actors and actresses beautifully because it was all make-believe and there were no real stakes, but once you got Joe offstage or -screen and made him deal with actual human beings and the interplay between them, that, according to my mother, was intolerable for Joe. He asked his niece to go upstairs, she felt, because that's how the scene played out best in his mind, with her discovery of the body, and him getting to play the role of the comforting uncle, as well as the grieving husband. Anything else was, literally, unimaginable. (Of course, there is a simpler explanation for his behavior: namely, that Joe sensed what was in that bedroom and asked his niece to go up first because he wasn't prepared to see his wife's dead body.)

Afterwards, Joe behaved the way a well-behaved male character in a Joseph L. Mankiewicz movie would: he held his niece tight in his arms in the hallway outside the bedroom, patted her hair gently, soothed her and told her it was all right: how horrible, how utterly horrible, he was so sorry, so inexpressibly sorry . . . But my mother's unease over the way the afternoon had played out was only underscored when she remembered, later, that as she and Joe pulled up to the house, Bennett Cerf's limousine was already parked in the driveway. Joe had known, he'd have to have known Rosa was already dead.

By the time Chris arrived at the apartment later that night back in the city, there was his father, wearing an expression full of misery, repeating again and again, "Oh dear, oh dear." Of course there were matters to tend to: Rosa was a Catholic, and an official verdict of suicide would have precluded a proper burial, and Joe wanted the fact of the suicide kept out of the papers, and so, despite the Mount Kisco police having seen what was from all indications a terse suicide note addressed to Joe—

Instead he dillydallied for many hours, finding no one except your mother, whom he finally pressured into going with him."

"The first honest sentiment I've heard here tonight": Chris Mankiewicz, c. 1957–58

what can it have said?*—strings were pulled, calls were made, Governor Harriman was involved—and all of this was happening in what my mother described as a fairly "party atmosphere" back in the Park Avenue apartment that evening. Joe was seeing to details and Averell Harriman was waving the magic wand the rich and powerful possess to keep the whole thing out of the papers. Chris stared at his father sullenly, thinking, "You fucking phony," and now, finally, it is dawn, and Chris is heading back to Columbia to try to get some sleep, and the current family psychiatrist, Dr. Kubie,† perhaps seeing a chance for a quick consultation, joins him in the elevator. On the way down, Kubie says, "Tell me, Chris, how do you feel about all this? Tell me your feelings." It would be hard to blame Chris if he felt put off by this question, asked during an early-morning elevator ride of a son whose mother has just been found dead of a suicide. But Chris, unfazed, answers: "You know, Dr. Kubie, it'll sound perhaps a little wrong, but I feel great relief, almost happiness, that her agony is over." The man looks at Chris and says, "That's the first honest sentiment I've heard here tonight."

After the funeral, my mother remembered seeing Joe make an almost involuntary decision, which she called "the only time I ever saw Uncle Joe betray true emotion." The family and a few mourners—not many, Rosa didn't know very many people outside Joe's circle, and Joe didn't want a large crowd—had driven out to the burial site, and according to custom, three people with shovels had dug in their spades and thrown dirt on the coffin. Joe was one of them. He took the shovel and stuck it into the earth symbolically then returned to join the rest of the group at some

---

* The note, which according to *The New York Times* of September 28, 1958, was largely indecipherable, though police were quoted as saying, "Mrs. Mankiewicz indicated that 'she was tired,'" soon vanished.

† Chris had himself been in and out of therapy for much of his teen years, ending it when he arrived home not long after one appointment to find his father irate: "How could you tell your doctor that?!" Chris decided that any doctor with a direct line to his father was probably not one he'd care to visit.

folding chairs. Mom remembered that he came back and sat down and then stood back up almost immediately. He clapped his hands together and said, "Enough. Let's go."

Mom found it heartbreaking. It was as if Joe, in clapping his hands together, was sealing off that painful period of his life forever. "He was putting an end to it: it was over. Her death, her life, it was all over, and he'd had enough. He couldn't sit there another minute."

In later years, Rosa would come to be almost as invisible a presence in Joe's life as his first, long-forgotten wife Elizabeth Young. Over the years he would send Tom or Chris whatever keepsakes he would come across of their mother, and after he'd remarried he certainly didn't keep any pictures of her around.* She was removed from his life, almost as if she could be removed from his life story.† Finally, in the mid-1970s, Tom Mankiewicz was visiting his father on his way to London for one of the James Bond movies. They were having drinks before dinner with Rosemary, Joe's third and final wife, when Joe turned to her and said, "Would you excuse us for a moment?" Rosemary stood and left the room, as Tom's heart raced. He thought, "Okay, something big is about to happen here." What could it be? A shocking revelation? An expression of remorse? A too-late but welcome apology for being a distant father?

It was none of these. Instead, Joe Mankiewicz said, "It's about your mother." *Oh my God.* Tom took a breath. Joe went on: "I've been paying for her grave every year . . . and I was wondering if this was something you might want to take over?" Tom was stupefied. "Pay for Mother's grave?" Joe nodded. It wasn't very much money, about $2,500 a year, and Tom agreed to do it. He took on the task and continued it until his own death.

And so, after nineteen years of marriage and another decade and a half of paying for the upkeep of her grave, Joe Mankiewicz had divested himself of Rosa Stradner for good.

---

* Still, on one occasion, Alex heard her father muttering to himself that his relationship with Rosa had been the most significant of his life.

† There is more than a whiff of Stalin-era whitewashing of history here, ironic for several reasons, not the least of which is that Herman had died on the same day as the Russian dictator. This odd coincidence prompted a classic Mankiewiczian remark from my uncle Don, who had broken the news to his younger brother Frank over the phone: "Well, Pop died this morning, but so did Joe Stalin, so we split the double-header."

———— ⚓ ————

BUT AFTER HER DEATH, JOE COULD NO MORE OUTRUN THE HOR-
rors of his life with Rosa than he could the resentments he'd long harbored
toward Herman and Franz. Once Rosa was in fact gone and buried, he
had returned to work with a vengeance, with one more movie to make
before the 1950s ended, and it was probably the best of them. *Suddenly,
Last Summer* was a brutal stew of neurosis, psychosis, misplaced sexual
longing, and rage—an adaptation of Tennessee Williams's southern gothic
mystery-melodrama. In it, a wealthy widow, Mrs. Venable (Katharine
Hepburn) tries to bribe a young psychosurgeon Dr. Cukrowicz (Montgomery Clift) working at a cash-starved mental hospital into lobotomiz-
ing her distressed niece, Catherine Holly (Elizabeth Taylor). In the wake
of Rosa's suicide, Joe must have found the prospect of guiding these gifted
actresses through two such psychologically complicated roles irresistible.

Something else that may have appealed to Joe was that for the first
time since Darryl Zanuck, he would be working with a strong producer,
Sam Spiegel, coming off a string of hits, including *The Bridge on the River
Kwai* and *The African Queen*. Although it meant that the film would not
be a Figaro production, Joe appreciated the chance to focus on directing and welcomed Spiegel's strong hand, though he did take to referring
to the producer as "Suddenly Sam Spiegel" for his habit of showing up
on the set unannounced. Too, because the source material for the film
was a one-act play with heavy "homosexual content," it had to be both
expanded and sanitized for the screen, a job that fell to the project's
screenwriter, Gore Vidal. Again Joe welcomed another strong hand to
play against, and he and Vidal worked well together, meeting in the Figaro
offices in New York and "opening up the play," which had all taken place
in the ornate Venable home in New Orleans, to include other locations
and make from the one-act a legitimately cinematic experience. Despite
cleansing the script almost entirely of intimations of homosexuality, the
film still packed an emotional wallop: under the steady guidance of the
persistently compassionate Dr. Cukrowicz (even the name must have appealed to Joe), Mrs. Venable gradually reveals that her sensitive young
son Sebastian died "suddenly, last summer" in Spain, in the company of
his cousin Catherine. Mrs. Venable has had the cousin institutionalized
upon her return to the United States; the poor girl's incoherent, hysterical
accounts of what happened seemed too shocking to believe, and upset
Sebastian's mother too much, thoroughly contradicting her "official ver-

sion" of how Sebastian died. The movie focused on the varying emotional responses the two women had to Sebastian's death.

Joe had good reason to be proud of the performance he helped Elizabeth Taylor achieve in the difficult role of Catherine Holly. She was a young woman traumatized both by witnessing her cousin's death and by being locked up in mental institutions.* Ultimately, working with Dr. Cukrowicz, she overcomes her memory block and tells the story of Sebastian's seduction of a group of boys, who then chase him in a frenzy, pounding on musical instruments like some kind of Dionysian rite, finally killing Sebastian and cannibalizing his flesh. That Taylor made this extraordinary story believable was no small feat, and Joe would proudly say that "it was the best screen performance Elizabeth Taylor ever gave." In addition to Joe's usual way with actresses (whether we believe Tom's contention that his father and Taylor were having an affair during the filming), Joe helped her performance during this critical monologue through a smart lighting scheme he devised with the film's cinematographer, Jack Hildyard (hired by Spiegel, another sign that Joe was helped by a strong producer). As Catherine recounts the horrors of the previous summer and repressed memories come flooding back to her, the film alternates between light and dark close-ups of Taylor, with her face gradually moving to the edge of the frame to allow the powerful flashback to take over the screen.

Joe also helped tame Taylor's legendarily disruptive behavior on film sets. When she arrived at 11:30 a.m. on her first day of shooting, more than two hours late, she found the set completely empty and a note taped to the camera: "Dear Elizabeth, We were all here at nine. So sorry to have missed you. Love, Joe." She was never late again.

Katharine Hepburn presented different challenges. Joe had known the actress for decades, and at first, he enjoyed directing her in the quasi-Oedipal role, that of an older woman made to feel young and adored, both by her son and society: "We were a famous couple. People didn't speak of Sebastian and his mother, or Mrs. Venable and her son. They said, 'Violet and Sebastian.'" Joe helped draw a remarkable performance out of Hepburn; her almost preternatural longing as she says these lines reveals the deep depression she has fallen into since her son's death. When she insists that she now believes her son's testament that he "saw God" the day they witnessed flesh-eating birds devour newly hatched sea turtles,

---

* Echoes of Rosa's agony surely reverberated for Joe.

we get a window into the kind of raw pain and despair that Hollywood films of the 1950s rarely trafficked in—this was a woman in true agony. The grief was nearly overwhelming.

But Hepburn regretted taking the part almost immediately after filming began. Interestingly, she later claimed it was Joe's poor treatment of Montgomery Clift, the troubled actor playing Joe's psychoanalytic stand-in Dr. Cukrowicz, that pushed her over the edge. Long tortured over having to hide his own homosexuality, and now addicted to drugs and alcohol after a painful car crash had permanently disfigured his face and nearly ruined his career a few years earlier, Montgomery Clift was a movie actor through and through, and he had difficulty memorizing the long lines the script called for. According to Hepburn, Joe was unrelenting, cruel, and unforgiving toward Clift. (Both Jack Hildyard and Taylor, a friend and confidante of Clift's for years, disputed Hepburn's account. They found Joe enormously patient with Clift, an observation supported by Ken Geist, who visited the set and saw Joe calm the actor's acute anxiety by speaking quietly to him and massaging his neck and shoulders.) More important, Hepburn found her own role so unsympathetic that she wanted to play Violet as insane, perhaps to distance herself from the character. Further, she was upset by the lighting scheme Joe had worked out with Hildyard. Joe decided to make Hepburn, then only fifty-two, look as young as possible when she discussed Sebastian's life, and then change camera angles and lighting after the truth of his death came out. "I wanted her suddenly to look old," Joe said. "In other words, the destruction of the legend about Sebastian, her son, destroyed her illusion of youth. Kate sensed what Jack and I were up to . . . and she didn't like what I was doing." It struck Hepburn as somehow uncompassionate—not to her; she was an actress known for her lack of vanity—but to the character herself. Although Joe and Hepburn had worked well together on *The Philadelphia Story,* and she'd even enjoyed him on *Woman of the Year,* no matter her disdain for the chauvinistic ending he'd grafted on, by now she had come to the conclusion that Joe Mankiewicz hated women, telling one friend "this director has got it in for women." Was it possible that Joe was working through his continuing anger at Rosa—for her life, her miseries, the distress she had inflicted on him, as well as her violent death—on his actresses? Hepburn may have thought so, as a legendary, potentially apocryphal story from the set makes clear. It has long been the custom on a movie set to applaud when a leading actor or actress finishes work. This happened on Hepburn's last day on the set, and she

"This director has got it in for women": Katharine
Hepburn, Montgomery Clift, and Elizabeth Taylor in
Suddenly, Last Summer, 1959

took in the applause of the crew and cast with a relieved smile. Then she
made sure to ask one of the production assistants, "Am I really done, are
my services truly no longer required?" Upon being told that yes, she was
finished on the film, she went to Joe Mankiewicz and, with cast and crew
watching in amazement, spat in his face.

She was not the only one upset by the movie. Tennessee Williams
himself publicly criticized the picture, saying that Hepburn and Taylor
were miscast and unhappily telling his biographer that "a short morality
play, in a lyrical style, was turned into a sensationally successful film that
the public thinks was a literal study of such things as cannibalism, madness, and sexual deviation." Joe himself defended the film by criticizing
the source material, saying that the play was "badly constructed and based
on the most elementary Freudian psychology."

It didn't matter. The film remains a powerful piece of work six decades
later and was a huge hit for Columbia Pictures. Both actresses were nominated for Oscars, though Joe, to his chagrin, was not. Still, with Taylor
now one of the world's most bankable movie stars, and the lure of her in
a famous publicity shot, pouting bewitchingly and spilling out of a one-
piece white bathing suit on a Spanish beach, the film brought Joe all the
way back. After a series of perfectly respectable films, Joe Mankiewicz was
now, once again, at the top of his game.

Did anyone care if the game was solitaire?

CHAPTER FIFTEEN

———⚲———

A RIVER IN EGYPT

You know it's possible, Octavian, that when you die, you will
die without ever having been alive.

—*CLEOPATRA*

IN THE MAINE HOUSE WHERE MY FATHER NOW LIVES THERE ARE TWO
drawers full of old photographs, in one of which is a white leather photo
album full of eight-by-ten pictures of the wedding day of Johanna Mankiewicz and her husband, Peter Davis. The photos are all in black-and-white.
Two nights earlier, the director George Cukor, who had become closer to
Goma since Herman's death, threw the young couple a dinner dance, and
many of the attendees at the wedding are Hollywood luminaries of one
kind or another; the pictures are full of famous or at least semi-famous
names: you can see a Selznick or two, a Hayward or two, maybe even a
Fonda. Though most of the photographs are staged, as was the custom
of the time, the actual pictures are surprisingly candid-looking, almost
as if the camera had been snapped a split second too early or too late. In
an almost astonishingly high percentage of the pictures my mother has
her eyes closed.

It was Sunday, September 13, 1959.

In one of the pictures, Mom is walking in on the arm of her uncle
Joe. She is on his right, smiling beneath her veil, and Joe is leaning down
toward her with a complaisant smile, as if confidently checking that all
is going well on his niece's perfect day. It is a warm picture, and easy
to imagine, had things gone a little differently, that either or both of
them might have framed the picture to keep in a prominent spot. My
mother loved her uncle, he had truly done everything one could have

hoped for after Herman's death. The checklist was easy to run down; he'd paid for Wellesley, sent her on a glorious trip to Europe the summer after graduation, and given her a delicious twenty-first birthday present: charge accounts at all the major New York department stores. "He was wonderful to me," she said. For more seriously, emotionally, he'd intervened when, at the age of nineteen, she'd become engaged to a man whom just about everyone thought was wrong for her,* and eventually he helped her extricate herself from that situation with such grace and courtesy† that

Mom and Uncle Joe on her wedding day, September 13, 1959

now, among the literally hundreds of telegrams that greeted the young couple after the ceremony was one from that former fiancé.

She was grateful too to Uncle Joe, because she knew it wasn't easy for him. After the events of last autumn—the word "suicide" would never be used in Joe's presence, any more, for that matter, than "Rosa" would—Josie had moved for a few months into the Park Avenue apartment, where Joe went through what she later termed a "gay Merry Widower" period, Uncle and Niece seeming to delight in each other's company, capped with his buying her a huge television set for Christmas. Then, when he went off to Europe for a month to clear his head and returned to sell the apartment and make a new start in a huge townhouse on East Seventy-first Street, she'd continued to serve as his unofficial hostess. Though he was not a man easy with his feelings, she believed his heart was in the right place, and she often remembered something her father said of Joe: "Uncle Joe is a nice man as long as he's reminded he is—but he needs to be reminded."

Her wedding day was certainly an occasion to reflect on what a wonderful surrogate father he had been. She and two of her bridesmaids

---

* For one thing, everyone said he had no neck, although as Mom asked, "Who in our family had a neck?"

† From Vietnam, where Joe got the news of the misguided engagement while he was working on *The Quiet American,* he "wrote [me] the most wonderful, understanding, supportive [letter], and dealt with my mother in a very helpful way."

would always remember the day their sophomore year at Wellesley when the school held a Father's Day. "I invited him," Josie said later, "and he came and he spent I would say ten straight hours with a bunch of giggling crazy girls. It was just marvelous . . . It meant everything to me . . . He'd been decent and wonderful and took a large group of my friends out. Unostentatiously, not looking for credit." He did it, she said, "out of love." It remained her fondest memory of him.

But too, there'd always been his strange insistence—and Josie sensed it had to do with why he'd acted as he had that horrible afternoon in Mount Kisco—on her knowing the truth about her father. "He was very concerned that I know the real facts of life. It was crucial to him that I understand that my father was this bad gambler and a big drinker, and he was constantly telling these stories. That [my father] was deeply unhappy, was the thing I had to understand." Sometimes, it seemed downright inappropriate, as with Joe's telling her why Herman didn't cheat on Sara. Joe told her that Herman *wanted* to sleep around, but he couldn't. "He insisted that my father was a Victorian in the worst ways." But nastiest of all was the afternoon when Joe showed his niece one of the few things that had been saved from the fire that had destroyed most of his files: a sheet of unpaid IOUs Herman had given Joe. "And that he had saved it to show to the daughter of the man who had written them [all those years before] . . . Why? Why not let go of those?" Josie sensed Joe's deep need, even now, to show the world who was who in the Mankiewicz family. Would what she called the "great resentment and great hostility" ever go away?

Still, Uncle Joe had supported her in every conceivable way, and there was no denying how good it was of him to come all this way and orchestrate the wedding so beautifully. He had been busy finishing his latest film, Josie knew—*Suddenly, Last Summer,* which she came to regard as the best movie Joe had done since *All About Eve,* probably due to the fact that its subject matter—madness, really, and lies and deception—was almost as close to Joe as the theater was. But more than his professional success was his impressive sense of control; when he arrived at the Jaffes' for the wedding rehearsal, he immediately took command, directing the proceedings and shunting aside the poor rabbi, who in Joe's view had gotten it all wrong. Joe decided that the bride and groom should not face *away* from their guests. "You!" he had barked at the rabbi. "Who do you think these people have come to see, Rabbi, you?" Joe instructed Johanna and Peter to turn around and face the guests, with the rabbi's back to the gathering, facing the swimming pool.

Wedding Day: Goma, Mom and Dad, and Erna
Stenbuck, née Mankiewicz, 1959

But something else distressed Johanna as she and Joe walked in. She thought back to earlier in the year, in the spring, when she had told Joe that she really was getting married this time, and to whom. She knew, or she thought she knew, that Joe liked Peter. This young man had everything someone like Joe would want; he was whip smart and had graduated from Harvard at twenty, his father was a screenwriter who'd worked with Joe at M-G-M, his late mother had been the novelist and screenwriter Tess Slesinger, and he was clearly a principled and intelligent young man with a promising future in journalism. There was really nothing *not* to like about Peter Davis, or so his besotted bride-to-be felt.

And yet. There it was, when Josie told her uncle of her plans, the grimace that he couldn't prevent from taking over his face. And it was so unfair, what Uncle Joe had said. *Thin?* The word made it seem like Peter would never amount to anything, it was so patronizing, and wrong, just plain wrong—and why? Because Peter was bad at word games? Because he had told her he wouldn't come over if the television was on? That may have been snobbish—hell, it *was* snobbish, but Joe was the one who hated television, whose dismissal of it in *All About Eve* had been so devastating. This is a serious, profound man I'm about to marry, Joe is wrong, anyone could see that, and it was desperately unfair. "I like Peter," Joe had said, tapping his pipe. "He's a perfectly nice guy, but he's a little . . ." She couldn't even think about it.

But still: *Just what the hell did he mean? Thin? Am I marrying an envelope?*

As Joe escorted her to the rabbi, along the side of a beautiful pool overlooking the entire town, the town over which her uncle and her father and their friends, now gathered here to celebrate her, held such dominion, she walked happily toward her groom. *This is a man I can live with. This is a man of smarts, of ambition, of drive . . .* Years later, she would describe her husband, who himself employed a jaw clench not unlike her uncle's, as always looking like he just stepped from a bracing shower . . . Ready to move forward into the world, to attack, to achieve . . . And of course Johanna Mankiewicz knew that some people weren't in fact like that. Some people are happy with what they have. They don't push and prod and seek always the next big thing, the next accomplishment, book, novel, assignment, job, movie—they take what is given them and form their lives cheerfully and without complaint. But she and her almost-husband came from stock where such behavior was virtually unthinkable, and as Josie stepped forward toward her groom, Joe watched with a grin, then resumed his place in the audience, having directed his niece in the way that she clearly wanted him to.

Josie was just beginning—her life, her career, her married life and building a family. But for Joe, watching and squinting into the sun as she took the vows, he had no way of knowing that at the age of fifty his own final act was about to begin. The seeds had been planted years earlier, but he would soon be embarked on the project that, if it didn't exactly kill him, so drained him of energy and life force that he never contested the fact that he was a very different man at the end than at the beginning. The saddest aspect of the whole sorry affair was that it took him so long to realize that he might well have been on his way to being a better one.

JOE HAD NEVER LIKED THE SUN, THE BEACH, VACATIONS OF ANY kind—but he was starting to understand why people loved the Bahamas so much. He had been down at Children's Bay Cay, the Bahamian retreat of actor Hume Cronyn for several weeks—Joe had first worked with the intelligent actor on *People Will Talk*—and he really did see the appeal. The rhythm of beach, work, pool, work, lunch, nap, work, had been successful—and he was enormously pleased that he was getting on so well with Jeanne Vanderbilt, the woman he'd brought along for the stay. Since Rosa's death, there had been a series of women, none all that serious, and he didn't think Jeanne, heiress to an enormous fortune, would last either (he was right). Still, Joe appreciated the ease they had around each other, and he was quietly excited about his new project: an ambitious adaptation of Lawrence Durrell's *Alexandria Quartet*. With four novels in all to adapt, Joe had written the equivalent of four screenplays, six hundred pages, and shown them to Durrell, who, according to Joe, had looked at him in amazement and said, "I really never thought anybody could do this." Joe felt the work was maybe the best of his career; the script demonstrated Joe's ability to look at things from

Hume Cronyn on the beach at Children's Bay Cay, with two friends

several different points of view; as with many of his films, it would be structured around several narrators' different accounts, and would in all tell a complete tale set during World War II with heavy mediations on memory and time, two things Joe loved to think and talk about.

Spending afternoons sipping drinks by the pool with Hume, with Jeanne and Hume's wife, Jessica Tandy, languidly swimming laps, Joe was content with the work, and eager to move on to preproduction and casting. One of the challenges, though, was that his producer on the picture, Walter Wanger, was beset by headaches on another film, the almost comically catastrophic *Cleopatra,* which Fox had started a few months back and which was generating stories of tremendous cost overruns and egos run amok. Joe was grateful that it wasn't his problem. He remembered one of his favorite lines of Herman's, that some of the films he'd worked on were so bad that "one should stay at least four city blocks away from where they are playing in case a sudden rain should drive you into the theater."

That's when the phone rang.

The story of the making of *Cleopatra,* like the stories of the Edsel, New Coke, or Apple's Newton computer, is a rich and complicated parable for American ambition and folly in the twentieth century. But for Joe Mankiewicz, the decision to take on the doomed project, into which Fox had already poured more than $5 million by the time he was asked to salvage the movie in January 1961, was a simple one which came down, in the end, to money. Joe was offered more than he'd ever earned in his life—"fuck-you" money, Chris called it. Throughout his entire career, he'd earned a weekly salary, even when he ran his own production company.

Taylor insisted Joe was the one man for the job.

Joe on *Cleopatra,* 1961–62

But the production of *Cleopatra,* which Fox had begun two years earlier and by the time of Josie's wedding to Peter Davis was well under way, with Elizabeth Taylor announced as the queen of the Nile amid a fanfare of publicity, was so important to Twentieth Century–Fox and its mercurial head Spyros Skouras, that Joe's agent Charlie Feldman was able to negotiate an almost unheard-of payment for Joe when he was offered to take over the directing duties from Rouben Mamoulian. Eager to get going on the *Alexandria Quartet,* Joe initially turned the project down. ("Why would I want to make *Cleopatra*? I wouldn't even go *see* Cleopatra.") But Liz Taylor, who had been impressed with Joe on *Suddenly, Last Summer* and was the world's biggest movie star, insisted that Joe was the only man who could bring shape to the material, and so Joe was summoned to New York from the Bahamas, and over lunch at the Colony, Skouras made his plea—and opened his checkbook: "Joe, I know you like the Riviera. Is there a house in particular you want? I hear you like yachts . . ." Persistence paid off, and Fox gave in to Feldman's demands. First, Fox bought his production company Figaro for the almost unheard of price of $3 million, equivalent to more than $25 million today. Joe would be so flabbergasted and exhilarated by the windfall that when his nephew Don's eight-year-old son John visited him in New York, Joe, after touring the young boy around the town house and thrilling

Joe's inimitable directing style, on *Cleopatra*

him with a ride in its elevator, opened his desk drawer and showed the boy an actual check for a million dollars.

Joe had proved with the adaptation of Shakespeare's *Julius Caesar* that he knew his way around antiquity, and the more he considered the material, with its psychologically complex heroine and its central male relationship between the proud and brilliant leader Julius Caesar and his ambitious successor Marc Antony (Herman, Joe; Margo, Eve; would it never end?), the more it appealed to his sensibilities. Even though the production was troubled, there was no script, the existing footage Mamou-

Joe with producer Walter Wanger (left) and Art Buchwald (right) during the filming of *Cleopatra*

lian had shot (which would have accounted for about twelve minutes of screen time) struck Joe as wooden and unusable, two of the three central roles had to be recast (Peter Finch and Stephen Boyd, the original Caesar and Antony, were no longer available), the sets looked garish and cheap, and there would not be nearly enough time to rewrite the script to his satisfaction, Joe said yes. As his agent said, "Hold your nose for fifteen weeks and get it over with."

In the end, *Cleopatra* took more than two years of Joe's life. It taxed his energy in a way that no film ever had, drastically affected his confidence, and effectively finished him off as a major director. The reaction to the film among critics was perversely, delightedly antagonistic. In my household, as I was growing up, *Cleopatra* was considered an almost gleefully epic disaster, and it was almost gospel that just as *Citizen Kane* was the best movie ever, *Cleopatra* was likely the worst. But an actual accounting of what went on from that fateful day in January 1961 when Joe agreed to do the film to the feeling he had going to the premiere in June of 1963 of "being carted to the guillotine in a tumbrel" (a feeling of course that does not come through in footage and photos of the event, where Joe is his customary grinning self), reveals that in some ways Joe Mankiewicz never did better work in his life. Given that the film was, as Joe later said, "conceived in a state of emergency, shot in confusion, and wound up in a blind panic," he had nothing to be ashamed of.

To begin with, that Joe came to a movie that was already under way proved far more complicated than if he'd taken on a new assignment, no matter how huge. The list of challenges that Joe would face was long, many of them due to Fox head Spyros Skouras's bizarre management style, where some decisions would be agonized over for months, and others made so hastily, as if the world depended on a yes-or-no answer by noon, that the end result was almost invariably penny-wise, pound-foolish. Elizabeth Taylor was getting a notoriously high salary of $50,000 a week,[*] and Spyros insisted that Joe start shooting before the revised script had even been completed, a decision that in the end cost the studio far more money than if they had just taken three months off and allowed Joe the time he needed to finish the complicated script, which was a nearly complete overhaul of the original.[†] In addition, Spyros had decided to

---

[*] More than $400,000 in 2021 dollars.

[†] Joe was dismayed by the sentimentality and feline symbolism of the original script and insisted on rewriting it based on historical sources like Plutarch and Suetonius.

Joe with the double-headed hydra:
Richard Burton and Elizabeth Taylor

take advantage of tax incentives and shoot the entire movie in England, which made no sense, given that the notoriously wet and un-Rome-like British weather made shooting outside, where the set designers had spent more than $1 million building a replica of the Roman Forum and Colosseum, virtually impossible. As a result, when Joe took over, the entire production had to be moved to Rome—the sets rebuilt from scratch, another cost overrun, this one in the millions, that would ultimately be used to tar Joe's reputation, but which was not his doing.

Worst of all, there was the double-headed hydra Liz-and-Dick, which became the most notorious love affair in the world and completely overshadowed the production. Taylor was more than merely a huge star by the time the film began shooting—she was a public personality and a massive celebrity. She was also such a notorious home wrecker, having "stolen" current husband Eddie Fisher away from her dear friend Debbie Reynolds (America's sweetheart, who had helped Liz through her own unhappy time after the death of her third husband Mike Todd in a plane crash),

---

Rather than portray Cleopatra as a virginal girl waiting for Caesar to deflower her, as Mamoulian had, Joe wanted his Cleopatra to be an intelligent young queen capable of winning the hearts of two of the world's greatest warriors. The costumes and scenery would make it an epic: Joe's script, he hoped, would provide psychological complexity. His intention was to make "an intimate epic."

that even the official Vatican newspaper, *L'Osservatore della Domenica*,
had denounced her "erotic vagrancy."
Now, with the international press
swarming, Elizabeth Taylor seemed to
be wrecking Richard Burton's marriage as well, and if not for a series of
bizarre illnesses that would tilt public
sympathy in her favor (and may well
have been botched suicide attempts),
she would have been even more reviled
than before. But Burton, who initially
saw Taylor as no more than another
notch in his happy Welshman's belt of
sexual conquests ("Gentlemen," Burton announced one day as he bounded
into the men's makeup trailer, "I've just
fucked Elizabeth Taylor in the back

Tom Mankiewicz celebrates his
twentieth birthday on the set of
Cleopatra with his father.

of my Cadillac!"), was stunned by his costar's notoriety. He found the
mountain of press scrutiny so enormous that he was heard to remark, "It's
like fucking Khrushchev! How did I know the woman was so famous!"

Through it all, Joe kept his equilibrium, though his health began to
break down. Stress caused his psoriasis to flare into such a serious derma-
tological disorder that the skin on his hands cracked open, forcing him
to wear the thin white film cutter's gloves both on the set and at night, as
he struggled to write the script in longhand and stay ahead of the work
he was doing each day. His humor never wavered, though. When one
Italian newspaper reported that the Taylor-Burton affair was a sham Joe
had concocted to cover up the *real* romance, which was between Taylor
and himself, Joe responded with a press release of his own: "The real
story is that I'm in love with Richard Burton, and Elizabeth Taylor is the
cover-up for *us*."

In time, as Tom, who took a year off from Yale to work on the film,
told me, "the picture nearly killed Dad." The almost impossibly taxing
task of directing by day and writing by night, a regimen Joe was forced
into adhering to for months, was so draining that by the end he required
daily vitamin B12 shots to keep going. When one shot missed its mark
and hit his sciatic nerve, Joe was barely able to walk. For thirteen months,

he got only two or three hours of sleep a night, and Hume Cronyn remembers thinking, "One day, he will die." But he didn't, and the production rolled along, costing nearly $60 million in the end, equivalent to more than half a billion dollars in 2021, more money than any movie before or since.* The waste, though, was hardly Joe's fault; the decision to shoot in Italy had opened the door for the kind of graft for which the nation was famous.† It became impossible to stay on top of the numbers. "If you wanted to buy some new dinnerware or a set of glasses for your house," Tom said later, "it was the easiest thing to put it on the budget of *Cleopatra*." Years later, Elizabeth Taylor, who was herself responsible for further waste in insisting that chili be shipped to Rome from Chasen's in Hollywood, was horrified when she saw the official studio accounting, which indicated that $100,000 had been spent on paper cups.

Other expenses were equally questionable. A massive replica of Alexandria had been built on the beach at Torre Astura, sixty miles from Rome and just ten minutes south of Anzio, where the Allies had made their successful amphibious landing in January 1944 in World War II. It wasn't till after the set had been built that anyone realized the harbor, where the film's Roman ships would be seen in the film, was still laced with live mines left over from the war. A costly "mine-dredging" expenditure was soon added to *Cleopatra*'s ledger. Making matters worse, the Alexandria set was not far from a NATO firing range, so filming would have to be confined to times, as producer Walter Wanger wrote in his diary, "when the big guns are not blasting."

Further delays were strictly the cause of Elizabeth Taylor, who was routinely late to the set and often kept everyone waiting for hours. What's more, as she felt she was playing the most beautiful woman in history, she wanted to look her best, so her contract stipulated that she was unable to shoot during her menstrual period. (Still, as Joe joked to Tom, no one

---

* The final budget number is deceptive. Because Fox had so few other films in production, nearly everything that went on in the studio was charged to *Cleopatra*. "If two people in Tokyo had dinner," Rosemary Mankiewicz says, "it went on *Cleopatra*'s cost report."

† In Tom's telling: "As wonderful as the Italians are at designing things, they have a natural proclivity for larceny. Once you start saying, 'All right, I need five hundred Praetorian guard outfits, I need six hundred Nubian slave outfits, I need ten thousand soldier outfits'—this is like an invitation."

knew when the contract was drawn up that the woman would wind up having three or four periods a month.)

Nor was the end of production even remotely the end of Joe's headaches. In June 1962, the Fox board of directors, more than a little alarmed by *Cleopatra*'s skyrocketing costs, forced Spyros Skouras out as head of the studio. In his place, they brought back Darryl Zanuck.

Zanuck, Zanuck, Zanuck! What are you two—lovers?

—*ALL ABOUT EVE*

Like most of his intense relationships, Joe's connection to Zanuck had been filled with both love and hate. In fact, his greatest success had come when he was working with Zanuck. It was Zanuck who had fixed "A Letter to Four Wives" by eliminating one of the wives, and Zanuck who had ridden herd over Joe as he edited *All About Eve.** (It was also Zanuck, Joe later liked to remind interviewers, who had urged Joe to cast Tallulah Bankhead as Margo Channing and Jeanne Crain as Eve, and who was dead set against casting Marilyn Monroe.) When Zanuck took over Fox from Skouras, Joe was relieved. At least now someone with a firm hand would be at the tiller, who knew how movies were made and what would make this one work. Gone would be the guesswork that had dominated the first part of the production.

But on one point Joe and Zanuck would never agree. In Joe's mind, the best way to salvage the film would be to do it as two separate movies, the first to focus on Caesar and Cleopatra, the second on Antony and Cleopatra. Joe had modeled his vision to some extent on Shaw's and Shakespeare's plays†—and in his view, two three-hour movies would have been perfect. But Zanuck was as adamant as Skouras had been on this point: he would hear none of it. First of all, he felt that no one would pay to see the film twice, and more than that, given the worldwide publicity over Taylor and Burton's affair, it made no sense to do Caesar and Cleopatra first, since Mark Antony was barely in it—and, as Spyros had

---

* It was Zanuck who had cut one of the flashbacks in *All About Eve,* a second viewing, from a different perspective, of Eve's crucial applause speech at Bill Sampson's birthday party. The excision made sense and kept the film's length down, but Joe, a huge fan of revisiting scenes from different angles, always regretted the cut.

† Shakespeare's *Antony and Cleopatra* had five acts; Shaw's *Caesar and Cleopatra* had four.

asked, who wanted to see Elizabeth Taylor make love to Rex Harrison for a whole movie?

Finally, on October 13, 1962, Joe screened his first cut for Zanuck in Paris, where Zanuck had his base of operations: a five-hour-and-twenty-minute version that Joe hoped would convince Zanuck of the wisdom of dividing the film in half and charging separate admissions for each. Instead, Zanuck's only response to the screening was to tell Joe at the end, "If any woman behaved toward me the way Cleopatra treated Antony, I'd cut her balls off." Joe fired back, "The picture isn't about you, Darryl," and the two men parted. The next day, Joe and Zanuck were scheduled to meet to discuss the cut. Zanuck cancelled the meeting. Less than two weeks later, Joe read in the trades that "after spending two years and $35 million of Twentieth Century–Fox shareholders' money," Joe Mankiewicz had earned a "well-deserved rest." Zanuck had fired him.

ONE OF TOM MANKIEWICZ'S CHERISHED POSSESSIONS AS A YOUNG man was a gift he'd received after working on his father's epic: a gold coin, mocked up on one side to look like an ancient Roman artifact, with bas relief profiles of the real Marc Antony and Cleopatra staring imperiously to the left—Antony is characteristically behind Cleopatra, whose visage dominates, complete with royal crown and proud nose. On the other side was a simple engraving curved around the outside rim: FROM ELIZABETH AND RICHARD—1962—"CLEOPATRA"—and best of all, in the center, one word: TOM. In the years after the film, Tom would bring out the coin and marvel at it, not merely for the craftsmanship with which an actual Roman coin had been replicated, but for what it meant about Hollywood. Tom felt that Burton and Taylor had liked him, but he was under no illusions—they had given out more than two hundred of these coins to members of the crew and cast. And yes, it was certainly a generous act, and he couldn't help feeling warmed by the gesture. The cast and crew of that monumental film had been through a lot because of the notoriety of the stars, and it was fitting and right, almost by way of apology, that the two had given such a thoughtful token to all involved. But what struck Tom when he thought of it later was just how much power the coin seemed to have. When he would show it to college friends, even the jaded Yalies would marvel at the almost religious nature of the artifact. Movie stars were like emperors and queens and kings themselves now ("All the religions in the world rolled into one," Margo Channing

"One of Tom's cherished possessions"

had said, "and we're Gods and Goddesses . . ."); their mere replications on a coin carried with it tremendous significance.

But as time passed and Tom made his way in the movie business, he became wistful about the change he felt the movie, and his cherished coin, represented. People were interested in his father's movie not because of the story it told of the woman who tried to remake the world in her own image, or the two men who tried and failed to tame her, or even really the story of the film's making, the colossally dramatic and messy way things happen in the real world of moviemaking. They were interested because it had two huge movie stars in it.*

Cleopatra, Tom knew, had contributed to the sorry state of the modern movie business. Hollywood films, in the years to come, would avoid trying to tell complex stories for large audiences. Yes, there would be the awards-bait movies every autumn, but these films were for smaller audiences now; the failure of *Cleopatra* had cemented the trend away from intelligence on screen for the masses. "The intimate epic" had not worked; no one wanted the intimate part, the psychology and human nuance Joe had hoped to bring to the screen. The epic side of the equation had won out; comic-book movies, movie star vehicles, and simpler genre films came to predominate. Despite the so-called *Easy Rider / Raging Bulls* revolution of the 1970s, in the end, no matter how great or talented the filmmakers, the compromises would keep coming, and the larger budgets

---

* An unapologetic name dropper, Tom loved to quote his friends Joan Didion and John Gregory Dunne on the subject, writers who, like many in the years since Herman's telegram, had come West for money to support their more "serious" work. After trying for years to wrangle a complicated subject—in this case, the tragic story of the newscaster Jessica Savitch and the perils of celebrity news journalism—into the movie that would eventually become *Up Close and Personal* in 1996, they remembered a producer interrupting them in a meeting where they'd been describing what the movie was about: it was about journalism, they said, it was about integrity, it was about the demeaning battle for ratings and how it—The producer snorted, cut them off, and explained as if to two children: "The movie is about Robert Redford and Michelle Pfeiffer."

would always go to simpler fare. As his own career progressed, Tom was happy to embrace these simpler movies—after all, he wrote James Bond and Superman movies, so he was reluctant to bite the hand that fed him*—but he missed the intelligence of a movie like *Cleopatra* that Joe had so labored to bring to the screen, and it pained him to see Joe's kind of picture being shunted aside. The intelligence, the wit, the richness of characterization . . . movies had become so debased now.

Tom went to his grave in 2010 thinking *Cleopatra* a horribly underestimated film.

> Do what you will, Caesar's done it first and done it better. Run where you will as fast as you can. You can't get out. There's no way out. The shadow of Caesar will cover you and cover the universe for all of time.
>
> —*CLEOPATRA*

> Peter Stone: Your brother, Herman, wrote *Citizen Kane*. Did he have any influence on you as a screenwriter?
> Joe Mankiewicz: None.
>
> —*INTERVIEW*, 1989

In late December of 1962, barely three months after Joe Mankiewicz had been unceremoniously dumped by Fox, *Variety* readers were surprised to read, under the headline "Zanuck and Mank End Tiff on Cleo," that Joe had been rehired. An immediate outcry had greeted Zanuck's decision to fire Joe—with support pouring in from people as disparate as Elizabeth Taylor, Richard Burton, and Billy Wilder.† But more than that: Zanuck quickly realized that the movie was a "monster hanging on [his] shoulder," and though he had no intention of leaving "picture making totally

---

* Tom explained his decision to focus on lighter genre fare as a way to distinguish himself from his father, for just as Joe felt he couldn't compete with Herman, and Herman with Franz—"Stick it, I'll never live up to that and I'm not going to try"—so Tom felt confounded by Joe's success.

† Wilder cabled Zanuck: "The sooner the bulldozers raze your studio, the better it will be for the industry." Burton told *The New York Times*, "What was done was vulgar." As for Elizabeth Taylor, she had been powerless to prevent Joe from being fired, but she did everything she could to make her preference clear: "Mr. Mankiewicz took *Cleopatra* over when it was nothing—when it was rubbish . . . and he certainly should have been given the chance to cut it. It is appalling."

Rex Harrison and Joe on the reshoots for *Cleopatra,* early 1963

in the hands of an artist," there was no one else other than Joe capable of wading into the complex mess of footage shot in the preceding two years and making anything remotely comprehensible out of it. In addition, Zanuck had realized that for continuity's sake, a number of other scenes needed to be shot, and he was worried that the cast, devoted to Joe, would not deliver their best performances with another director. Finally, at least according to Joe, Zanuck must have calculated that on some level the battle was already lost: there was no way *Cleopatra* was going to be the triumph Fox had once hoped for, and if Zanuck hired someone else to finish the picture, it would be Zanuck who would be blamed for the whole mess. This way, there was no doubt: it was a Joseph L. Mankiewicz picture, and Joe would be the one to bear the brunt of the blame.

Too late, Joe realized Zanuck had outsmarted him. "When he fired me," Joe said ten years later, "I should have stayed fired. It was a mistake to have shot those retakes, because it implied approval by me." Even so, Joe made a half-hearted attempt to take his name off the film, but to no avail.

Joe knew it was doomed, going so far as to joke about the film's fate on live television. On *The Tonight Show,* Johnny Carson had deputized Bert Parks to interview Joe live from the premiere in New York. Parks congratulated Joe as he entered the theater, declaring, "A wonderful, wonderful achievement!" Joe looked at Parks warily. "Well," he said with a hangdog smile, "you must know something I don't." But even Joe couldn't have guessed at the level of vitriol the reviews contained, most memo-

Joe and Roddy McDowell on the reshoots for *Cleopatra,*
early 1963

rably one by Judith Crist of the *New York Herald Tribune,* headlined "A
Monumental Mouse," that decried the film's script and called the whole
thing "an extravagant exercise in tedium."

But the truth is, Tom was right. His father's film is not nearly as bad as
its reputation. If talky and overlong, it is also at times genuinely moving,
and its first half in particular is filled with that combination of wit and
grandeur that Joe had hoped for as he aimed for his oxymoronic "intimate epic." And the performances are subtle and honest. The magnetic
Burton, though Joe felt the best parts of his performance didn't make it
into the finished film, effectively conveys a sexy if impotent and doomed
lush, overshadowed first by Caesar and then by Cleopatra.* Harrison
is a sophisticated and mature Caesar, quite obviously a brilliant man,
and his performance alone suggests the heights the film Joe aspired to—
something worthy of Shaw. Interestingly, among the leads, given Joe's
typical excellence with actresses and her own performance in *Suddenly,
Last Summer,* Taylor doesn't quite bring it home, coming off sometimes

---

* History forced Joe into a reversal of his standard Joe–Herman dynamic; here it is
the younger man who is the uncontrollable alcoholic and the older who is cold
and ambitious.

Joe on the reshoots for *Cleopatra,* early 1963

as more of a shrill and emotional fashion plate than a woman of queenly ambition.

Worst of all, Joe had been prescient about the script: he simply didn't have the time to get it right. Skouras's short-sighted invocation that "we're paying the girl fifty thousand a week, we got to get something on film" all but ordained that the film would wind up a lopsided epic. Beginning to shoot without a completed script meant that the first half of the movie would always be stronger; the second half never got the attention it needed. And since his editorial skills were always the weakest part of Joe's writing—even his best movies have speeches that go on too long, points that are made once too often, repetitions and duplications* that give truth to Ken Geist's assertion that as a filmmaker Joe didn't trust silence—the film's dragginess in the second half seems almost inevitable.

THANK GOD THEY WOULDN'T BE STAYING THE NIGHT IN THE CITY. There'd been some talk about it, and because of a couple of interviews Joe had scheduled with the press the next day, it might have been more convenient, but Jesus Christ, was he glad to get the hell out now. The evening had been a torture, start to finish. Zanuck had insisted that the NBC play was a brilliant move, and that getting the Johnny Carson show to do a live remote from the theater would put the movie in thirty mil-

---

* And reiterations and reverberations and redundancies.

lion homes—but how many of those homes weren't totally aware of this monstrosity? Everyone in the damned country knew about the movie, everyone knew about Liz and Dick and their shenanigans, everyone knew it was a disaster. Sitting in the theater while the thing played had proved impossible for Joe, but the lobby was no better as the reviews started to come in. As prepared as Joe felt he had been, as disappointed as he himself was in the film then unspooling in the Rivoli, the critics' bile was another level deeper, and somehow aggrieved and angry. It was as if they were taking it personally, that the country was so fascinated by Taylor and Burton and so eager to see their love scenes that when in the end those scenes were less than transportingly exhilarating, and the movie surrounding them less than a holy mash-up of *Gone with the Wind* and Beethoven's Fifth, someone's head had to roll. And as Joe knew they would, critics wouldn't take it out on Liz or Dick, or blame Zanuck or Fox or Spyros Skouras for the misshapen beast before them. It was Joe's head on the chopping block. Judith Crist was the worst. Standing near the popcorn concession, Joe scanned quickly, taking in phrases before he could bring himself to read the whole thing straight through: "At best a major disappointment . . . Mr. Mankiewicz, hitherto one of our most adult and literate screenwriters . . . the resultant mélange of clichés and pompous banalities is unworthy of him . . . We were led to anticipate a fresh and sophisticated character-oriented approach . . . Mr. Mankiewicz's heart is obviously not in the large-scale action . . . a strangely static epic . . . Mr. Mankiewicz frustrates the requirements of the wide screen . . . The mountain of notoriety has produced a mouse."

To the end of his life, Joe maintained that he knew that his career was essentially over at the age of fifty-four. The disaster of *Cleopatra* had been that immense. Joe knew that Fox had nearly gone bankrupt—and not just because of *Cleopatra*. Zanuck's own World War II picture *The Longest Day* hadn't helped, an almost equally profligate epic, but *Cleopatra* had been the center of all attention—and so now, Joe knew there was no chance the studio would commit to the *Alexandria Quartet,* which Joe would later call "the great disappointment of my life." He was practically numb from fury.

NEVER AGAIN WOULD JOE MANKIEWICZ THROW HIMSELF SO COM-pletely into a production. "After thirty years," Joe said two and a half angry decades later, "I thought I'd seen all the infighting and dirt." But

Rosemary Matthews

it was nothing—*nothing*—like *Cleopatra.* The entire experience, he said, left him "with a deep distaste for the making of films." The regret was total. As Tom said, "I think instinctively he knew it was wrong for him. But it was just too much money to turn down." As a result, and it was as if the whole family knew it, Joe would never be the same.

But one good thing had come out of the whole sordid endeavor, and to any careful onlookers on *Cleopatra*'s opening night, it would have been observable. At the end of the night, Joe didn't retreat alone to his new house in Mount Kisco. He drove there with his new wife, Rosemary. As the car sped upstate—to home, a place of comfort and rest—Joe Mankiewicz relaxed.

Thirty-three-year-old Rosemary Matthews was the efficient and pulled-together daughter of an English archdeacon. With a clipped but gentle accent, she had first impressed Joe when she worked as a dialogue coach for Rossano Brazzi on *The Barefoot Contessa,* and she had worked off and on for Figaro in various capacities ever since, serving as one of the production's secretaries on *Cleopatra.* Joe admired her reserve, her aristocratic good looks, and her common sense. She was "possibly the only Englishwoman," he said, "with an awareness that coffee is more than just any brown liquid, heated." And there was a crucial difference between Rosemary and other women Joe had been involved with. She was not an actress. Nor, crucially, was she unstable. In fact, Rosemary, growing up in a solid home, her father a British prelate and her mother a surgeon, was well-educated, reserved, and, by proving herself through almost a decade of devotion and friendship, indispensable. As Hume Cronyn said, at that point in Joe's life, after the humiliations of *Cleopatra,* Joe "mistrusted everything about himself and his emotional functioning."

In the end, the truth may have been simpler than anything anyone could have imagined. After years of pushing himself, to compete, to be better than everyone else, to be smarter than everyone, more successful than Herman, wittier than Wilder, more sophisticated than Lubitsch, to be wiser and saner than his women, to show them all that he cared about their problems and neuroses, maybe he didn't want, or need, to challenge

"I did find her in the original contact sheets." Mom
peeks through at Joe and Rosemary's wedding.

himself in every arena. In this one area of his life, at home, for the first
time, Joe looked at Rosemary and saw a woman who accepted him, and
a future that might be uncomplicated.

And so on December 14, 1962, before a small crowd in front of a New
York City judge, after nearly two years of shooting on *Cleopatra,* just two
weeks before Zanuck rehired him to do the reshoots and finish the editing, and less than six months before the film opened, Joe married again.
Three years after orchestrating and virtually directing the wedding of Herman's daughter, now Joe looked happy, content, even twinkly. Johanna
Davis gripped the arm of her husband and watched Joe and Rosemary
greet the judge with professional élan. Her uncle seemed not to care, at
least for the moment, about *Cleopatra,* about which Joe had told his niece
so many horror stories.

But it's likely that Josie's mind was not on Joe's career for the moment, or for that matter her own. As she watched Joe and Rosemary take
their vows, it's hard to imagine, no matter her gratitude for all that her
uncle had done for her, that she was paying careful attention.[*]

For the beam that seemed to emanate from Johanna Mankiewicz Davis
that afternoon had very little to do with Joe and Rosemary and everything
to do with what was happening inside her. Should she be more focused

---

[*] Interestingly, my mother appears in none of the printed photos taken at the wedding and party afterwards. I did find her in the original contact sheets, though,
peeking through in one image of Joe and Rosemary as they read congratulatory
telegrams after the ceremony.

on her career? God knows, that's what Joe would want, if he knew, if she trusted him enough to tell him the good news—but whenever she thought about her father, she was less sure. Of course it was practically legend how little Herman had cared about the Hollywood game, but it was deeper than that. It wasn't specific to Hollywood, or moviemaking. It had to do with priorities, or what people in other parts of the country called "values." Herman Mankiewicz, yes, cared so much about achievement and accomplishment, and like all Mankiewiczes, he would forever want to know exactly what had happened to the missing three points. But more than that, as she remembered her father, which she tried to do at least once a day, Josie Davis knew that he would be absolutely thrilled and made wildly, enormously, instantly tearful by the news of what would be arriving next summer, perhaps a month or so after *Cleopatra*.

Herman Mankiewicz was about to become a grandfather.[*]

---

[*] Not for the first time. Don had already had two children: Jane, born in 1950, and John, born in 1954; and Frank's son Josh had been born in 1955.

CHAPTER SIXTEEN

---❧---

LEGACY

A fellow will remember things you wouldn't think he'd remember. You take me . . . One day, back in 1896, I was crossing over to Jersey on a ferry and as we pulled out, there was another ferry pulling in—and on it, there was a girl waiting to get off. A white dress she had on—and she was carrying a white parasol—and I only saw her for one second and she didn't see me at all—but I'll bet a month hasn't gone by since that I haven't thought of that girl . . .

—*CITIZEN KANE*

ONE SUNDAY MORNING IN APRIL 2018, AT THE HOLLYWOOD ROOSEVELT Hotel theater in downtown Los Angeles, the Turner Classic Movies festival hosted a panel called "Growing Up Mankiewicz." Many of the 120 or so assorted guests had come because of their devotion to TCM's movie host, Ben Mankiewicz, though Ben, Herman's grandson and Frank's son, wouldn't host this event but serve as a panelist, alongside his brother Josh and his cousins John, also Herman's grandson and Don's son, and Alex, Joe's only daughter.

The theme of the event, and indeed the question that haunted the lives of the descendants of Franz Mankiewicz, was simple: What kind of pressure does it put on a person to grow up in such a family? For an hour, the panelists circled the question, sometimes trying to answer directly, sometimes skirting it with charming, self-conscious evasiveness. The burden, as Ben put it, required them to be merely the funniest, smartest, most clever people in any room. By John's account, the pressure to succeed was "stealth," passed from generation to generation like a gene that mutates from "the missing three points" to "how come you don't have a show on HBO?" John, a TV writer with credits ranging from *Miami Vice* to *House*

Growing up Mankiewicz: Josh, moderator Illeana
Douglas, Ben, John, and Alex Mankiewicz

of Cards, told of an interesting birthday present he'd once received from
his screenwriter father Don,[*] who gave him three picture frames: the
first displayed Herman's nomination certificate for Best Screenplay for
The Pride of the Yankees; the second held an Oscar nomination Don had
received for Best Screenplay for writing the 1958 Susan Hayward movie *I
Want To Live!* The third picture frame, of course, was blank.

Josh and Ben had taken a different path to avoid comparisons with
their legendary ancestors. Their father Frank had himself taken Herman's
warnings to heart and escaped Hollywood altogether, eschewing entertainment for politics and public service, going to law school, serving
as regional director of the peace corps in Latin America, and becoming Robert Kennedy's press secretary (famously sharing the news of the
senator's assassination with the world in June 1968) before serving in the
ill-fated McGovern presidential campaign and then becoming the head
of National Public Radio and later a lobbyist in Washington, D.C.[†] So

---

[*] Herman's older son Don carved out a successful career as a writer for film and
television, writing and creating shows like *Ironside* and *Marcus Welby, M.D.* (the
doctor's name, or so Don told impressionable nephews, was a loose rearrangement
of the phrase "make us be well").

[†] This sentence makes brief work of a colossally talented man. Frank Mankiewicz
deserves his own biography; in fact, when he passed away in 2014 at the age
of ninety, Ben and Josh joked that he had been working on his autobiography,
entitled "I Wasn't Listening Then and I Can't Hear You Now," a title which hints

Josh and Ben had been raised far from the movie business, and while both went into journalism, the long arm of Hollywood brought them back to entertainment anyway. After beginning as a political reporter, Josh became a popular correspondent on NBC's long-running *Dateline* program, where he made a "happy career out of interviewing murder suspects and raising a skeptical eyebrow."* Ben, twelve years Josh's junior, worked his way up through local news before finding himself at the intersection of journalism and entertainment in the TCM job, where it became his pleasant task to introduce old movies from the Golden Age of Hollywood and serve as kind of keeper of the flame, not just of the family's legacy but the entire industry's.

So it seemed that the harder one tried to deny it—destiny, the pressure to succeed, writing, being a Mankiewicz and explaining the missing three points—the less likely it was one could escape. A tale from Joe's daughter Alex, who made a life for herself as a graphic artist on Australia's Eastern Shore, a scant 7,500 miles from Hollywood, made it clear. When she was in college in the 1980s, with little or no idea what she wanted to do with her life, she was shocked to pick up a copy of a book called *Hollywood Dynasties,* read a chapter on her family, and find in it the simple declaration from her father: "My daughter is in college. She's going to be a writer, she just doesn't know what kind yet."† There was no escaping any of it.

JOE'S MARRIAGE TO ROSEMARY BROUGHT, AT LEAST TO HIS PERSONAL life, a calm that had hitherto been utterly unknown. They settled an hour

---

at the classic Mankiewiczian traits of humor, intelligence, and the inability to get close to people.

* By the late 2010s, Josh was well known enough to be lampooned by comedian Bill Hader, who delighted in imitating Josh's response to a murder suspect who had a curiously passive response to finding the body of his dead wife: "Most people would call 911. But you didn't do that, did you?" The line—"but you didn't do that, did you?"—was spread widely on Twitter, where few if any recognized the curious echoes across Mankiewicz family history.

† Something else I shared with Alex: when I was eight, my mother inscribed a copy of her novel to me with words—"To Nicky, from one writer to another. All my love, Mommy"—that I found shocking and almost horrifying. Her labeling me a "writer" served, when combined with her untimely death a year later, as an unintentional recipe for decades of anxiety and self-doubt (and it may well be part of the reason for this book's nearly two-decade gestation).

Joe and Rosemary with Alex, c. 1967

from the city, first in Pound Ridge and then in Bedford, New York, where they would live for the remainder of Joe's life, until his death in 1993. And not long after they'd moved there, Rosemary had become pregnant. Like Herman, Joe, a father again at the age of fifty-seven, found himself delighted and invigorated by his baby girl, Alexandra, and, also like Herman's, Joe's daughter would grow up in the twilight of her father's career.

Joe was sick of moviemaking. He had taken to referring to himself as the oldest whore on the beat, but he was tired of turning tricks. It was too damn complicated, and the new generation ascendant in Hollywood had no use for Joe's kind of movie. And given the problems he'd faced on *Cleopatra,* he never wanted to begin a film again until absolutely everything was in place: the script, a production plan, maybe even the knowledge of what country the movie would be shot in. Moviemaking was no longer really possible like this; now the trains were constantly leaving the station before the seats were bolted down for the passengers—but Joe insisted, so his next few projects ended up taking longer than they should have, and he never had much affection for them. *The Honey Pot* he knew was a cranky and overlong, if amusing and intelligent adaptation of Ben Johnson's *Volpone.* And then came what Joe called "Joe Mankiewicz's goddamn Western," *There Was a Crooked Man . . . ,* which he himself deemed almost unwatchable to an interviewer a decade after he finished it.*

It would be nice to say, though, that Joe had mellowed, that despite the professional setbacks, his domestic tranquility brought him, for the first time, a kind of peace. It would be nice, but it would be wrong. The films, especially *The Honey Pot,* reveal a snobbishness that frequently curdles into genuine contempt for other people. Fox, the film's arrogant schemer, played with condescension by Rex Harrison, gives sneering voice to many of Joe's most cherished opinions about the utter banality of modern life: television is for the "witless and undemanding," and he excoriates the

---

* Still, he was proud of having made the first Western to introduce a new level of reality to the movies: "It was the first film to show horseshit in the streets."

"little people" for their abuse of that precious commodity, time itself:
"How little you people value time . . . Like everything else, you'll choose
what's more, not what's better."*

Of course he could not get away from his own unconscious mind, but
it doesn't take a Dr. Hacker to see the hostility in Joe's giving the shallow
character whom he's talking to about time—the one who, when he asks
her, "Do you know what the hell I am talking about?" says, "Honestly,
no"—the name Sara, the name of his brother's widow.

Unfair? Maybe. But then was it unfair of Joe to have sent word to
my mother, when she returned from her honeymoon in October 1959,
that the charge accounts at the department stores Joe had set up for her
had been cancelled? Now that she was married, Joe decided he would no
longer pay for her shopping sprees. Josie Davis, newlywed, wasn't some
kind of mad shopper, she had spent maybe $200 on the accounts—but
the curt note from Joe's secretary left her with the guilty feeling that he
felt she'd been taking advantage of him. Later, when she thought about
all those IOUs of Herman's Joe had showed her, it occurred to her that
while she didn't *think* Joe wanted her to repay him for her father's debts,
the trust between them had eroded so much that she couldn't be sure.

In the years after her marriage, with Mom and Dad settling in Greenwich Village, it is easy to imagine an alternate life where her kindly uncle
Joe, who had cared for her so thoughtfully after her father's death, would
have been a continuing presence in her life. But it was not to be. Instead
there was a quiet but firm, growing estrangement, and while my mom was
never entirely clear what had caused it—Rosa's suicide? Joe's guilt over his
behavior that afternoon? Josie's marriage to the alleged "thin" man? Joe's
to Rosemary?—there was an undeniable rift, during which no real contact
was had. Joe had invited Mom and Dad to the opening of *Cleopatra* in
1963, as well as his wedding, but there was no regular communication at
all. The split was such that until Alex was born in April 1966, Mom didn't
even know Rosemary was pregnant.

In the opening newsreel sequence of *Citizen Kane,* a short cartoon
depicts the growing of the Kane empire: a series of radio towers that rise
over various American cities demonstrating the reach of Charles Fos-

---

* In fact, mortality was clearly much on Joe's mind. "Does a clock give a damn what
  kind [of time] it measures? No. But we do—we special ones. We slow down for
  the good—we sip it, second by second, like a great wine—and we speed up the
  bad. You little people—you chumps—swallow time like a hamburger."

Joe and Alex on the Martha's Vineyard ferry, c. 1971

ter Kane's media domain. My mother always imagined Herman's steady descent as being like the second half of the animation, where Kane's empire collapses and the radio signals whimper and flicker out. And the same was true of Joe's career, in deeper eclipse as the years went on, and, as Mom thought about it, the same was true of the gossamer-thin connections between members of the family, little animated ripples that no longer made it from one person to the other.

In the early seventies, Mom spent an evening with her cousin Tom. By then the cold war with Joe was more than a decade old, though Mom had had the satisfaction at least of seeing Joe send my father a fawning congratulatory note after one of Dad's documentaries aired to acclaim on CBS. While it may not have made up for the "thin" comment, it was a certain kind of eating crow, which pleased her. She asked Tom, gently, "Does he ever, you know, mention me . . . ?"

Tom said, "Yes, he asks how you are now and then."

"What do you think his feeling is about me, why this total lack of interest?"

Tom hesitated, then told the truth: "Well, I think you kind of failed him. He sees you as having failed him."

Mom was stunned. *She* had failed *him*? How?

Mom and me, c. 1970

Tom said, "Well, he always thought you'd be a star."

Mom looked at Tom, and considered Joe, living his life in Bedford—all those movies but so few friends, and to have pushed away the few people who actually cared about him. She told Tom, "I kind of feel like I am a star. I've had two children, and a happy marriage, and I'm writing a novel."

But to Joe, that wasn't being a star. Being a star meant succeeding at the highest levels—of show business, academia, whatever field it was—displaying to the world an intelligence and brilliance that it hadn't seen before. Domestic concerns were secondary.

"He always thought you'd be a star": Johanna Davis, c. 1973

IN 1971, TOM AND JOE MANKIEWICZ BOTH FOUND THEMSELVES working in London at Pinewood studios. Tom was working on the James Bond movie *Live and Let Die,* and Joe was directing *Sleuth,* an adaptation of the play by Anthony Shaffer starring Laurence Olivier and Michael Caine, and father and son frequently shared a car to and from the studios. With Tom making good money and a name for himself in Hollywood, he said he didn't need anything from his father anymore and claimed that the two of them had settled into a good relationship. Still, it's hard to imagine that things were free and easy between them, given Joe's attitude toward Hollywood and that his son was now working on the very kind of picture Joe blamed for everything that was wrong with the industry. In fact, as Tom pointed out, while the entire set of *Sleuth* fit in one soundstage in Pinewood, the Bond movie consumed seven such massive stages. Joe wandered onto one of them one afternoon while on a break, looked around at the huge sets, the submarines and men with machine guns, a massive lagoon, an underground cave, an inflatable version of the actor Yaphet Kotto bobbing up and down near the roof, and he said, "My God, what the hell do you people do in here all day long?"

Shortly afterwards, one evening as they were walking back to Joe's hotel—Joe liked to walk in the evenings and had the car drop him off a few blocks away—Joe said quietly, "Tom, if this one works out, I think

I may just hang it up." Tom objected: "No, Dad, you're just tired," but Joe was firm. And sure enough, the success of *Sleuth* gave Joe what he most seemed to want: a good one to go out on. The film was like the anti-*Cleopatra,* a non-spectacle with a cast of two, a tightly constructed thriller, full of reversals and double crosses, concerning—what else?—a younger man scheming to undercut an older man and take everything that is most precious from him. While the film may be a little long—it is, after all, a Joseph L. Mankiewicz film—it is also entertaining and suspenseful, regardless of such curious directorial touches as cutting to Olivier's collection of miniature figurines whenever things get tense. Joe was nominated yet again for an Academy Award for Best Director, and as he told Ken Geist, referring to his "oldest whore on the beat" theory, "Suddenly you get hot, and the wrinkles go out of your face, and you are a young beauty again." For Joe, it was, again, a success, and that seemed to sustain him. Why risk putting himself out there? It would have to be something extraordinary to cause him to take the chance.

It never came.

IT WAS AN EPIC CASE OF WRITER'S BLOCK. THAT'S HOW ALEX describes it, what hit Joe in the years after *Sleuth,* and how others in the family thought of it. *Uncle Joe can't write anymore; he isn't writing. Nothing's happening.* There were a number of false starts on various projects in the seventies, and some movies that he was offered to direct, foremost among them *All the President's Men,* on which project he met a number of times with Robert Redford, who had bought the film rights to the best-selling book, each time asking more and more questions that were so baffling to Redford that he finally moved on to Alan J. Pakula. Joe met with Paul Newman, who lived in nearby Westport, on a few different projects. He toyed with an adaptation of *Macbeth* to star Marlon Brando and Maggie Smith, though he must have known it was a long shot, Shakespeare having fallen even further out of favor with audiences in the years since *Julius Caesar.* Most frustratingly, for years, Joe wrestled to adapt a film out of *Jane,* a novel by Dee Wells about a young woman who has an affair with three men and doesn't know whose baby she's pregnant with, a ripe possibility for one of Joe's multiple-flashback, multiple-point-of-view scripts. And there were meetings, so many meetings, one with a Hollywood producer who offered Joe the chance to direct a hot new literary property, though he worried Joe would find the material beneath

Joe directs Laurence Olivier on the set of *Sleuth*.

him. When Joe said, "Try me," the man produced the latest airport novel by Jacqueline Susann, and was surprised when Joe didn't bat an eyelash. Joe said he was still game, but in this case, it would have to be what was known as a "step deal," which would give the producer the right to terminate the deal after prenegotiated specified steps, like a first draft. The producer said, fine, what's the first step? Joe said, "The first step is how much will you pay me just to *read* that piece of shit?"

His contempt for Hollywood never softened. The rage deepened, and the feeling of having been used and abused by an entire industry took hold. As a result, as the years passed Joe knew as well as anyone that the chances of his ever making another movie again were slim. Still, even though in Tom's mind Joe was pretending—there was no way he was going to direct another film—he never stopped working, or trying to write. He had ideas for plays and books—one grand idea no less than a history of the actress, which he would trace all the way from Renaissance theater through Sheridan down to the present day—and so every morning found him at his desk in the office in Bedford, sitting down with a notebook or at the typewriter.

But nothing came. For the longest time, absolutely nothing. Joe was never someone who had easily tossed off anything, but this was profound, and crippling. Over the years, Joe and Rosemary had developed a delightful ritual at Christmas; he was usually too consumed and busy to do any real shopping, so she would buy and wrap the gifts for herself, and then Joe would compose marvelous, witty Mankiewiczian Christmas cards to affix to the presents, weaving cryptic hints about what was inside. Even these simple ditties were now, painfully, beyond his reach. And it wasn't for lack of trying. Every day, the same routine—and every day the same result: nothing.

YEARS LATER, AFTER JOE HAD DIED AND ALEX WAS IN HER MID-twenties, she started thinking about her lineage, and she realized that while she knew quite a lot about Franz, his standards and ideals, the source of all misery—the domineering patriarch who insisted on perfection and would accept nothing less—she knew very little of the original Johanna Mankiewicz, Franz's wife. Who was she? What was she like? Can she really have been such a cipher? Sara had insisted that Herman and Joe inherited their wit from her, and Heaven knows there isn't a mound of evidence that it came from Franz, so if a lightning bolt of drollness hadn't come out of the blue sky to strike Herman and Joe and their descendants, then surely Johanna cannot have been the simple hausfrau that Joe and Herman spoke of, or didn't speak of.

Alex knew the bare facts: Johanna had survived Franz and ended up in a nursing home in California, living there for three years until her death. Herman and Joe had rarely visited. But where had Johanna been buried? Luckily Joe's final assistant, a woman who knew next to nothing about movies or Joe's actual work, had kept immaculate files, which told the tale. Johanna's body had been sent back to New York and been buried in a large Jewish graveyard in Queens. Franz had been buried in Mount Tremper in the Catskills, in Ulster County, New York, where he and Johanna had spent a few summers with their children, on a mountain overlooking a stream, now the site of a Buddhist monastery. Herman's ashes had been scattered there too. But Johanna, Alex learned, ended up in the vast borough of Queens, where she had never lived, amid the most religious of all Jewish graves.

One day in the mid-1990s, Alex and Rosemary went out to Queens to look for the grave, stopping first in the caretaker's hut at the edge of the cemetery, where the man blew dust off a huge leather tome, opened it to find the plot number, and told them, "I have to warn you. That grave hasn't been tended to in some time." Rosemary and Alex made their way down the rows of religious gravestones, simple slabs for the most part, and finally found an old stone headstone, ivy wrapped around the name, still legible despite decades of exposure to the elements. The original Johanna Mankiewicz, a woman who had insisted on a Jewish burial, resting till eternity next to strangers. To another family, it might have seemed an unfathomable mystery. But, as Alex knew, no Mankiewicz is buried next to any other Mankiewicz.

The family members are buried, as they lived, separately.

THE DISTANCE IN THE FAMILY AND THE ENDLESS STRIVING, AS WELL as the emphasis on career above all else, would last to the bitter end, a sad fact which was borne out when Tom died of cancer in 2010 at the age of sixty-eight. The way Tom's death was greeted by a London paper was emblematic of the whole competitive mess, Franz's legacy in a nutshell, for the second sentence of Tom's obituary, after listing his work on the James Bond and Superman films, read: "Such credits could hardly rival the achievements of his father, Joseph Mankiewicz, who won four Oscars, including two for writing and directing *All About Eve* (1950)." As if that wasn't bad enough, the article continued: "And even Joe Mankiewicz remains overshadowed by Herman Mankiewicz, Tom's uncle, who cowrote *Citizen Kane* (1941) with Orson Welles." Of course, such a chain could go on forever. Herman was overshadowed by Welles, Welles was overshadowed by Mozart, Mozart by Shakespeare, Shakespeare by Jesus, etc., etc. . . .

That competition would not only poison a person's life, but also his death, seemed painfully unfair—and then I talked to Chris. Having spoken to them separately for the book already, I knew this set of Mankiewicz brothers hadn't been terribly close, but I had no idea the depth of the resentments that lingered through the decades. The same afternoon my father called me with the news about Tom, I'd gotten a voice message from Chris, asking me to call. When I reached him, I said that I knew why he was calling, I'd heard about Tom. There was a brief pause on the other end of the phone, then Chris said, "Dammit! My thunder's been stolen." We kept talking for a while, and Chris said, "Of course I know it's terribly boring to get a call like this out of the blue, telling you that someone you didn't know very well and didn't really care about has died." I started to object: I liked Tom a lot, I may not have gotten a chance to see him very much—but Chris cut me off. With exquisite timing and classic Mankiewicz humor, he said, "No, I was talking about *my* feelings for the guy."

So that's what it came down to, this horrible nonstop competitiveness. Was there no room for compassion, for caring? The drive to achieve, to

Joe may not have loved where his industry was going, but younger directors never failed to pay homage: with Martin Scorsese, at a restaurant in New York, 1991

compete, to make jokes and demonstrate your own brilliance, at the expense not just of the idiots you work with, but the entire industry, your own family, your brother . . . It can lead to an ambition that is founded on absolutely nothing but itself.

IN HIS FINAL YEARS, PARALYZED and unable to produce, Joe found he was competing not just with his own high standards, but with his own past successes, and with each passing year, even the modest *Sleuth* came to seem like something he could never top.* And so the silence continued, and so too the almost hermetic existence of a man still young enough to travel, to write, to teach, and to attend film festivals. He sat for interviews, was the willing subject of retrospectives and television profiles, traveled with Rosemary and Alex and other old friends, and ventured forth on occasion to teach at programs such as the nearby Eugene O'Neill Theater Center in Connecticut. But his life was more and more circumscribed. Joe had long criticized the "ivory ghetto" of Hollywood for having little relationship to the real world outside it, but as he retreated more and more into himself in his Bedford estate, he was as isolated as anyone, his interaction with others, which he had never greatly valued, at an all-time low.

He settled comfortably into the role of a man whose bitterness was reaching new depths. Interviewers routinely referred to him now as cranky or irascible, though some professed profound agreement with his scathing attacks on current films, filmmakers, and filmmaking theories: Joe

---

* He also seemed increasingly haunted by the specter of Herman, even though in most people's minds his late brother's accomplishments paled next to his own. In the late 1980s, the town of Wilkes-Barre approached Joe with the idea of holding a film festival to celebrate the two brothers. Joe shut it down immediately; the idea of sharing a bill with Herman was intolerable.

Joe with Rosemary and actor John Candy on the set
of *Delirious,* directed by Tom Mankiewicz, 1990

claimed, "I could blow out of my nose" better stuff than Woody Allen's
and Neil Simon's output; Spielberg's and Lucas's movies were "a series of
visual explosions that hurt my ears and give me a headache"; and "There's
nothing new about the director with his jacket draped over his shoulder
and the pseudo-philosophical cop-outs—'What do you mean, where
are the tennis balls? Life is a tennis game without tennis balls . . .'" He'd
greet interviewers outside his big brick house, accompanied by his black
Labrador, Cassius, still lean and hungry, and run through the contours
of his life and career (though always careful to remind them that his own
autobiography would be forthcoming, they shouldn't expect to be able
to capture his whole life—Geist had tried, and it was impossible, the
book was excrement). He felt it could fairly be said that he "was there in
the beginning, and that [he] saw the rise, peak, collapse, and the end of
the talking picture." He refused to speak of *Cleopatra* by name, calling it
only "the humiliating experience," but in the next breath he'd point to
the house and say, "It bought us this!" Still, he wasn't shy about sharing
regrets. He told one interviewer he'd had "more talent than I've played
fair with—I've pissed away a lot of talent." And though he said it was far
too early ("by several generations") to say that film was Art, he was firm
about what he had tried to do in his own work, namely "look at the truth
of the milieu in which I live and work—look at it wittily." That was the
important thing: "You have to look at it with wit, because otherwise you'd
cry." The world remained full of idiots. We were all now "living in an age
of illiteracy," and he loved to quote Dr. Johnson's famous dictum, which

Joe's later years were filled with honors—here
he receives the Erasmus Award in the city of
Rotterdam in 1984.

he said his father had drilled into him early on: "Relieve your mind of
cant." Don't think foolishly.

To the last, he was proud to play the snob, telling visitors that he wasn't
"all that involved with the unwashed and the unwanted. Granted, they've
got their problems—they're dreadful, and I want to help in any way I
can. But I don't want to write about them . . . Why must we always write
about the lowest common denominator of humanity?"

He took particular, wicked delight in one idiocy that he was proud to
have played a role in birthing, a theatrical award called the Sarah Siddons
Award, so named after the award at the center of *All About Eve,* given
annually to the best performance by an actress on stage in Chicago ("that
meat-oriented metropolis," Joe called it, "where the winds of culture blow
cold"). Had they so totally missed the point of the movie? Did they not
see that he had built his greatest film around a creature who was devoted
to earning "this meaningless totem," with "its implications as a sort of
cockamamie immortality," as an object of *satire*? "Could anyone con-
ceivably have been taken in by such an 'Award'? . . . It would seem," he
concluded about this real-life award that had gone to the likes of Helen
Hayes, Carol Channing, and most delectably *All About Eve*'s own Celeste
Holm, "that the idiocies of theater-folk within their world share with
the idiocies of the outsiders, 'the private people,' within their world, one
common characteristic: they are continuing, self-perpetuating idiocies."

It was during this period that I met Joe for the only time as an adult.
Whatever his feelings about awards, this one was being given at the French
consulate in Manhattan, and I tagged along with my father. In the years

since, I've wished to go back to that moment and talk more with him, or somehow download my brain to find the memories of the day that must be stored there. But all I remember is Claudette Colbert at the door with the French ambassador, and the elegant, short, and pudgy older man who at that point was just my distant Great Uncle Joe, making a few choice, funny remarks when presented with the award.* Afterwards, Joe looked happy and a little cuddly. What lingers most of all from the afternoon was a warmth and what seemed for all the world like a gentle authenticity.

I saw, in other words, what Joe wanted everyone to see, a seemingly happy and benign man with a keen intellect and a quick wit.

There was no sense then, that this was a man who was cut off from others, that he had been driven so strenuously to compete, to win, to defeat anything and everything he ever came into contact with that he'd tied himself in so many knots and for well over a decade hadn't written a word. No sense of the storm that had always raged, if not inside him, at least around him, even as he fought so desperately to keep it away. No sense of the man who was telling one of his relatives that he'd started ingesting large quantities of codeine, just because he could and because it helped stave off pain.

And yet I have one other memory of the man, vivid and frankly sensual. There was, quite simply, a smell about my Great Uncle Joe that afternoon at the French consulate that I have never been able to shake; more than mere halitosis, a sour and dyspeptic odor was emanating from him that had the feel of something rotten, something deep within the man consuming itself.

So in walking back through Central Park with my father that afternoon, and hearing the answer as to why exactly we had never really seen Joe while I was growing up, I was more than prepared to be judgmental and unsparing in my thoughts about the old guy. When Dad told me about Rosa's suicide, and Mom's feeling that Joe had set her up to find her aunt's dead body, I was quick to write him off as an unfeeling brute. And heck, I figured, maybe that's why the old man was so stenchy: he had no soul.

---

* Neither the French consulate nor my own memory has been able to locate the precise content of these remarks. Though my father admits his own memory may be faulty, he contributes one choice, telling witticism Joe made about the honor he was getting: "This award," Dad remembers Joe saying, "is more real to me than any of you."

Where we came in: Joe with Rosemary at the French consulate on the 1988 afternoon when I remet him

But who was the soulless one? The accomplished writer-director who had brought millions to laughter, tears, and a better understanding of the human condition, or the entitled youth who had learned all the wrong lessons from his moderately celebrated relatives and so, though he had no idea what to do with his own life, considered himself superior to everyone he came across, even one of the very men who had planted this unearned arrogance? Not for years, decades—not until I realized that only by learning as much as I possibly could about Joe and his older brother, reading through the accounts of both their lives as well as hundreds and hundreds of pages of transcripts of interviews conducted with people who had actually known them and spent time with them, and then allowing the facts and stories to merge with my own imagination, could I approach fathoming the complexity of these two men. As Joe said, "I don't think anybody exists as one pure note of music, or one color—people are fragmented."

Nothing was as simple as I'd thought.

WHAT HE MISSED MOST WERE THE ACTRESSES. SEEING THEM UNSURE of themselves in a scene, he would go to them, and quietly take them aside, look into their eyes with his own crystal blues, and softly ask them what was wrong. The entire apparatus of the movie set would be whirring and humming around them, but it didn't matter. Everything else would come to a standstill when Joe worked with an actress. What he loved most, what he missed most, was the feeling that the two of them were the only people in the world. When he was with an actress, or an actor, time would simply stop. And when he'd made the bond with them—relaxed Linda, soothed Bette's nerves, made sure Liz knew what she was supposed to do, calmed Monty down enough to at least get the poor man through the next take—he'd step back behind the camera, and in the same tone of voice he'd been using all along, just say, "Whenever you're ready." Not for Joe the booming, unnecessary and terrifying "Action!" A simple nod of the head to the camera operator to start rolling, and then a word or two to the actors, and the make-believe would begin.

JOE DIED IN FEBRUARY 1993, FOUR YEARS AFTER I'D SEEN HIM LAST. Even though I'd dismissed him as second-rate Herman and barely considered him a relative, still I preened at the obituary on the front page of the *New York Times,* thrilling at the phrase "literate skeptic of the American cinema." A few days later, at the funeral in Joe's adopted hometown in Bedford, New York, I was pleasantly diverted by the sight of the elegant Hume Cronyn mourning so openly, crying and walking slowly through the crowd, though I was somewhat chagrined when I nearly knocked the old guy down the front steps of the church. ("Aren't we Jewish?" one of the cousins asked as we left the church and headed back to Joe's house.)

There, the house filled with Joe's cronies (and Cronyns) milling about, exchanging pleasantries and memories. With the stone fireplace and half-staircase, and the well-dressed guests from another era, it was almost as if the party in *All About Eve* had never ended, just mellowed a bit through the decades.

At one point in the afternoon, I wandered off down the hall to Joe's study and found myself standing alone with the four Oscars and the musty smell of decades of pipe smoke. Looking around at the mementos, I marveled at the lack of respect Joe had received from his family—no one seemed to like him very much, or treat him like what he so obviously was: one of the most successful movie makers of the twentieth century. And as I stood there, having accepted that my future would inevitably lie in some of the same fields that Joe had seemed to conquer to so much effect in the outside world—and so little in his own family—I realized that whether I wanted to or not, I would of course be competing with Joe as surely as he had with Herman. There was no avoiding it.

But then something caught my eye, on a big mahogony desk: Joe's Rolodex.

It was opened, oddly, to Paul Newman's name and number, neatly typed. It was exquisitely suggestive—had Joe been on the verge of a comeback, a movie with Paul Newman, when he died? I looked through the Rolodex—so many luminaries, so many well-known people, accomplished people in the arts—and then I realized that quite instinctively I was looking up my own name.

It was there. My name, my address. The electric jolt that ran through my body cannot be overstated. I wandered back down the hall to rejoin the party (flipping the Rolodex away from my name first), bursting idiotically with the image of Uncle Joe instructing his secretary to type up a card with my name and address and phone number. *He cared!*

I thought back to the cuddly old man with the pipe at the French consulate, and wished to God I'd known who he really was. I realized now that one of the reasons I'd always rooted for Herman in thinking about the two brothers was because he'd had a family—a wife, two sons, a daughter—whom he must have cared about, more than he might ever have admitted. His life was full of struggles and unpleasantness, and his desires to do something else, *anything else,* had been pronounced and even legendary, but what he did do, what was undeniable, was create a family, and out of that family had come my uncles, and my cousins, and my mother, and my brother, and me.

But Joe had done the same thing. Watching Rosemary, speaking to her for this book, feeling her passionate devotion to Joe, seeing the wisdom in Tom's declaration that being with Rosemary had added ten years to Joe's life, hearing my mom on tape, despite all her problems with Joe, say "Rosemary's just the best thing that's happened to him . . ." And sensing Alex's care and love for her father's memory . . . Feeling in my bones the genuine love that emanates off the thousands of photographs boxed up in a storage cage in Rosemary's nursing home . . . It was real. In those final years, decades really, with his work at a virtual dead end, what was sustaining him if not family? Joe loved his wife and daughter to the end, in whatever way he could; it was inarguable.

And maybe that was the best the Mankiewiczes could do, this house of strangers—we'd live separately, die separately, be buried separately, but through it all, if we were lucky, the people we decided to spend our lives with, our friends and husbands and wives and children, we would try to curb our Franz-like tendencies to turn everything into a contest, resist the urge to label everyone else an idiot if they disagreed with us, and do what we could, if possible, to let people in, behind the armor and the wit.

JOE MANKIEWICZ WAS NOT A RELIGIOUS MAN, AND WHEN HE USED the word epiphany one autumn day in 1992 at the age of eighty-three, he did so with a gently self-chiding laugh. But there was no denying what had happened to him that afternoon, and Alex was moved and almost honored to be there to hear about it. The season had been an unusually

cold one, and Joe, who had
recently returned from a trip
to Europe, had been out for
a brief walk with the dog that
afternoon, on the gentle country roads around his house in
Bedford. When he came back
into the house, his cheeks were
ruddy, and he told his daughter he'd had an epiphany. He
shook his head with a kind of

"It was all over in about an hour":
Joe in his study

dazed expression and said that he finally realized he'd done some good
things in his life.

Alex held her breath, cautiously hopeful. Her whole life, she had tried
to reconcile his searing self-criticism—he should have written a good
book, or two; he should have written a play; the movies were no good,
nowhere near good enough—with the fact that he had been feted and
celebrated all over the world. Of course, like all the Mankiewicz offspring,
she knew about Franz and the impossible standard he had upheld—she'd
heard firsthand about Joe coming home to Harlem having gotten a 97
on a test, and Pop grilling him about the goddamn three points—and
so she knew where it had all come from, but she'd long thought it was
ridiculous. Of course, she hadn't argued with him about it—he could be
a "steamroller" when he felt opposed. But Alex had quietly, strenuously
disagreed with her father's objections to his own work. "I should have
written one good book, dammit." It was madness.

Now here he was, a little out of breath, though from the epiphany
or the autumn air she couldn't tell, finally softening. Yes, he saw, it was
absurd to carry on. The work had been fine. He sat there in his dear old
red cardigan, shaking his head from side to side. Alex said, "It was all over
in about an hour."

The next morning, a new man. It was like an enormous weight had
been lifted. Joe went to his study and for the first time in years, began
to write. He began taking notes for his autobiography. And he started
to go through mounds of mail that needed tending to, answering letters that had been staring at him from his desk for more than a decade.
In the final few months of his life, Alex says, it was like he was having
a reconciliation—with himself, his accomplishments, the specter of his
father.

The work had been good. And it was more than the work. He was just a man, not a perfect creature, not by any measure . . . But the same human being who had carried inside him such a hunger to be loved, and to love, to see his mother laugh at his bathrobe performances . . . "Flee with me to my hacienda." She had loved him, and Pop had too, in his own strange fashion. Pop had wanted to be a poet. Why did we all forget that? He'd come to America and left two sisters in Germany, and he'd thought he'd make his name in the field of poetry. What kind of craziness was that? He was only seventeen years old, trying to build a life in a country where he barely spoke the language. But he drove himself, when the poetry dream vanished—such lunacy, he must have hated himself for ever indulging the dream—to become a leading academic. A thinker. A respected professor who barely had time for his children. That man had a soul too, ended up terrifying his son, the poor boy had to hide in the closet. We're all just human beings, where in the hell is it written we have to make it all so damn complicated?

Joe sat at the typewriter. It was a beautiful old Underwood; he'd been given it when he first got to Hollywood. The ribbons were sometimes tricky, but Joe didn't mind much. He liked the smudge of the ink on his forefingers and thumbs, and he didn't even really care when he'd find splotches on his pages at the end of a day. He rubbed his hands together, an unconscious habit he'd picked up from Herman, the papery sound of two palms being rubbed back and forth. It always put him in a good mood to hear the sound and think of Herman again, the way he'd stood up to Pop. Good God, what courage.

The warmth was real. The closeness, the deep and honest compassion . . . There were so many stories left to tell.

Acknowledgments

I am indebted to so many for so much, in part because this book took so long, but more because help came from such an absurd number of sources.

The first thanks go to my dear late uncle, Frank Mankiewicz, who got the ball rolling without realizing it—because in the beginning was the word, and the word was a newspaper interview in 2002 in which I made Herman sound so much like the Foster Brooks of Hollywood's Golden Age that Uncle Frank called me the day the article appeared to chide me, gently, and suggest there was a lot more than "the white wine came up with the fish" to know about his father. Thank you, Uncle Frank, for that and so much more.

The next chronological thanks go to Susan Lacey, who, when she ran PBS's nonpareil biography series *American Masters,* was intrigued enough to commission a proposal for a documentary about Herman and Joe, and she provided enough funds for me to conduct interviews with some of their descendants and friends. Susan's enthusiasm for the project never dimmed, even as the odds of a film documentary became longer, the price of movie clips proving to date an all-but-intractable obstacle.

At a Christmas party that December, I mentioned the possible documentary to my friend the agent Bill Clegg. "That's a book," he said, and I assumed he meant a kind of companion book to the film. Eighteen years later, there is still no film, but at least we have redefined "companion." Agents are frequently described as tireless and indefatigable, and Bill is both those things, and he is also shrewd and funny; his shepherding of this book and its author through this long process has been incredible to behold.

Anyone writing a book about these two brothers is standing on the shoulders of two giants: Richard Meryman, whose *Mank,* published in 1977, helped reinvigorate Herman's reputation as a writer and larger-than-life wit; and Ken Geist, whose biography of Joe, *Pictures Will Talk,* was published the following year and remains the definitive portrait of Joe at his crankiest. I was lucky enough to get to know Ken before his death, and he was generous enough to share not only an extremely off-color story about my mother (for another book perhaps) but also all the original audio interviews he had conducted for *Pictures Will Talk.* Dick Meryman was similarly generous before he passed away in 2015, maybe because he was also a dear family friend, so beloved when I was growing up that Mom called him "The Man." He was kind, gentle, and extremely enthusiastic about this project, and he also shared boxes of all the transcripts he had conducted for *Mank,* as well as a trove of old reel-to-reel interviews. I am forever indebted to Dick, and his wife Liz, for sharing these treasures with me.

Attention must also be paid to Dick's sister-in-law Whitney Hansen, and the entire Hansen family, for encouragement and love during the years of this book's germination and, maybe more important, in the decades that preceded it when it was, quite obviously, growing without my knowledge, during which time Whitney was more than a surrogate mother, and her son Brooks far more than a non-brother brother. The Hansen family's impact on me, and this book, is incalculable.

Inspiration comes in many forms, often from friends like Melissa Marks and Vicente Caride, and David Dishy and Stefanie Roth; sometimes from the gang in On Thin Ice, who provided memories that have lasted a lifetime; sometimes from companions who don't know they're providing it, which I hope allows me to list JT and MM. It would also be wrong not to acknowledge David Fincher, whose gorgeous meditation on Herman at Victorville hit home theaters as this book was being copyedited and is indisputably a deep and lasting contribution to Mankiewicziana.

Others must be thanked for their myriad direct and indirect contributions to the manuscript: Maddy Cohen, for two summers helping me in a hundred little and big ways, not the least of which was sorting through the story of *The Philadelphia Story;* Dan Wilhelm, for a gentle read when the book still didn't know what it was; Meredith Coleman, for *Mad Dog of Europe;* Michael Gately, for inestimable help with sourcing; Sam Millstein, for silent film titles; Peter Kaufman, for pitching the seventh inning; Al Tapper and Bobby Haas, for patronage on other projects that permitted this one to grow; Michael Kantor, for modeling menschiness among so many other things; Andrew Solomon, for friendship always and in particular a meaningful week in 2012 when his generosity allowed my family to take in the sights of London while I wrote at his house and in whatever they call coffee shops over there; and Jerry Weisfogel and Matonah Rubin, for wisdom and guidance way beyond the call of duty.

Thanks too to two large-hearted writers who helped early on. Erik Simon provided research assistance and infused his Midwestern amiability into the book. Before that, Larry Maslon helped with the initial proposal, and, oh yes, the title.

My gratitude extends to many who will probably forever be unaware of their contributions to this book, but who spoke to me from Ken Geist's and Dick Meryman's tapes and transcripts. The full list of those consulted for this book is here:

Emanuel Aaronson, Rita Alexander, Brooks Atkinson, Richard Barr, Anne Baxter, Nathaniel Benchley, Robert Benton, B. A. Bergman, Irving Berlin, Abraham Bienstock, Judge and Mrs. John Biggs, Albert Boni, Richard Brooks, Lewis Buckman, Bernhard F. Burgunder, Val Burton, John Byram, James M. Cain, Michael Caine, Bent Cardan, Kitty Carlisle, Ruth Chase, William Chase, Shirley Potash Clurman, Joseph J. Cohn, Marc Connelly, Mr. and Mrs. Sheldon Coons, Joseph Cotten, Robert Coughlan, Joan Crawford, Hume Cronyn, George Cukor, Nat Curtis, Frank Davis, Isabelle Davis, Johanna Mankiewicz Davis, Ossie Davis, John De Cuir, Howard Dietz, Kirk Douglas, Rebecca Drucker, Philip Dunne, Peggy Cummins Dunnett, William Eckhardt, Florence Eldridge, C.O. Erickson, Chester Erskine, William Fadiman, Geraldine Fitzgerald, Henry Fonda, John Fox, Mattie Fox, Dr. Saul Fox, Sidney Freeman, Martin Gang, Sidney Ganis, Louis Gensler, Sir John Gielgud, Gail Gifford, Max Gordon, Marius Goring, Cary Grant, Edith Mayer Goetz, John Green, Nancy Green, Gerald Greene, John Groth, Alice Guinzburg, Mel Gussow, Dr. Frederick J. Hacker, Francis Hackett, Jack Haley, Adrienne Hall, Maurice Hall, Jed Harris, Rex Harrison, Helen Hayes, Rose Hecht, Jo Hennessey, Dr. Maurice Herzmark, Jack Hildyard, Celeste Holm, Brooke Hayward Hopper, William Hornbeck, Mr. and Mrs. Arthur Hornblow, Jr. , John Houseman, Kenneth Hyman, Paul Jacobs, Mildred and Sam Jaffe, George Jessel, Nunnally Johnson, Pauline Kael, Bronislau Kaper, Joe Kastner, Alfred Katz, Danny Kaye, Elia Kazan, Edwin Knopf, Mildred Knopf, Arthur Kober, Milton Krasner, Fritz Lang, Jennings Lang, Martin Landau, Robert Lantz, Charles Lederer, Sammy Leve, Charles Levy, Robert G. Levy, Rachel Linden, Clinton M. Long, Simon Long, Mary Anita Loos, Joseph Losey, Roddy McDowall, Barbara McLean, John Lee Mahin, Harold Mankawitz, Frank Mankiewicz, Sara Mankiewicz, Tom Mankiewicz, Fredric March, Lester Markel, Rear Admiral G. Markey, USNR (Ret.), Samuel Marx, Pamela Mason, Phil McAniff, Roddy McDowall, "Doc" Merman, Gary Merrill, Lewis Milestone, Mike Mindlin, Oswald Morris, Henry Myers, David Newman, George Oppenheimer, Murdock Pemberton, Nat Perrin, Ralph R. Perry, Ada Persoff, Tommy Phipps, Robert Pirosch, Vincent Price, Eileen Pringle, Sidney Poitier, Otto Preminger, Dr. and Mrs. Marcus H. Rabwin,

Decla Dunning Radin, Sir Michael Redgrave, Gottfried Reinhardt, Walter Reisch, Alan Rivkin, Edward G. Robinson, Jill Robinson, Yosal Rogat, Lin Root, Welles Root, Arthur Ross, Harry Ruby, Joseph Ruttenberg, Morrie Ryskind, Richard Sale, George Schaefer, Dore Schary, Stanley Scheuer, Joseph Schoenfeld, Ad Schulberg, Bud Schulberg, Stuart Schulberg, Sigrid Schultz, Si Seadler, George Seaton, George Seldes, Danny Selznick, Irene Mayer Selznick, Sonia Shaplin, Arthur Sheekman, Madeline Sherwood, Sol C. Siegel, Estherlea Silverman, Jonathan Silverman, Murray Silverman, Jean Simmons, Pearl Sindel, Walter Slezak, Bella Spewack, Mrs. Dorothy Steiner, Erna Mankiewicz Stenbuck, George Stevens, Donald Ogden Stewart, Ann Marlow Strauss, Howard Strickling, Frank Sullivan, Blanche Sweet, Jessica Tandy, Norman Taurog, Irma May Templar, Marian Spitzer Thompson, Judy Tolmach, Regis Toomey, Marietta Tree, Mr. and Mrs. Hawley Truax, Henry Tuck, King Vidor, Adelaide Thorp Wallace, Richard Watts, J. Watson Webb, Arnold Weissberger, Orson Welles, William Wellman, Lyle Wheeler, Katharine White, Billy Wilder, Richard Wilson, Robert Wise, Abel Wolman, Gordon Wolman, Peggy Wood, William Wright, Collier Young, Frederick Young, Arthur L. Zerbey, and Sam Zolotow.

These people never knew I was listening as they sat for their interviews in the early 1970s, but I was privileged and honored to be a time-traveling fly on the wall during those remarkable sessions.

My special thanks to Joe's late agent, Robbie Lantz, for a memorable interview one afternoon in the Autumn of 2002.

At Knopf, thanks go to the incredible team of Kathy Zuckerman, Amy Hagedorn, Marc Jaffee, and Jenny Carrow.

Professional thanks also go to all those who passed through the halls of Nick Davis Productions during the long years of this book's gestation, especially those whose work intersected with the project, foremost among them Stephanie Esposito, Vanessa Longley-Cooke, and the incomparable Leyla Brittan, who didn't know what she was signing up for but helped expertly with pictures, captions, research, and much else; and also the trusted long-time colleagues, too numerous to mention, whose excellent work allowed me sometimes to disappear into the book while they held down the fort, in particular my two secret weapons, Mark Rosenberg and Josh Freed.

It goes without saying, but my thanks go most especially to my Great Uncle Joe and my Gopa Herman (though of course I never called him that), and all those members of their families, living or not, not limited to the following people who spoke with me either on or off the record, whether they even knew it was for the book, and whether Geist or Meryman had spoken with them first: Alex Mankiewicz, Tom Mankiewicz, Chris Mankiewicz, Max

Reynal, and Rosemary Mankiewicz; and Don Mankiewicz, Carol Mankiewicz, Ilene Korsen Mankiewicz, Holly Jolley Mankiewicz, Lee Mankiewicz, Jack Mankiewicz, Molly Mankiewicz, and Katie Mankiewicz.

Special mention goes to my beloved first cousins. I share a profound bond with them all, and they are each remarkable people whose tender intelligence and wit have inspired and sustained me, each in different ways, heroes and companions all: John Mankiewicz and Jane Mankiewicz, and Ben Mankiewicz and Josh Mankiewicz.

Five-plus decades of gratitude to my father, Peter Davis, who has been helpful in more ways than he knows, the biggest fan on the block, and always keenly ready to forgive any missing three points. My in-laws, Fred and Leatrice Mendelsohn, in addition to giving me the greatest gift of all, provided years of warmth and encouragement and steadfast love, and I miss them every day.

And my brother, Tim, after a childhood of our competing in ways both loud and quiet, has proven time and again that he is not the idiot, but a rock, and the best big brother anyone could ever have.

I listed Mom earlier, among those interviews I was lucky enough to get from Ken Geist and Dick Meryman, but I think maybe I'm allowed to thank her again. Thank you, Mom.

As for my editor, Vicky Wilson, she may well be the perfect combination of patient and terrifying, and she has my eternal gratitude.

Finally, I thank the family I have created with the woman whose loving warmth, sly wisdom, and calm genius are the foundation of my life. My wife, Jane, sees things so deeply and clearly it's staggering; whenever we talk, I often get the feeling that she's expressing thoughts that I might arrive at if you gave me a year or two, and she is kind enough not to complain when I then act as if the ideas were mine all along. She is my miracle. Our daughters, Lily and Grace, are equally brilliant and beautiful and astonishing. Without these three, nothing means a thing.

NOTES

The two pillars of Mankiewicz biography while I was writing this book were *Mank,* written by Richard Meryman and published in 1977, and *Pictures Will Talk,* by Kenneth Geist, published the following year. Both men were extremely generous with me, and both shared all the original audio interviews they conducted for their work, including mountains of rich material that didn't make it into their published books. Thus, while I conducted a variety of original interviews for this book during the past eighteen years, the bulk of my interviewees spoke to me from the early 1970s—many have passed away, but their voices imbue this project on every page.

ABBREVIATIONS:

CM Chris Mankiewicz
ER Erna Mankiewicz
FM Frank Mankiewicz
JM Joseph Mankiewicz
JMD Johanna Mankiewicz Davis
RM Rosemary Mankiewicz
SM Sara Mankiewicz
TM Tom Mankiewicz

Prologue

x   "than Meets the Eye": Andrew Sarris, *The American Cinema* (1968), 161.
xv   "as much fun as he wants": Ben Hecht, *A Child of the Century* (1954), 479.

PART 1

1   "Your only competition is idiots": Hecht, 466.

Chapter One: ROSEBUD

3   told a psychoanalyst: Richard Meryman interview with Fred Hacker.

5 "not good unless it's your best": Robert Coughlan, "15 Authors in Search of a Character Named Joseph L. Mankiewicz," *Life* (March 12, 1951), 158–173; 163.

5 "just a characteristic": ibid., 163.

6 "tremendously industrious": ibid., 163.

7 "Promises, promises": author interview with Peter Davis.

7 "for the grace of God, goes God": Pauline Kael, *The Citizen Kane Book,* 31.

8 "is it 'veeya' or 'veal'?": author interview with Frank Mankiewicz.

8 "a round little woman": *Life,* 163.

8 "too strong a word": Meryman interview with Sara Mankiewicz.

8 "concentrated very hard": Meryman, *Mank* (1978), 23.

9 need not worry: Meryman interview with Fred Hacker.

10 "Rosebud was pure Mank": Peter Bogdanovich, "Interview with Orson Welles," in James Naremore, ed., *Orson Welles' "Citizen Kane": A Casebook* (2004), 25. (I remember vividly that as a boy, while first investigating Herman, I read something about Orson Welles using the memorable phrase "Rosebud was pure Mank" and have so quoted it in the text.)

11 "bulldog Herman": Meryman, 25.

11 "terrifying and destructive": ibid., 23.

12 promised him a bicycle: ibid., 20–21. The Rosebud-bicycle story is told many other times, including in Tom Mankiewicz's droll but notoriously fact-averse (at least in the family) memoir, *Growing Up Mankiewicz,* as well as in Geist.

13 "going to the library": Meryman interview with SM.

Chapter Two: GERTRUDE SLESCYNSKI

14 first memories: Geist interview with Joe Mankiewicz.

15 "Herman complex": ibid.

16 "my idiot brother": Kael (1971), 33.

17 "*why* I gamble"; "and I hate her": Meryman, 199.

17 "fiercely ambitious": *Life,* 163.

18 "is a real shit": author interview with Peter Davis.

20 "never shouts"; "starts out": *Life,* 160.

20 "well-nigh perfect": Richard Burton, in Geist, *Pictures Will Talk* (1978), xiii.

20 "bloody marvelous": Michael Caine, *Acting in Film* (1997), 121.

20 "Mankiewicz is a genius": Sam Staggs, *All About "All About Eve"* (2000), 113.

20 "always adored him": Geist interview with Erna Mankiewicz.

20 kidding and jokes: author interview with Tom Mankiewicz.

21 "very internal guy": Geist, 1.

21 "Dad was so controlled": author interview with TM.

22 "such a sweet child": author interview with Chris Mankiewicz.

23 pride and hope: Geist interview with JM and Geist, 16.

23 "father figure I wanted": Meryman, 142–143. Interestingly, Joe's interviews with his brother's biographer Meryman reveal a much warmer attitude toward Herman than those he conducted with his own, Geist.

23 loose change: Meryman interview with JM.

24 prevented him from attending: Meryman, 27.

25 "Are you related": author interview with Frank Mankiewicz.

25 "what are you doing these days?": the Cagney story is a Mankiewicz chestnut, related in my interview with FM and in *Life*, 163.

25 "no time for him": ibid.

26 "to my hacienda": Geist, 16–17.

27 "write that down": Meryman interview with Mildred Jaffe.

27 "moving all the time": Geist, 18.

27 "no contact today": *Life*, 163.

27 "He had friends": Geist interview with ER.

28 "When anybody blew": Meryman, 31.

29 "they don't drink": Meryman interview with Fred Hacker.

29 would phone Franz: Meryman, 29.

30 "rained on or not": ibid., 31.

30 "real contempt for money": *Life*, 163.

31 "hip-pocket lending library": Meryman, 31.

31 "darting into entryways": ibid., 32.

31 "Show me a rule": Meryman interview with Frank Perry.

32 "push his food on his fork": Dorothy Kahn, in Meryman, 32.

33 "what England seems": Meryman, 29.

34 "almost professional": Richard Rodgers, *Musical Stages* (1975), 35.

36 "particularly clever": "Columbia's Review a Bright Satire," *New York Times*, April 13, 1916.

36 "very famous doctor": Geist, 18.

37 "some thwarted violence": Meryman, 18.

Chapter Three: THE NEW YORKER

38 "one day you wake up": Meryman, 315.

40 "too competitive": Simon Louvish, *Monkey Business: The Lives and Legends of the Marx Brothers* (1999), 165–166.

40 "wanted me to be funny": Meryman, 120–122; Meryman interview with SM.

41 "in a dream world": Meryman, 35.

41 an *X* through the rest: ibid., 37.

41 "zero flying aptitude"; "if need be, die": ibid., 38.

42 "fanciful lies": ibid., 39.

42 "too pure for words": ibid., 40.

42   "never live up": *Life*, 163.

43   then leave the theater: author interviews with FM and TM.

44   "The sun will be shining": Meryman, 44–45.

45   "Which one is the bride?": ibid., 45.

45   "a nice, noisy wedding": Meryman interview with SM.

45   "slept in another bed": ibid.

46   "an old marriage": Meryman, 45-46.

46   "no nothing"; "more than okay!": ibid., 46.

49   "has his faults": ibid., 43.

49   "with my money": ibid., 47.

49   almost lascivious: ibid., 48.

50   "boy whores": Meryman interview with SM.

51   had to find a job: Meryman, 51.

52   life in Berlin: ibid., 51–53.

52   "no illusions": Meryman interview with Rebecca Drucker.

53   "if you picket": Meryman, 54; "a way of looking": Meryman, 55.

54   lock him inside: Meryman interview with Sigrid Schultz.

54   poker buddies: Meryman, 65.

54   "partly for his wife": ibid., 55; "Your stuff is great": ibid., 58.

56   "carried off the honors": Meryman interview with SM.

56   "Schnooks, where are you?": Meryman, 56.

56   "to a tiny baby?": ibid., 61.

57   "an *expressioniste* of beauty": Andrew Hewitt, *Social Choreography: Ideology as Performance in Dance and Everyday Movement* (2005), 273.

57   "surprised at Yesenin": Meryman, 62.

58   "laughed boisterously"; "checks in Russia": ibid., 63.

58   "impossible to keep up"; "railed at him": ibid., 64.

59   "prospective return"; close enough: ibid., 65.

Chapter Four: YES, *THE NEW YORKER*

61   "liveliest and most amusing": Stanley Walker, *City Editor* (1961), 41.

62   "Where is it written": Meryman, 98.

62   "what do you know!": ibid., 98.

63   "until you are Swopen to": ibid., 68.

63   "seldom makes literature": Hecht, 393.

64   "first real exposure": Meryman, 70–71, and Meryman interview with SM.

64   "Even his enemies laughed": Hecht, 393.

64   "life of every party": Meryman interview with SM.

66   "acted obeisant": James R. Gaines, *Wit's End* (1977), 28.

66   "do this every day?": Margaret Case Harriman, *The Vicious Circle* (1951), 7.

66   "collection of unsalable wit": ibid., 20; Marion Meade, *Dorothy Parker* (1988), 74.

66 "Who's in a hurry?": Nathaniel Benchley, *Robert Benchley* (1955), 3.

66 "Why so it does": Gaines, 30; Meade, 85.

66 "So do you": Harriman, 145; Meade, 76.

67 "people telling jokes": Alden Whitman, "Dorothy Parker, 73, Literary Wit, Dies," *New York Times,* June 8, 1967.

68 "used piece of soap": Meryman, 84.

69 "every other writer": Meryman interview with SM.

69 script dragged on: Meryman, 126.

69 "sixteen bottles of Scotch": Kael, *Raising Kane and Other Essays*, 191.

70 "sit in a box seat": Meryman, 125.

70 "like a saloon brawler": Hecht, *Charlie* (1957), 141.

71 "mad about": Meryman interview with SM.

71 "new theatrical year": *The New Yorker* (August 15, 1925), 13.

71 "who has never been there": *The New Yorker* (January 16, 1926), 19.

71 "let her prepare": *The New Yorker* (August 8, 1925), 15.

71 "not among his worst": *The New Yorker* (July 18, 1925), 15.

71 "read a bad book": *The New Yorker* (January 2, 1926), 20.

72 "one of the greatest joys": *The New Yorker* (October 24, 1925), 20.

72 "one-tenth ability": *The New Yorker* (June 20, 1925), 15.

72 "filled with trash": *The New Yorker* (February 6, 1926), 16.

72 "The Big Game": *The New Yorker* (November, 14, 1925), 11-12.

73 "saturated with the theatre": Meryman, 91.

74 "for women and fairies": ibid., 123.

74 lost all the money: ibid., 124.

74 "colored, pretty bungalows": ibid.

75 whacked Ross's desk: ibid., 125.

PART 2

77 "whole equation of pictures in their heads": F. Scott Fitzgerald, *The Last Tycoon* (1994), 3.

Chapter Five: HOLLYWOOD

79 "course in neoclassicism": Geist, 19.

80 "ragpickers"; "pissants"; "Jew tailors"; "blintze brains": Meryman, 161.

81 little German one-act: Geist, 20.

82 "in the money": Meryman, 129.

84 "wash in private": ibid., 131.

84 "fragrant mystery": *Intolerance* (1916).

84 "supposed to be Russian?": *The Last Command* (1928).

84 they were gambling: Meryman, 137.

85 "a badge of honor": Meryman interview with Ben Schulberg.

85 "On football wagers": Meryman, 136.

85 "or it doesn't": This particular gambling story was told many times, by every family member who traffics in such tales, each time with slight variations. One good recent print source is Tom Mankiewicz, *My Life as a Mankiewicz* (2012), 9.

85 "Look! No hands!": Meryman, 129.

86 "he stops learning"; "Send Your Boy to an Eastern College": ibid., 153.

86 "can't fire me": ibid., 137.

86 "seldom written": Hecht, 478.

86 "half the women"; "tricky essentials": Meryman, 131.

86 "Tell them to repaint it!": ibid., 153.

87 "only competition is idiots": Hecht, 466.

87 "for a few days": Meryman, 134.

88 setbacks of his plays: ibid., 132.

88 "Fresh Air Fund": ibid., 138.

88 Graduation day: Geist, 21.

90 "horrified and nauseated me"; "total failure": *Life,* 164.

90 joined a fraternity: Geist, 19.

90 "Lie down with idiots": author interview with FM.

91 "Eckstein in lights"; "you're in it": Geist, 20.

91 "my brother's name": Geist, 20.

91 "fistfight with Zeppo"; "perhaps develop": Geist, 21.

92 "succumb to the blandishments": Geist, 21.

92 "intoxication of theater": ibid., 22.

92 "Everything that Paris was described as": *All About Mankiewicz,* dir. Luc Béraud (1983). www.youtube.com/watch?v=oaTNbVyI2Gc

92 "come out to Hollywood!": Geist, 23.

92 "discovered Tutankhamen's tomb"; "I *knew* that back": Joe told the story of his first night in Hollywood many times in many different ways, the best two in Béraud's film and at Geist, 23.

92 "an illusion shattered"; "one Hollywood pro": Geist, 24.

Chapter Six: TRAPPED

95 establish the jeopardy: Geist interview with JM; Geist, 25-28.

96 "strongly impressed": Geist, 37.

96 "very apologetically": ibid., 37.

96 "the kind of guy": Meryman, 140.

96 "bachelor's table": ibid., 131.

97 "eaten by wolves": ibid., 142.

97 "never lasts": ibid., 144.

97 "patronized him": *Life,* 164.

98   "everything he has": Meryman, 144.

98   "ruins you for anyone else": Geist, 39.

99   "the big ham bit": Geist, 41.

100 "all clowns": author interview with FM.

101 limousine on Halloween: Mom told my brother and me about her chauffeur-driven Halloweens, a lightly fictionalized version of which appears in her novel *Life Signs*.

101 "literate people": author interview with FM.

101 "what has he got to say": author interview with FM.

102 "give up this crap": Geist, 37.

103 "Napier": Meryman, 176.

103 "zoomed away": Geist, 51.

103 "fuck a star": author correspondence with Peter Davis.

104 reattach his foreskin: Meryman interview with JM.

105 become his bride: Geist, 70.

106 parting on good terms: ibid., 85.

107 "wrote a syllable": ibid., 49.

109 "my little chickadee": *All About Mankiewicz* (1983), film.

110 "asbestos pants": Meryman, 145.

110 "bedlams of shouted ideas": ibid., 145.

111 "picks up spit"; "punctured his pretensions": ibid., 148.

112 "make your dinner party": ibid., 207.

112 "How much can a gun eat?": ibid., 212.

112 "wonderful times": Meryman, 175.

112 "more respectable version": Meryman interview with Marion Spitzer; Meryman, 143.

112 "More regimented": Meryman interview with John Lee Mahin.

112 "color of my environment": Geist, 18.

112 "infantile regression": Meryman interview with Fred Hacker.

113 "terrified of Herman": Meryman, 177.

113 "Here lies Herm": *Life*, 164.

114 Adolf Mitler: "*The Mad Dog of Europe*," screenplay by Lynn Root.

118 jeopardize their German business: Ben Urwand, *The Collaboration: Hollywood's Pact with Hitler* (2013), excerpted in *The Hollywood Reporter* (August 9, 2013). www.hollywoodreporter.com/news/how-hollywood-helped-hitler-595684

Chapter Seven: MONKEYBITCH

120 "pictures smell of rotten bananas": Fitzgerald, 140.

121 "whole equation in his head": ibid., 3.

121 "learn to crawl": Geist, 73.

122 "women's picture": ibid., 92.

123 "carry light and music": Hamilton, *Writers in Hollywood* (1990), 149; Matthew J. Bruccoli, ed., *Three Comrades: F. Scott Fitzgerald's Screenplay* (1978), 44.

123 "tired of the best scenes": Hamilton, 150; *The Letters of F. Scott Fitzgerald*, ed. Andrew Turnbull (1963), 563.

124 "spat on the American flag": Hamilton, 148; Jacques Bontemps and Richard Overstreet, " 'Measure for Measure': Interviews with Joseph Mankiewicz," *Cahiers du Cinema in English* 18 (February 1967), 31.

125 "doesn't he know": Hamilton, 152; Sheila Graham, *Beloved Infidel* (1959), 197.

125 "My only hope": Hamilton, 150.

126 "ever be wrong?": ibid.

126 "collaborator's typewriter": Meryman, 158.

126 "you just left": ibid., 152.

126 "neurotic inertia": ibid., 154.

127 "allowed alone in a room": Wilk, *The Wit and Wisdom of Hollywood* (1971), 144.

127 "a loafer is a loafer": Meryman, 154.

127 "stands where they are sitting": ibid., 163.

127 "twelfth drink": Meryman interview with Gottfried Reinhardt.

128 follow her out: Meryman, 167.

128 "poor Sara": ibid., 136.

129 "never came close to her": Meryman interview with Fred Hacker.

129 "frumpy English secretary": Meryman interview with SM.

130 "needlessly extravagant": letter, Sara to Herman, late 1930s. (I found this undated letter slipped mysteriously into a folder containing transcripts of Richard Meryman's interviews with Sara.)

130 "smart about those things": Meryman interview with SM.

131 "listening to a baseball game": Meryman interview with Don Mankiewicz.

131 "picture of a moonbeam": Meryman, 202.

132 "never got over": Meryman interview with SM.

134 "Get in here!": Meryman interview with Johanna Mankiewicz Davis.

134 butterfly kisses: Johanna Davis, *Life Signs* (1973).

134 "you knew that he loved you": Meryman interview with JMD.

135 "white wine came up with the fish": Meryman, 15.

136 the European memories: author interview with Alex Mankiewicz.

137 considerable amount of alimony: Geist, 85.

138 portrait of a gangster: Meryman, 172.

138 "wishing I was back in New York": ibid., 289.

139 less than a week: ibid., 173.

139 relief came at last: ibid., 174–175.

139 black-and-white to color: Kenneth Von Gunden, *Flights of Fancy* (1989), 216.

PART 3

Chapter Eight: *AMERICAN*

146 "take good care": Meryman, 239.

146 never to return: ibid., 236.

147 left the lunch feeling: Meryman interview with Houseman.

147 Welles started a thriller: Callow, 477.

148 $200 a pop: Meryman, 241.

148 no grandson should ever: Sara's interview contains phrases like "magnetic, absolutely" and she describes how Welles would tell her "move over" as he climbed into bed with her.

150 took credit for everything: Carringer, 16; Meryman, 241.

151 great work at last: Carringer, 17–18; Meryman, 248–251.

153 long film script: Carringer, 18; Meryman, 257.

154 blamed on Kane: Carringer, 19–21.

154 uncredited work: ibid., 24.

155 unofficial cast gatherings: Meryman, 259.

155 "shall be deemed the author": Carringer, 32.

156 "completely without film!": Meryman, 263.

156 pretty good: Meryman interview with Rita Alexander.

156 "save Mankiewicz from disaster": Meryman, 258.

157 had to fire Jedediah: Meryman interview with Welles.

158 beachheads for lawsuits: Meryman, 269.

158 spent the nickel: ibid., 247; author interview with FM.

159 "do something drastic": Meryman interview with SM.

160 The phrase "resident loser-genius" is a terrific one that I am stealing from Pauline Kael. Pauline Kael, "Raising Kane," *The New Yorker*, February 12, 1971.

160 hobbled around: Meryman, 277.

160 "written in Mr. Welles's absence": ibid., 273.

161 "I don't think I'll ever": Geist, 109.

161 "producer at Metro": ibid.

Flashback: FRATRICIDE

163 the movie version: Geist, 100–106.

165 classic comedic tableau: Cavell, 133–160.

167 "cut you down to size": Geist, 105; Tom Mankiewicz, 20. This is a story Joe told, characteristically, different ways at different times.

168 "a cup of coffee": Geist, 106.

168 "worst bunch of shit": ibid., 107.

169 "couldn't change it fundamentally": Ring Lardner interview, Archive of American Television (2000), https://interviews.televisionacademy.com/interviews/ring-lardner-jr

Chapter Nine: A NEW HEART

171 "doesn't your stomach turn": Meryman interview with JM.
171 "let loose a colossal belch": Meryman interviews with JM and SM.
172 "what can I bring you": Meryman interview with SM.
174 "part of the chemistry": Geist, 97.
175 "only thing I could say": author interview with TM.
176 "all the ladies at M-G-M": Geist, 89.
176 "absolutely irresistible": Geist, 89.
176 "part of anything": Geist interview with JM.
177 "an intellectual game": author interview with CM.
178 "marvelous girl": Geist interview with JM.
179 "When you're Judy Garland": Carey and Mankiewicz, *More About All About Eve*, 23.
179 "most remarkably bright": Geist, 110.
179 "close the book on Judy": Clarke, 181.
180 "enjoyed being myself": Clarke, 134.
180 harboring unconscious hostility: Geist, 111.
181 same renowned Freudian: ibid., 111.
181 "willing to negotiate": author interview with Peter Davis.
182 stormed out: Geist, 112–113.
183 "love an animal": Clarke, 181.
183 "so, so sorry": author interview with TM.
184 "a little happy, a little sad": Clarke, 191.
185 glittering in triumph: ibid., 213.
185 "dimmer and dimmer": ibid., 212.
185 "remember an emotion": ibid., 212.
185 "only one role is available": Carey, 32.
186 if she stepped aside: Geist, 118.
186 pleaded with the studio: Geist interview with Nunnally Johnson.
186 "failed in all things": *The Keys of the Kingdom,* trailer copy.
187 arm in arm: Geist, 120.
188 "wouldn't have lasted": Geist interview with Johnny Green.
188 "sit there sobbing": Geist, 120.

Chapter Ten: SHIPS IN THE NIGHT

192 "strike two, you're out!": author interview with FM.
192 "He should drink": Meryman, 280.
192 "a loathsome person": ibid., 279.
192 "here comes crazy Mank": ibid., 235.
192 "something marvelous": Geist interview with JMD.

193 "impressed and depressed": Meryman, 177.

193 "seen the year before": ibid., 178.

193 "What's the matter, kid?": Meryman interview with EM.

193 "surrender gesture": Meryman interview with Fred Hacker.

193 "warning to their children": *Life,* 164.

194 "so embarrassing": Meryman interview with JM.

194 "Dwight Taylor sober": Meryman, 282; "the little boy in me": Meryman, 281.

194 "monitor ass": Meryman, 15.

194 "admit what I'm writing": ibid., 287.

194 "why would you go": Meryman interview with Houseman.

194 "write me out of it": ibid., 287.

195 "all worthwhile contributions": Meryman, 284.

195 "wasting the best years": ibid., 285.

196 "at your disposal": Geist interview with Arthur Miller.

196 "what I was thinking": Geist, 121.

196 "earned your wings": ibid., 132.

197 "shall be the last": ibid., 136.

198 "take my chances"; "one wife too many": Geist, 138.

199 "without even trying": *Time* (January 17, 1949), 86.

Chapter Eleven: EVE

203 a mean cut: Meryman, 282.

204 drunkenly plowed into; "so we have hopes": Meryman, 283.

205 "on his way home": ibid., 284.

206 "quirks and frailties": Carey, 8.

207 "marriage of writer and material": Geist, 161.

208 "goldmining camp and ivory ghetto": Carey, 11.

209 "oldest whore on the beat": among many sources, Andrew Sarris, "Mankiewicz of the Movies" (1970), in Dauth, 27.

209 "love letter to Thespis": Geist interview with Celeste Holm.

209 went off, alone: Geist, 167.

210 "where God goes on vacation": author conversation with John Mankiewicz, 2003.

210 "the world is full of Eves": Carey and Mankiewicz, *More About All About Eve,* 98.

211 "servicing a bottomless pit": Carey, 29.

211 keep the deep voice: *All About Mankiewicz.*

212 "I've been there": Carey, 29.

213 "because I am bored": "George Sanders, Film Villain, A Suicide," *New York Times,* April 26, 1972.

213 "predictable, conforming": Carey, 41.

214 "Waldo Lydecker School": Les Fabian Brathwaite, "Hays'd: Decoding the Classics—'All About Eve,' *IndieWire*, April 25, 2014.

215 "done as a short": Geist, 168; "really going on": author interview with CM.

216 "boy was she provoked!": Geist interview with JMD.

217 "propensities of creative talents": Carey, 51.

217 "nothing to do with": Geist, 161; "it doesn't get to him": Geist interview with JMD.

217 "Absurd": author interview with Rosemary Mankiewicz.

219 most sparked: Meryman, 313–314.

220 "every top star": ibid., 313.

220 "layman and fathead": ibid., 313.

222 "pushed me aside": Sam Staggs, *Close-Up on Sunset Boulevard* (2003), 183; Staggs quotes a letter from Chris Mankiewicz.

223 "I miss the boys": Meryman interview with SM.

224 life has moved on: Johanna Davis, *Life Signs,* 47–49.

225 "It won't be long": Davis, 49.

PART 4

227 "belong to herself": Davis, 182.

Chapter Twelve: NO WAY OUT

230 "stop dreaming": *Hollywood Round Table,* 1963. Motion Picture 306–1757; Records of the U.S. Information Agency, Record Group 306; National Archives at College Park, College Park, MD. www.youtube.com/watch?v=1u27coFlGXg

230 "house of Edwin Knopf": Geist, 175.

231 "put in concentration camps": Greg Mitchell, "Winning a Battle but Losing the War Over the Blacklist," *New York Times,* January 25, 1998.

231 "least politically minded": Geist, 174.

232 "slandered, libeled, persecuted": ibid., 180.

232 "nobody appointed DeMille": Mitchell, *New York Times,* January 25, 1998.

232 "Mankiewicz Will Not Sign Oath": *Daily Variety,* October 11, 1950.

233 "ballot to recall": Geist, 183.

233 "impeached, my boy": James Ulmer, "A Guild Divided," *DGA Quarterly,* Spring 2011. www.dga.org/Craft/DGAQ/All-Articles/1101-Spring-2011/Feature-Loyalty-Oath.aspx

234 "out of the water": Geist, 189.

234 "act of contrition": Mitchell, *New York Times,* January 25, 1998.

235 "rather soiled linen": Geist, 194.

235 "only one that got wet"; "Fleddie Zinnemann"; "or how big": Mitchell, *New York Times,* January 25, 1998.

235 "a thing you stand for": Ulmer, *DGA Quarterly.*

Chapter Thirteen: HOORAY FOR THE BULLDOG

237 "*see my husband*": Meryman interview with SM.

238 "how lucky Sara was": ibid.

238 "Italian, of course": Meryman, 321.

239 didn't want to be interrupted: ibid., 322.

239 "What the hell am I doing"; "an absolute vision": Meryman interview with SM.

240 what time it is: Tom Mankiewicz interview with JM; didn't get the part: Geist, 118.

241 "it can never be the play": ibid., 148.

241 "murderous fights": ibid., 167.

241 whatever he was now: author interview with CM.

242 frankly crazy behavior: author interview with TM.

242 "Get the butler": author interview with Robbie Lantz.

Chapter Fourteen: MAN-ABOUT-TOWN

244 thinking of his own boys: author interview with RM.

245 "Hollywood bullshit": author interview with CM.

246 "You think you're Leonard Bernstein": author interview with Peter Davis.

246 "nobody wants to listen": author interview with CM.

247 predicting precisely how: Tom Mankiewicz, 6.

248 "I don't like Jeanne Crain": Geist, 209n3.

248 "very pleasant, very shy": Carey, 69–70.

249 "going to be difficult": author interview with CM.

249 "great character comedienne": Carey, 70.

249 "wrapped for a gift": *Life* (March 12, 1951), 160.

249 "as a fiddler would a Stradivarius": Carey, 70.

250 "as if the theater were the one woman": *All About Mankiewicz* (1983), film.

251 "appeared to be well directed": Geist, 219.

251 "remnants of many broads": Geist, 225.

252 "taken his set back": Tom Mankiewicz, 43.

252 "brilliant" and "electrifying": Bosley Crowther, " 'Julius Caesar' and Two Other Arrivals," *New York Times,* June 5, 1953.

253 "with an astonishing lack of subtlety": Klinowski, Jacek; Garbicz, Adam, *Feature Cinema in the 20th Century: Volume One: 1913–1950: a Comprehensive Guide.* (2012).

253 "Angry at too many things": Derek Conrad, "Joseph Mankiewicz, Putting on the Style," in Dauth, *Joseph L. Mankiewicz: Interviews* (2008), 25.

254 "hate each other worse than": author interview with TM.

254 "He's drunk": Tom Mankiewicz, 29.

255 "kind of a pig": Geist interview with JMD.

256 "Mother yelling": ibid., 28.

257 "neither have I": Carey, 94.

258 "When Mumbles is through rehearsing": Geist, 258n8; James Bacon, *Hollywood Is a Four-Letter Town* (1976), 203.

259 "most intelligent man": Vincent Canby, "40 Years of Cinematic Magic," *New York Times,* November 20, 1992.

260 "always needed a villain": Meryman, 260.

261 all very psychosomatic: author interview with Robbie Lantz.

261 "Johanna took the answer": Bettman, "Einstein's Answer to Student's Geometry Question," May 17, 1952, photograph. Getty Images, www.getty images.com/detail/news-photo/may-17-1952-when-15-year-old-johanna -mankiewicz-solved-her-news-photo/517257104

262 "I turned it down": Meryman, 319–320.

262 "never had a bad one": Meryman interview with JM.

263 "closer to loving Herman": Meryman, 322.

264 has a play on Broadway: my phrasing comes from anecdotal Broadway history. Geist quotes Kaufman slightly differently: "I intend to live until Joe Mankiewicz has done his first play on Broadway"; Geist, 291. Or "Don't worry, I'm not going to die until Joe Mankiewicz writes his first play": Tom Mankiewicz, 37.

264 still but not too still: Geist interview with JMD.

264 an orchestration: author interview with CM.

265 "desperately insecure": Geist interview with JMD.

265 "dillydallied": author interview with CM.

265 Bennett Cerf's limousine: Geist interview with JMD.

266 "You fucking phony": author interview with CM.

266 The note: "Mrs. Mankiewicz Is Found Dead," *New York Times,* September 28, 1958.

266 "first honest sentiment": author interview with CM.

266 "betray true emotion"; "it was over": Geist interview with JMD.

267 "paying for her grave": author interview with TM.

267 "split the double-header": author conversation with John Mankiewicz.

268 expanded and sanitized: Geist, 293.

269 "best screen performance": ibid., 299.

269 having an affair: Tom Mankiewicz, 46.

269 "sorry to have missed you": Tom Mankiewicz, 46.

270 unforgiving toward Clift: William J. Mann, *Kate* (2006), 409; Geist, 294.

270 "what I was doing": Geist, 298.

271 "Am I really done?": A. Scott Berg, *Kate Remembered* (2003), 238; Geist, 298.

271 "literal study": Tennessee Williams, "Five Fiery Ladies," *Life* (February 3, 1961), 88.

271 "elementary Freudian psychology": Geist, 293.

Chapter Fifteen: A RIVER IN EGYPT

273 "wonderful to me": Geist interview with JMD.

273 former fiancé: author conversation with Peter Davis.

273 "needs to be reminded": Geist interview with JMD.

273 "had a neck": ibid.

274 "not looking for credit"; "the real facts"; "great hostility": ibid.

274 barked at the rabbi: author conversation with Peter Davis.

275 "perfectly nice guy": Geist interview with JMD.

277 "never thought anybody": Jeff Laffel, "Joseph L. Mankiewicz," *Films in Review* (July-August 1991, September-October 1991); Dauth, *Interviews*, 199.

277 story of the making: this chapter relies on Geist, 302-345; David Kamp, "When Liz Met Dick," *Vanity Fair* (April 1998); and the AMC documentary *Cleopatra: The Film That Changed Hollywood* (2001).

278 "wouldn't even go *see*": Peter Stone, "All About Joe," *Interview* (August 1989); Dauth, *Interviews*, 183.

279 "you like yachts": Dauth, *Interviews*, 183.

279 an actual check: author interview with John Mankiewicz.

280 "Hold your nose": Geist, 310.

280 "conceived in a state of emergency": David Lewin, "It All Depends on Cleo," *Daily Mail* (10 June 1963); in Lower and Palmer, *Critical Essays* (2001), 211.

282 "erotic vagrancy"; "back of my Cadillac": Kamp, *Vanity Fair* (April 1998).

282 "real story": Kamp, *Vanity Fair* (April 1998).

283 "he will die": *Cleopatra: The Film That Changed Hollywood* (2001), video.

283 "on *Cleopatra*'s cost report": author interview with RM.

283 "the easiest thing": author interview with TM.

283 "big guns": Kamp, *Vanity Fair* (April 1998).

283 "natural proclivity for larceny": author interview with TM.

284 three or four periods: author interview with TM.

285 "cut her balls off"; "well-deserved rest": *Vanity Fair* (April 1998).

286 two huge movie stars: author interview with TM.

286 as if to two children: ibid.

287 so debased now: ibid.

287 "None": Dauth, *Interviews*, 182.

287 "given the chance": ibid., 330.

288 "hands of an artist": Geist, 332.

288 "implied approval": ibid., 336.

288 "something I don't": Kamp, *Vanity Fair* (April 1998).

291 "produced a mouse": Judith Crist, "Cleopatra: A Monumental Mouse," *New York Herald-Tribune,* June 13, 1963.

291 "great disappointment": Geist interview with JM.

292 "deep distaste": Geist, 333.

292 "too much money": author interview with TM.

292 "brown liquid, heated": Carey, 7.

Chapter Sixteen: LEGACY

295 hosted a panel: "Live from TCM Classic Film Festival: Growing Up Mankiewicz" (August 28, 2018), Turner Classic Movies, Inc. www.facebook .com/watch/live/?v=10156296179465396

297 "skeptical eyebrow": ibid.

297 "doesn't know what kind": Farber and Green, 259.

298 first film to show horseshit: *All About Mankiewicz* (1983), film.

299 all those IOUs: Geist interview with JMD.

300 Herman's steady descent: author interview with Peter Davis.

301 "feel like I am a star": Geist interview with JMD.

301 "what the hell": Tom Mankiewicz, 152.

302 "you're just tired": author interview with TM.

302 "young beauty again": Geist, 395.

303 "just to *read* that": author interview with FM (story told many times).

305 buried next to: author interview with Alex Mankiewicz.

305 "remains overshadowed": "Tom Mankiewicz," *The Telegraph,* August 3, 2010. www.telegraph.co.uk/news/obituaries/culture-obituaries/film-obi tuaries/7925042/Tom-Mankiewicz.html

305 "about *my* feelings": author phone call with Chris Mankiewicz, August 1, 2010.

307 "out of my nose": Geist, 399.

307 "series of visual explosions": Peter Stone, "All About Joe," *Interview* (August 1989); Dauth, *Interviews,* 180.

307 "without tennis balls": Andrew Sarris, "Mankiewicz of the Movies," *Show Magazine* (March 1970); Dauth, *Interviews,* 34.

307 black Labrador: Paul Attanasio, "Joe Mankiewicz, Master of the Movies," *Washington Post* (June 1, 1986); Dauth, *Interviews,* 160.

307 "rise, peak, collapse": Beaver, *100 Years of American Film* (2000), 352.

307 "pissed away": Geist, 11.

307 "look at it wittily"; "lowest common denominator": *All About Mankiewicz* (1983), film.

308   "meat-oriented metropolis": Carey, 108.

308   "self-perpetuating idiocies": ibid., 108–109.

309   "more real to me than any of you": Peter Davis email to author.

310   "people are fragmented": *All About Mankiewicz* (1983), film.

311   "literate skeptic": "Joseph L. Mankiewicz, Literate Skeptic of the Cinema, Dies at 83." *New York Times,* February 6, 1993. (My memory inserted the word "American" into the headline.)

312   added ten years: author interview with TM.

312   "just the best thing": Geist interview with JMD.

312   epiphany; "over in about an hour": author interview with Alex Mankiewicz.

314   old Underwood: author interview with RM.

Selected Bibliography

Agee, James. *Agee on Film: Criticism and Comment on the Movies.* New York: Modern Library, 2000.

Andrew, Geoff. *The Director's Vision: A Concise Guide to the Art of 250 Great Film-makers.* Chicago: A Cappella Books, 1999.

Auiler, Dan. *Hitchcock's Notebooks: An Authorized and Illustrated Look Inside the Creative Mind of Alfred Hitchcock.* New York: HarperCollins, 1999.

Bacon, James. *Hollywood Is a Four-Letter Town.* Chicago: Henry Regnery Co., 1976.

Beaver, Frank Eugene. *100 Years of American Film.* New York: Macmillan Library Reference USA, 2000.

Behlmer, Rudy, ed. *Memo from Darryl F. Zanuck: The Golden Years at Twentieth Century–Fox.* New York: Grove Press, 1993.

———. *Memo from David O. Selznick.* New York: Modern Library, 2000.

Benchley, Nathaniel. *Robert Benchley: A Biography.* New York: McGraw-Hill, 1955.

Béraud, Luc, and Michel Ciment. *All About Mankiewicz.* Janus Film/Filmedis (France), 1983.

Berg, A. Scott. *Goldwyn: A Biography.* New York: Riverhead Books, 1989.

———. *Kate Remembered.* New York: G. P. Putnam's Sons, 2003.

Bogdanovich, Peter. *Pieces of Time.* New York: Arbor House, 1981.

———. *Who the Devil Made It.* New York: Alfred A. Knopf, 1997.

Brady, Frank. *Citizen Welles: A Biography of Orson Welles.* New York: Charles Scribner's Sons, 1989.

Brownlow, Kevin. *David Lean: A Biography.* New York: St. Martin's Press, 1996.

———. *The Parade's Gone By . . .* Berkeley: University of California Press, 1968.

Bruck, Connie. *When Hollywood Had a King.* New York: Random House, 2003.

Burns, Kevin, and Brent Zacky. *Cleopatra: The Film That Changed Hollywood.* AMC documentary, 2001.

Caine, Michael. *Acting in Film: An Actor's Take on Movie Making.* New York: Applause Books, 1997.

Callow, Simon. *Orson Welles: The Road to Xanadu.* London: Jonathan Cape, 1995.

Carey, Gary, and Joseph L. Mankiewicz. *More About All About Eve*. New York: Random House, 1972.

Carringer, Robert L. *The Making of Citizen Kane*. Berkeley: University of California Press, 1985.

Cavell, Stanley. *Pursuits of Happiness: The Hollywood Comedy of Remarriage*. Cambridge, MA: Harvard University Press, 1981.

Clarke, Gerald. *Get Happy: The Life of Judy Garland*. New York: Random House, 2000.

Corey, Melinda, and George Ochoa. *The American Film Institute Desk Reference*. New York: Dorling Kindersley Publishing, 2002.

Coughlan, Robert. "15 Authors in Search of a Character Named Joseph L. Mankiewicz." *Life* (March 12, 1951), 158–173.

Crawford, Christina. *Mommie Dearest*. New York: Berkley, 1979.

Curtis, James. *Between Flops: A Biography of Preston Sturges*. New York: Harcourt Brace Jovanovich, 1982.

———. *W. C. Fields: A Biography*. New York: Alfred A. Knopf, 2003.

Dauth, Brian, ed. *Joseph L. Mankiewicz: Interviews*. Jackson: University of Mississippi Press, 2008.

Davis, Johanna. *Life Signs*. New York: Atheneum, 1973.

Dos Passos, John. *Manhattan Transfer*. Boston: Houghton Mifflin Company, 1953.

Farber, Stephen, and Marc Green. *Hollywood Dynasties*. New York: Ballantine Books, 1985.

Fitzgerald, F. Scott. *The Love of the Last Tycoon*. Edited with notes by Matthew J. Bruccoli. New York: Scribner, 1994.

Frank, Gerold. *Judy*. New York: Da Capo Press, 1999.

Fraser-Cavassoni, Natasha. *Sam Spiegel*. New York: Simon & Schuster, 2003.

Friedrich, Otto. *City of Nets: A Portrait of Hollywood in the 1940s*. New York: Harper & Row, 1986.

Gabler, Neal. *An Empire of Their Own: How the Jews Invented Hollywood*. New York: Anchor Books, 1988.

Gaines, James R. *Wit's End: Days and Nights of the Algonquin Round Table*. New York: Harcourt Brace Jovanovich, 1977.

Geist, Kenneth L. *Pictures Will Talk: The Life and Films of Joseph L. Mankiewicz*. New York: Charles Scribner's Sons, 1978.

Gussow, Mel. *Don't Say Yes Until I Finish Talking: A Biography of Darryl F. Zanuck*. New York: Doubleday, 1971.

Halliwell, Leslie. *Halliwell's Filmgoer's and Video Viewer's Companion*, 9th ed. New York: Perennial Library, 1990.

Hamilton, Ian. *Writers in Hollywood, 1915–1951*. New York: Harper & Row, 1990.

Harriman, Margaret Case. *The Vicious Circle: The Story of the Algonquin Round Table*. New York: Rinehart & Co., 1951.

Hart, Moss. *Act One: An Autobiography*. New York: Random House, 1959.

Hecht, Ben. *Charlie: The Improbable Life and Times of Charles MacArthur*. New York: Harper & Brothers, 1957.

———. *A Child of the Century*. New York: Simon & Schuster, Inc., 1954.

Hepburn, Katharine. *Me: Stories of My Life*. New York: Alfred A. Knopf, 1991.

Hewitt, Andrew. *Social Choreography: Ideology as Performance in Dance and Everyday Movement*. Durham, NC: Duke University Press, 2005.

Houseman, John. *Run-Through: A Memoir*. New York: Simon & Schuster, 1972.

———. *Unfinished Business: A Memoir*. New York: Applause Books, 1989.

Kael, Pauline, Herman J. Mankiewicz, and Orson Welles. *The Citizen Kane Book*. Boston: Little, Brown, and Company, 1971.

Kael, Pauline. *Conversations with Pauline Kael*. Edited by Will Brantley. Jackson: University Press of Mississippi, 1996.

———. *5001 Nights at the Movies*. New York: Henry Holt and Company, 1991.

———. *For Keeps: 30 Years at the Movies*. New York: Dutton, 1994.

Kamp, David. "When Liz Met Dick." *Vanity Fair*, April 1998.

Kanfer, Stefan. *Groucho: The Life and Times of Julius Henry Marx*. New York: Alfred A. Knopf, 2000.

Kerr, Walter. *The Silent Clowns*. New York: Alfred A. Knopf, 1980.

Louvish, Simon. *Monkey Business: The Lives and Legends of the Marx Brothers*. London: Faber and Faber, 1999.

Lower, Cheryl Bray, and R. Barton Palmer. *Joseph L. Mankiewicz: Critical Essays with an Annotated Bibliography and a Filmography*. Jefferson, NC: McFarland & Company, 2001.

Mankiewicz, Tom, and Robert Crane. *My Life as a Mankiewicz: An Insider's Journey Through Hollywood*. Lexington: University Press of Kentucky, 2012.

Mann, William J. *Kate: The Woman Who Was Hepburn*. New York: Henry Holt and Company, 2006.

The Marx Brothers: Monkey Business, Duck Soup and A Day at the Races. London: Faber and Faber, 1993.

Marx, Groucho. *Groucho and Me*. New York: Da Capo Press, 1995.

McBride, Joseph. *Frank Capra: The Catastrophe of Success*. New York: St. Martin's Press, 2000.

McGilligan, Patrick, ed. *Backstory: Interviews with Screenwriters of Hollywood's Golden Age*. Berkeley: University of California Press, 1986.

Meade, Marion. *Dorothy Parker: What Fresh Hell Is This?* New York: Villard Books, 1988.

Meryman, Richard. *Mank: The Wit, World, and Life of Herman Mankiewicz*. New York: William Morrow and Company, 1978.

Mitchell, Greg. "Winning a Battle but Losing the War over the Blacklist." *New York Times,* January 25, 1998.

Naremore, James, ed. *Orson Welles' "Citizen Kane": A Casebook*. New York: Oxford University Press, 2004.

Nasaw, David. *The Chief: The Life of William Randolph Hearst*. New York: Houghton Mifflin Company, 2000.

Robinson, David. *Chaplin: His Life and Art*. New York: HarperCollins, 1992.

Rodgers, Richard. *Musical Stages: An Autobiography*. New York: Random House, 1975.

Roth, Henry. *Call It Sleep*. New York: Picador, 1991.

Russo, William. *A Thinker's Damn: Audie Murphy, Vietnam, and the Making of The Quiet American*. Philadelphia: Xlibris, 2001.

Sandomir, Richard. *The Pride of the Yankees: Lou Gehrig, Gary Cooper, and the Making of a Classic*. New York: Hachette Books, 2017.

Sarris, Andrew. *The American Cinema: Directors and Directions 1929–1968*. New York: Dutton, 1968.

Schatz, Thomas. *The Genius of the System: Hollywood Filmmaking in the Studio Era*. New York: Pantheon, 1988.

Schulberg, Budd. *What Makes Sammy Run?* New York: Random House, 1990.

Staggs, Sam. *All About "All About Eve."* New York: St. Martin's Press, 2000.

———. *Close-Up on Sunset Boulevard*. New York: St. Martin's Press, 2003.

Stempel, Tom. *Frame Work: A History of Screenwriting in the American Film*. 3rd ed. Syracuse, NY: Syracuse University Press, 2000.

Stevens, George, Jr., ed. *Conversations with the Great Moviemakers of Hollywood's Golden Age at the American Film Institute*. New York: Alfred A. Knopf, 2006.

Sturges, Sandy, ed. *Preston Sturges by Preston Sturges: His Life in His Words*. New York: Touchstone, 1991.

Thomson, David. *"Have You Seen . . . ?": A Personal Introduction to 1,000 Films*. New York: Alfred A. Knopf, 2008.

———. *The New Biographical Dictionary of Film*. New York: Alfred A. Knopf, 2002.

———. *Rosebud: The Story of Orson Welles*. New York: Alfred A. Knopf, 1996.

———. *Showman: The Life of David O. Selznick*. London: Abacus, 1993.

———. *The Whole Equation: A History of Hollywood*. New York: Random House, 2004.

Truffaut, François. *Hitchcock*. New York: Simon & Schuster, 1995.

Urwand, Ben. *The Collaboration: Hollywood's Pact with Hitler*. Cambridge, MA: Harvard University Press, 2013.

Von Gunden, Kenneth. *Flights of Fancy: The Great Fantasy Films*. Jefferson, NC: McFarland & Company, 1989.

Walker, Stanley. *City Editor*. Baltimore, MD: Johns Hopkins University Press, 1961.

Welles, Orson. *This Is Orson Welles / Orson Welles & Peter Bogdanovich*. Jonathan Rosenbaum, ed. New York: HarperCollins, 1992.

Wilk, Max. *Schmucks with Underwoods: Conversations with Hollywood's Classic Screenwriters*. New York: Applause Books, 2004.

Wilk, Max, ed. *The Wit and Wisdom of Hollywood*. New York: Atheneum, 1971.

Index

HM refers to Herman Mankiewicz; JM refers to Joe Mankiewicz. Page numbers in *italics* refer to illustrations.

Photographic Credits

Courtesy of Rosemary Mankiewicz: x, 6, 20, 95, 102, 103, 121, 122, 125, 137, 138, 176, 178, 193, 198, 200, 208, 216, 223, 247, 253, 254, 255, 257 (both), 258, 259, 260, 266, 277, 278 (both), 279 (bottom), 279 (top) Photograph by Tazio Secchiaroli, 281, 282, 288, 289, 290, 292, 293, 298, 300 (top), 303, 306, 307, 308, 310, 313.

Theatre Magazine, October 1930. Photograph by Vandamm: 61

The Museum of Modern Art / Film Stills Archive: 80

Paramount Pictures / Photofest: 84, 107

MGM / Photofest: 99, 101, 124, 166, 168, 179

Ralph F. Stitt: 109

RKO Radio Pictures, Alexander Kahle: 144

Publicity shot: 181

Twentieth Century-Fox / Photofest: 185, 197, 199, 214, 215, 249

Picture Post / Hulton Archive / Getty Images: 252

United Artists / Photofest: 256

Bettmann / Getty Images: 262

Columbia Pictures/ Photofest: 271

All other photographs are from the author's private collection

A NOTE ABOUT THE TYPE

This book was set in Adobe Garamond. Designed for the Adobe Corporation by Robert Slimbach, the fonts are based on types first cut by Claude Garamond (ca. 1480–1561). Garamond was a pupil of Geoffroy Tory and is believed to have followed the Venetian models, although he introduced a number of important differences, and it is to him that we owe the letters we now know as "old style." He gave to his letters a certain elegance and feeling of movement that won their creator an immediate reputation and the patronage of Francis I of France.

Typeset by North Market Street Graphics,
Lancaster, Pennsylvania

Printed and bound by Berryville Graphics,
Berryville, Virginia